About AFREPREN

The African Energy Policy Research Network (AFREPREN) is an African initiative on energy, environment and sustainable development supported by the Swedish International Development Cooperation Agency (SIDA) and the Swedish Agency for Research Cooperation with Developing Countries (SAREC). It brings together 97 African energy researchers and policy makers who have a long-term interest in energy research and the attendant policy-making process. AFREPREN has initiated policy research studies in 19 African countries: Angola, Botswana, Burundi, Eritrea, Ethiopia, Kenya, Lesotho, Malawi, Mauritius, Mozambique, Rwanda, Seychelles, Somalia, South Africa, Sudan, Tanzania, Uganda, Zambia and Zimbabwe. The Network also maintains close collaborative links with energy researchers and policy makers from Côte D'Ivoire, Ghana, Nigeria, Sierra Leone and Senegal. The key objective is to strengthen local research capacity and to harness it in the service of energy policy making and planning. Initiated in 1987, AFREPREN is a collective regional response to the widespread concern over the weak link between energy research and the formulation and implementation of energy policy in Africa. AFREPREN is funded by SIDA.

T0348045

African Energy Policy Research Series

African Energy: Issues in Planning and Practice
AFREPREN (1990)

Energy Management in Africa
M. R. Bhagavan and S. Karekezi (eds) (1992)

Rural Electrification in Africa
V. Ranganathan (ed) (1992)

Energy Options for Africa: Environmentally Sustainable Alternatives
S. Karekezi and G. Mackenzie (eds) (in association with the UNEP Collaborating
Centre on Energy and Environment) (1994)

Biomass Energy and Coal in Africa
D. O. Hall and Y. S. Mao (eds) (1994)

Energy Utilities and Institutions in Africa
M. R. Bhagavan (ed) (1996)

Transport Energy in Africa
M. R. Bhagavan (ed) (1996)

Renewable Energy Technologies in Africa
S. Karekezi and T. Ranja (1997)

Biomass Energy Policy in Africa
D. L. Kgathi, D. O. Hall, A. Hategeka, C. V. Mlotshwa & M. B. M. Sekhwela
(1997)

Planning and Management in the African Power Sector
V. Ranganathan (ed) (1998)

Petroleum Marketing in Africa
M. R. Bhagavan (ed) (1999)

Reforming the Power Sector in Africa
M. R. Bhagavan (ed) (1999)

Capacity Building for a Reforming African Power Sector
M. Teferra and S. Karekezi (eds) (2002)

Renewables and Energy for Rural Development in Sub-Saharan Africa
Maxwell Mapako and Abel Mbewe (eds) (2004)

Energy Services for the Urban Poor in Africa
Bereket Kebede and Ikhupuleng Dube (eds) (2004)

Energy Services for the Urban Poor in Africa

Issues and Policy Implications

Edited by

Bereket Kebede and Ikhupuleng Dube

Contributing authors

O. Kalumiana
J. Kyokutamba
M. Katyega
S. Karekezi
L. Majoro

Zed Books Ltd
LONDON & NEW YORK

in association with

African Energy Policy Research Network
(AFREPREN)

Energy Services for the Urban Poor in Africa
was first published in 2004 by
Zed Books Ltd, 7 Cynthia Street, London N1 9JF, UK and
Room 400, 175 Fifth Avenue, New York, NY 10010, USA
www.zedbooks.co.uk

in association with

the African Energy Policy Research Network (AFREPREN),
PO Box 30979, Nairobi, Kenya
www.afrepren.org

Contact: Stephen Karekezi, Director
African Energy Policy Research Network (AFREPREN/FWD)
PO Box 30979, 00100 Nairobi GPO, Kenya
Tel: +254-20-566032 or 571467
Fax: 254-20-561464/566231
Email: afrepren@africanonline.co.ke
or
StephenK@africaonline.co.ke

Distributed in the USA exclusively by Palgrave, a division of
St Martin's Press, LLC.,
175 Fifth Avenue, New York, NY 10010

Cover design by Sophie Buchet
Typeset by Long House, Cumbria, UK

A catalogue record for this book
is available from the British Library

ISBN Hb 1 84277 558 8

Contents

List of Tables   ix
List of Figures   xiv
List of Abbreviations and Glossary   xvi
Acknowledgements   xix
Notes on Contributors   xx

PART 1 INTRODUCTION
Bereket Kebede and Ikhupuleng Dube   1

Study objectives   2
Major findings and policy implications   4
Who captures the subsidies?   6
How does energy pricing affect the informal sector?   7
What is the impact of subsidies on utilities and public finance?   8
Energy pricing and related issues   9

Part 1 • Notes and References   11

PART 2 REGIONAL REPORT
Stephen Karekezi and Lugard Majoro   13

Regional profile   14

1 IMPACT OF URBANIZATION ON ENERGY CONSUMPTION
   PATTERNS   15
   Stephen Karekezi and Lugard Majoro

2 ENERGY USE AMONG THE URBAN POOR   22
   Consumption patterns and the cost of household energy   22
   Energy use in the informal sector – small and micro-enterprises   26

3 KEY TRENDS   32

Part 2 • Notes and References   35

PART 3 RESEARCH METHODOLOGY AND
APPROACH
Bereket Kebede and Ikhupuleng Dube   41

4 RESEARCH METHODOLOGY AND APPROACH   43
   Subsidies and access of the urban poor to modern energy   43
   Subsidies and leakages to the non-poor   45
   Energy subsidies and public finance   45
   Energy subsidies and small and micro-enterprises (SMEs)   46

Part 3 • Notes and References   47

PART 4 ZAMBIA
Oscar Kalumiana   49

    Country Profile   50

  5 Introduction   51
    Overview of economic developments and indicators   52
    Poverty in urban households   53
    Energy consumption patterns among urban households   54
    Organisation of the energy sector in Zambia   55
    Subsidies in the energy sector   57
    Urban household expenditure   59

  6 Impact of Energy Pricing on Affordability of Modern Forms
    by the Urban Poor   60
    Methodology   60
    Findings   61
    Conclusions   69

  7 Energy Subsidies Captured by Different Household Categories   71
    Methodology   71
    Findings   71
    Conclusions   75

  8 Impact of Energy Subsidies on Public Finances   76
    Methodology   76
    Findings   76
    Conclusions   79

  9 Policy Options and Recommendations   80
    Issues to be addressed by policy   80
    Policy options   83
    Policy implementation   84

    Part 4 • Appendices   89

PART 5 ZIMBABWE
Ikhupuleng Dube   103

    Country Profile   104

 10 Introduction   105
    Rationale of the study   105

 11 Do the Urban Poor Need Subsidies to Access Modern Energy?   108
    Research approach   108
    Findings   108

 12 Are Subsidies for Upfront Costs a Better Option?   113
    Research approach   113
    Findings   113

13   Who Captures the Subsidies?   121

14   What is the Impact of Subsidies on Utilities and Public Finance?   125
     Research approach   125
     Findings   126

15   What are the Implications of Subsidies on the Informal Sector?   131

16   Policy Options and Recommendations   135
     Impact of subsidies on affordability of modern forms of energy
     by the poor   135
     Distribution of subsidies amongst different income groups and
         their impact on public finances   142
     Pricing of electricity to small and micro-enterprises   144

     Part 5 • References   146
     Part 5 • Appendices   149

PART 6   ETHIOPIA
Bereket Kebede
(with Elias Kedir, Aselefech Abera and Solomon Tesfaye)

(with Elias Kedir, Aselefech Abera and Solomon Tesfaye)   157

     Country Profile   158

17   Introduction   159
     Rationale of the Study   159
     The pattern of urban energy demand in Ethiopia   160

18   Expenditures of the Urban Poor and Costs of Energy   164

19   Who Captures Energy Subsidies?   175
     Methodology   175
     Empirical results   175

20   Energy Subsidies and Public Finance   182

21   Electricity Tariffs and Informal Sector Enterprises   188

22   Policy Options   193

     Part 6 • Notes and References   197
     Part 6 • Appendices   199

PART 7   TANZANIA
Maneno J. J. Katyega (with Norbert Kahyoza)

Maneno J. J. Katyega (with Norbert Kahyoza)   209

     Country Profile   210

23   Background to the Study   211

24   What is the Impact of Subsidies on Utilities and Public Finance?   212

25   Who Captures the Subsidies?   219

26   Subsidies and the Informal Sector   221

27   Policy Options   224

     Part 7 • Notes and References   226
     Part 7 • Appendices   228

PART 8 UGANDA
Joan Kyokutamba 231

    Country Profile 232

28 Introduction 233
    Rationale of the Study 233

29 Do the Urban Poor Need Subsidies to Access Modern Energy? 235
    Affordability of energy by the urban poor – with subsidies 235
    Affordability of energy by the urban poor – without subsidies 237

30 Are Subsidies for Upfront Costs a Better Option? 240

31 Who Captures the Subsidies? 246

32 What is the Impact of Subsidies on Utilities and Public Finance? 249
    Subsidies from setting the tariff below the LRMC 249
    The subsidy on electricity consumption bills 252
    The subsidy on capital cost contribution (upfront costs) 255
    Effect of capital cost contribution subsidy on GDP 256
    Effect of capital cost contribution subsidy on budget deficit 256
    Effect of subsidies on the long-term debt of the UEB 258

33 What Are the Implictions of Subsidies for the Informal Sector? 260
    Research approach 260
    Findings 260

34 Policy Options and Recommendations 267
    1: Initiate and promote appropriate demand-side management
    (DSM) and energy efficiency mechanisms 267
    2: Increase the lifeline tariff to at least 40 kWh to satisfy the basic
    minimum energy required by poor households 268
    3: Amortize upfront costs of electricity with monthly bills 269
    4: Increase support to the Sustainable Energy Use in Households and
    Industries (SEUHI) programme for the promotion of improved
    charcoal stoves 270
    5: Review wiring standards and other service connections by
    promoting Single Wire Earth Return (SWER) 271
    6: Reform the metering system and enable consumers to purchase
    the power they can pay for at full cost recovery 272
    7: Design tariffs to ensure equitable tariff rates for SMEs 273

    Part 8 • Notes and References 275
    Part 8 • Appendices 278

INDEX 291

List of Tables

2.1 Earnings (Z$ millions) and employees (000s) in urban areas of
     Zimbabwe in 1997   16
2.2 Gini Coefficient for urban areas in four African countries (1991–7) 17
2.3 Percentages of households and urban income by five expenditure
     groups in Ethiopia   18
2.4 Energy expenditure as percentage of urban household income
     in selected African countries   23
2.5 Urban household energy consumption and expenditures in
     relation to monthly income, 1988   23
2.6 Access to energy sources by households for different income
     categories in urban areas and nationally, Zimbabwe   24
2.7 Households before and after electricity connection in
     Pamodzi Ndola, Zambia   25
2.8 Upfront cost of using a 12 kg cylinder in Kenya   25
2.9 Cost of buying and refilling different gas cylinder sizes in Kenya 26
2.10 Comparison of household energy use by activity in Zimbabwe   28
2.11 Household-based enterprises in Botswana   29
2.12 Commercial activities employing or owned by the urban poor in Africa 30
2.13 Boundaries of urban income groups (income per month) in Zimbabwe   35

ZAMBIA
4.1 Real overall GDP and sectoral growth rates, 1995–2000   53
4.2 Fuels used by urban households for cooking and lighting –
     1996 and 1998   55
4.3 Domestic electricity tariffs compared to LRMC and ACBT, 1998   58
4.4 Estimated average *per capita* urban household expenditure on
     different fuels, 1998   63
4.5 Mean urban household energy budget, 1998   64
4.6 Mean household monthly energy consumption expressed as
     useful electricity unit equivalents, 1998   65
4.7 Household monthly energy expenditure compared to
     unsubsidized electricity costs at the ACBT   66
4.8 Calculation of monthly cost of devices for the year 1998   66
4.9 Household total monthly energy expenditure converted to
     unsubsidized electricity at 4.5 US cents/kWh   66
4.10 Mean monthly household energy consumption (equivalent useful
     kWh of electricity) in Ethiopia and Zambia   68
4.11 Amortized monthly energy and capital costs (1998) spread over
     a 10-year period   68
4.12 Comparisons of the poor urban household energy budget share of
     income with other countries   69

4.13   Existing household monthly *per capita* subsidies on electricity, 1998   72
4.14   Price build-up of kerosene, 1998 (per litre)   72
4.15   Distribution of the electricity subsidy among urban households   74
4.16   Actors in the implementation of policy options on energy subsidies   85
4.17   Actors in the implementation of policy options on leakages of the electricity subsidy   86
4.18   Actors in the implementation of policy options on subsidies and public finances   86
A4.1   Gross Domestic Product (GDP) real growth rates (%) in SADC Countries, 1981–99   89
A4.2   Total electricity generation in Zambia (GWh), 1980–2001   90
A4.3   Petroleum imports in Zambia, 1989–2000   90
A4.4   Mean percentage share of urban household expenditure on different items, 1996 and 1998   91
A4.5   Capital costs for urban electricity connections, 1998   91
A4.6   Existing *per capita* subsidies on kerosene captured by each household per month, 1998   91
A4.7   Annual subsidy levels for electricity consumers, 1998   92
A4.8.1 Ownership of durable items in Pamodzi and Twapia townships, 1996, % of total households   95
A4.8.2 Energy use and charcoal consumption before and after electricity connection in Pamodzi   96
A4.8.3 Types of appliances owned by households as ranked percentages   97
A4.8.4 Electricity consumption and payment of bills in the project households (Pamodzi) and non-project connections (Twapia)   98
A4.10 Selected time series data – Zambia   100

ZIMBABWE
5.1   Percentage access by households to energy sources by poverty status   106
5.2   Comparison of the current monthly household energy cost and the monthly cost without subsidies   109
5.3   Comparison of energy subsidies to household expenditure and income indicators   111
5.4   Device and upfront costs of basic electrical devices   114
5.5   Cost of kerosene devices   114
5.6   Upfront costs of LPG and associated devices   114
5.7   Comparison of upfront cost and device cost to household incomes and budget reserves   115
5.8   Comparison of monthly LPG recurrent cost to recurrent cost of electricity and kerosene   116
5.9   Ownership of electrical devices by urban households   117
5.10 Maximum amount buyers are willing to pay for total energy compared to the true cost of energy   118
5.11 Preferences for different energy sources (%)   119
5.12 Lifeline tariff subsidy charge   121
5.13 Monthly lifeline tariff subsidy distribution   121
5.14 Monthly subsidies to the domestic sector due to pricing below LRMC   123
5.15 Annual subsidies to other customer categories   124
5.16 Service fee connection subsidy   126
5.17 Kerosene subsidies   126
5.18 Comparison of energy subsidies to public sector finances   127

5.19   GDP growth and inflation rates forecasts for some SADC countries   128
5.20   Comparison of government expenditure and the level of subsidies   129
5.21   Sectoral distributions of small and micro-enterprises   131
5.22   Location of SMEs   132
5.23   ZESA classification of small and micro-enterprises using electricity   132
5.24   Comparison of unit charges for the different customer categories   133
5.25   Filtering of draft policy options   145
A5.1   Energy consumption patterns and costs for the urban households
       by source of energy   150
A5.2   Household consumption expenditure by key items   152
A5.3   Selected time series data – Zimbabwe   154

ETHIOPIA
6.1   Mean annual energy consumption of all households converted into
       kerosene   165
6.2   Mean annual energy consumption of all households converted into
       electricity   166
6.3   Costs of using kerosene and energy expenditures of all poor and
       non-poor households   168
6.4   Costs of using electricity and energy expenditures of all poor and
       non-poor households   170
6.5   Ratios of total present value of costs to expenditures for poor
       households   172
6.6   Ratios of total present value of costs to expenditures for poor
       households (2% inflation and 5% income growth)   174
6.7   Total and mean kerosene and electricity subsidies for poor and
       non-poor households (in Birr)   176
6.8   Total and mean kerosene and electricity subsidies for *per capita*
       expenditure deciles (in Birr)   176
6.9   Quantile (median) regressions of kerosene and electricity subsidies
       on total household expenditures and household size   177
6.10   Total and mean kerosene and electricity subsidies by urban centres
       (in Birr)   179
6.11   Coefficients of quantile regressions for kerosene and electricity
       subsidies on expenditure and household size   180
6.12   Tariff rates between 1994 and 1998 and marginal costs in 1994   183
6.13   Electricity subsidies per kWh between 1994 and 1998 (in Birr)   184
6.14   Total subsidies in Birr by electricity blocks and by sector
       (August 2000–July 2001)   186
6.15   Tariff–marginal cost ratios by customer categories and electricity
       blocks (1994–8)   189
6.16   Estimate of average monthly value of energy expenses of informal
       sector establishments by industry type, 1996   191
A6.1   Cost of kerosene use with and without subsidy and mean
       energy expenditures of households by urban areas   199
A6.2   Cost of kerosene use with and without subsidy and mean
       energy expenditures by *per capita* expenditure deciles   200
A6.3   Costs of electricity use with and without subsidy and mean
       energy expenditures of households by urban areas   201
A6.4   Costs of electricity with and without subsidy and energy
       expenditures of *per capita* expenditure deciles   202

A6.5   Present value of costs of electricity and energy expenditure
of poor households with and without subsidy (6% interest rate)   203
A6.6   Current and discounted present values of electricity costs with and
without subsidy and energy expenditures, by *per capita* expenditure
deciles (6% interest rate)   204
A6.7   Current and discounted present values of electricity costs with and
without subsidy and energy expenditures of poor households   205
A6.8   Selected time series data – Ethiopia   206

TANZANIA

7.1   Current tariff levels compared to long-run marginal cost, 2000   212
7.2   Electricity subsidies and leakage in energy terms, 2000   214
7.3   Electricity subsidies and leakage in monetary terms, 2000   215
7.4   Expenditures on rural electrification programmes, 1995–2000
(in million TShs)   216
7.5   Impact of electricity subsidies on public finances (US$ million) 217
7.6   Extent of electricity leakage to the non-poor in 2000   220
7.7   Electricity tariffs in Tanzania, May 2002–June 2003   220
7.8   Home-based micro-enterprise energy consumption and cost patterns
in 2001   222
7.9   A suggestion on year 2003 tariff structure segmentation   224
A7.1 Selected time series data – Tanzania   228

UGANDA

8.1   Energy consumption situations in Uganda, 1999–2001   233
8.2   Categories of electricity subsidies   235
8.3   Household energy expenditure by income group   236
8.4   Mean monthly energy expenditure for average households converted
to buy various energy sources   236
8.5   Mean annual energy expenditure for all poor, moderately poor, very
poor and extremely poor households converted into electricity   237
8.6   Level of subsidy available for domestic electricity consumers   237
8.7   Household ability to purchase electricity at non-subsidized prices 238
8.8   Projection of basic costs of using electricity in a typical urban poor
household   238
8.9   The cost of switching from other sources of energy to electricity,
and its effect on annual energy budgets for poor urban households   241
8.10 Cost of wiring a two-roomed house by SWER   243
8.11 Loan repayment schedule for household electricity connection   244
8.12 Number of households connected to grid electricity in 1999   246
8.13 Summary of the domestic electricity tariff, true cost and subsidy (1993) 247
8.14 Urban poor household expenditure on energy converted to
electricity and level of subsidy captured relative to the total
subsidy offered (1993 tariff)   247
8.15 The UEB tariff schedule (1993)   250
8.16 Tariff frequency analysis for subsidized energy for the year 1999 252
8.17 Amount of electricity subsidy in each tariff code   253
8.18 Summary of the effect of subsidies on public finances   254
8.19 The effect of electricity subsidies on the national budget in 1999/2000 257

8.20	Selected performance indicators for the Uganda Electricity Board, 1999–2000 (in millions of UShs)	258
8.21	Typical power consumption in enterprises	263
8.22	Energy usage in commercial enterprises	264
A8.1	Average monthly energy expenditure for the three categories of urban poor households (in UShs)	278
A8.2	Capital contribution (1993)	278
A8.3	Revised scheme costing schedules, Dec. 2001	279
A8.4	Materials needed for wiring a two-roomed house	279
A8.5	Upfront costs of electricity for a new house	280
A8.6	Market prices for energy appliances	280
A8.7	Loan repayment schedule: A	281
A8.8	Loan repayment schedule: B	281
A8.9	Loan repayment schedule: C	282
A8.10	Loan repayment schedule: D	282
A8.11	Activities of micro-enterprises and energy technology used	283
A8.12	Informal sector activities that provide income for the urban poor (home-based micro-enterprises and other small enterprises)	284
A8.13	Uganda Electricity Distribution Company Ltd	284
A8.14	New tariff rates for electricity consumed in Uganda with effect from 1 September 2002	286
A8.15	Performance indicators for Uganda Electricity Board (UEB)	287
A8.16	Selected time series data – Uganda	288

List of Figures

2.1	Urbanization by region	15
2.2	National population growth compared to urban population growth (1990–2001)	16
2.3	Percentage of urban population living below the poverty line (1998–9)	17
2.4	Energy sector capital budget shares (%) and total budget shares (million Birr), 1990–2000	19
2.5	Percentages of urban households electrified	20
2.6	Employment (000s) in the informal sector in Kenya (1998–2002)	27
2.7	Commercial activities in small and micro-enterprises in Nairobi, Kenya	28
2.8	Changes in the commercial activities before and after electrification	32

ZAMBIA

4.1	Changes in proportions of poor and non-poor households in urban areas	54
4.2	Final energy consumption (Toe) by source, 1999	56
4.3	Proportion of energy expenditure (excluding cost of firewood and charcoal) of total monthly household expenditure, 1995	60
4.4	Total monthly energy budget as % of total income for ten urban household expenditure deciles	64
4.5	Percentage decrease/increase of current monthly energy budget if all households exclusively used unsubsidized electricity instead of different fuels	67
4.6	Monthly share of the kerosene rebate among urban households, US$	73
4.7	Charcoal licence fee as a proportion of the retail price, July 2001	73
4.8	Percentage share of the electricity subsidy (Kwacha) gained by various consumer categories	74
4.9	Proportion of total energy subsidies to central government deficit and GDP for Uganda, Zambia and Zimbabwe	78
4.10	Total electricity subsidy as compared to ZESCO net current assets and net profit for 1998	78
A4.3	Petroleum imports in Zambia, 1989–2000	90
A4.10.1	Zambia: Modern energy consumption (kgoe) per US$ of GDP (US$), 1992–2001	101
A4.10.2	Zambia: Electricity consumption (kWh) per US$ of GDP (US$), 1992–2001	101
A4.10.3	Zambia: Modern energy consumption (kgoe) per US$ of merchandise export (US$), 1992–2001	102

A4.10.4 Zambia: Electricity consumption (kWh) per US$ of merchandise
         export, 1992–2001   102

ZIMBABWE
5.1   Rural and urban electrification rates in Africa   105
A5.3.1   Zimbabwe: Modern energy consumption (kgoe) per US$
         of GDP, 1992–2001   155
A5.3.2   Zimbabwe: Electricity consumption (kWh) per US$ of GDP,
         1992–2001   155
A5.3.3   Zimbabwe: Modern energy consumption (kgoe) per US$ of
         merchandise export, 1992–2001   156
A5.3.4   Zimbabwe: Electricity consumption (kWh) per US$ of merchandise
         export, 1992–2001   156

ETHIOPIA
6.1   Share of electricity and energy from total cost of informal sector
         monthly expenses   191
A6.8.1   Ethiopia: modern energy consumption (kgoe) per US$ of GDP,
         1992–2001   207
A6.8.2   Ethiopia: Electricity consumption (kgoe) per US$ of GDP,
         1992–2001   207
A6.8.3   Ethiopia: modern energy consumption (kgoe) per US$ of
         merchandise export, 1992–2001   208
A6.8.4   Ethiopia: Electricity consumption (kgoe) per US$ of merchandise
         export, 1992–2001   208

TANZANIA
7.1   Impact of electricity subsidies on public finance   218
A7.1.1   Tanzania: modern energy consumption (kgoe) per US$ of GDP,
         1992–2000   229
A7.1.2   Tanzania: Electricity consumption (kWh) per US$ of GDP,
         1992–2000   229
A.7.1.3 Tanzania: Modern energy consumption (kgoe) per US$ of
         merchandise export, 1992–2000   230
A7.1.4   Tanzania: Electricty consumption (kWh) per US$ of merchandise
         export, 1992–2001   230

UGANDA
A8.16.1 Uganda: Modern energy consumption (kgoe) per US$ of GDP,
         1992–2001   289
A8.16.2 Uganda: Electricity consumption (kWh) per US$ of GDP,
         1992–2000   289
A8.16.3 Uganda: Modern energy consumption (kgoe) per US$ of
         merchandise export, 1992–2001   290
A8.16.4 Uganda: Electricity consumption (kWh) per US$ of merchandise
         export, 1992–2000   290

List of Abbreviations and Glossary

A	Ampère
ACBT	Average cost-based tariff
ADB	African Development Bank
AFREPREN	African Energy Policy Research Network
BOZ	Bank of Zambia
CAPCO	Central African Power Corporation
CBO	Community-based organization
CEC	Copperbelt Energy Company
CSA	Central Statistical Authority
CSO	Central Statistics Office
DoE	Department of Energy
DSM	Demand side management
EA	Enumeration area
EE	Energy efficiency
EELPA	Ethiopian Electric Light and Power Authority
EEPCO	Ethiopian Electric and Power Company
ERA	Electricity Regulatory Authority
ERB	Energy Regulation Board
ESKOM	Electricity Supply Commission (South Africa)
ESMAP	Energy Sector Management Assistance Programme
GDP	Gross domestic project
GNESD	Global Network on Energy and Sustainable Development
GRZ	Government of the Republic of Zambia
GTZ	Gesellschaft für Technische Zusammenarbeit
GVA	Gigavolt ampère
GWh	Gigawatt-hour
HBS	Household Budget Survey
HEPP	Houshold Energy Planning Programme
HV	High voltage
ICS	Interconnected system
IPTL	Independent Power Tanzania Limited
K	Kwacha (Zambian currency) (US$1=K2,113.23 in 1998; US$1=K4,000 in January 2002)
KCJ	Kenya Ceramic Jiko
kg	Kilogram
kgoe	Kilogram of oil equivalent
kV	Kilovolt
kWh	Kilowatt hour (1,000 Wh)
l	Litre

LFS	Labour Force Survey (Botswana)
LPG	Liquefied petroleum gas
LRMC	Long-run marginal cost
LSE	Large-scale enterprise
LV	Low voltage
MEDaC	Ministry of Economic Development and Cooperation
MEWD	Ministry of Energy and Water Development
MFNP	Ministry of Finance and National Planning
MJ	Megajoule (1,000,000,000 joules)
MME	Ministry of Mines and Energy
MoE	Ministry of Energy and Mineral Development (Uganda)
MoFED	Ministry of Finance and Economic Development
MSE	Medium-scale enterprise
MW	Megawatt
NBS	National Bureau of Standards
NEP	National Energy Policy
NGO	Non-governmental organization
NOCZIM	National Oil Company of Zimbabwe
ODA	Official Development Assistance
OECD	Organization for Economic Cooperation and Development
OLS	Ordinary least squares
OMC	Oil-marketing company
PAP	Poverty Alleviation Programme
PAYE	Pay As You Earn
PV	Photovoltaic
REA	Rural Electrification Agency
REPOA	Research on Poverty Alleviation
SADC	Southern African Development Community
SCS	Self-contained system
SEI	Stockholm Environment Institute
SEUHI	Sustainable Energy Use in Households and Industry
SIDA	Swedish International Development Cooperation Agency
SME	Small and micro-enterprise
SMEs	Small and medium-sized enterprises
SRMC	Short-run marginal cost
SSE	Small-scale enterprise
SUPCO	Supply company
SWER	Single Wire Earth Return
TANESCO	Tanzania Electric Supply Company
Toe	Tonnes of oil equivalent
TRA	Tanzania Revenue Authority
TShs	Tanzania shillings
UBOS	Uganda Bureau of Statistics
UEB	Uganda Electricity Board
UEDCL	Uganda Electricity Distribution Company Limited
UIPE	Uganda Institute of Professional Engineers
UNDP	United Nations Development Programme
UNHS	Uganda National House Survey
UPE	Universal primary education
UShs	Uganda shillings

VAT	Value-added tax
ZCCM	Zambia Consolidated Copper Mines
ZESA	Zimbabwe Electric Supply Authority
ZESCO	Zambia Electricity Supply Corporation
ZNOC	Zambia National Oil Company Ltd
ZRA	Zambezi River Authority
ZW$	Zimbabwean dollar

Acknowledgements

The publication of this book has been made possible through the kind support of the Swedish International Development Cooperation Agency (SIDA).

The editors wish to thank the contributors to this volume who are AFREPREN principal researchers in the Energy Services for the Urban Poor Theme Group. The quality of the reports was greatly enhanced by reviews provided by a group of external reviewers, namely: Mr. Robert Bailis, Dr. Jonathan Scurlock, Dr. Robert Van Buskirk, and by S. Karekezi, and L. Majoro at the AFREPREN Secretariat. Special thanks also go to AFREPREN staff and interns who cross-checked energy data and information, namely: E. Manyara, C. Oloo, L. Ojiambo, S. Wakenga, R. Wachira, D. Matimu, and S. Leyian. In addition, the editors wish to thank the following AFREPREN Secretariat staff and interns who provided logistical and coordination support to the AFREPREN Energy Services for the Urban Poor Theme Group: W. Kithyoma, J. Kimani, J. Wangeci, J. Muthui, P. Musyoki, A. Maina, J. Lwimbuli, M. Gichohi, K. Muzee, O. Onguru, T. Ongesa, D. Kedemi, R. Serem, S. Mwongela, S. Khakata, E. Kisilu, J. Kinyua, L. Luchinga, P. Muendo, J. Odero, F. Muthoni, L. Makokha, C. Gakenia.

Notes on Contributors

The views expressed in this volume are the authors' own and should not be attributed to the institutions and organizations in which they are employed.

Bereket Kebede holds a DPhil in Economics and an MSc in Agricultural Economics from Oxford University, a BA in Economics from Addis Ababa University and a Certificate in Environmental Economics from Gothenburg University, Sweden. He is currently a postdoctoral fellow at the University of Bath, UK, has lectured at Addis Ababa University and was Vice-President and Administrative Secretary of the Ethiopian Economic Association. A manager, coordinator and researcher in various research projects, he has published papers on energy ecosystems, agricultural households models, institutional economics and petroleum pricing, taxation and marketing in Africa.

Ikhupuleng Dube is a principal research engineer in the Zimbabwe Electricity Supply Authority (ZESA), with an MSc in Electrical Engineering from the Technische Hochschule Zwickau University in Germany. A technical committee member of the Standard Association of Zimbabwe and a member of the Zimbabwe Institution of Engineers, he has participated in a number of energy studies, particularly on long-term supply and demand forecasts, system reliability, energy efficiency and the application of renewable energy technologies by power utilities. He has also participated in studies on power sector reform as a principal researcher with AFREPREN.

Oscar Kalumiana holds a BSc in Natural Resources from the University of Zambia. He has held the post of energy and environment consultant, coordinated a project on the provision of electricity through energy services companies, and acted as consultant for various biomass energy projects. He has published manuals and papers on biomass energy and the environment, charcoal production in earth kilns, the demand and supply of firewood and charcoal, and, charcoal storage.

Joan Kyokutamba works as Principal Human Resource and Administration Officer with the Uganda Electricity Board (UEB). She is a social scientist by training and holds a BA in Education from Makerere University, Kampala, as well as a Diploma in Human Resources Management (DHRM) from the Uganda Management Institute. Currently pursuing a Masters Degree in Ethics and Development Studies at the Uganda

Martyrs University, Nkozi, she is a principal researcher with AFRE-PREN's 'Energy for the Urban Poor Theme Group' and has conducted a number of studies for the energy sector in Uganda.

Maneno Katyega holds an MSc in Energy Engineering from George Washington University, USA, a BSc in Applied Hydrology from the University of Dar-es-Salaam, Tanzania and a Diploma in Hydropower Development from the Norwegian Institute of Technology. He has also attended various courses on energy management, environment and renewables. He has worked as the demand-side management project manager, planning hydrologist and hydrologist/energy engineer at the Tanzania Electric Supply Company (TANESCO), where he is currently Senior Energy Analyst with responsibility for research and development. The author of various publications on renewables and the power sector, his most recent publication was on innovative rural electrification strategies for Tanzania.

Stephen Karekezi, BSc, MSc, is Director of the African Energy Policy Research Network (AFREPREN) as well as Executive Secretary of the Foundation for Woodstove Dissemination (FWD) in Nairobi. He graduated as an engineer and has postgraduate qualifications in management and economics. In 1995 he was appointed to the Scientific and Technical Advisory Panel (STAP) of the Global Environment Facility (GEF), co-managed by the World Bank, UNDP and UNEP. He has written, co-authored and edited some 87 publications, journal articles, papers and reports on sustainable energy development. In 1990 he received the Development Association Award in Stockholm in recognition of his work on the development and dissemination of the Kenya Ceramic Jiko, an energy-efficient cooking stove.

Lugard Majoro holds a BSc in Agriculture from Makerere University, Uganda and is currently pursuing an MBA at the United States International University-Africa (USIU-A), Kenya. He is an energy analyst and a research fellow at the AFREPREN Secretariat, where his responsibilities have included backstopping AFREPREN's 'Energy Services for the Urban Poor' Theme Group. He has written and co-authored several research papers, publications and reports on the provision of modern energy to Africa's urban poor, energy and transport, and the power sector.

Part I

INTRODUCTION

Bereket Kebede and Ikhupuleng Dube

The majority of the population in developing countries in general and in sub-Saharan Africa in particular live in rural areas. But conditions are changing fast with high rates of urbanization – and these rates are especially high in sub-Saharan Africa, compared with other regions of the world. Urbanization entails changes both in production and consumption structures and these in turn alter energy use patterns.[1] In addition to the growth in the size of the urban population the fact that most modern (commercial) forms of energy concentrate in urban areas also underscores the importance of studying urban energy. There is thus a need to study the pattern of energy use in urban areas in its own right, as it has different characteristics from conditions prevailing in rural areas.

Even though the supply of modern energy resources in urban areas is far better than in rural areas in developing countries, this does not automatically imply that the poor in urban areas have access to them. In sub-Saharan African countries particularly, a significant proportion of the urban poor do not access modern energy sources despite their residence in metropolitan and other urban centres that are well supplied with modern energy resources compared with rural areas. For example, of the estimated one third of Africa's population who live in urban areas, only about 25 per cent have access to electricity (Tomlinson, 1999; World Bank, 2003b). Urban household electrification levels are generally below 30 per cent. Between 1970 and 1990, Africa's population increased by about 150 million, but over this period the number of persons with access to electricity increased by only about 60 million. Over a 20-year period (1970–90) the number of urban inhabitants who lacked access increased from slightly below 40 million to close to 96 million, and by 2000 the number had increased to over 100 million. This is equivalent to the whole of Nigeria, the most populous country in Africa, lacking electricity.

Studies systematically analyzing this seemingly paradoxical situation in urban areas are still rare. The studies compiled in this volume attempt to fill this literature gap. The country studies focus on interrelated issues in the provision of modern energy to the urban poor in five sub-Saharan African countries: Zambia, Zimbabwe, Ethiopia, Uganda and Tanzania. The main objectives of the studies are presented in the next section.

Study objectives

The provision of modern energy resources to the urban poor is an important policy challenge, especially with the rapid rate of urbanization and the recent focus on poverty alleviation in developing countries. Significant numbers of the urban poor in sub-Saharan Africa are without access to modern forms of energy, especially electricity. This has resulted in poor urban households relying on non-electrical forms of energy, such as fuelwood, charcoal, kerosene and dung cakes as their main sources of energy. Subsidies are widely used to improve the access of the poor to modern energy resources and change this heavy reliance on traditional forms of energy. Policy makers and energy service providers generally perceive the incomes of poor urban households to be too low to access modern forms of energy. But whether this is actually the case has not been properly examined; the studies presented in this volume systematically analyze whether urban poor households have the purchasing power to access unsubsidized modern forms of energy.

In addition to recurrent costs (for example, monthly electricity bills) households have to incur fixed costs (for example, connection fees or the cost of electrical equipment) to access modern forms of energy. Examining the importance of fixed costs in relation to overall energy costs is important since, in general, they require relatively large lump-sum expenditures and, as such, may become important constraints for the urban poor. The research studies examine the role of fixed energy costs in two main contexts – considering these costs when incurred as lump-sum expenditures, but also as they would apply if amortized over the lifespan of the equipment.

The only tangible policy response by most governments in developing countries has been to provide blanket energy subsidies, usually in the form of lifeline tariff or kerosene subsidies. The provision of blanket subsidies has some inherent problems: leakage to non-targeted groups, for example, can be large if the items subsidized are also consumed by the non-targeted group. Whether these leakages are significant in the energy subsidies of the five sub-Saharan African countries is examined in the country case studies included in this volume.

Ultimately, the cost of subsidies has to be covered by some sectors of the economy. Hence, energy subsidies create a financial burden on those sectors that provide them; in the case of energy subsidies, the costs may be borne by the government, by energy utilities or by other consumers if there are cross-subsidies. The financial burden created by energy subsidies is also examined in the country case studies.

The rapid rate of urbanization in sub-Saharan Africa has not been accompanied by a corresponding expansion of the formal sector. This has resulted in the growth of urban unemployment on one hand and a thriving informal sector on the other. In addition to contributing significantly to the economy as a whole, the informal sector has become an important source of income and provides employment to the urban poor. The urban poor are engaged in a variety of economic activities in the form of small and medium enterprises (SMEs). The welfare of the urban poor can be affected significantly by the policy environment in which the small and micro- enterprises operate: energy pricing is one significant element in this policy environment. The welfare of the urban poor can be affected negatively if the electricity tariffs of a country are unfavourable to SMEs. Tariff structures can create a condition where SMEs become the source of energy subsidies to the other economic sectors and the non-poor. The tariff structures of the five sub-Saharan African countries are examined to assess how favourable they are to SMEs.

To recapitulate, then, the study objectives of the five country case studies presented in this volume are to examine:

- if poor urban households can afford modern energy sources without subsidies; and the role of upfront fixed energy costs in affecting the affordability of modern energy by the urban poor;

- if energy subsidies are well targeted to the urban poor;

- the impact of energy subsidies on public finances;

- how electricity tariffs affect the operations of SMEs.

The African Energy Policy Research Network (AFREPREN) organized a thematic group on energy for the urban poor to tackle these important issues. The study was carried out by researchers from five sub-Saharan African countries: Ethiopia, Tanzania, Uganda, Zambia and Zimbabwe. The inclusion of many countries helps to analyze both common features and differences that exist among African countries. In addition to the cross-country nature of the studies, that the countries are found at different levels of development also helps to identify patterns that emerge with economic growth. It helps to identify peculiar features of countries at relatively lower and relatively higher levels of development: for example, the gap between the *per capita* gross domestic product (GDP) of Ethiopia and Zimbabwe is significant and, correspondingly, the difference in the extent of modern energy use (for instance, level of electrification) is large.

As with most other studies in developing countries in general and sub-Saharan African countries in particular, the lack of appropriate data to tackle the research issues was an important constraint. For example, getting appropriate information on urban poverty, on tariffs dis-aggregated by income levels of urban customers, or on the energy costs of SMEs is very difficult. Hence, either similar information that can stand in for the unavailable data is used, or estimates are made in an indirect way.

The next section summarizes the major findings and policy implica-tions from the country case studies.

Major findings and policy implications

As indicated in the previous section, the country case studies focus on four interrelated research issues. The major findings and policy implications from the country studies are summarized in the following subsections. Similarities and differences in the findings as well as the different policy implications are discussed.

Do the urban poor need subsidies to access modern energy? And are subsidies for upfront costs a better option?
Generally, governments provide subsidies in relation to the recurrent rather than the fixed costs of energy use. For example, many sub-Saharan African governments provide kerosene subsidies[2] that lower the price of the fuel but do not undertake initiatives that decrease the cost of stoves. In the case of electricity, two forms of subsidies exist. First, the lifeline tariff is deliberately kept low in the expectation that most poor households use an amount of electricity below the lifeline level. Second, even tariffs above the lifeline level are kept below the long-run marginal cost (LRMC) of supplying electricity. But initiatives attempting to decrease the upfront costs of electricity (like connection fees, internal wiring and the purchase of electrical equipment) are rare.

The country studies show that government subsidies, generally ignoring upfront (fixed) costs, are not decisive in changing costs of modern energy such as kerosene, liquefied petroleum gas (LPG) and electricity. In other words, the average poor urban household has the purchasing power to access modern forms of energy even without subsidies. But the studies further analyze the effect of including fixed (upfront) costs on the affordability of the energy sources to poor urban households.

As indicated above, in addition to the recurrent components of modern energy (for example, monthly electricity bills) households incur fixed or upfront costs. In contrast to the recurrent costs, the fixed costs are used for relatively long periods of time, depending on the lifespan of the equipment. The country studies compared the purchasing power of households with the total cost of modern energy, including upfront costs. This is done both with and without amortizing upfront costs over the lifespan of the fixed equipment, and including and excluding the current subsidies on recurrent costs. In other words, the discounted value of purchasing power and total costs of modern energy are compared by including and excluding existing energy subsidies.

Upfront costs are found to be a significant part of the costs incurred to access modern energy, particularly electricity. Generally, the comparison of the discounted purchasing power with costs without subsidies indicates that the average poor urban household can afford electricity. This result indicates that given a mechanism that can spread costs over relatively long periods of time, poor households seem to afford electricity even when supplied without subsidy. Spreading upfront costs over recurrent bills is one way of spreading fixed costs over longer periods of time. The provision of credit to poor urban households is another mechanism that can help them spread the fixed costs.

Hence, if government gives priority to the dissemination of electricity among the poor, it seems advisable to focus on the issue of spreading fixed costs over longer periods of time or providing credit. A component part of the fixed cost of electricity that is directly under the control of most governments in sub-Saharan Africa is connection fees, since electricity supply is mainly dominated by government-owned utilities. Spreading connection fees into electricity bills minimizes the down-payment households have to make to access electricity. A case in point from the five countries is Uganda; the Uganda Electricity Board subsidizes 79 per cent of the connection fees if households are located within 80 metres of an existing low-tension line. This policy option is not expected to impose a financial burden on utilities as the full cost is to be recovered. It increases the risk of customers defaulting on payments – since bills will increase by the amortized amount of connection fees – but as long as the utilities supply the electricity they have the means to enforce collections. Rigid standards in internal wiring can set the hurdle of high connection fees even higher. Simplifying these standards without compromising safety can prevent the barrier becoming insuperable.[3]

In addition to connection fees, the fixed costs of electricity include the purchase of electrical equipment. Directly subsidizing the purchase of electric equipment for poor households is one policy option, though its practical implementation will be difficult as the private sector supplies electrical equipment to households. Alternatively, the government can establish a fund to which poor households can apply if they are interested in but cannot afford the purchase of electric equipment. In another variation on the theme the government can enter into an arrangement where suppliers are compensated for the sale of their equipment at lower prices to poor households. In addition to creating a strain on government resources these options are very difficult to put into practice. They need an efficient targeting system that identifies the poor and avoids corruption. If poor households can purchase electrical equipment at subsidized prices, a secondary market where the poor re-sell the equipment could develop on the margin between subsidized prices and resale at a higher figure closer to market value. In cases where these conditions can be controlled, such a policy may repay the experiment.

Governments can also use tax or similar fiscal incentives to encourage private sector suppliers either to extend credit or spread fixed cost – tax relief, for example, for equipment suppliers with particular initiatives that spread the cost of equipment. Since the administration and monitoring of these initiatives is demanding, ways of minimizing these costs have to be carefully planned.

Other innovative arrangements by governments and NGOs should also be encouraged. For instance, in most government- and NGO-sponsored welfare programmes, energy is not considered as a priority in the livelihood of the poor. In integrating energy as an essential element of the livelihood of the poor, micro-credit programmes – a typical component of anti-poverty strategies – can be targeted to cover fixed costs of electricity.

In the long run, falling prices of electricity and electrical equipment are the best guarantee that they will become accessible to larger segments of the population. Improvements in efficiency and higher levels of competition in electric generation, transmission and distribution, as well as in the marketing of electrical equipment, are required to achieve that outcome. Improvements in efficiency decrease marginal costs and, as long as the pricing principle of equating marginal cost with marginal revenues is maintained, this pulls electricity tariffs down. The monopoly of utilities in generation and distribution of electricity may have to be terminated to increase competition. A regulatory institutional framework that maintains competitive conditions in the electricity sector is required.

In addition to examining whether unsubsidized modern energy can be afforded by poor urban households, the country studies investigate who captures the energy subsidies: the targeted group – the poor – or the non-poor. The main results and policy implications of this investigation are summarized in the next subsection.

Who captures the subsidies?

Having ascertained the role of subsidies in enabling poor urban households to access modern forms of energy, the country studies then examined the question of the distribution of subsidies amongst different income groups. The findings show that both kerosene and electricity subsidies are mostly captured by the well-to-do; higher-income households get the larger portion of the energy subsidies. This implies that if the subsidies are removed, most of the cost will be borne by richer urban households; the social cost of subsidy removal will not be high as it will hurts mostly the relatively well-to-do.

In relation to kerosene, abolition of subsidies is probably the advisable policy option. First, the empirical findings show leakage to non-poor households is high and hence, as indicated above, the social cost of kerosene subsidy removal is low. Second, the kerosene subsidy does not play an important role in improving affordability to the poor. Since kerosene is subsidized by higher taxes from other fuels (for example, in Ethiopia), the abolition of kerosene subsidies will have the added advantage of decreasing the burden on consumers of other fuels.

In relation to electricity, the fact that lifeline tariffs are fixed at relatively high rates creates a problem. For example, in Ethiopia in 2001, 74 per cent of electricity consumers were consuming less than the lifeline tariff. Hence, many of the customers that are subsidized by the lifeline tariff are non-targeted groups. This leakage to non-targeted groups can be minimized by decreasing the lifeline tariff to a level that realistically approximates the consumption level of poor households.

A related problem is that households consuming more than the lifeline tariff will also enjoy the subsidy for the first amount of electricity below the lifeline rate. This is another form of leakage to non-targeted groups. In addition to decreasing the level of the lifeline tariff, it is necessary to redesign it so that it applies only to the target group. A variable tariff rate can help to do that. All households consuming a larger amount of electricity than the lifeline threshold can be made to pay a higher tariff even for the first units of electricity below the lifeline. To avoid sudden jumps in payment for those who are just consuming above the lifeline threshold, a smoothing procedure that slowly increases the rate at the threshold can be introduced.

The resources that can be saved by the removal of subsidies can better be utilized to minimize the constraints households face in relation to upfront (fixed) costs, as indicated in the previous subsection.

The pricing policy and tariff structures in a country affect productive activities as well as consumption. The studies examined how electricity tariffs affect the performance of informal sector enterprises. The next subsection presents the main results.

How does energy pricing affect the informal sector?
In some of the case countries (for example, Ethiopia) the electricity tariff structure is designed to favour consumption in the economy. Since some of the informal sector enterprises are located inside households, it is likely that this policy has also subsidized them, as long as their consumption of electricity is not relatively high. But generally, a tariff favouring consumption at the expense of productive activities is not favourable for economic growth. This condition has to be redressed.

In other countries (for example, Zimbabwe) large-scale users such as high-voltage industrial, mining, commercial and agricultural customers are charged below their respective LRMCs and are being subsidized by other customer categories, including small-scale enterprises. Small-scale enterprises (which probably are more important for the welfare of the urban poor) subsidize large commercial firms and there is no apparent reason why this is allowed. This distorted tariff structure can be particularly damaging for smaller enterprises if their electricity expenditure is proportionally larger, as is the case in Zambia.

Governments must carefully examine the effects of distorted tariff structures and monitor their possible negative impacts, particularly on those sectors that are more relevant for the welfare of the urban poor.

In addition, since most small and micro enterprises are owned by or employ the urban poor, initiatives that improve their energy access are likely to lead to better income for the urban poor. These enterprises are principally found in the informal sector, which has received minimal support from governments.

In most high-density areas, it is common to find several households with power supply from a single source. 'Backyard dwellers' obtain electricity from the main house and share the same meter. Similarly, in the informal sector, a survey of SMEs carried out in Nairobi, Kenya by AFREPREN showed that in most fabricating workshops, the power source and specialized equipment such as lathe machines and arc welders were owned by an individual who would rent them out at an agreed fee (AFREPREN/FWD, 2003). These flexible mechanisms allow intermittent provision of electricity, which matches the irregular incomes of most of the urban poor.

Two studies separately carried out in South Africa by Mehlwana (1997) and the National Electricity Regulator (1996) showed that in the shanty towns where the urban poor live it was common practice to find 'illegal' power supply cables running across the road. In most cases, the fees charged for power supply were exorbitant, in addition to restrictions on the type of appliances that one could use.

The power utilities in South Africa and in Zimbabwe have partially tackled this problem by introducing compact ready boards.[4] However, this cannot entirely solve the problem, especially for backyard dwellers and SMEs that have low consumption levels and irregular incomes. A more effective way of dealing with the problem in the long term would be to legalize informal power distribution. The power utility would concentrate on ensuring that the power is supplied safely, by insisting on a set of minimum standards. The informal power distribution would then be allowed to set tariffs that reflect the risk and income profiles of their consumers.

Energy subsidies have to be financed by resources from certain sectors of the economy. Generally these resources are drawn either from government budgets or from energy utilities. The next subsection summarizes the impacts of subsidies on energy utilities and public finance.

What is the impact of subsidies on utilities and public finance?

The total amounts of subsidies in the countries under study are significant. For example, for the financial year 1999/2000 the total electricity subsidy in Uganda was about 6 per cent of GDP and 22 per cent of the government budget deficit respectively. But the empirical results also indicate that a significant proportion of these energy subsidies are financed by cross-subsidization. For example, in Zimbabwe a significant proportion of the subsidies is made up by the customers paying tariffs above the LRMC. In Ethiopia, the kerosene subsidy is financed by additional taxes collected from other fuels, mainly from gasoline. This means that the direct effect of energy subsidies on government finances is minimized. But energy utilities may not be compensated directly for these subsidies, weakening their financial position.

Even though the direct effects of subsidies on public finances may be minimized by cross-subsidization, indirect effects that may be transmitted through relative price changes can be significant. For example, the additional taxes imposed on the other fuels to cross-subsidize kerosene in

Ethiopia decrease their demand, indirectly decreasing the taxes that can be collected from them. Depending on demand elasticities and other feedback effects, these indirect effects may be significant. Although identifying such indirect effects is beyond the scope of the studies presented in this book, policy makers should be aware of them when assessing cross-subsidizations.

The final subsection of this introductory part touches on pricing and some related issues.

Energy pricing and related issues
The LRMC is generally taken as the true reflection of the cost of electricity. And generally, subsidies exist if tariff rates are less than the LRMC. In the computation of the LRMC, current costs of electricity generation, transmission and distribution are considered. Provided there are inefficiencies in these systems, the current practice of including actual costs of utilities probably inflates the LRMC. There is a need to re-examine the method used to determine the LRMC, since actual costs are expected to be higher than efficiency costs. The computation of the LMRC must be based on best practice.

Even though the studies focused on the provision of modern energy to the urban poor, biomass is likely to be the dominant form of energy used by the urban poor in Africa, and hence policy should also focus on its efficient utilization. In other words, policy makers should not only be concerned about improving the access of the poor to modern forms of energy, but should also accept that traditional fuels will be important, at least in the short run, for the urban poor. Interventions aimed at providing efficient technologies and appliances for biomass use should be promoted. This will reduce the energy expenditure of the urban poor and, in addition, ensure that available biomass resources are used more efficiently.

At the household level, improved charcoal stoves that are designed to reduce heat loss, increase combustion efficiency and attain higher heat transfer would be appropriate for dissemination. Despite these advantages, improved stove dissemination is still relatively low in most countries in the region. The main reason for the low dissemination among the urban poor is the high cost of the stove. An improved stove is about twice the cost of the traditional metal stove.

One way of increasing dissemination of improved stoves among the urban poor could be to introduce innovative financing schemes that would reduce the upfront cost of improved biofuel stoves. For instance, a hire purchase system could be introduced through stove manufacturers and distributors. Technical changes to the improved stoves could also lower the cost of acquisition. For example, the Kenya Ceramic Jiko (KCJ) has been modified to reduce the amount of metal cladding required for its manufacture (AFREPREN/FWD, 2001), reducing its cost. Improved institutional stoves have also been disseminated in several East and

Southern African countries, and would be ideal for small and micro-enterprises such as food kiosks and informal sector outside caterers. A financing scheme for institutional stoves could lower the upfront cost and enhance dissemination.

The rest of the book is organized in the following way. While Part 2 presents a review of the issues at the regional (African) level, Part 3 outlines the common methodological approaches used in the country studies. The subsequent parts present the country studies for Zambia, Zimbabwe, Ethiopia, Uganda and Tanzania.

Part I • Notes and References

Notes

1   A more detailed discussion of the effect of urbanization on energy patterns is given in Part 2.
2   Or, as in the cases of Tanzania, Zambia and Zimbabwe, lower taxes are levied on kerosene instead of subsidies.
3   The use of Single Wire Earth Return (SWER), pre-paid meters and/or compact ready boards is suggested by the Uganda study to simplify internal wiring.
4   A compact ready board is a unit that has a bulb holder, a socket outlet and a main switch. Use of the board eliminates the need for internal wiring.

References

AFREPREN/FWD, 2001. Newspaper cuttings and internal surveys carried out by the RETSCAP. Nairobi: African Energy Policy Research Network/ Foundation for Woodstove Dissemination.
——, 2003. *African Energy Database Handbook*. Nairobi: African Energy Policy Research Network/Foundation for Woodstove Dissemination.
Mehlwana, A. M., 1997. 'The Anthropology of Fuels: Situational Analysis and Energy Use in Urban Low-Income Townships of South Africa', in *Energy for Sustainable Development – The Journal of the International Energy Initiative*, Vol. 3 No.5. Bangalore: International Energy Initiative Inc.
National Electricity Regulator, 1996. *Lighting up South Africa, 1996 – Progress Report on Electrification*, Pretoria: National Electricity Regulator.
Tomlinson M., 1999. 'Access to Energy Services – a Brighter Future?', in *Energy after the Financial Crises*, Washington, DC: World Bank/ESMAP.
World Bank, 2003. *World Development Indicators 2003*. Washington DC: World Bank.

Part 2

REGIONAL REPORT

Stephen Karekezi and Lugard Majoro

REGIONAL PROFILE
Sub-Saharan Africa
(excluding South Africa):
SELECTED INDICATORS

- Area (km²): 22,405,000 (2001)
- Population (million): 631.3 (2001)
- Urban population (million): 209.6 (2001)
- Urban population growth rate (%): 4.9 (average 1990–2001)
- GNP *per capita* (US$): 300 (2001)
- Number of people living below US$1 a day (%): 50 (1998)
- Number of people living below US$2 a day (%): 81 (1998)
- Kerosene consumption *per capita* (litres): 13.96 (1997)
- Commercial energy consumption *per capita* (Kgoe): 669 (2000)
- Electricity consumption *per capita* (kWh): 112.8 (2000)

Sources: World Bank, 2000a; World Bank, 2003a; World Bank, 2003b; AFREPREN/FWD, 2003a; Karakezi *et al.*, 2002

1

Impact of Urbanization
on Energy Consumption Patterns

Stephen Karekezi and Lugard Majoro

While most of Africa is still essentially rural, the continent's towns and cities are growing rapidly. As shown below (Figure 2.1), sub-Saharan Africa has the highest urban grown rate. It is estimated that for most African countries the urban growth rate is close to double the national population growth rate (Figure 2.2). Large urban centres are growing rapidly and dominate their respective national economies. Examples include Cairo, Lagos, Nairobi, Dar-es-Salaam, Kampala, Lusaka, Harare and Gaborone. The second largest city in most African countries is usually much smaller and rarely known outside the country.

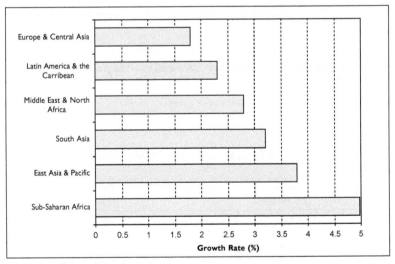

Figure 2.1 Urbanization by region

Sources: World Bank,, 2000; World Bank,, 2003a

In many ways, the urbanization patterns that are emerging in Africa are somewhat similar to those prevalent in much of Latin America today, namely heavily urbanized countries dominated by a single city that is often both the nation's political and economic capital. In a number of

Latin American countries, high urbanization rates are the norm and the capital city can account for as much as 60 per cent of the national population. For example, Bolivia, Colombia, Chile and Argentina have urban populations that account respectively for 63, 75, 86 and 88 per cent of the national populations (World Bank, 2003b).

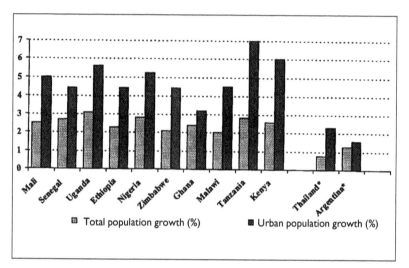

Figure 2.2 National population growth compared to urban population growth (1990–2001)
* Data for Thailand and Argentina is 1995–2000
Sources: World Bank,, 2000; World Bank, 2003a; UNHABITAT website

Table 2.1 Earnings (Z$ millions) and employees (000s) in urban areas of Zimbabwe in 1997

Town	Earnings (Z$ millions)	% of total	Employees	% of total
Harare	14,843.10	60.59	363.10	56.30
Bulawayo	4,687.40	19.13	147.10	22.81
Matare	1,196.70	4.89	35.30	5.47
Gweru	1,064.10	4.34	30.00	4.65
Kwekwe	831.00	3.39	20.00	3.10
Masvingo	703.20	2.87	17.30	2.68
Kadoma	523.20	2.14	13.70	2.12
Marondera	345.30	1.41	9.00	1.40
Chinhoyi	304.30	1.24	9.50	1.47
Total	24,498.30	100.00	645.00	100.00

Source: CSO, 1999c

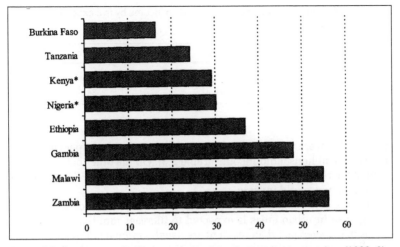

Figure 2.3 Percentage of urban population living below the poverty line (1998–9)

*Data for 1992
Source: World Bank, 2003c

Similar trends are emerging in Africa. For example, in Zimbabwe the two towns of Harare and Bulawayo dominate economic activities and account for about 79 per cent of the country's earnings and employment (Table 2.1). In Botswana, out of 15,346 operational business establishments in the country, 6,679 (about 43 per cent) are found in two towns, Gaborone and Francistown (CSO, 1998c).

Rapid urban population growth rate in sub-Saharan Africa has been accompanied by high levels of urban poverty. As shown in Figure 2.3, the levels of poverty[1] in most urban areas are fairly high, which underlies the importance of focusing on the urban poor.

Table 2.2 Gini Coefficient for urban areas in four African countries (1991–7)

Country	Gini Coefficient
Ethiopia	56
Kenya	51
Zambia	40
Uganda	35

Note: Gini coefficient is a measure of disparity in the distribution of incomes.
Source: World Bank, 2003a

The distribution of income in most countries in Africa shows a large disparity between the poor and the non-poor (see Table 2.2). In Ethiopia (Kebede, 2001) the Central Statistical Authority (CSA) classified urban households into five income groups and found that 47.7 per cent of the

Table 2.3 Percentages of households and urban income by five expenditure groups in Ethiopia

	Very poor	Poor	Medium	Rich	Very rich
% of households	8.3	39.0	11.5	28.4	12.8
% of income	0.9	14.1	7.3	34.8	42.9

Source: Kebede, 2001

households were very poor and poor, and control only 15 per cent of the overall urban household income (Table 2.3). On the other hand, 41.2 per cent of the rich and very rich households controlled up to 77.7 per cent of the urban household income.

In spite of the high levels of poverty, urbanization is accelerating, and energy use in urban areas is expected to increase rapidly. Typical activities of the average urban resident are usually more modern and energy-intensive than the activities of a rural resident. Consequently, the ongoing rural–urban demographic shift is expected to result in a large increase in modern energy consumption (Karekezi, 2002a).

Conventional thinking argues that as the population moves from rural communities to increasingly crowded urban cities, their energy use patterns change (Barnes, 1995). Charcoal, kerosene and LPG replace wood as the primary cooking fuels. The three-stone fire is abandoned and charcoal braziers, kerosene stoves and LPG cookstoves become the cooking devices of choice. New energy devices are acquired. Examples include electric lights, radios, televisions, fans, refrigerators and air conditioners. The demographic shift to urban areas is supposed not only to trigger changes in the type and form of energy used but also to imply a much higher demand for energy. *Per capita* use of energy increases significantly as the population moves from rural communities to urban conglomerations (Karekezi, 2002b).

As the urbanization of Africa gathers pace, sub-Saharan Africa's energy sector will probably begin to acquire the characteristics prevalent in Northern Africa and Latin America. This implies major increases in demand for modern energy services. This would, however, be subject to rising real incomes for the majority of inhabitants. Otherwise, the increase will be met by unprocessed and environmentally unsound biofuels (Karekezi and Majoro, 1999).

Urbanization in many Latin American and Asian countries generally also implied a greater degree of industrialization and trading as production and commercialization became more centralized. Consequently, a rapid increase in energy demand for the industrial and commercial sectors was experienced. Energy demand for productive activities in urban areas often requires modern fuels and energy services, largely provided by centralized energy generation plants. The transition to clean modern energy in urban areas relies heavily on increased incomes – a trend that is found in only a few African cities (Karekezi, 1993). Stagnation in the economies of most African countries results in failure to generate the expected level of increased demand for energy (Karekezi and Majoro, 1999).

Although the bulk of current energy investments in Africa are aimed at serving the urban population, not all segments of the urban population benefit equally. There is some evidence that a larger proportion of government financing, subsidies and international development aid is aimed at developing modern energy infrastructure that largely serves the needs of the urban-based formal sector, commercial and industrial sectors and the medium- and high-income urban households. For example, data from Ethiopia comparing energy sector capital budget shares of different energy sources shows that the allocation for the traditional energy and petroleum products that meet the bulk of the energy needs of the urban poor is on average 10 per cent of the total allocation (see Figure 2.4). Energy services for the urban poor are not a major concern that is high on the development agenda.

As shown in Figure 2.5, urban electrification levels are low in most sub-Saharan African countries. The limited available evidence indicates that the situation is even worse in low-income urban households. This is particularly troubling since the low-income areas are usually not very far from major electricity transmission and switching stations. Low-income areas are often close to the city centre and are densely populated: the associated transmission and distribution costs of electricity extension are

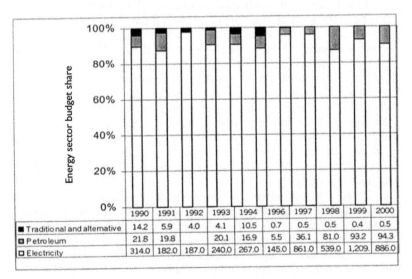

	1990	1991	1992	1993	1994	1996	1997	1998	1999	2000
■ Traditional and alternative	14.2	5.9	4.0	4.1	10.5	0.7	0.5	0.5	0.4	0.5
▫ Petroleum	21.8	19.8		20.1	16.9	5.5	36.1	81.0	93.2	94.3
▫ Electricity	314.0	182.0	187.0	240.0	267.0	145.0	861.0	539.0	1,209.	886.0

Figure 2.4 Energy sector capital budget shares (%) and total budget shares (million Birr), 1990–2000

Source: Wolde-Ghiorgis, 2002

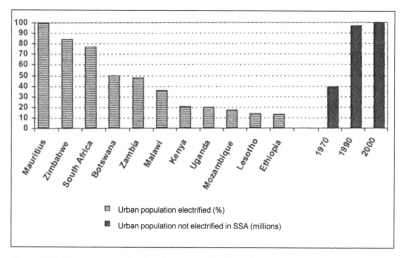

Figure 2.5 Percentages of urban households electrified

Sources: AFREPREN, 2003a; Dube, 2002; Teferra, 2002; Kyokutamba, 2002; Kalumiana, 2002; Katyega, 2003; World Bank, 2002; IEA, 2002; Okumu, 2003; Kinuthia, 2003

therefore not high. In many cases, the costs are lower than the cost of extending electricity to low-density high-income areas.

Current trends indicate that the increase in urban energy consumption will be in the form of traditional biofuels. Of the estimated one third of Africa's population who live in urban areas, only about 25 per cent have access to electricity (Tomlinson, 1999; World Bank, 2003b). As shown in Figure 1.5, urban household electrification levels are generally below 30 per cent. Between 1970 and 1990, Africa's population increased by about 150 million, but over this period the number of persons with access to electricity increased by only about 60 million. Over a 30-year period (1970–2000) the number of urban inhabitants that were not electrified increased from slightly less than 40 million to close to 96 million by 1990, and by 2000 the number had increased to over 100 million – the equivalent of the whole of Nigeria, the most populous country in Africa, going without electricity.

Energy demand patterns of the urban poor largely revolve around household energy end uses such as cooking and lighting as well as energy services for small-scale and informal commercial and productive activities. At the household level, most low-income households in urban areas of sub-Saharan African countries rely on biofuels for cooking (often charcoal in East Africa and wood in Southern Africa), while coal is a main source of energy in certain Southern African countries such as Zimbabwe, South Africa, Swaziland and Lesotho. LPG is rarely used in low-income households. Kerosene is usually the fuel of choice for lighting

(Kebede, 2003; Dube, 2002; Katyega, 2003; Kyokutamba, 2002). As mentioned earlier, electricity continues to be a rarity in many low-income urban households.

An important aspect of urbanization, particularly in Africa, is the growth of the informal sector. The informal sector is one of the largest employers in most African cities. Informal sector activities are essentially dominated by the urban poor. While most informal sector enterprises are characterized by energy use at low to medium intensity, they are an important group to consider. Currently, many informal sector enterprises extensively use unprocessed biofuels and residual oil products. Some studies have shown that provision of efficient and affordable energy could lead to improved performance in the informal sector (Hosier, 1994).

Typical commercial energy applications in the informal sector include use of electricity, kerosene and charcoal for cooking and lighting in small restaurants, food kiosks, shops, bars and video halls. Another important informal sector activity is urban transport, particularly mini-buses for commuter transport and pick-ups for freight delivery (Karekezi *et al.*, 2003). It should, however, be pointed out that the transport energy question, although important, is not be addressed in this book. There are other important energy applications in the informal sector, including the fabrication of simple household items and various mechanical and electrical repair services.

In general, urban energy in Africa is characterized by the following features (Karekezi, 1993):

- *per capita* energy consumption much higher than in rural areas;

- an urban energy consumption spectrum with two extremes: on one hand the energy-intensive heavy industry generally classified as the formal sector, on the other the informal sector and the low-income households with low-to-medium energy consumption levels;

- disparity between the rich and the poor in urban areas and concomitant wide disparity in provision and access to energy services – discussed in the next section.

2

Energy Use
among the Urban Poor

With the growing rate of urban poverty and limited development of modern energy infrastructure in low-income areas, the cost of modern energy services is increasingly becoming prohibitive for low-income households and informal sector enterprises (the informal sector is often the largest source of employment for low-income urban residents). Many low-income urban households are faced with the difficult and almost daily choice of apportioning dwindling urban incomes between essential food purchases and cooking fuel. The increasingly desperate measures that many low-income urban dwellers and informal sector enterprises resort to in an attempt to procure modern energy services are indicative of the suppressed demand and increasing relative cost of modern energy services. Examples include the frequent and growing problem of illegal electricity connections and repeated attempts to avoid the high duty placed on petroleum fuels (Karekezi, 1993).

For ease of analysis, urban energy consumption patterns in sub-Saharan Africa are discussed at two levels: households and the informal sector (made up of small and micro-enterprises, or SMEs).

Consumption patterns and the cost of household energy

As shown in Table 2.4, lower-income groups pay a much higher proportion of income to meet their energy needs compared to higher-income groups. This is corroborated by a study carried out by Barnes (1995) in 45 cities in 12 developing countries, which classified the households by income per person per month. It showed that the lowest earners (US$7–11 per person per month) spent about 22 per cent of their income on energy while the highest earners (US$107–216 per person per month) used 9 per cent of their income.

Several other studies (Hosier, 1994; Barnes, 1995; Smith, 1998; Qase and Annecke, 1999; and Dube, 2001) confirm that the urban poor pay more for each unit of energy consumed. This is partly attributed to the low-grade fuels used by the poor. Dube (2001) and Smith (1998) demonstrate that the use of modern energy by the poor is hampered by the upfront costs of acquiring the requisite appliances. For example, in Zimbabwe connection to grid electricity using a compact ready board is about 300 per cent higher than the poor households' average income.

Table 2.4 Energy expenditure as percentage of urban household income in selected African countries

Income level	Energy expenditure as % of urban household income			
category	Uganda	Ethiopia	Zimbabwe	Zambia
Low-income	15.00	10.00	7.70	7.89
High-income	9.50	7.00	4.80	5.86

Sources: Kebede, 2001; Dube, 2001; Kyokutamba, 2002; Kalumiana, 2003

Table 2.5 Urban household energy consumption and expenditures in relation to monthly income, 1988

Country	Income/person (US$/month)	Energy consumption (kgoe/month)	Energy expenditures (US$)	As % of total income
Thailand	117.50	10.82	8.85	7.53
Bolivia	68.33	10.79	4.43	6.48
Philippines	60.10	6.92	4.93	8.21
Indonesia	24.45	8.51	2.40	9.81
Burkina Faso	35.12	10.48	4.36	12.51
Mauritania	25.34	10.83	6.18	24.40
Uganda*	71.83	N/A	14.00	19.39
Zambia	23.04	16.48	3.76	16.31

*Data for 1990
Sources: Reddy, Williams and Johansson, 1997; Okumu, 2003

A similar trend is observed at national level (Table 2.5). The poor countries tend to spend a larger proportion of their income on energy compared to the relatively richer countries.

The high energy costs that the poorer households incur indicate the prevalent use of biofuels, which have low energy content per unit of input. For example, 1 kg of fuelwood produces markedly less energy than the equivalent quantity of LPG.

This disparity underlines the equity dimension of the urban energy question. Tyler (1994) cites three factors that explain why the poor spend more on energy than the non-poor, namely:

- low-quality fuels that burn less efficiently when used, so that more fuel is required to perform the task;

- purchasing fuel in small quantities at the end of a chain of small distributors, resulting in higher retail prices; and

- energy subsidies, for example on electricity, that are largely captured by high-income groups.

Energy consumes a substantial portion of the income of the urban poor. Even at national level, household energy expenditure in Africa accounted for 7–18 per cent of the total household income (ADB, 1996). The data may be dated, but the underlying pattern is unlikely to have changed significantly. As mentioned earlier, the higher energy expenditure also results from the purchase of lower-grade fuels rather than smaller quantities of modern fuels – a choice dictated by the low and irregular income of most urban households.

The study by Barnes (1995) shows that for countries with close to 100 per cent electrification, the poor households pay less for lighting than the rich households, for example in Thailand. This is attributed to the fact that the poor pay a lifeline tariff. In countries with low electrification, on the other hand, the poor households pay more for lighting than the richer households. For example, the study cites lighting costs in Cape Verde where the poorest households pay about US$1.40 per kilolumen hour compared to US$0.85 for the highest-income households. A similar pattern emerges with respect to the cost of cooking energy. For example, in Philippines the urban poor paid US$1.79 per kgoe while the rich paid US$0.66 per kgoe. This is explained by the use of low-quality fuels such as wood, where 10–15 per cent of the energy is utilized. By contrast, LPG and electric cookers, commonly used by the high-income households, deliver energy efficiencies of the order of 50–65 per cent.

A case study carried out in Nairobi by Gitonga (1999) showed that the main fuels the urban poor households use were, in order of importance, charcoal, kerosene and fuelwood. A notable aspect of the survey is that all households visited that had a charcoal stove also possessed a kerosene stove. The reason was that kerosene is used mostly in the morning for breakfast, while charcoal is used for the 'hard foods' that take long to cook. A similar pattern is found in most countries of the region. In some countries such as Zimbabwe, however, electricity is the main fuel for cooking, reflecting improved access (Table 2.6). In the cases of both Kenya and Zimbabwe, kerosene is still an important fuel and is ranked second for its ease of use, affordability and suitability for both cooking and lighting.

Table 2.6 Access to energy sources by households for different income categories in urban areas and nationally, Zimbabwe

Energy source	Urban (%)		National (%)	
	Poor	Non-poor	Poor	Non-poor
Access to electricity	73.1	81.9	19.0	52.8
Cooking fuel				
Electricity or gas	47.6	60.8	11.7	38.3
Kerosene	39.7	33.7	10.2	25.4
Wood or coal	12.7	5.4	78.1	36.3

Source: CSO, 1998a

The use of kerosene, wood and charcoal seems to predominate in areas without adequate access to electricity. Introduction of electricity tends to change the energy consumption pattern, as demonstrated in a Zambia case study (Table 2.7). After connection to electricity, the use of kerosene, wood and charcoal decreased, the largest drop being in the use of kerosene because it is principally used for lighting and cooking of 'light' foods. However, there is a marked increase (about 7 times) in the use of candles. This could be explained by the fact that the candles are used as back-up lighting during blackouts.

Table 2.7 Households before and after electricity connection in Pamodzi Ndola, Zambia

	Before connection (1995)	After connection (1997)
Households using kerosene (%)	97	50
Households using candles (%)	11	80
Households using wood (%)	37	5
Households using charcoal (%)	100	85

Source: Arvidson et al., 1998

LPG – one of the most efficient, convenient and clean fuels – is used in many urban areas of Africa. The major users are households, government institutions and the commerce/industrial and manufacturing sectors. Because of its relatively high upfront cost, it is mainly used for cooking in high-income urban households and small and medium-scale enterprises/institutions.

The high upfront costs of LPG are attributable to the fact that in most countries in the region both the fuel and devices are imported. The typical costs of the 12 kg cylinder of LPG commonly used for cooking are shown in Table 2.8. A comparison of the upfront cost of using LPG to the mean monthly energy expenditure of poor urban households in selected countries in the region (US$17) demonstrates the unaffordability of LPG.

To partially counter this problem, smaller gas cylinders have been introduced on the market in both Kenya and Uganda. The different sizes of cylinders have enabled the petroleum companies, principal marketers

Table 2.8 Upfront cost of using a 12 kg cylinder in Kenya

Device	Cost (US$)	As % of mean monthly energy expenditure of urban poor households in the region
LPG cylinder ready-to-use (12kg)	66	388
LPG cooker (with 2 plate)	40	235
Total	106	623

Source: AFREPREN/FWD, 2003b

of LPG, to reach lower-income groups. Essentially, the upfront cost of using LPG has been reduced by about 48 per cent. In addition, the smaller cylinders have a dual function: lighting, cooking, or both. The dual-purpose cylinders can fitted with either a cooking kit or a lighting kit. To purchase both kits in Kenya currently costs about US$52.

If the above upfront cost of US$52 is compared to the mean monthly household energy expenditure of US$17 of the urban poor in the region, it is clear that LPG is still an expensive option for the average urban poor household. As shown in Table 2.9, even for the smallest cylinders, the up-front cost is a major hurdle for the urban poor. However, the refilling cost of US$3–15 seems within the reach of many poor urban households. A subsidy on cylinders and cookers and/or amortizing the cost of appliances in the fuel price of LPG could increase the urban poor's access to LPG substantially.

Table 2.9   Cost of buying and refilling different gas cylinder sizes in Kenya

Weight (kg)	Price				
	Selling price of ready-to-use cylinder (KShs)	Selling price of ready cylinder (US$)	Refilling (KShs)	Refilling (US$)	Sector that mainly uses the cylinder
50	13400	178	4485	60	Industry
22	8500	113	1950	26	Industry
12	4960	66	1120	15	Households & SMEs
6	3440	46	540	7	Households & SMEs
3	1480	20	270	4	Households

Source: AFREPREN/FWD, 2003b

Energy use in the informal sector – small and micro-enterprises (SMEs)

The informal sector (largely made up of small and micro-enterprises – SMEs) is a major producer of goods and services for the urban poor and an important source of employment. The main legal feature of SMEs in most African countries is that they are neither registered with the Registrar of Companies nor (in most cases) recorded in official or tax records. Often their operators do not have licences from the relevant authorities. The level of organization is generally low, with little access to organized markets, formal credit, education and training.

According to the 1995/6 Labour Force Survey (LFS) undertaken in Botswana (CSO, 1999b) an establishment is referred to as an informal activity if it has the following characteristics (this is also true for most countries in the region):

- not a registered company;
- not registered with a professional association;
- has less than 10 employees and the employees are casually hired;
- has an informal account or none;
- its expenditure is not easily distinguishable from household expenditure;
- is temporary or mobile or located in owner's home/plot.

The high employment creation potential in the informal sector is partly attributed to the use of simple and inexpensive technologies (inclusive of energy technologies) requiring rudimentary skills; ease of entry and exit; low capital investment; and the absence of registration and other official formalities. In Kenya, the informal sector accounted for about 75 per cent of employment (Figure 2.1).

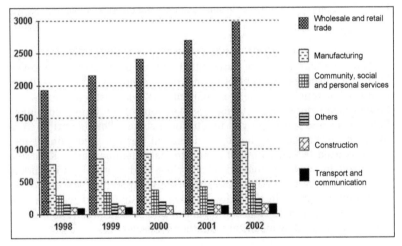

Figure 2.6 Employment (000s) in the informal sector in Kenya (1998–2002)

Source: CSO, 1990a, 2003

A survey carried out in Nairobi, Kenya showed the distribution of SMEs depicted in Figure 2.7. The informal sector is one of the fastest-growing economic subsectors in many sub-Saharan African countries. It is also one of the largest employers. While its energy needs are modest, the informal sector can play a crucial role in providing energy services as well as the manufacture and distribution of low-cost clean energy technologies. In Kenya, for instance, the whole improved stove manufacturing process is carried out by the informal sector, as well as the production of kerosene stoves and lamps commonly used by the urban poor.

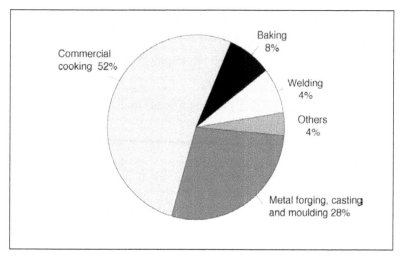

Figure 2.7 Commercial activities in small and micro-enterprises in Nairobi, Kenya

Source: Gitonga, 1999

The same Nairobi survey showed that up to 50 per cent of the surveyed businesses used 14 per cent of their profits on energy while 10–20 per cent used as much as 40 per cent (Gitonga, 1999). Most food kiosks and home-based caterers were using large versions of the improved household stoves and not improved institutional stoves. This is attributed to the high upfront cost of the stoves. Charcoal was the predominant fuel and was used for hardening of metals to make hammer mills. Kerosene was used for welding instead of acetylene and oxygen gas cylinders because of the prohibitive capital cost of the equipment.

A similar survey in Zimbabwe showed that fuelwood was the predominant fuel in both households and home-based SMEs (Table 2.10). This was followed by electricity and then kerosene.

Table 2.10 Comparison of household energy use by activity in Zimbabwe

Energy source	Typical household use (%)	Home-based SMEs (%)
Wood	93.95	84.10
Electricity	2.72	7.71
Kerosene	2.46	4.90
Other	0.88	2.30
LPG	0.00	1.00

Source: Dube, 2001

Energy demand patterns of urban households, especially the poor, largely revolve around household energy end uses such as cooking and lighting as well as energy services for home-based commercial and productive activities. Most SMEs are home-based and are involved in a wide range of activities. A survey carried out in Botswana showed the range of activities listed in Table 2.11. The most common activities in order of frequency were property rentals, hawking/vending and brewing/selling of beer.

Table 2.11 Household-based enterprises in Botswana

Activities	No. of enterprises
Property rentals	6,791
Hawker/vendors	3,864
Brewing/selling of beer	2,908
Making/selling of clothes	2,274
Selling crops, fruits, vegetables	620
Cooking/selling of food	587
Taxi service	430
Building/plumbing etc.	391
General dealers	344
Other repairs	286
Gathering, catching of fish etc.	284
Vehicle repair/panel beating	248
Haircutting/dressing	208
Making/selling furniture	208
Selling poultry, livestock etc.	151
Selling milk, eggs, other livestock	105
Making craftwork	62
Blacksmith/tinsmithing	29

Source: CSO, 1994

The prevalence of household-based enterprises could explain the wide variation in household energy consumption, illustrating the overlap between energy use at the household level and at the level of the informal enterprise.

Table 2.12 lists commercial activities that are commonly found among the urban poor. The activities are broadly categorized into:

- commercial/service/community;
- production/manufacturing.

A further attempt is made to identify the major energy input, the conventional technology device used, and the alternative energy technology options available for each activity.

Access to modern energy services is an important impetus to regeneration of low-income urban areas. The absence of electricity appears to be an important barrier to informal sector entrepreneurial activities. In

Table 2.12 Commercial activities employing or owned by the urban poor in Africa

Activity	Main energy input	Services Energy device used	Alternatives
Food kiosks	Charcoal, kerosene	Stoves	LPG, efficient biofuel stoves
Small restaurants	Charcoal, kerosene, electricity, LPG	Stoves, electric cookers	Efficient biofuel stoves, and more efficient electricity stoves
Small shops	Kerosene, electricity	Fridges, stoves, lanterns	More energy efficient devices
Laundry	Charcoal, electricity, solar	Flat iron, washing board	
Tailoring	Animate, electricity	Sewing machines, flat irons	Sewing machines with efficient motors
Beer bars /halls	Kerosene, electricity	Fridges, stoves, electric cookers	LPG, efficient biofuel stoves & more efficient electric cookers
Informal video halls	Electricity		Time of day electricity tariffs
Taxi service	Petroleum	Petrol & diesel engines	Efficient internal combustion engines, improved engine tuning & maintenance
Commercial pick-up transport	Petroleum	Petrol & diesel engines	Efficient internal combustion engines, improved engine tuning & maintenance
Vehicle repair	Electricity, LPG, animate	Welding equipment grinders, compressors	Efficient motors
Electrical goods repair	Electricity	Soldering equipment	
Butcheries	Animate, electricity	Incandescent lights	Tubes and CFLs
Tyre repair	Kerosene	Heaters, compressors	Efficient heaters and motors
Urban clinics	Electricity	Sterilizers, water boiling equipment, fridges	Solar water heaters, efficient equipment, tubes and CFLs
Churches & mosques	Electricity	Incandescent lights	Tubes and CFLs
Social halls & youth centres	Electricity	Incandescent lights	Tubes and CFLs
Local govt. offices	Electricity	Incandescent lights	Tubes and CFLs

Table 2.12 cont.

| Activity | Production/manufacturing activities | | |
	Main energy input	Energy device used	Alternatives
Metal works	Electricity, gas	Welding equipment, lathe machines, grinders, incandescent lights	Efficient electric motors, tubes and CFLs
Metal household items	Charcoal, electricity	Heaters	Use of efficient heaters, and electricity
Pottery/clay products	Animate, woodfuel	Rollers	Solar dryers, electric rollers
Woodwork and furniture	Animate, electricity	Cutting and planing equipment	Efficient motors
Basket makers	Animate	sewing machines, flat irons	Efficient motors
Construction	Electricity		
Grain milling	Electricity, diesel	Electric motors	Efficient motors
Paint manufacture	Animate, electricity	Mixers, incandescent lights	Efficient motors, tubes and CFLs
Bakeries	Electricity, animate	Mixers	Efficient motors and ovens
Fabric manufacture	Electricity, animate	Motors	Efficient motors
Coffee processing	Electricity, firewood	Heaters, blowers, motors	Efficient dryers, blowers and motors

Sources: AFREPREN/FWD, 2003b; Dube, 2001; Katyega, 2001; Kalumiana, 2002; Kebede, 2001; Kyokutamba, 2002

Southern Africa, floodlights have been used successfully to provide lighting services to the urban poor. High-density low-income areas have a floodlight located in the centre of a cluster of about 300 houses and it lights up the whole area (Dube, 2001). This is principally for security and cuts down substantially on the cost of community lighting. The urban poor usually set up SMEs near the floodlight in the evenings.

A study carried in Elandskraal, South Africa tracked the number of activities before and after electrification, and the changes are shown in Figure 2.8 (Fakira, 1994).

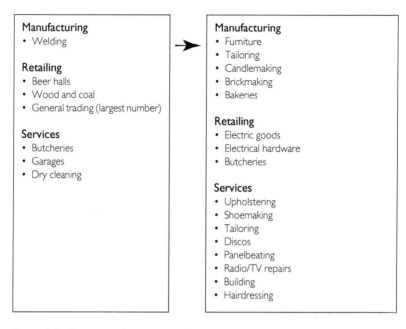

Figure 2.8 Changes in the commercial activities before and after electrification
Source: Fakira, 1994

3

Key trends

The rate of urban growth in most countries in the region is double the national population growth. This rapid urbanization has major implications for the consumption of energy, particularly modern energy.

Urban poor households in most cities of the region constitute over 50 per cent of all households. In Zimbabwe, which is considered to be better off than most countries in the region, urban poor households account for 73 per cent of the total urban population. Most households are involved in some form of income–generating activity. However, the overview available from the data does not differentiate between energy use for these activities and for normal household needs.

With the exception of South Africa, Zimbabwe and Mauritius – with 77, 84 and 100 per cent electrification levels respectively – most urban areas have low electrification levels of less than 30 per cent. Estimates carried out by AFREPREN give the average urban electrification for East and Southern Africa as 38 per cent. However, if Zimbabwe, South Africa and Mauritius are excluded, the average drops to less than 25 per cent.

Except in Zimbabwe, South Africa and Mauritius, biofuels are the main source of urban energy for most countries in the region, followed by kerosene. Kerosene plays a major role because of its dual use as a lighting and cooking fuel, while electricity is excluded from common use by its high cost and unavailability. Urban poor households spend 10–20 per cent of their income on energy. In contrast, the non-poor spend about 5–7 per cent of their income on energy.

Findings from AFREPREN studies in East and Southern Africa, and earlier studies carried out in South Africa, show that the major hurdle to electricity access is the high upfront cost of connection and appliances. Connection to grid electricity using a compact ready board, one of the cheapest ways of connecting a house, is estimated by Dube (2001) to be close to 300 per cent the monthly income of poor households in Zimbabwe. This has lead to high levels of electricity theft through illegal connections.

The impact of electrification was demonstrated by two studies carried out in South Africa and Zambia. In the former, electrification resulted in a dramatic increase of enterprises offering a variety of services, while in the latter consumption of charcoal, wood and kerosene reduced by 15, 32 and 47 per cent, respectively.

The informal sector is increasingly becoming a key player in the region's urban economy. For instance, in Kenya it accounts for about 75 per cent of employment. In almost all countries in the region, even those with high GNP *per capita* such as Botswana, the informal sector is a key employer of the urban poor. The main source of employment in the informal sector is the SMEs, and the household-based micro-enterprises. SMEs spend a substantial amount of their profits on energy. A survey carried out in Kenya showed that 60 per cent of the enterprises spent 10–50 per cent of their profits on fuel costs.

In brief, energy use among the urban poor is characterized by the following (Tyler, 1994):

- low-quality fuels that burn less efficiently when used, so that more is required to perform the same task;

- purchasing fuel in small quantities at the end of a chain of small distributors, resulting in higher retail prices; and

- energy subsidies, for example on electricity, that are largely captured by high-income groups.

The country case studies discussed in the chapters included in this volume provide detailed data and evidence confirming the above key characteristics of the urban energy subsector in Africa. But before the presentation of the country case studies, the next chapter outlines the main methodological approaches employed.

Note

1 The parameters used to determine urban poverty levels vary from country to country. Generally, the measurement of poverty can be based on either money-metric measures or on non-money-metric approaches. The former measures include income and consumption expenditure adjusted to reflect differences in households, while the latter approaches include access to social services, with qualitative and participatory assessments (CSO, 1998a). The money-metric approaches facilitate the quantification of the depth and severity of poverty, and allow consistent comparisons to be made across subgroups of households. On the other hand, the non-money-metric measures provide details on the poor, their conditions and other non-financial dimensions of poverty.

Table 2.13 shows the monthly income (money-metric measure) that is used to classify the urban income groups in Zimbabwe, ranging from extremely poor to very high-income households.

Table 2.13 Boundaries of urban income groups (income per month) in Zimbabwe

Extremely poor	Poor	Moderate	High income	Very high income
< Z$3,000	Z$3,000–8,000	Z$8,000–15,000	Z$15,000–30,000	> Z$30,000
< US$75	US$75–200	US$200–375	US$375–750	> US$750

Source: Dube, 2001

References

AFREPREN/FWD, 2001. Newspaper cuttings and internal surveys carried out by the RETSCAP. Nairobi: African Energy Policy Research Network/Foundation for Woodstove Dissemination.

——, 2003a. *African Energy Database Handbook*. Nairobi: African Energy Policy Research Network/Foundation for Woodstove Dissemination.

——, 2003b. *Internal Surveys Carried Out in Various Suburbs of Nairobi*. Nairobi: African Energy Policy Research Network/Foundation for Woodstove Dissemination.

ADB, 1996. *Household Energy Consumption Pattern in Africa*. Energy Sector Technical Paper Series, Technical Paper No. ES10, Abidjan: African

Energy Programme, African Development Bank.

Arvidson, A., A. Ellegard and F. Mwale, 1998. 'Electrification of Low-income Households in Developing Countries – Experiences from a Pilot Project in Ndola, Zambia', in A. Arvidson, (ed.), *Renewable Energy for Development*, 11, 2 (November 1998), Newsletter of the Energy Programme, Stockholm: Stockholm Environment Institute (SEI).

Barnes, D., 1995. 'Consequences of Energy Policies for the Urban Poor', in Rachel English (ed.), *Energy Issues, FPD Energy Notes*, 7 (November 1995), Washington: World Bank Group.

Bureau of Statistics, 1988. *Population Census: National Profile – Basic Demographic and Socio-economic Characteristics*, Dar-es-Salaam: Bureau of Statistics, President's Office, Planning Commission.

CSO, 1994. *Household Budget Survey – Total Household Consumption, Employment and Income*, Lusaka: Central Statistical Office.

——, 1995a. *Household Budget Survey 1993/4*, Lusaka: Central Statistical Office.

——, 1995b. *Inequality among Households in Zimbabwe: an Assessment Using the 1990/1 Income Consumption and Expenditure Survey*, Harare: Central Statistical Office and Centre for the Study of African Economies, University of Oxford.

——, 1996. *Gender Statistics Report*, Lusaka: Gender Statistics Unit (December).

——, 1998a. *Poverty in Zimbabwe*, Harare: Central Statistical Office.

——, 1998b. *Selected Socio-economic Indicators*, Lusaka: Central Statistical Office.

——, 1998c. *Statistical Bulletin*, 23, 4, Gaborone: Government Printer, Republic of Botswana.

——, 1999a. *Economic Survey 1999*. Nairobi: Central Bureau of Statistics, Office of the President/Ministry of Planning and National Development.

——, 1999b. *Labour Statistics*, Gaborone: Central Statistical Office.

——, 1999c. *Quarterly Digest of Statistics – June 1999*, Harare: Central Statistical Office.

——, 2003 . *Economic Survey 2003*. Nairobi: Central Statistical Office, Office of the President/Ministry of Planning and National Development.

Dube, I., 2001. 'Energy Services for the Urban Poor in Uganda', short-term study report for the AFREPREN Theme Group on 'Energy Services for the Urban Poor', Nairobi: AFREPREN/FWD.

——, 2002. 'Energy Services for the Urban Poor in Uganda', final report, short-term study report for the AFREPREN Theme Group on 'Energy Services for the Urban Poor', Nairobi: AFREPREN/FWD.

Fakira, H., 1994. *Energy for Micro-enterprises*, Cape Town: Energy Development Research Centre, University of Cape Town.

Gitonga, S., 1999. *Energy Services for the Urban Poor: the Kenya Country Study*, Nairobi: IT Kenya Energy Programme, study funded by the Department for International Development (DfID), London.

Hosier, R. 1994. *Informal Sector Energy Use in Tanzania: Efficiency and Employment Potential*, Energy, Environment and Development Series, No. 25, Stockholm: Stockholm Environment Institute (SEI).

IEA, 2002. *World Energy Outlook: Energy and Poverty 2002*, Paris: International Energy Agency.

Kalumiana, O., 2002. 'Energy Services for the Urban Poor: the Case of Zambia', medium-term study report for the AFREPREN Theme Group on 'Energy Services for the Urban Poor', Nairobi: AFREPREN/FWD.

——, 2003. 'Should Modern Energy Services be Subsidised for the Poor? The Case of Urban Households in Zambia', *Journal of Energy in Southern Africa* (Cape Town), Vol. 14, No. 20.

Karekezi, S., 1993. 'Sustainable Energy Use in Urban Areas of Developing Countries', Working Paper No. 9, Nairobi: AFREPREN/FWD.

——, 1999. 'Access to Modern Energy – a View from Africa', in E. McCarthy, and F. Martin (eds), *Energy After the Financial Crises*, Washington, DC: World Bank/ESMAP.

——, 2002a. Poverty and Energy in Africa – a Brief Review, *Energy Policy*, 30, 11–12 (Oxford: Elsevier Science Ltd).

——, 2002b. 'Renewables in Africa – Meeting the Energy Needs of the Poor', *Energy Policy*, 30, 11–12 (Oxford: Elsevier Science Ltd).

Karekezi, S. and L. Majoro, 1999. 'Energy and Environment Linkages in African Cities', in *Energy–Environment Linkages in African Cities – Final Report of the Regional Workshop*, Nairobi: United Nations Centre for Human Settlements (Habitat).

Karekezi, S. and T. Ranja, 1997. *Renewable Energy Technologies in Africa*, London: Zed Books Ltd/AFREPREN/FWD/SEI.

Karakezi, S., M. Mapako and M. Teferra, 2002, 'Africa – Improving Modern Energy for the Poor', *Energy Policy*, Vol. 30, No. 11–12. Elsevier Science, UK.

Karekezi, S., L. Majoro and T. Johnson, 2003. *Climate Change Mitigation in the Urban Transport Sector – Priorities for the World Bank*, Washington, DC: World Bank.

Katyega, M., 2001. *Energy Services for the Urban Poor in Tanzania*, Nairobi: AFREPREN/FWD.

——, 2003. *Electricity Subsidies and the Urban Poor in Tanzania*, Nairobi: AFREPREN/FWD.

Kebede, B., 2001. 'Modern Energy and the Urban Poor in Ethiopia: Literature Review and Empirical Analysis', medium-term study report for the AFREPREN Theme Group on 'Energy Services for the Urban Poor', Nairobi: AFREPREN/FWD.

——, 2002. 'Energy Subsidies and the Urban Poor in Ethiopia: the Case of Kerosene and Electricity', medium-term study report for the AFREPREN Theme Group on 'Energy Services for the Urban Poor', Nairobi: AFREPREN/FWD.

—— 2003. 'Energy Subsidies and the Urban Poor in Ethiopia: The Case of Kerosene and Electricity. Energy Services for the Urban Poor Theme Group', Nairobi: AFREPREN/FWD.

Kinuthia, P., 2003. *Data and Statistics Compilation*, data collected for the Eastern Africa Study funded by the Global Network on Energy and Sustainable Development (GNESD), Nairobi: AFREPREN/FWD.

Kyokutamba, J., 2002. 'Energy Services for the Urban Poor: The Case of

Uganda', short-term study report for the AFREPREN Theme Group on 'Energy Services for the Urban Poor', Nairobi: AFREPREN/FWD.

Ministry of Energy and Water Development, 1996. *Energy Statistics Bulletin – 1974–1996*, Lusaka: Ministry of Energy and Water Development.

Ministry of Finance and Economic Development, 1998. *Economic Report*, Lusaka: Ministry of Finance and Economic Development.

National Electricity Regulator, 1996. *Lighting up South Africa, 1996 – Progress Report on Electrification*, Pretoria: National Electricity Regulator.

———, 2001. *National Electricity Regulator Annual Report 2000/2001*, Pretoria: National Electricity Regulator.

———, 2003. *National Electricity Regulator Annual Report 2002/2003*, Pretoria: National Electricity Regulator.

Office of the President, 1995. *Economic Report, 1995*, Lusaka: National Commission for Development Planning.

Okumu, D., 2003. *Energy Expenditure Data for Uganda*, data collected for the Eastern Africa Study funded by the Global Network on Energy and Sustainable Development (GNESD), Nairobi: AFREPREN/FWD.

Qase, N. and W. Annecke, 1999. *Energy Provision for the Urban Poor: South African Country Case Study*, Cape Town: Energy and Development Research Centre, University of Cape Town, study funded by the Department for International Development (DfID), London.

Reddy, A., R. Williams and T. Johansson, 1997. *Energy after Rio: Prospects and Challenges*, New York: United Nations Development Programme (UNDP)/International Energy Initiative/Stockholm Environment Institute (SEI).

Smith, N.,1998. *Low-cost Electrification: Affordable Electricity Installation for Low-income Households in Developing Countries*, London: Intermediate Technology Publications.

Teferra, M., 2002. *Data and Statistics Compilation*, AFREPREN Energy Sector Reform Theme Group, Nairobi: AFREPREN/FWD.

Tomlinson M., 1999. 'Access to Energy Services – a Brighter Future?', in *Energy after the Financial Crises*, Washington, DC: World Bank/ESMAP.

Tyler, S., 1994. 'Household Energy Use and Environment in Asian Cities: an Introduction', *Energy*, 19, 5 (special issue on Energy Use in Asian Cities, eds. S. Tyler, J. Sathaye and N. Goldman, Oxford: Elsevier Science Ltd): 503–5.

UNDP, 2000. *Human Development Report 2000*, New York: United Nations Development Programme/Oxford University Press.

UNHABITAT website.

http://www.unhabitat.org/habrdd/conditions/soeastasia/thailand.htm

http://www.unhabitat.org/habrdd/conditions/southamerica/argentina.htm

Wolde-Ghiorgis, W., 2002. 'Renewable Energy for Rural Development in Ethiopia: the Case for New Energy Policies and Institutional Reform', in S. Karekezi, M. Mapako and M. Teferra (eds.), *Africa: Improving Modern Energy Services for the Poor*, double issue of *Energy Policy Journal*, 30, 11–12 (September, Oxford: Elsevier Science Ltd).

World Bank, 2000. *Entering the 21st Century: World Development Report 1999/2000*, Washington, DC: World Bank.

———, 2001. *African Poverty at the Millennium: Causes, Complexities and*

Challenges (eds. Howard White and Tony Killick in collaboration with Steve Kayizzi-Mugerwa and Marie-Angelique Savane), Washington, DC: World Bank.

——, 2002. *African Development Indicators 2002*, Washington, DC: World Bank.

——, 2003a. *African Development Indicators 2003*, Washington, DC: World Bank.

——, 2003b. *World Development Indicators 2003*, Washington, DC: World Bank.

——, 2003c. *World Development Report 2003 – Sustainable Development in a Dynamic World: Transforming Institutions, Growth and Quality of Life*, Washington, DC: World Bank.

Part 3

RESEARCH METHODOLOGY AND APPROACH

Bereket Kebede and Ikhupuleng Dube

4

Research Methodology and Approach

The AFREPREN research group working on the urban poor started its work by identifying a common methodological approach for examining the issues in all the countries covered by the study. This common approach facilitated the identification of regional commonalities as well as contrasts and helped to analyze the policy challenges faced by the different countries. The adopted methodology took into consideration issues such as common definitions of urban areas, urban poverty levels, micro-enterprises, etcetera. Differences in data availability, the energy context of each country and country-specific policies were also given space in this approach. This meant that each researcher carried out the study following a common methodological approach while taking into account country-specific conditions. The following is a summary of the main approaches followed in the studies. Specific approaches relevant for each country are presented in the country reports.

Subsidies and access of the urban poor to modern energy

One of the main issues addressed by the studies is whether urban poor households have the purchasing power to access modern forms of energy without subsidies. Urban poor households generally are defined as those whose income falls below the national poverty line. In addition to classifying households into poor and non-poor by using the national poverty line, in most studies the poor themselves are classified into further groups (very poor, extremely poor, and so on).

To address the question of affordability, on one hand, the amount of money poor urban households can expend on modern energy – their purchasing power – and, on the other hand, the costs of modern energy fuels have to be estimated. The mean energy expenditures of households – that is, mean energy budgets – are used as proxies of purchasing power for a particular fuel. Since households actually expend that amount of money for energy on all types of fuels, it is logical to assume that they can afford to expend the same amount on a particular fuel as long as they get the same level of energy.[1]

In the estimation of the costs of fuels, first the mean physical amounts of the different energy items used by the relevant households are identified. For the sake of illustration, imagine the relevant average poor urban household is consuming firewood, charcoal and kerosene. In the initial stage, the amounts of firewood and charcoal in kilograms and kerosene in litres are identified.

Second, using the conversion efficiencies of the fuels, the net total energy used by the households is derived. Even though the average household has used the total (gross) amounts of firewood, charcoal and kerosene identified at the first stage, the useful energy consumed depends on the conversion efficiencies of the respective fuels. For example, the typical efficiencies of firewood, charcoal and kerosene are 0.1, 0.2 and 0.3 respectively (Hosier and Kipondya, 1993). In other terms, while only 10 per cent of the energy from firewood is usefully used for cooking (90 per cent being 'wasted') the proportion increases to 30 per cent for kerosene. Summing up the net energy from firewood, charcoal and kerosene gives total net energy used by the average household.

Third, the total amount of modern energy – say electricity – that can provide an equivalent amount of the calculated total net energy can be identified by dividing the amounts from the second stage by the energy content[2] of electricity. Continuing our illustration, if the total net energy used by the representative household is divided by the energy content of a kilowatt hour of electricity, the total kilowatt hours of electricity that can provide the same amount of energy is known.

Fourth, since the amount of electricity computed at stage three is in net terms it has to be divided by the conversion efficiency of electricity to arrive at the gross figure. This provides the gross kilowatt hours of electricity needed by the average household to maintain the same level of energy consumption as they currently get from different energy sources (firewood, charcoal and electricity).

Fifth, multiplying the gross kilowatt hours by the electricity tariff (price) gives the amount of money required to purchase the amount of electricity that provides an equivalent amount of the energy households currently use. This amount is used as an estimate of the cost of modern energy. The cost of modern energy is estimated with and without subsidies in order to examine how far subsidies change this cost and make it affordable to urban poor households.

In addition to the recurrent cost of modern energy, additional fixed costs such as connection fees and the purchase of equipment are also considered. Adding fixed costs to recurrent cost provides the total cost of the modern energy system under consideration. The fixed costs are included in the total cost both in the case of one-off payments and alternatively in the case of costs amortized over the lifespan of the system. If households are required to pay the total amount of fixed costs as a one-off down payment, the first scenario better captures the immediate costs households incur. But the second approach captures the fact that systems are used for longer periods.

Hence, the analysis involves comparing average energy expenditure for a representative sample of urban poor households with the cost of the modern energy system under consideration. If the former is greater than the latter, that modern energy system is deemed to be affordable by the urban poor. Making the comparisons with and without energy subsidies indicates the importance of the subsidies in making modern energy affordable to the urban poor. Subsidies are considered important for affordability if the cost of energy without subsidies is higher than purchasing power, and the inclusion of subsidies significantly changes the comparison.

Subsidies and leakages to the non-poor

An important issue in the provision of subsidies is to ascertain that they are captured by the targeted group. Mistakes in targeting can appear as mistakes of exclusion (targeted group not covered by the subsidy) or inclusion (non-targeted groups getting the subsidy). In the case of electricity, for example, because most urban poor households do not get electricity they are excluded from the benefits of the lifeline tariff and other subsidies. On the other hand, since non-poor households benefit from the lifeline tariff there is also a problem of including non-targeted groups. The studies in this volume mainly focus on the latter kind of targeting problem, while the first one is directly related to the limited dissemination of modern energy.

In cases where there is information on the amount of modern energy resources consumed by households, the amount of energy subsidy captured by households is used to examine how much of the total subsidy is captured by non-poor households. Where household-level information is not available, the electricity consumption in the country by tariff category, blocks or steps is used to estimate the amount of energy subsidy captured by the non-poor. The analysis involves establishing the total number of customers and the amount of energy consumption in each electricity block or step. Using tariff data the level of subsidy inherent in each block is identified in order to get an estimate of the total subsidy for different household groups.

Energy subsidies and public finance

The estimated amounts of subsidies, derived by the methods outlined above, are compared to different financial indicators used to analyze energy utilities and the public sector. These indicators include revenues, debt, the expenditures of energy utilities and the gross domestic product. Subsidies are considered too great a burden if the ratio of subsidies to the aforementioned indicators is significantly high. Such a methodological approach obviously cannot be used to ascertain the social costs and benefits of subsidies. These are considered to be beyond the scope of the studies.

Energy subsidies and small and micro-enterprises (SMEs)

The studies examined how electricity tariffs affect the operations of small and micro-enterprises (SMEs). Surveys of SMEs were conducted in some of the study countries. The categorization of the SMEs was made according to standard definitions of such activities in each of the countries.

The tariff structures of individual countries are examined to ascertain whether they discriminate in favour of or against SMEs. Higher tariff rates for SMEs relative to the long-run marginal cost (LRMC) of electricity and the tariffs of other sectors of the economy are taken as indications that SMEs are not favoured by the electricity pricing of the country.

Part 3 • Notes and References

Notes

1 A limitation of this method is that it ignores substitution between energy and other (non-energy) household expenditures.
2 The energy content is the amount of energy that can be derived from a unit of fuel – for example, from a kilowatt hour of electricity 409.65 kilojoules of useful energy can be derived (Hosier and Kipondya, 1993).

References

Hosier, R. H. and W. Kipondya, 1993. 'Urban Household Energy Use in Tanzania: Prices, Substitutes and Poverty', *Energy Policy*, 21, 5, May, Oxford: Elsevier Science Ltd.

Part 4

ZAMBIA

Oscar Kalumiana

COUNTRY PROFILE
Zambia

SELECTED INDICATORS

Land area (km²): 753,000
Capital city: Lusaka
National population (millions): 10.38 (2001)
National population growth rate (%): 1.7 (2001)
Urban population (millions): 4.0 (2001)
Urban population growth rate (%): 2.6 (2001)
Urban population as % of national population: 38.5 (2001)
GDP growth rate (%): 5.23 (2001)
GNP *per capita* (US$): 320 (2001)
Gini index: 52.6 (1998 Survey year)
Official exchange rate (US$: Kwacha): 4,685 (September, 2003)
Economic activities: Agriculture, forestry, fishing, mining, manufacturing
Modern energy consumption *per capita* (kgoe): 106 (2001)
Modern energy production (000 toe): 1,200 (2001)
Energy sources: Biomass, imported petroleum, hydro, solar, wind,
Installed capacity (MW): 1,786 (2001)
Electricity generation (GWh): 9,110 (2001)
Electricity consumption per capita (kWh): 474.4 (2001)
Urban electrification rates (%): 48 (2001)
System losses (%): 27 (2001)

Sources: AFREPREN/FWD, 2003a; Chandi, 2003; EIU, 2001; IEA, 2003; Kalumiana, 2003; Mbewe, 2003; Phelan, 2003; UNDP, 2003; World Bank, 2003a; World Bank, 2003b.

5

Introduction

One of the challenges facing Zambia is using energy as a vehicle for poverty reduction. In 1998, only 48 per cent of urban households had access to electricity (CSO, 1998: 127), despite the fact that the country has surplus generating capacity of 450 MW. In its recently adopted Poverty Reduction Strategy Paper (MFNP, 2002: 172–3), the government seeks to invest US$114 million in the energy sector between 2002 and 2005 in order to reduce poverty. It is intended that by 2010 the urban household electricity access rate will have risen to 70 per cent.

There is growing debate about the role of energy policy in tackling poverty. In its Energy and Development Report for 2000, the World Bank raises the following pertinent questions: *Do energy policies and projects have a positive role to play in alleviating poverty? If they do, what kind of policies and projects are likely to have the most beneficial and sustainable impact? In addition, in which areas should energy sector policy advisers focus their efforts?* (ESMAP/World Bank, 2000: 4–5).

The standard poverty alleviation strategies – macroeconomic growth, human capital investment and income redistribution – do not address poverty as it relates to energy (UNDP, 1997: 12). If the patterns of energy use result in adverse effects on nutrition, health, productivity and the environment, for example, the benefits of economic growth are likely to be absorbed only very slowly by poor people. In contrast, programmes that focus directly on creating opportunities for poor people to improve their energy services by increasing their use of energy carriers can enable poor households to enjoy both short-term and self-reinforcing long-term improvements in their living standards.

While poor rural households usually have access to *free* biomass fuels (by collecting firewood, for example), urban households have to purchase most of their energy requirements. Conditions for improving energy services for the urban poor therefore ought to be understood in order to be able to develop programmes that can alleviate *energy poverty* in urban households. For this reason, The African Energy Policy Research Network (AFREPREN), with financial support from the Swedish International Development Cooperation Agency (SIDA), in 1999 embarked on a research programme intended to build on its long-term interest in energy research and the attendant policy-making processes. The programme, to run for three years (1999–2002), among other things included investigations into issues related to *energy services for the urban poor*. This aspect is intended to assess, among other factors, how energy subsidies can affect the provision of energy services for the poor.

Overview of economic developments and indicators

During the period 1995–2000 the government's objectives were set to achieve a sustained annual economic growth rate of 4.5 per cent, reduce inflation gradually to 15 per cent or less, and increase foreign exchange reserves to at least two months of import cover. These objectives were to be achieved through continued implementation of structural reforms aimed at removing supply-side bottlenecks as well as pursuing appropriate fiscal and monetary policies. Of particular importance was the acceleration of structural reforms principally related to the privatization programme, reduction of poverty, internal and external liberalization of the economy, strengthening of the banking sector and rehabilitation of major infra-structure, especially the road network.

In spite of the positive strides made in implementing economic reforms and improving the policy environment for private-sector-led development, economic growth over the period averaged a meagre 1.6 per cent, compared to the desired and anticipated average of 4.5 per cent. In 1998, for example, Zambia registered a negative real increase in GDP. Within the Southern African Development Community (SADC), only the Democratic Republic of Congo (DRC) and Lesotho registered such negative growth (see Appendix 4.1).

Over the same period the population grew at an average annual rate of 3.1 per cent. As rapid economic growth is an essential though not a sufficient condition of poverty reduction, the generally weak performance of the economy during the period contributed to an increase in the incidence of poverty from 69.2 per cent in 1996 to 72.9 per cent in 1999. It is therefore imperative to work out mechanisms for linking economic growth to poverty eradication or alleviation.

Although there was contraction in economic activity in most major sectors of the economy in 1998, the greater pull-down on aggregate output was exerted by the significant decline in the primary sectors of mining and agriculture. Value-added in the mining sector fell by 11 per cent as a result of low metal production at the Zambia Consolidated Copper Mines (ZCCM) and a fall in metal prices. The fall in metal production was partly due to delays in the privatization of the mines under ZCCM. The delays in privatization reduced new investments and capitalization of the mines, thereby reducing output in subsequent years. Value-added in the agriculture sector fell by 6 per cent in the wake of the *El Nino* climate cycle and a resultant drought.

Economic activity picked up slightly in 1999, however, when a growth rate of 2.4 per cent was recorded. This was largely in response to favour-able weather conditions that affected the agricultural sector positively and also reflected the positive performance of the manufacturing, construction and service sectors. Historically, domestic growth in the services sector has remained steady, despite economic liberalization and the stiff competition that domestic service providers faced from foreign investors and providers of services.

A notable feature of the composition of domestic output during the period was the transformation of the structure of GDP, with the share of the mining sector, traditionally the backbone of the economy, falling significantly from 16.7 per cent in 1994 to 6.6 per cent in 1999. The wholesale and retail trade sector made important gains, with its share rising from 14.8 per cent in 1994 to 19.4 per cent in 1999, making it the biggest contributor to GDP. This can be attributed to the liberalization of the economy as well as the decline of the mining sector in the period.

Positive developments were also recorded in the area of inflation control as the rate of inflation dropped from 46 per cent in 1994 to 20.6 per cent in 1999. However, the rate of inflation, though assuming a downward trend, tended to fluctuate under the impact of shocks such as drought and falling metal prices. The fall in inflation was facilitated by supportive fiscal and monetary policies.

Table 4.1 Real overall GDP and sectoral growth rates, 1995–2000

	1995	1996	1997	1998	1999	2000
Overall GDP	−2.1	6.6	3.3	−1.9	2.4	3.58
Agriculture	4.5	−0.12	−0.88	0.28	2.24	−
Mining	−4.6	0.35	0.26	−2.97	−2.24	−
Manufacturing	−0.04	0.55	0.50	0.18	0.30	−
Construction	−0.17	−0.54	1.19	−0.52	0.53	−
Energy	−0.05	−0.18	0.12	−0.08	0.09	−
Services	−2.15	6.55	2.11	1.22	4.77	−

Source: MoFED, 2000a, 2000b; MFNP, 2002

Poverty in urban households

In Zambia, the measurement of poverty begins with the construction of a poverty line which forms the cut-off point between the poor and non-poor. In determining the poverty line, expenditure has mainly been preferred, as households are more likely to report expenditures accurately than incomes. Thus expenditure has been the main measurement of poverty. In measuring poverty, the Central Statistical Office (CSO) takes into account the size and ages of the household members by assigning a weight to each member of the household according to their age, known as the *adult equivalent scale*. The CSO scale is given as:

Age	Adult equivalent scale
Child 0 years	0
Child 1–3 years	0.36
Child 4–6 years	0.62
Child 7–9 years	0.78
Child 10–12 years	0.95
Adult (13+ years)	1.00

In 1988, the poverty lines were fixed at K32,861 and K47,188 (per adult equivalent unit per month) for extremely poor and moderately poor respectively. Extremely poor persons were therefore those persons in households with an expenditure on food below K32,861 per month. Moderately poor persons were those persons in households with an expenditure on food equal to or above K32,861 but lower than K47,188 per month. Non-poor persons were those persons in households with an expenditure on food equal to or above K47,188 per month. In urban areas, 48.6, 46 and 56.5 per cent of the people were poor in 1991, 1996 and 1998 respectively. Figure 4.1 shows these household poverty levels.

Energy consumption patterns among urban households

The CSO defines an urban area in terms of its population size and economic activities. In this regard, an urban area is one with a minimum population of 5,000 people. The main economic activity must be non-agricultural, as in the case of wage employment. In addition, the area

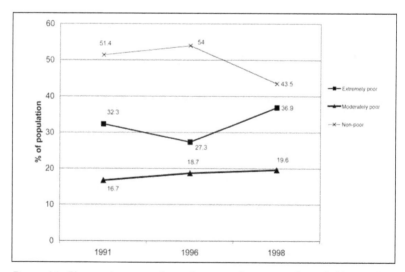

Figure 4.1 Changes in proportions of poor and non-poor households in urban areas

Source: MFNP, 2002

must have basic modern facilities such as piped water, tarred roads, post offices, police stations and health centres. The urban population in 1998 was 38 per cent of the total national population (CSO, 1999: 3). The total national population having electricity has risen from 15 per cent in 1995 to 20 per cent in 2000 (Department of Energy, unpublished).

Urban households rely on four main fuels: electricity, charcoal, firewood and kerosene. To some extent candles are used for lighting purposes. Table 4.2 shows the proportions of households using specified fuels for lighting and cooking. Lighting for urban households is predominantly provided by electricity, followed by kerosene. Between 1996 and 1998, the proportion of households meeting their lighting needs from kerosene declined by 4 per cent, while the number reliant on electricity increased by 3 per cent. The 'missing' 1 per cent probably substituted candles for kerosene, as evidenced by an increase of 1 per cent in candle usage over the same period. Cooking by urban households is dominated by charcoal, followed by electricity and firewood. Between 1996 and 1998 the proportion of households meeting their cooking energy needs from electricity increased from 36 to 39 per cent, while the number using charcoal declined by 2 per cent and the number using firewood declined by 1 per cent.

Table 4.2 Fuels used by urban households for cooking and lighting – 1996 and 1998

Energy source	Proportion (%)of urban population using it for			
	Cooking		Lighting	
	1996	1998	1996	1998
Electricity	36	39	45	48
Kerosene	–	–	39	35
Charcoal	51	49	–	–
Firewood	13	12	–	–
Candles	–	–	15	16
Diesel	–	–	1	1
Total	100	100	100	100

Source: CSO, 1996, 1998

Organization of the energy sector in Zambia

Zambia is endowed with many types of energy sources, including woodlands and forests, hydropower, coal, and new and renewable sources of energy. Woodland and forests are estimated to cover about 66 per cent of the total land area, with the standing stock and annual growing stock being equivalent to 4.3 billion and 120 million tonnes, respectively. The hydropower resource potential is estimated at 6,000 MW. The total installed capacity is 1,715.5 MW. Hydroelectric plants represent 92 per cent of the installed capacity and account for 99 per cent of electricity production (Appendix 4.2). Proven coal reserves are estimated at 30 million tonnes with several hundred million tonnes of probable reserves. Petroleum is the only energy source that is imported. Total imports in 1999 amounted to 421,100 metric tonnes of crude oil (Appendix 4.3). A limited quantity of refined petroleum products are also imported into the country. Solar radiation averages 4.5 kWh/m^2/day, with up to 3,000 sunshine hours annually. Wind speeds are low, however, averaging 2.5 metres per second at 10 metres above the ground (MEWD, 1994: 10). The total energy supply averages 4.5 million tones of oil equivalent (Toe) annually. For households, woodfuel is the largest source of energy (Figure 4.2).

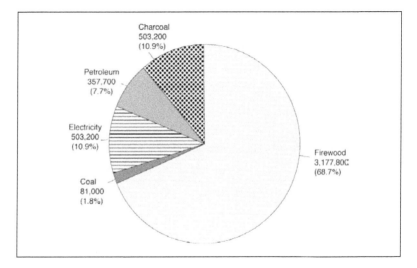

Figure 4.2 Final energy consumption (Toe) by source, 1999

Source: DoE, 2000

The Ministry of Energy and Water Development (MEWD) has the overall responsibility to develop, articulate and implement policy on energy. The National Energy Policy (NEP) document, adopted in 1994, seeks to *promote optimum supply and utilization of energy, especially indigenous forms. The policy also seeks the facilitation of the socio-economic development of the country and the maintenance of a safe and healthy environment.* The Department of Energy (DoE) is the chief adviser to the Minister of Energy and the executive arm of government in all policy-related energy matters. The Zambia National Oil Company Ltd (ZNOC), a government-owned company formerly responsible for the importation of crude petroleum products and the bulk sale of petroleum products to oil-marketing companies (OMCs), was liquidated in early 2002.

TAZAMA Pipelines Ltd is responsible for transporting spiked crude petroleum (crude petroleum with additives for easing its passage through pipelines) from Dar-es-Salaam to Ndola through 1,701 kilometres of pipeline. Zambia and Tanzania jointly own the company through a shareholding structure (Zambia 67 per cent and Tanzania 33 per cent). The INDENI Petroleum Refinery Co. Ltd is responsible for refining the spiked crude petroleum into finished products. The refinery, located at Ndola, has the capacity to process 1.1 million tonnes of spiked crude annually. Zambia, Totalfinael of Italy and private shareholders own the refinery on a 45–50–5 per cent basis. The following OMCs operate in Zambia: BP (Zambia) Ltd, AGIP, Total, Mobil, Caltex, Engen, Ody's and Jovenna.

The Zambia Electricity Supply Corporation (ZESCO) Ltd is a publicly owned utility responsible for generation, transmission, distribution and supply of electricity in the country. The company previously had monopolistic powers established under the Zambia Electricity Supply Act. This Act was repealed in 1995 by the passing of a new Electricity Act. ZESCO Ltd is now established under the Companies Act. The Copperbelt Energy Company (CEC) is a private electricity distribution company that buys power from ZESCO in bulk for sale to the mines located on the Copperbelt.

Kariba North Bank Company Ltd (KNBC) is a company responsible for running the 600 MW Kariba North Bank Power Station on the Zambezi, the river that forms Zambia's border with Zimbabwe. The Zambezi River Authority (ZRA) is the successor to the Central African Power Corporation (CAPCO) and is jointly owned by Zambia and Zimbabwe on a 50–50 basis. It is responsible for managing the section of the Zambezi River that forms the common border. The Energy Regulation Board (ERB) was established through the Energy Regulation Act (No. 16 of 1995). The ERB is the sole licensing authority for operators in the energy sector and is responsible for close monitoring and supervision of such operators. It seeks to promote competition and ease of entry into the energy sector, as well as safeguarding consumer interests.

Subsidies in the energy sector

The following are some of the most frequently cited of the many arguments against energy subsidies.

- Most energy subsidies are poorly targeted and do not reach the intended beneficiaries.

- Subsidies are often indiscriminately applied to consumption levels well above those applicable to the poor.

- Subsidies are overly restrictive with respect to end use, depriving users of choice.

- Misdirection of subsidies become almost inevitable as different interest groups attempt to capture them.

Since subsidies are usually paid for by the public sector, they can be considered to be a waste of public resources, in that they do not filter to the target group. Especially in a poor country like Zambia, *unproductive* subsidies can be considered a burden on public resources, as the available scarce resources have many competing needs. Energy subsidies in contemporary Zambia are discussed below.

Electricity
Electricity units are charged below the long-run marginal cost (LRMC). The LRMC is defined as *the incremental cost per kilowatt-hour (kWh) of supplying an additional kW of demand, with the projected requirement of additional generation capacity.* The costs therefore include the cost of planned additional investments in generation with a horizon of at least six to ten years. The levels of the tariffs are also influenced by the burden imposed on the system and the load factors of specific customers.

Prevailing tariffs are also below the *average cost-based tariff* (ACBT). This is the tariff level at which the utility is able to cover all its total annual costs – operational, administrative and capital costs (depreciation and rate of return on net assets) – for generation, transmission and distribution. The ACBT does not include the future cost of expanding the power system but has a 6 per cent return rate (after tax) on net fixed asset value (which is the performance target given to ZESCO Ltd by the government). Since the difference in the real tariff rate and the charge that customers pay for electricity is a cost to the utility, it is considered a subsidy. Hence subsidies constitute the difference between the prevailing tariff and the real tariff.

In 1998, residential customers paid a tariff of 3.1 US cents per kWh on consumption up to 700 kWh, while those consuming above 700 kWh paid 5.1 US cents per kWh. The LRMC was 6.5 US cents per kWh for consumption up to 1,000 kWh and 11.6 US cents per kWh for consumption above 1,000 kWh. The ACBT was 4.5 US cents per kWh for consumption up to 1,000 kWh and 8.8 US cents per kWh for consumption above 1,000 kWh. The margins by which the tariffs fell below the LRMC and ACBT are shown in Table 4.3.

Table 4.3 Domestic electricity tariffs compared to LRMC and ACBT, 1998

Tariff category	LRMC	ABCT	Applicable tariff	Tariff as % of LRMC	Tariff as % of ACBT
Up to 50 kWh	19.8	17.6	3.1	15.7	17.6
51–1000 kWh	6.5	4.5	3.1	47.7	68.9
Above 1000 kWh	11.6	8.8	5.1	44.0	57.9

Source: Survey by author

Kerosene
There is no official subsidy on kerosene. The government forgoes revenue on kerosene, however, due to the existing tax regime as follows:

- The road levy of 15 per cent of the retail (pump) price applicable on petrol and diesel is not charged on kerosene;

- Value-added tax of 17.5 per cent is not charged on kerosene;

- Customs duty on kerosene is 10 per cent instead of 45 per cent applicable to other petroleum products.

Urban household expenditure

Household expenditure is an important measure of domestic sector welfare. The share of food expenditure in total income or expenditure, for example, is one of the indicators of household welfare. Households in the lower-income groups tend to spend more of their incomes on food. The CSO does not assess energy expenditure separately; instead it is lumped into the housing category, which includes rent, energy, water and housing maintenance. Mean urban household expenditure for this category was 10 per cent of total household income in both 1996 and 1998 (see Appendix 4.4).

The research objective of the study has been outlined in Part 3. Here in Part 4 we present the research approach and findings in the context of the Zambian situation.

6

Impact of Energy Pricing on Affordability of Modern Forms by the Urban Poor

Methodology

In determining the affordability of energy in poor urban households, it was necessary to determine, among other things, the total household income as well as the proportion of income spent on energy by households. For this purpose secondary data on household living conditions from the Central Statistical Office 1998 survey were re-analyzed to capture the desired variables. The survey covered 8, 223 urban households.

The CSO data are available on CD Rom in various statistical packages. Out of 8,223 households surveyed in 1998, 2,381 were extremely poor, 1,528 moderately poor and 4,314 non-poor. Since the available data only show the average household monthly consumption per household category, it was assumed that this figure was representative of all households in each category. The intra-household differences were therefore ignored, as it was not possible to compute them. The average household size, calculated for the households actually surveyed, was 7.0,

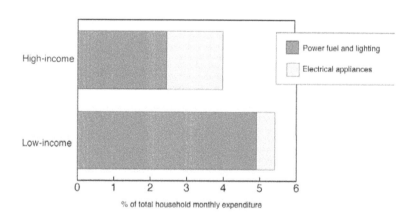

Figure 4.3 Proportion of energy expenditure (excluding cost of firewood and charcoal) of total monthly household expenditure, 1995

Source: CSO, 1995

6.2 and 4.9 persons for extremely, moderately and non-poor households. Extremely poor urban households fell within the first four expenditure deciles, moderately poor households into deciles four to six, and non-poor households into deciles six to ten.

As an additional data source, the CSO 1995 household budget survey results were also taken into account. The survey categorized two types of urban households: high-income and low-income. As a proportion of the total household budget, the energy-related expenditure of these households (excluding spending on charcoal and firewood), was 4 per cent for high-income and 5.4 per cent for low-income households, respectively (Figure 4.3).

In assessing whether the poor urban households' energy budget share can accommodate the cost of modern energy services, the mean monthly amounts of fuels used by households (electricity, charcoal, firewood and kerosene) were converted to the equivalent useful energy value of electricity. Using the cost of this electricity equivalent, the energy budget share for subsidized electricity was computed.

The subsidy was considered to be the difference between the prevailing tariff and the LRMC or the ACBT. Since the tariffs have been depressed for such a long time, it would require a minimum of 13 years at real tariff increase (in dollar terms) to reach the LRMC (ZESCO, 1999). Therefore, the ACBT was used.

Findings

The first hypothesis assessed the relationship between incomes and household energy budget shares of the urban households. This was to ascertain how expenditure on different sources of energy affected household incomes. The analysis involves the comparison of expenditure by the households on traditional forms of energy (charcoal and firewood) and corresponding expenditure by similar households on modern energy forms (electricity and kerosene). The analysis also involves the discussion of policy intervention measures that could be effected to ensure access to modern forms of energy by the poor household groups. To test the hypothesis, monthly household expenditure on all fuels used was assessed. The assessment covered household expenditure on electricity, firewood, charcoal, kerosene and candles.

Household per capita *expenditure on energy*

ELECTRICITY
In 1998, the average amount of money spent by households on electricity among the extremely poor, moderately poor and non-poor categories was K2,963.53 (US$1.40), K10,870.99 (US$5.14) and K18,952.57 (US$8.97) respectively. The prevailing tariff categories were as follows: up to 700 kWh – 3.1 US cents per month; above 700 kWh – 5.1 US cents per month

(ZESCO, internal report). In reality, none of the household categories consumed above 300 KWh per month. The average *per capita* consumption was found to be 45 kWh, 166 kWh and 289 kWh by extremely poor, moderately poor and non-poor households respectively. Non-poor households spent about six times more money on electricity than extremely poor households, and twice as much as moderately poor households (Table 4.4).

FIREWOOD
The mean household expenditure on firewood is shown in Table 4.4. The average expenditure by households in the extremely poor, moderately poor and non-poor categories was K2,721.94 (US$1.29), K2,000.14 (US$0.95) and K500.98 (US$0.24) respectively. The prevailing mean firewood price in 1998 was K50/kg (US$0.024/kg). The average *per capita* monthly consumption of firewood by the extremely poor, moderately poor and non-poor households was estimated at 54.4 kg, 40 kg and 10 kg respectively. Poor households spent about four times more money on firewood than non-poor households.

CHARCOAL
The urban household *per capita* expenditure on charcoal was highest for extremely poor households at K10,203.26 (US$4.83) per month. This was followed by an expenditure by the moderately poor households of K5,089.78 (US$2.41) and by the non-poor households of K3,644.44 (US$1.72) per month respectively. The prevailing price of charcoal in 1998 was K8,000 per 45kg bag (DoE, 2000: 43) or K177.78/kg. This price level translated to monthly *per capita* consumption of 57.6kg, 28.6kg and 20.5 kg of charcoal by the extremely poor, moderately poor and non-poor household categories, respectively. The extremely poor households consumed about twice as much as moderately poor households, and three times as much as non-poor households (Table 4.4).

KEROSENE
As with firewood and charcoal, the extremely poor households consumed the bulk of the kerosene, on which they expended K1,461.97 (US$0.69) per month, compared to K643.90 (US$0.30) and K256.72 (US$0.12) for moderately poor and non-poor households respectively. At the prevailing price of K640.37 per litre, the *per capita* monthly expenditures were equivalent to 2.4, 1 and 0.4 litres for the extremely poor, moderately poor and non-poor household categories, respectively (Table 4.4).

CANDLES
As urban households also use candles for lighting, the total monthly expenditure for this energy source was also estimated. All households spent less than a quarter of a dollar on candles. Extremely poor households spent K500.79 (US$0.24) per month, compared to K468.78

Table 4.4 Estimated average *per capita* urban household expenditure on different fuels, 1998

Poverty category	No, of households covered	Monthly expenditure, K	Monthly expenditure, US$	Mean monthly consumption
Electricity				
Extremely poor	1576	2,963.53	1.40	45 kWh
Moderately poor	1121	10,870.99	5.14	166 kWh
Non-poor	3534	18,952.57	8.97	289 kWh
Firewood				
Extremely poor	3319	2,721.94	1.29	54.4 kg
Moderately poor	2007	2,000.14	0.95	40.0 kg
Non-poor	3407	500.98	0.24	10.0 kg
Charcoal				
Extremely poor	3319	10,203.26	4.83	57.6 kg
Moderately poor	2007	5,089.78	2.41	28.6 kg
Non-poor	3407	3,644.44	1.72	20.5 kg
Kerosene				
Extremely poor	3319	1,461.97	2.4	0.69
Moderately poor	2007	643.90	1.0	0.30
Non-poor	3407	256.72	0.4	0.12

Notes
Exchange rate = K 2,113.23 to US$1.
Firewood price in 1998 = K50/kg (Kalumiana, 2000)
Charcoal price in 1998 = K8,000/45kg = K177.78/kg
Kerosene price = K640.37/litre

Source: Survey by author

(US$0.22) and K152.84 (US$0.07) for moderately and non-poor per month, respectively.

TOTAL HOUSEHOLD *PER CAPITA* ENERGY EXPENDITURE

The total household *per capita* monthly household energy budget is shown in Table 4.5. The mean total urban household monthly income in 1998 was estimated at K226,290, K309,341 and K401,269 for extremely poor, moderately poor and non-poor households, respectively. In both 1996 and 1998, 48 per cent of total household income was spent on food. In 1998, all household categories, on average, spent less than 10 per cent of income on energy services. Extremely poor households spent 7.9 per cent, while moderately poor and non-poor households spent 6.2 per cent and 5.9 per cent of their total expenditure, respectively.

Using the average total monthly expenditure per household category, an estimate of the proportion of the energy budget to total household

Table 4.5 Mean urban household energy budget, 1998

Household status	Monthly household income	Monthly expense on					Total energy budget	Expenditure as % of total income
		Electricity	Charcoal	Firewood	Kerosene	Candles		
Very poor	226,290.83	2,963.52	10,203.26	2,721.94	1,461.97	500.79	17,851.5	7.9
Moderately poor	309,341.57	10,870.99	5,089.78	2,000.14	643.90	468.78	19,073.59	6.2
Non-poor	401,269.81	18,952.57	3,644.44	500.98	256.72	152.84	23,507.55	5.9

Source: Survey by author

income was made for the 10 expenditure deciles. This is shown in Figure 4.4. The figure shows that the poor spend higher proportions of their income on energy. Although non-poor households spend a relatively small proportion of their income on energy, they consume more energy than the poor.

To find out if poor urban households can afford unsubsidized modern energy services (excluding the cost of energy devices), the total energy consumed by each household has to be converted to one energy unit. In this case electricity was used. The mean monthly amounts of fuels used by different household categories were converted to useful electricity equivalent units (Table 4.6). In this scenario, extremely poor households

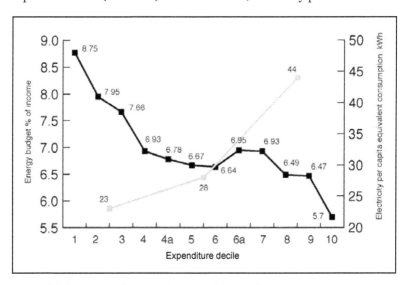

Figure 4.4 Total monthly energy budget as % of total income for ten urban household expenditure deciles

Note: Deciles 1-4 = extremely poor, 4a-6 = moderately poor, 6a-10 = non-poor. The points for per capita consumption represent mean values for the household categories).
Source: Survey by author

use 163 kWh, moderately poor households 172 kWh and non-poor households 216 kWh, respectively. From Figure 4.4, it can also be deduced that the non-poor households consume about twice as much energy as poor households.

To find out if the current households energy expenditure could accommodate the cost of unsubsidized modern energy, the total electricity

Table 4.6 Mean household monthly energy consumption expressed as useful electricity unit equivalents, 1998

Extremely poor

	Unit	Mean fuel used	Energy content (MJ/ unit) (a)	Total energy consumed	Efficiency(b)	Useful energy equivalent, kWh
Electricity	kWh	45	3.6	162	0.6	27.0
Firewood	Kg	54.4	15.5	843.8	0.1	23.4
Charcoal	Kg	57.6	32.6	1879.1	0.2	104.4
Kerosene	Litre	2.3	43.3	98.8	0.3	8.2
					Total	163.0

Moderately poor

	Unit	Mean fuel used	Energy content (MJ/ unit) (a)	Total energy consumed	Efficiency(b)	Useful energy equivalent, kWh
Electricity	kWh	166	3.6	1011.6	0.6	99.6
Firewood	Kg	40.0	15.5	620	0.1	17.2
Charcoal	Kg	28.6	32.6	933.3	0.2	51.8
Kerosene	Litre	1.0	43.3	43.8	0.3	3.7
					Total	172.3

Non-poor

	Unit	Mean fuel used	Energy content (MJ/ unit) (a)	Total energy consumed	Efficiency(b)	Useful energy equivalent, kWh
Electricity	kWh	289	3.6	1717.2	0.6	173.
Firewood	Kg	10.0	15.5	155.6	0.1	4.3
Charcoal	Kg	20.5	32.6	668.3	0.2	37.1
Kerosene	Litre	0.4	43.3	17.3	0.3	1.4
					Total	215.3

Sources: DoE, 2000; Kaoma and Kasali, 1993; Hibajene and Kaweme, 1993.

equivalent consumed was compared to the LRMC and the ACBT. Compared to the LRMC, the energy expenditure of all household categories would not cover the cost of the unsubsidized modern energy. To be able to afford the cost of unsubsidized modern forms of energy, the extremely poor, moderately poor and non-poor would have to increase their energy budgets by 25.5, 24.1 and 26.4 per cent, respectively.

The energy budget share was compared to the ACBT of 4.5 US cents per kWh (Table 4.7). The results show that the *per capita* monthly household energy budget share of the extremely poor, moderately poor and non-poor households is 13, 14 and 12 per cent, respectively, less than the total expenditure on electricity.

The monthly cost of cooking devices is shown in Table 4.8. These range from US$1.79 for a 4-plate cooker to US$0.11 for the charcoal *mbaula*.

Table 4.7 Household monthly energy expenditure compared to unsubsidized electricity costs at the ACBT

Household category/Energy cost	Extremely poor	Moderately poor	Non-poor
Useful electricity equivalent consumed, kWh	163.1	172.3	216.3
Total unsubsidized cost, US$	7.34	7.35	9.73
Total unsubsidized electricity cost, Kwacha	15,506.14	16,386.71	20,568.54
Current subsidized energy budget, Kwacha	17,851.50	19,073.59	23,507.55
% unsubsidized energy cost below current expenditure	−13.1	−14.1	−12.5

Source: Survey by author

Table 4.8 Calculation of monthly cost of devices for the year 1998

Device	1998 prices (K)	1998 prices (US$)	Estimated lifespan (months)*	Monthly cost (US$)
Two-plate cooker	39,951.77	18.91	36	0.53
Four-plate cooker	454,299.80	214.98	120	1.79
Kerosene lamp	5,303.33	2.51	12	0.21
Charcoal *mbaula*	5,702.51	2.7	24	0.11

Source: * Hibajene and Kaweme, 1993

Table 4.9 Household total monthly energy expenditure converted to unsubsidized electricity at 4.5 US cents/kWh (ACBT and equipment cost)

Household category/Energy cost	Extremely poor	Moderately poor	Non-poor
Monthly useful electricity equivalent consumed, kWh	163.1	172.3	216.3
Energy unsubsidized cost, US$	7.34	7.35	9.73
Monthly cost for 4-plate cooker, US$			1.79
Monthly cost for 2-plate cooker, US$	0.53	0.53	
Unsubsidized energy cost plus cost of equipment, US$	7.87	8.28	11.52
Unsubsidized energy cost plus cost of equipment, Kwacha	16,626.26	17,506.84	24,351.81
Monthly energy budget, Kwacha	17,851.50	19,073.59	23,507.55
% unsubsidized energy cost below current expenditure	−6.9	−8.21	+3.5

Source: Survey by author

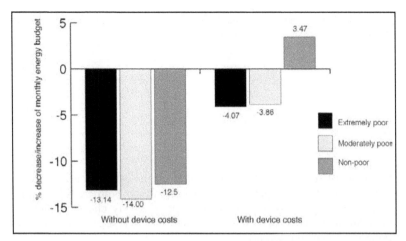

Figure 4.5 Percentage decrease/increase of current monthly energy budget if all households exclusively used unsubsidized electricity instead of different fuels

Source: Survey by author

When the cost of energy devices (Table 4.8) is included, the analysis shows that the poor households would still be able to afford electricity (Table 4.9). The expenditure of the non-poor households would be more than the 1998 monthly budget by about 4 per cent. These households are already using electricity, however, so they are able to meet the cost of cooking devices. The savings in household energy monthly budgets are summarized in Figure 4.5.

Household energy expenditure (inclusive of cooking devices)
In order to compare the impact of end-use devices on energy affordability, the following assumptions were made:

- all poor households will use the 2-plate cooker;

- all non-poor households use the 4-plate cooker;

- since all households use electricity, kerosene will not be used for lighting;

- poor households will not use charcoal either.

From Table 4.9 it can be seen that, even when the cost of electrical cooking stoves is included, poor households will still be able to afford the unsubsidized cost of electricity. Only the non-poor households will exceed their 1998 total energy budget share by 3.5 per cent (Figure 4.5). If they also use the 2-plate cooker, they too will be able to afford the cost of unsubsidized electricity. Compared with other countries, however, it would appear that poor households in Zambia are consuming relatively higher levels of energy than, for example, poor households in Ethiopia

Table 4.10 Mean monthly household energy consumption (equivalent useful kWh of electricity) in Ethiopia and Zambia

Household category	Poor		Non-poor	
	Annual	Monthly	Annual	Monthly
Ethiopia[a]	592.4	49.4	1335.2	111.3
Zambia[b]	1956.7	163.1	2595.6	216.3
Difference	1364.4	113.7	1260.4	105.0

Sources: [a]Kebede, 2001; [b]this study

(Table 4.10). This could be an indication of the relative cost of energy within household budgets in the two countries. Both traditional and modern energy forms in Zambia are comparatively cheaper, allowing poor households the ability to consume relatively larger amounts than their Ethiopian counterparts.

Household energy expenditure (inclusive of initial capital cost)
Households without access to electricity have to meet other capital costs before they are connected. The most significant ones are wiring and connection fee costs. In 1998, the average wiring costs were as follows: high cost (four-bedroomed house) K2 million; medium cost (two- to three-bedroomed house) K1 million; and low cost (one- to three-bedroomed house) K500, 000. It is assumed that these cost categories apply to the non-poor, moderately and extremely poor households, respectively. The average connection cost was K187,000. In carrying out further analysis,

Table 4.11 Amortized monthly energy and capital costs (1998) spread over a 10-year period

Household category/Energy cost	Extremely poor	Moderately poor	Non-poor
Total unsubsidized energy expenditure[a]	15,506.14	16,386.71	20,568.54
Cost of electrical stoves	1,120.01	1,120.01	3782.68
Connection fee	1,562.50	1,562.50	1,562.50
Wiring costs	4,166.67	8,333.33	16,666.67
Total energy and capital costs	22,355.32	27,402.55	42,580.39
Current subsidized energy expenditure	17,851.50	19,073.59	23,507.55
Cost differential, K[b]	4,503.	82 8,328.96	19,072.84
Cost differential, %	−25.23	−43.67	−81.13
Monthly income	226,290.83	309,341.57	401,269.81
Total unsubsidized energy expenditure as % of monthly income[c]	6.9	5.3	5.1

[a] Total monthly cost of unsubsidized electricity at 4.5 US cents/kWh.
[b] Difference between total cost of unsubsidized electricity, electrical stoves, wiring, connections and cost of subsidised electricity.
[c] Total cost of unsubsidized electricity, electrical stoves, wiring and connections as % of current income.
Source: Survey by author

the costs were discounted over a ten-year period and at a discount rate of 10 per cent. This was to derive the amortized monthly costs. The results of the analysis are shown in Table 4.11.

To afford the total cost of energy and capital costs required, the extremely poor, moderately poor and non-poor households would have to raise their energy budgets shares by 25, 44 and 81 per cent respectively. Most poor households are unable to meet these upfront capital costs all at once. They would be able to meet them, however, if the costs were spread over a period of time. If the capital costs applicable to 1998 were spread over ten years, the extremely poor households would need to increase their monthly energy budget share in total monthly income from 7.9 per cent to 9.9 per cent. Moderately poor households would have to raise their energy budget share of income from 6.2 per cent to 8.9 per cent.

Comparisons of these figures with data from other countries show that poor households in other countries spend relatively large proportions of their income on energy. In Uganda, for example, extremely poor households expend 22 per cent of their income to meet their energy needs (Table 4.12). This comparison would suggest that it is possible that poor urban households in Zambia can still increase their energy budget share in the face of rising energy prices. Removal of energy subsidies could be one cause of rising energy prices.

Table 4.12 Comparisons of the poor urban household energy budget share of income with other countries

Country/household category	Zambia	Uganda	Zimbabwe	Ethiopia	Tanzania
Extremely poor	9.9	22			
Very poor		13.5			
Moderately poor	8.9				
Poor		10.2	12.0	10	20.3

Sources: Kyokutamba et al., 2001; Kebede, 2001; Katyega, 2001; Dube, 2001

Conclusions

From the analysis it is clear that, in 1998, poor urban households could afford unsubsidized electricity at the ACBT but not at the LRMC. For the ACBT, households would have spent less on energy if they exclusively used electricity. It was even possible in 1998 to raise electricity tariffs above the ACBT of 4.5 US cents by 1.5, 0.9 and 0.5 US cents for extremely poor, moderately poor and non-poor households, respectively.

The main hindrance preventing poor households from using electricity is the upfront cost of internal wiring and connection fees. If these costs could be spread over time, then poor households would be able to afford both the energy and the capital costs of using electricity. Similar findings appear to have been made in Ethiopia and Zimbabwe. In Ethiopia, for example, poor urban households can afford kerosene and electricity without subsidies, provided the fixed costs are spread over time (Bekeret and Kedir, 2001). In Zimbabwe, urban households do not consider energy subsidies to be decisive for the affordability of modern energy services (Dube, 2001).

From these findings it can be concluded that if poor households can be assisted to obtain electricity connection, they will be able to pay for unsubsidized electricity. It is therefore not necessary to subsidize electricity below the ACBT, as long as the urban poor can be assisted to afford electrical cooking devices, house wiring and connections fees. Poor households could afford the upfront costs if these were amortized. Currently, households actually pay more for traditional energy sources that they would if they used electricity.

It can be concluded, then, that the energy expenditure of the poor is sufficient to cover the unsubsidized cost of modern energy services at the ACBT, but not sufficient to cover the unsubsidized cost of modern energy services at the LRMC.

7

Energy Subsidies Captured by
Different Household Categories

Methodology

The objective was to ascertain the proportion of the subsidies captured by different income categories. The total subsidy on electricity was used to determine the leakage of subsidies to the non-poor. Only the subsidy on the ACBT was considered, as it is currently not feasible to reach the LRMC in the short term. The value of the subsidy captured by each household category was then computed.

Based on the value of subsidy captured by each household category, the group capturing the largest share of subsidy was then ascertained. The analysis focused on the critical analysis of the non-poor households' need of the electricity subsidy. Further, it ascertained the impact of the affordability by the urban poor of modern forms of energy, in the absence of subsidies.

Findings

Distribution of subsidies amongst different household categories focused on electricity, as there are no direct subsidies on kerosene, firewood and charcoal. Government forgoes revenue on kerosene in the form of reduced taxes. Forgone revenue on firewood and charcoal is in the form of uncollected revenue. The electricity subsidy arising from the ACBT is considered in the analysis. For clarity's sake, kerosene and charcoal pricing are also discussed.

Electricity subsidy
Electricity subsidies are indirect, in the sense that electricity is sold below the LRMC, which for households was 6.5 US cents per unit in 1998. The ACBT was 4.5 US cents per unit. Urban household tariffs were in two categories, namely consumption up to 700 kWh costs (3.1 US cents per unit) and above 700 units (5.7 US cents per unit). None of the household categories consumed above 700 units per month, hence all household categories were paying below the ACBT.

Non-poor households captured the largest portion of the monthly *per capita* electricity subsidy at US$4.035 per month, representing 60 per cent of the total subsidy on electricity. This further represents 45 per cent of their mean total monthly expenditure on electricity. The moderately poor households captured 31 per cent of the total electricity subsidy at US$2.06 per month, which represents 37 per cent of their total expenditure on electricity. The extremely poor households captured less than US$1 per month, representing only 9 per cent of the total electricity subsidy, or 44 per cent of their total expenditure on electricity (Table 4.13).

Table 4.13 Existing household monthly *per capita* subsidies on electricity, 1998

Poverty category	Mean monthly consumption with subsidy, US$ (A)	Estimated monthly consumption by kWh (B)	Estimated mean monthly expenditure without subsidy, US$ C = (Bx0.045)*	Amount of subsidy/ month, US$ D = (C–A)
Extremely poor	1.40	45	2.025	0.625
Moderately poor	5.41	166	7.47	2.06
Non-poor	8.97	289	13.005	4.035

*ACBT = 4.50 US cents per kWh
Source: Survey by author

Forgone revenue on kerosene
Several tax rebates are imbedded in the cost of kerosene. The price of subsidized kerosene in 1998 was K640.37/litre compared to the actual true price of K869.77 (inclusive of taxes). Table 14.4 shows the kerosene price build-up in Zambia.

Table 4.14 Price build-up of kerosene, 1998 (per litre)

With full taxes		With partial taxes	
ZNOC wholesale price	458.8	ZNOC wholesale price	458.8
VAT by ZNOC to OMCat 17.5%	80.29	VAT by ZNOC to OMC at 17.5%	
Excise duty at 45%	68.82	Excise duty at 15%	68.82
Road levy at 15%	68.82	Road levy at 0%	
ERB levy	2.1	ERB levy	2.1
Terminal fee	4.1	Terminal fee	4.1
Oil company margin	56.1	Oil company margin	56.1
Dealer margin	50.45	Dealer margin	50.45
Pump price VAT at 17.5%	80.29	Pump price VAT at 0%	
Total unsubsidized price Kwacha	869.77	Total subsidized price Kwacha	640.37
Total unsubsidized price US$	0.4116	Total subsidized price US$	0.30
Price differential for unsubsidized kerosene US$/litre			0.11

Source: Survey by author

The total tax rebate on kerosene amounted to 29 per cent of total household expenditure on kerosene. The extremely poor households captured the largest portion of the kerosene tax rebate of US$0.69 per month, representing 63 per cent of the total rebate on kerosene. The moderately poor households captured 26 per cent of the total rebate of US$0.10 per month. The non- poor households captured 11 per cent of the total tax rebate of US$0.04 (Figure 4.6).

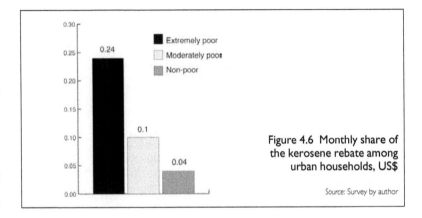

Figure 4.6 Monthly share of the kerosene rebate among urban households, US$

Source: Survey by author

Charcoal

There is no subsidy on charcoal. However, due to the failure by the Forest Department to collect legal fees, there is a lot of forgone revenue. Less than 5 per cent of all transporters acquire licences and virtually no producer acquires any licence at all. Figure 4.7 shows the applicable licence fees as of July 2001. A production licence costs K5, 400 per cord and K360 per bag. This translates to US$0.24 for production and US$0.11 for transportation. The forgone revenue on each bag of charcoal was therefore in the order of $0.35/bag. With a minimum of 15 million bags consumed annually and a 5 per cent levy compliance rate, the forgone revenue is in the order of US$5.25 million annually.

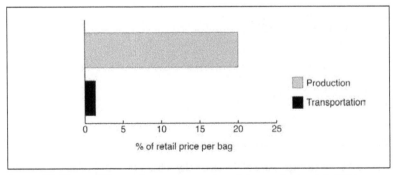

Figure 4.7 Charcoal licence fee as a proportion of the retail price, July 2001
Source: Survey by author

Total annual electricity subsidy

The total annual household subsidy for the 124,500 urban households in 1998 amounted to US$5,031,618 (K10,632,961). Of this total subsidy, the extremely poor households captured K72.1 million, which was less than 1 per cent of the total subsidy. The moderately poor households captured K1.8 billion, or 17 per cent of the subsidy. On the other hand, non-poor households accounted for 83 per cent of the total subsidy (K8.8 billion) (Table 4.15).

Table 4.15 Distribution of the electricity subsidy among urban households

Household category	No. of consumers	Monthly subsidy	Total monthly subsidy, US$	Total subsidy captured, ZK	% of subsidy	Total annual subsidy, ZK
Extremely poor	4,547	0.625	2,841.88	6,005,535.51	0.7	72,066,426.08
Moderately poor	34,203	2.06	70,458.18	148,894,339.72	16.8	1,786,732,076.66
Non-poor	85,750	4.035	346,001.25	731,180,221.54	82.5	8,774,162,658.45
Total	124,500	6.72	419,301.31	886,080,096.77	100	10,632,961,161.19

Source: Survey by author

The total annual subsidy in 1998 for all electricity consumers amounted to US$49.5 million (K104.6 billion). The total share gained by urban households was 10 per cent of the total (US$5 million or K10.6 billion). Figure 4.8 shows the distribution of electricity subsidies amongst the different consumer categories.

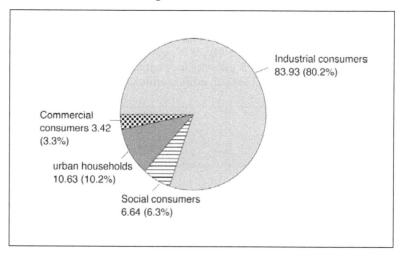

Figure 4.8 Percentage share of the electricity subsidy (Kwacha) gained by various consumer categories
Source: ZESCO, 2002

Conclusions

The analysis shows that in 1998 the non-poor households captured the largest proportion of the electricity subsidies (83 per cent). The subsidy to the domestic sector, comprised of all the consumer categories, was only 10 per cent of the total subsidy. Whilst subsidies to the commercial and industrial sectors can be justified for productive purposes, subsidies to the households cannot be justified, since such subsidies benefit mainly the non-poor households and not the targeted group, the extremely poor households.

8

Impact of Energy Subsidies
on Public Finances

Methodology

To evaluate the impact of subsidies on public finances, the total value of energy subsidies was compared to the following financial indicators:

1. proportion of GDP arising from the energy sector compared to electricity and gas oil exports in the year;

2. central government revenue;

3. central government budget deficit.

Since the bulk of the subsidies are in the electricity sector, the level of subsidies was compared to the profitability of the national electricity utility, ZESCO Ltd. In addition, the level of subsidy was compared to the utility's 1998 current assets and net profit. This was to ascertain if the utility was in a position to shoulder the burden of providing subsidies. The prevailing level of subsidies was also compared to the level of energy subsidies in other countries.

Findings

The third hypothesis examined the impact of subsidies on public finances. The argument behind the research question is that, since public finances support subsidies, subsidies can only be sustained if there are sufficient public resources to finance them. It is therefore important to assess energy subsidies in relation to national financial indicators. To access the impact of energy subsidies on public finances, the study considered the proportion of subsidies compared to the various finance indicators discussed below (MoFED, 2000a, 2000b; BOZ, 2000).

National income from the energy sector
The analysis focused on how subsidies relate to public income from energy services. The two issues addressed are the contribution of energy to GDP and also the revenue from electricity exports. The total GDP in 1998 amounted to K6,044.118 billion (US$2,860 million). The contribution to GDP by electricity, petroleum products and water accounted for K67.9 billion (US$32.1 million), a growth rate of –0.08 per cent. In the

same year, electricity exports by ZESCO Ltd amounted to K12.8 billion (US$6.1 million) (BOZ, 2000: 26). When compared to the above indicators, it is clear that, the amount of electricity subsidies was eight times more than total electricity export earnings.

As for the proportion of the energy sector's contribution to GDP, the total level of subsidies was 1.5 times more. This means that, had there been no energy subsidies, the electricity sector's contribution to GDP would have been higher than US$32.1 million. The level of subsidies was equal to 1.7 per cent of the GDP.

Central government revenue from domestic goods and services
Another financial indicator used in the analysis was revenue that accrued to central government from domestic goods and services. This revenue amounted to K411 billion (US$194.5 million) in 1998 (BOZ, 2000: 32). The total subsidy was 25.4 per cent of the total central government revenue from domestic goods and services.

Central government budget deficit
The central government budget deficit is an important indicator of government capacity to finance its expenditure, since subsidies are a form of expenditure. In 1998, the central government budget deficit amounted to K186 billion (US$88.0 million) (BOZ, 2000: 35). The electricity subsidies were 56.2 per cent of this deficit.

In summary:

- Total subsidies on electricity amounted to 1.7 per cent of total GDP in 1998.

- Total subsidies on electricity amounted to more than 8 times the value of electricity exports of US$6.1 million. As a result, GDP real growth rate in the energy sector amounted to –0.08 per cent.

- Total subsidies on electricity amounted to 56.2 per cent of central government deficit.

- Compared to GDP, the subsidy is very small. It is, however, a significant proportion of government deficit. When compared to Uganda and Zimbabwe, the impact of electricity subsidies on GDP cannot be considered as burdensome, as the level is lower than in these two countries (Figure 4.9). Zambia's electricity subsidy of 56.2 per cent of the government deficit is quite high when compared to that of the other two countries. Although the years being compared are different, they are close enough to give a good picture of the prevailing circumstances.

- The high proportion of the subsidy indicates the relative importance of the electricity subsidy in Zambia's budget deficit as compared to Uganda and Zimbabwe. In this context, the subsidy can be considered to be a burden on public finances.

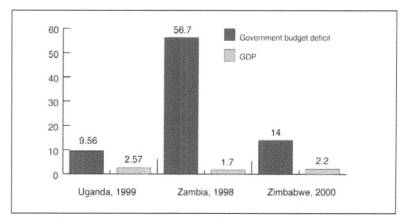

Figure 4.9 Proportion of total energy subsidies to central government deficit and GDP for Uganda, Zambia and Zimbabwe

Sources: Kyokutamba et al., 2001; Kalumiana, 2003; Dube, 2001

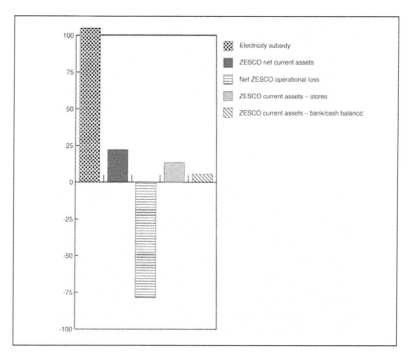

Figure 4.10 Total electricity subsidy as compared to ZESCO net current assets and net profit for 1998

Source: ZESCO, 2002

Subsidies compared to the utility's financial indicators
As the electricity subsidy is directly paid for by the national electricity utility, ZESCO Ltd, its impact on the utility's finances was also assessed. The following were the findings (Figure 4.10):

- The electricity subsidy in 1998 was five times the utility's total net current assets.

- The electricity subsidy in 1998 was almost twenty times the utility's bank/cash balance.

- The electricity subsidy in 1998 was eight times the utility's net current assets in the form of *stores*.

Facing an unfavourable financial environment, the utility made a loss of K78.6 billion in the same year.

Conclusions

The above analyses have shown that the levels of total energy subsidies constitute a large proportion of public financial indicators. Amongst the indicators are central government deficit and the operational profitability of the national electricity utility. Although in 1998 the electricity sector grew by 1.5 per cent, the real energy GDP declined by 0.1 per cent, whilst the total GDP fell by 1.9 per cent. With such an economic scenario, it is not in the best interests of the economy to maintain unprofitable subsidies like those enjoyed by non-poor households, as they are a burden on public finances. Furthermore, the utility has no resources to maintain the current electricity subsidies, hence the operational losses incurred.

9

Policy Options and Recommendations

The policy options recommended take into account the existing policy on energy service provision in Zambia, contained in the NEP (MEWD, 1994). In terms of household energy the policy document outlines the following:

Electricity

- Increased household access to electricity through:
- Encouragement of adoption of low-cost methods of power distribution and home wiring;
- Reducing the capital cost charged to customers before installation of power supply.

Kerosene

- Financing supplies on cash basis;
- Complete divestment of government in distribution.

Charcoal and firewood

- Ensure sustainable supply of charcoal to urban households;
- Support efforts aimed at finding alternatives to charcoal and firewood.

Issues to be addressed by policy

From the findings of this study, the following points have emerged:

- Between 1996 and 1998, the proportion of urban households using kerosene for lighting declined by 4 per cent, whilst that of electricity users increased by 3 per cent. The use of candles increased by 1 per cent. It is clear that electricity and candles are being substituted for kerosene. Since only 10,000 households countrywide are connected annually (ZESCO, internal report), this rate of connection is equivalent to the average annual growth in urban households, estimated at 1.5 per cent. This implies that only the incremental portion of households is connected to electricity annually. Since the households connected annually include those in rural areas, the rate of urban household annual electrification is lower than 10,000.

- Between 1996 and 1998, the proportion of urban households using electricity for cooking increased from 36 to 39 per cent, whilst corresponding use of charcoal was reduced by 3 per cent and use of firewood by 1 per cent. This shows that urban households are shifting towards using more electricity than charcoal and firewood, a shift in energy use that is occurring under the government's new electrification targets.

- If lighting is used as an indicator of households connected to electricity, then the difference between the proportion using electricity for lighting and cooking could be used as a proxy of households unable to use electricity for cooking. In 1998, this proportion was 9 per cent for the households connected to the grid. Since these households are already connected and could afford the cost of electricity for cooking, the only barrier preventing their access to electricity for cooking is the cost of cooking devices.

Amortization of stoves

As mentioned above, these developments occur at a time when the government has set new target rates for electrification. For urban areas, the goal is to increase the electrification rate from 48 per cent in 1998 to 70 per cent by 2010. This will entail a six-fold increase in the number of annual household connections, from 10,000 to 60,000. It is therefore recommended that the costs of cooking devices be amortized.

This is a feasible option in Zambia as demonstrated in the Pamodzi Low Cost Electrification Project, which used a deferred payment system to enable poor urban households to own 2-plate cookers for which they pay over time (Arvidson and Ellegard, 1998; Mehlwana, 1999). In the Pamodzi project, households using charcoal and firewood were reduced by 15 and 32 per cent respectively, showing the impact of enabling households to access both electricity and stoves (Arvidson and Ellegard, 1998; Mehlwana, 1999: Appendix 13).

Amortization of capital costs

It is also clear from the findings that the costs of connection and house wiring are beyond the reach of poor households. A mechanism to connect households on a deferred payment scheme will be beneficial to these households. The Pamodzi Project pilot project used this approach. The deferred payment scheme for connection costs should be pursued as a matter of policy and incorporated into the urban electrification programme. The issue of house wiring, however, is more problematic. A low-cost credit scheme can assist poor households to afford the cost of house wiring.

Currently ZESCO loses a lot of money in carrying out rural electrification. Between 1994 and 2001, ZESCO Ltd spent K50 billion (about US$24 million in 1998) on rural electrification on behalf of the government. In order to avoid this expenditure burden on the utility, it is proposed that a

Rural Electrification Agency (REA) be established that will implement these projects. ZESCO can still implement rural electrification projects, however, if returns on investment are justified from a business perspective. This will leave the electricity utility with adequate resources to invest in its township/urban electrification programme. As this programme targets poor households, it will enable these households to access electricity quickly.

For this to be successful, the utility needs to carry out market surveys to determine which customers, at any particular time, are willing to be connected under the deferred payment scheme. The biggest shortcoming of the township electrification programme has been the indiscriminate connection of poor households, regardless of whether they want to be connected or not, as long as they reside in an area the utility and government want to connect. A study carried out in Twapia Township in November 1996 revealed this weakness (Kalumiana, 2003).

In order to allow for increased connections, independent power distributors should be encouraged to participate in power distribution in the urban market. Increased urban connections will benefit rural electrification: more funds will accrue to the REF, because it is financed by a 3 per cent levy on the bills of existing consumers.

Improvement of charcoal stoves efficiency
The analyses have also shown that significant savings on the poor household energy budget can be made if the efficiency of firewood and charcoal cooking devices is improved. This is important, as electricity connections will take time to reach all poor households – and households with electricity will still use charcoal when cooking certain foods such as beans, as it is claimed that charcoal improves the taste of beans (personal communication). Charcoal is also used as security for unreliable electricity supply (Chidumayo, *et al.*, 2002). Improving charcoal stove efficiency is therefore another policy option.

Gradual reduction of subsidies
Two types of electricity subsidies appear to exist. Costing electricity below the LRMC reflects one type; the other one consist of pricing electricity below the ACBT. As it is not feasible in Zambia to have electricity tariffs reflecting the LRMC, the ACBT subsidy was considered in the analysis. The ultimate policy goal would be to increase tariffs progressively to the ACBT and later to the LRMC to ensure that electricity consumers enjoy reliable energy services, whilst at the same time enabling the utility to realize a positive return on its investment. As this policy goal will take time to achieve, the current subsidy need to be redesigned so that, as far as possible, it benefits the poor. To do this it is recommended that 100 kWh be considered a lifeline tariff, which should move progressively to the ACBT, while consumption above 100 kWh should be charged above the ACBT until the LRMC is reached.

Leakage of the electricity subsidy
Since the bulk of the subsidy (78 per cent) is captured by the non-poor, this portion of the subsidy should be reduced progressively as subsidies place a great burden on public finance. The shift in the lifeline tariff recommended above will also ensure that the subsidy captured by the non-poor is gradually reduced.

Policy options

Energy subsidies
The following are the policy recommendations:

1   Create an environment where poor urban households can afford to use electricity for cooking through a low credit scheme for cooking devices. For this policy option to be successful, it is necessary for government to encourage independent power distributors. The electricity utility's capacity to implement a deferred payment scheme needs to be strengthened through sensitization of management and training of personnel. The policy option is viable as experience from the Pamodzi Project has shown that more electricity consumers in a deferred payment scheme were paying their bills than those connected in the conventional way.

2   Enable more poor urban households to access electricity through new connections. A deferred connection scheme can assist in achieving this. This policy option requires an environment that can allow for the operation of credit schemes accessible to poor urban households. Electricity distributors need to include the connection costs in the tariff rate so as to reduce the upfront costs. Again, the Pamodzi Project has shown the way. It can be asumed that such consumers will appreciate the need to pay more for increased access to electricity.

3   Create an environment where poor urban households can afford the cost of house wiring. As with the first option, a suitable credit scheme can enable the implementation of such a policy option.

4   Encourage a demand-driven township electrification programme. The current institutional framework is sufficient to implement this policy option. However, the involvement of independent power distributors will accelerate the rate of new connections. The current utility has sufficient manpower to implement this policy option – but the utility should be encouraged to connect customers based on ability and willingness to pay. This can be determined through market surveys. Government should make viability of new connections a condition in its performance contract with ZESCO.

5 Create a Rural Electrification Agency so that ZESCO does not implement unviable rural electrification projects. This policy option will entail creating an institution (the REA) responsible for rural electrification projects, so as to ensure that ZESCO concentrates on urban electrification. The REA, being financed by public funds, will in most cases be subsidized. Subsidies are required for most rural electrification projects, but the REA's activities should be sustainable in the long run. Such a scenario would free the existing utility, which has been connecting relatively few new urban customers, to redirect its resources from rural electrification to what is now clearly defined as its main role: increasing urban customer connections.

6 Carry out a charcoal stove efficiency improvement programme as well as awareness building among charcoal consumers. There is already sufficient institutional capacity, through NGOs, to implement this policy option. Although successful stove programmes are few, well-planned ones have made a positive impact on the urban poor. Learning from such experiences will increase the chances of this policy option being implemented viably.

Leakage of the electricity subsidy to the non-poor
The following are the policy recommendations:

1 Progressively reduce the level of the electricity subsidy. The current institutional arrangement is sufficient to implement this policy option.

2 Maintain an electricity lifeline tariff at the ACBT. Its implementation will lead to increased revenue for the electricity utility as compared to current levels. Utility employees need to be trained in tariff determination and management.

3 Charge electricity consumption of more than 100 kWh per month at cost above the ACBT. The cost of this consumption level should move progressively towards the LRMC. As with the new lifeline tariff, its implementation will lead to increased revenue for the electricity utility as compared to current levels. Again, utility employees need to be trained in tariff determination and management.

Impact of subsidies on public finances
Progressively reduce the electricity subsidy for non-poor households (the same recommendation as has been made against leakage above).

Policy implementation

Tables 4.16, 4.17 and 4.18 indicate who would be responsible for each aspect of the recommendation to ensure successful implementation.

Table 4.16 Actors in the implementation of policy options on energy subsidies

Policy option	Actors	Role(s)
1 Create an environment in which poor urban households can afford to use electricity for cooking through electrification schemes based on low-cost deferred payment	Ministry of Energy and Water Development	a Adopt policy option as part of national electrification strategy b Finance further research into deferred payment schemes c Encourage utilities to adopt deferred payment schemes
	ZESCO Ltd	Adopt deferred payment schemes
2 Enable poor urban households to afford wiring costs	Independent power distributors	Adopt deferred payment schemes
	Micro-financiers	Finance low-cost loan schemes
3 Enable poor urban households to afford connection costs	Ministry of Commerce and Industry and Energy Regulation Board	License Independent power distributors
4 Encourage a market-based township electrification programme using conventional means	Ministry of Energy and Water Development	Make profitability a condition of the government performance contract with ZESCO
	ZESCO Ltd	Carry out consumer market surveys before new connections are made
5 Create rural electrification agency so that ZESCO does not implement unviable rural electrification projects	Ministry of Energy and Water Development	a Create the REA, whose sole role is to carry out rural electrification projects b Ensure ZESCO Ltd does not carry out unprofitable rural electrification projects
6 Carry out a charcoal stove efficiency improvement programme as well as awareness building among charcoal consumers	Ministry of Energy and Water Development	Provide financing for implementing this policy option
	NGOs (e.g., Care international)	Implement improved stove projects
	Donors	Provide financing for implementing this policy option
	Research institutions (National Institute for Scientific and Industrial Research)	Carry out research in improved stoves Adapt proven foreign stoves to Zambian conditions

Source: Survey by author

Table 4.17 Actors in the implementation of policy options on leakages of the electricity subsidy

Policy option	Actors	Role(s)
1 Progressively reduce the current electricity subsidy	ZESCO Ltd	Implement an effective tariff system that ensures that the bulk of the subsidy is captured by the poor
2 Maintain an electricity lifeline tariff at the ACBT	ZESCO Ltd	Manage the lifeline tariff to ensure it never sinks below the ACBT
3 Charge electricity consumption above 100 kWh per month at a cost above the ACBT. This consumption level to move progressively towards the LRMC	ZESCO Ltd	Implement a tariff system that ensures household electricity consumption above 100 kWh is paid for above the ACBT. Progressively move the cost of this consumption level towards the LRMC.

Source: Survey by author

Table 4.18 Actors in the implementation of policy options on subsidies and public finances

Policy option	Actors	Role(s)
Progressively reduce the electricity subsidy for non-poor households	ZESCO Ltd	• Strengthen capacity to deal with complex tariff issues • Restructure tariff system to take into account proposed policy option • Carry out regular tariff studies to ensure successful setting and management of new tariffs • Sensitize consumers on need to have progressive upward tariff adjustments
	Energy Regulation Board	• Approve higher tariff applications from ZESCO

Source: Survey by author

Part 4 • References

AFREPREN/FWD, 2003. *African Energy Data Handbook.* Nairobi: AFREPREN/FWD.

Arvidson, A. and E. Ellegard, 1998. 'Electrification of Low-income Households in Developing Countries. Experiences from a Pilot Project in Ndola, Zambia', paper for the Stockholm Environment Institute.

Bereket, K. and E. Kedir, 2001. 'Energy Subsidies and the Urban Poor in Ethiopia: The Case of Kerosene and Electricity: Ethiopia', unpublished document, Nairobi: AFREPREN/FWD.

BOZ, 2000. *1999 Annual Report*, Lusaka: Bank of Zambia, pp. 13–37.

Chandi, L., 2003. 'Country Data Validation: Zambia', unpublished, Nairobi: AFREPREN/FWD.

Chidumayo, E. N, I. Masialeti, H. Ntalasha and O. S. Kalumiana, 2002. 'Charcoal Potential for Southern Africa. Zambia Final Report', University of Zambia/European Union, INCO-DEV 1998–2001, pp. 37–42.

CSO, 1995. *Household Energy Budget Report*, Lusaka: Central Statistical Office.

——, 1996. *Living Conditions in Zambia, 1996,* Lusaka: Central Statistical Office, pp. 125–47.

——, 1997. *The Evolution of Poverty in Zambia, 1991–1996*, Lusaka: Central Statistical Office, pp. 11–26.

——, 1998. *Living Conditions in Zambia, 1998*, Lusaka: Central Statistical Office, pp. 72–3, 126–8.

——, 1999. *Zambia in Figures*, Lusaka: Central Statistical Office, p. 3.

——, 2000. *National Accounts Statistical Bulletin No. 71994–1999*, Lusaka: Central Statistical Office, pp. 5–7.

DoE (Anonymous). Internal Reports, Lusaka: Department of Energy.

——, 2000. *Energy Statistics Bulletin, 1980–1999*, Lusaka: Ministry of Energy and Water Development, pp. 2, 43.

Dube, I., 2001. 'Energy Services for the Urban Poor in Uganda', short-term study report for the AFREPREN Theme Group on 'Energy Services for the Urban Poor', Nairobi: AFREPREN/FWD.

ESMAP/World Bank, 2000: *Energy Services for the World's Poor*, Washington DC: Energy Sector Management Assistance Programme/ World Bank, pp. 4–5.

Hibajene, S. H. and S. Kaweme, 1993. *Electrification of Low-income Households: the Use of Low-cost Approaches*, Energy, Environment and Development Series No. 5, Stockholm: National Council for Scientific Research/ Stockholm Environment Institute, pp. 18–24.

IEA, 2003. *Energy Balances of Non-OECD Countries, 2000–2001*, Paris: International Energy Agency.

Kalumiana, O. S., 1997. *Demand and Supply of Firewood and Charcoal in*

Lusaka Urban Market, Lusaka: Provincial Forestry Action Programme/ FINIDA.

——, 2000. 'Charcoal Potential In Africa – Zambian Study Component', progress report (draft).

——, 2003. 'Country Data Validation: Zambia', unpublished, Nairobi: AFREPREN/FWD.

Kaoma J. and G. Kasali, 1993. *Efficiency and Emission Characteristics of Two Zambian Cookstoves Using Charcoal and Coal Briquettes*, Energy, Environment and Development Series No. 7, Stockholm: National Council for Scientific Research/Stockholm Environment Institute, pp. 8–17.

Katyega, M., 2001. *Energy Services for the Urban Poor in Tanzania*, Nairobi: AFREPREN/FWD.

Kebede, B., 2001. 'Energy Subsidies and the Urban Poor in Ethiopia: the Case for Kerosene and Electricity', medium-term study, Nairobi: AFREPREN/FWD.

Kyokutamba, J., A. Matovu and I. P. Dasilva, 2001. 'Government Policies and Grid Extension as Solutions for Energy for the Urban Poor – Uganda', medium-term study, Nairobi: AFREPREN/FWD.

Mbewe, A., 2003. 'Country Data Validation: Zambia', unpublished, Nairobi: AFREPREN/FWD.

Mehlwana, M., 1999. *Electrification of a Low-income area in Zambia. Evaluation of the Pamodzi Project*, Cape Town: Energy and Development Research Centre, University of Cape Town.

MEWD, 1994. *National Energy Policy for Zambia*, Lusaka: Ministry of Energy and Water Development, pp. 1–12.

MoFED, 2000a. *Year 1999 Economic Report*, Lusaka: Ministry of Finance and Economic Development, pp. 3–7.

——, 2000b. *Public Expenditure Review*, Lusaka: Ministry of Finance and Economic Development, pp. 6–10.

MFNP, 2002. *Poverty Reduction Strategy Paper*, Lusaka: Ministry of Finance and National Planning, pp. 99–103, 172–3.

Phelan, J. (ed.), 2003. *African Review Journal*, 39, 8, London: Alain Charles Publishing Ltd.

UNDP, 1997. *Energy after Rio, Prospects and Challenges*, New York: United Nations Development Programme, pp. 10–17.

——, 2003. *Human Development Report, 2003*, Oxford, New York: Oxford University Press/United Nations Development Programme.

World Bank, 2000. *Entering the 21st Century: World Development Report 1999/2000*, Washington, DC: World Bank.

——, 2003a. *African Development Indicators 2003*, Washington, DC: World Bank.

——, 2003b. *World Development Indicators 2003*, Washington, DC: World Bank.

ZESCO 1999. *ZESCO Electricity Tariff Study*, Swedpower Final Report, Lusaka: Zambia Electricity Supply Corporation, pp. 41–50.

——, anonymous. ZESCO internal reports. Lusaka: ZESCO.

——, 2002. *Statistics Yearbook of Electric Energy – 2001/2002*. Lusaka: Zambia Electricity Supply Corporation, pp. 3–22.

Part 4 • Appendices

Appendix 4.1

Gross Domestic Product (GDP) real growth rates (%) in SADC Countries, 1981–99

Country	1981–90	1996	1997	1998	1999	1990 weight
Angola	2.1	12.1	5.9	1.7	2.0	6.5
Botswana	16.9	7.0	6.9	8.3	5.2	2.5
DRC	0.7	0.9	-6.4	-3.5	0	6.6
Lesotho	3.9	12.7	3.5	-5.8	4.0	0.4
Malawi	2.2	12.0	5.3	6.2	4.0	1.3
Mauritius	4.9	6.0	5.2	5.6	5.5	1.9
Mozambique	0.1	6.4	6.0	9.9	6.0	1.4
Namibia	-0.6	2.1	2.4	2.6	3.0	1.7
Seychelles	3.6	1.5	7.9	3.0	3.0	0.3
South Africa	1.5	3.1	1.7	0.6	1.0	67.7
Swaziland	6.6	3.9	3.8	2.5	3.0	0.6
Tanzania	3.3	4.2	3.3	4.0	4.0	2.6
Zambia	1.0	6.5	3.5	-1.8	2.4	2.6
Zimbabwe	4.2	7.0	2.0	1.6	1.0	3.9
SADC Total	1.6	4.1	2.2	0.9	1.5	100.0
Sub-Saharan Africa	2.3	5.5	3.9	2.7	2.9	–
Africa total	2.5	5.8	3.1	3.4	3.1	–
Developed countries	2.4	3.2	3.2	2.2	2.8	–

Source: MoFED, 2000a

Appendix 4.2

Total electricity generation in Zambia (GWh), 1980–2001

Year	Inter-connected hydro	Decentralized hydro	Total hydro	Diesel	Total generation	% hydro
2001	9,059	33.5	9,093	17.4	9,110	99.8
2000	8,168	26.5	8,195	16.5	8,211	99.8
1999	7,746	35.5	7,782	16.3	7,798	99.8
1998	7,604	38.9	7,643	14.5	7,657	99.8
1997	7,816	35.2	7,851	17.2	7,868	9978
1996	7,035	39.1	7,074	14.6	7,089	99.8
1995	7,769	41.4	7,810	14	7,824	99.8
1994	8,037	64.6	8,102	12.9	8,115	99.8
1993	8,001	68.9	8,070	12.4	8,082	99.9
1992	6,412	92.6	6,505	12.8	6,517	99.8
1991	8,799	107.4	8,906	10.7	8,917	99.9
1990	7,668	124.7	7,793	10.4	7,803	99.9
1989	6,179	113.1	6,292	10.2	6,302	99.8
1988	8,010	108.2	8,118	9.4	8,128	99.9
1987	7,829	101	7,930	8.8	7,939	99.9
1986	9,486	98.1	9,584	6.9	9,591	99.9
1985	9,763	98.2	9,861	8	9,869	99.9
1984	9,428	88.8	9,517	9.7	9,527	99.9
1983	9,725	88.7	9,814	10.3	9,824	99.9
1982	10,147	86	10,233	9.8	10,243	99.9
1981	9,725	78.8	9,804	9.9	9,814	99.9
1980	8,991	70.2	9,061	9.3	9,071	99.9

Source: ZESCO, 2002

Appendix 4.3

Petroleum imports in Zambia, 1989–2000

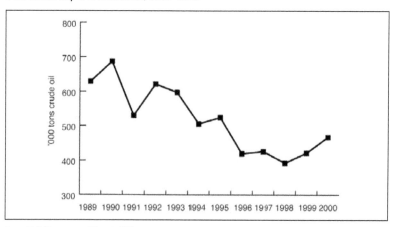

Source; DoE (Department of Energy), 2000.

Appendix 4.4

Mean percentage share of urban household expenditure on different items, 1996 and 1998

Item	1996	Change	1998
Food	48	0	48
Housing	10	0	10
Clothing	6	+1	7
Transport	12	−3	10
Remittances	5	−2	3
Education	3	+2	5
Medical care	3	−1	2
Personal services	9	+1	10
Alcoholic beverages & tobacco	4	0	4
Entertainment	*	−	1
Total	100		100
No. of households surveyed	661,000		680,000

* Not assessed separately
Source: CSO, 1996, 1998

Appendix 4.5

Capital costs for urban electricity connections, 1998

Cost item	Extremely poor	Moderately poor	Non-poor
Total connection fee	187,500	187,500	187,500
Connection fee spread over 10 years (K/month)	1,562.50	1,562.50	1,562.50
Total wiring costs	500,000	1,000,000	2,000,000
Wiring costs spread over 10 years (K/month)	4,166.67	8,333.33	16,666.67
Total	5,729.17	9,895.83	18,229.17

Source: Author's survey

Appendix 4.6

Existing *per capita* subsidies on kerosene captured by each household per month, 1998

Poverty category	Current price with subsidy, US$/litres	Consumption litres	Mean expenditure with rebate	Current prices without US$/litres	Estimated mean US$	Amount of rebate/month US$
	A	B	C	D	E (B*D)	F=(E–C)
Extremely poor	0.30	2.3	0.69	0.41	0.93	0.24
Moderately poor	0.30	1.0	0.30	0.41	0.41	0.10
Non-poor	0.30	0.4	0.12	0.41	0.16	0.04

Source: Author's survey

Appendix 4.7

Annual subsidy levels for electricity consumers, 1998

Consumer type	Number	Consumption, kWh	Subsidy US$/kWh	Total subsidy, US$	Total subsidy, ZK	% of total subsidy
Urban households	124,500			5,031,616	10,632,961,880	10.16
Commercial up to 1000kWk	12,873	22,099,821	0.06	1,348,089.08	2,848,822,289	2.7
Commercial above 1000kWk	3,091	90,807,593	0.003	272,422.78	575,691,989	0.5
Sub-total	**140,464**	**112,907,414**		**6,652,127.86**	**14,057,476,158**	**13.36**
Industrial up to 300kVA	3,523	265,561,981	0.02	5,311,239.62	11,223,870,902	10.7
Industrial 300-2000kVA	297	236,952,572	0.05	11,136,770.88	23,534,558,335	22.2
Industrial 2000-7500kVA	24	167,140,649	0.04	7,521,329.21	15,894,298,516	15.2
Above 7500 kVA	8	224,983,104	0.07	15,748,817.28	33,280,873,141	31.8
Sub-total	**3,852**	**894,638,306**		**39,718,156.99**	**83,933,600,894**	**79.9**
Social services - water	342	182,046,211	0	–	–	
Social services - health	1,535	63,167,143	0.02	1,579,178.58	3,337,167,540	3.2
Social services - street lighting	1,792	18,183,091	0.09	1,563,745.83	3,304,554,592	3.2
Sub-total	**3,327**	**263,396,445**		**3,142,924.41**	**6,641,722,132**	**6.4**
TOTAL	**147,643**	**1,270,942,165**		**49,513,209**	**104,632,799,183**	**100**

Source: ZESCO, 1999.

Appendix 4.8

Description of the Pamodzi Low Cost Electrification Project (courtesy of Anders Arvidson, 1998)

The overall objective of this project was to contribute to a more rapid and sustainable electrification of Zambia's peri-urban areas. This was to be achieved by tests and modification of new methods for more cost-efficient and feasible solutions, both on the technical side (using ready boards) and at the organizational level (credit scheme, consumer training). The target of this pilot project was to electrify 200 households.

Initially, the main emphasis was on the technical aspects, investigating the use of ready boards, but as project negotiations extended over a long time, these became well-known appliances on the market, and the focus shifted to organizational aspects. Ready boards are nowadays used extensively in South Africa, and are reported to be working well for low-income households. They have been used in various types of houses, from mud-plastered homes to concrete blockhouses. A ready board is a single multi-socket outlet fixed in a room, into which cables for various uses can be plugged. Savings of the order of 75 per cent can be realized if a ready board is used instead of the conventional methods.

The credit scheme consists of two parts. The first part is a credit provided to ZESCO for the purpose of covering the actual costs of connection. SIDA (through the SEI) provided this. The condition for providing the credit was that ZESCO could show that the second part was working: that consumers had been connected and that they had contributed the required down payment. This is the only way in which the two parts of the credit scheme are connected, implying that ZESCO takes the responsibility to honour the credit with SEI regardless of whether or not its clients honour their obligations with ZESCO.

The credit from SEI was on similar terms to those undertaken by consumers (repayment over five years), but was given in foreign currency. The annual interest rate was 5 per cent (based on US$) instead of the 25 per cent requested on the consumer credits (based on ZMK). Thus ZESCO incurs a foreign exchange risk in the credit, but is to some extent insured against inflation losses. The repayment of the credit to SEI goes into a revolving fund for the benefit of further electrification projects. The revolving fund is managed by a commercial bank, and governed by a committee consisting of representatives of ZESCO and the government of Zambia through the Ministry of Energy and Water Development.

Consumer assistance was also introduced into the scheme by appointing a local facilitator (a woman in one of the households of the compound) and a local contact group. The facilitator and contact group were trained by ZESCO personnel. The facilitator was trained in simpler maintenance and supervision tasks, and had responsibility for keeping a complaints book. For more complicated tasks the facilitator would contact the local ZESCO office for the necessary service and repairs.

A cooker, a pressing iron and a light socket were included in the installation packet, in order to provide useful energy services right from the beginning, and also to encourage people to become more attractive consumers for ZESCO.

The pilot project was implemented in the Pamodzi township of Ndola. This township was constructed as a part of the 'site and service' scheme in the 1970s, with the houses situated along parallel roads that form a well-organized grid. All houses have access to piped water and sewage, but, before the project, none had power. The houses have the same plan, with one bedroom, one living room and a kitchen. Initially the houses were owned by the Ndola City Council, but in the wake of economic restructuring they were being sold to the public. The project mainly attracted households in the privately owned houses, partly because they are slightly wealthier, and partly because a tenant is understandably hesitant to make large investments in other people's property. In order to evaluate the effect of the project, several surveys were undertaken in Pamodzi, both before and during the project. In order to gather data for comparison with the use of the standard procedure, a survey was also carried out in a neighbouring compound, Twapia.

Organization of the revolving fund
In order to be able to supply the consumers with a credit towards the connection costs, a revolving fund is part of the project. While some of the problems of the revolving fund have been solved, some remain to be settled. The size of the revolving fund is based on the calculated cost of connecting 200 households. ZESCO achieves a disbursement of the fund after showing that they have connected fifty households. Thus the total sum in the fund is divided into four credit agreements, to be serviced separately.

The total cost for the installation was put on the level of the connection fee charged by ZESCO in late 1996, with the addition of the cost for appliances (cooker, pressing iron). The total sum charged this way was ZMK540,000 per installation (at the time equivalent to US$430). This charge was already slightly lower than that required to recover all the costs, but it was deemed psychologically impossible to charge a higher rate for the 'low-cost' connection than ZESCO was already charging for the 'standard' connection.

Prospective customers were required to make a down-payment of 25 per cent of the total installation cost of ZMK540,000, which was ZMK 135,000. The size of the down-payment was determined both by ZESCO's requirements and the ability of the household to pay. Based on an initial market survey it was concluded that 70 per cent of the households in the area would be able and prepared to pay such an amount for electrification. At that time, this sum was equal to about US$85. This was a substantial amount for a low-income household, but was deemed necessary if ZESCO was to risk extending credit to such households. The remainder of the connection cost (ZMK405,000) was then to be repaid through additions to the bill in five years' time. In order to make this simple, a fixed amount, representing the average interest over the whole period, plus the repayment of the capital, is shown in the agreements. The addition that each customer has to pay is ZMK9,267 per month (slightly less than US$6).

In order to make it attractive to repay the amount at an earlier date, the whole repayment schedule over five years was in the contract for each customer. This shows that the sum repaid at any time is much less than that paid in the end if the repayment scheme is followed. Still, few people have opted for this, most likely in the absence of funds, but perhaps also because there was an awareness of inflation. It may well be that inflation makes it more profitable to remain with the credit scheme until the end, in spite of the relatively high interest rate.

Social and economic differences between Twapia and Pamodzi
An initial survey in Pamodzi gave information on pre-electric energy use, social conditions and the cost of electricity connection deemed feasible by the households. This helped to guide the design of the credit scheme. A market survey carried out before installation started indicated that most households (92.5 per cent) wished to have electricity and were willing to be connected. These households were estimated to be able to pay their down-payments in a reasonably short time.

Compared to the households connected in Twapia, the households connected through the project in Pamodzi were better off in terms of social and economic status. Households were slightly smaller, with an average of 6.4 persons in Pamodzi against 7.4 in Twapia. Literacy among the respondents in Pamodzi was 93 per cent while in Twapia it was only 70 per cent. Households without literate persons amounted to only 5 per cent in Pamodzi against 22 per cent in Twapia. Households in Pamodzi owned more durable items than those in Twapia (Table A4.8.1).

Houses were of a unified standard in Pamodzi, with greater variation in standard in Twapia. Asbestos roofs were used on all houses in Pamodzi

Table A4.8.1 Ownership of durable items in Pamodzi and Twapia townships, 1996, % of total households

Item	Pamodzi	Twapia
Glass windows	100	63
Books	94	78
Sofa	94	58
Extra room	31	34
Bicycle	28	30
Car	5	11
Motorcycle	0	2

while most had iron sheets in Twapia. Mudbrick houses did not exist in Pamodzi, but made up 7 per cent of the houses in Twapia.

In terms of infrastructure there were major differences between the townships. Whereas all houses in Pamodzi had a separate kitchen and bathroom, piped water and a flush toilet, virtually none of these facilities were available in Twapia. The differences were smaller with respect to house tenure: overall, the majority owned their houses, though to a greater extent in Pamodzi (93 per cent) than in Twapia (70 per cent).

An interesting aspect of the relative status of the compound is the amount of rent paid, and the imputed rent value of the house. This shows that the actual, as well as the imputed rent in Pamodzi was about 50 per cent higher than in Twapia. Perhaps more revealing is the estimated actual rent value of the property, which was six times higher than that actually paid. This suggests that Ndola city council was making substantial losses through its rent policy.

Energy use in Pamodzi before and after electrification

Energy use patterns in electrified households in Pamodzi had changed dramatically after electrification (Table A4.8.2). Charcoal consumption had gone down to less than half what it had been, but the majority of the households were still using it to some extent. This might be explained by the fact that the survey was carried out in August, which was just at the end of winter in Zambia. Households are known to use charcoal for space heating purposes in the cold season. It is, however, likely that charcoal was still being used for some energy-consuming tasks in the household such as heating water, especially larger amounts required for washing. Kerosene use (mostly for illumination) was much less common, while the use of candles had increased, though mainly as a stand-by source of light during electricity failures.

One reason often given for embarking on the use of electricity is that it would greatly reduce the use of traditional fuels – mostly biomass fuels such as wood and, in the case of urban Zambia, charcoal. Such a reduction, it is said, would help to restrain deforestation and environmental

Table A4.8.2   Energy use and charcoal consumption before and after electricity connection in Pamodzi

Fuel type used/households	Before connection (1995)	After connection (1997)
Households using kerosene (%)	97	50
Households using candles (%)	11	80
Households using wood (%)	37	5
Households using charcoal (%)	100	85
Charcoal bags[a] per month (average)	2,3	1,0

[a] A charcoal bag is a re-used 90-kg grain bag. In the Copperbelt its content of charcoal is around 50 kg, while in the Lusaka area it is 40 kg.

degradation. The authors were unable to find documentary evidence that this effect has occurred anywhere in Africa, and therefore believe that it is based partly on wishful thinking and partly on misconceptions of problems and causes in the African context. In general, deforestation is not caused by harvesting timber for woodfuel purposes, but by the expansion of agricultural lands, against which urban electrification cannot be a remedy.

Benefits of the project approach to electrification

Pamodzi was electrified with a view to making the clients full and active users of electricity by supplying appliances right from the start. In Twapia, the households were required to purchase all equipment that they wanted to use. Given the lower economic status of the households in Twapia, this probably resulted in a restriction, so that a strict priority was applied to what was actually present at the time of the survey.

The list of appliances present in the households of the two townships (Table A4.8.3) illustrates the different priorities. The most common appliances (apart from lighting points) in Twapia were the radio and the television set. At least in the case of the TV, this was a substantial investment, and it is probably very important to note that it was bought before a cooker or a stove. Thus, households that were electrified through the project were able to start using electricity for conducting everyday tasks in general at a much earlier stage than households that were connected wholesale.

From the point of view of the households, perhaps the major improvement has been in light quality, which enhances the quality of life in the evening. In the project, it was also clear that women benefited, since they need no longer use charcoal for such tasks as cooking and ironing.

Table A4.8.3 Types of appliances owned by households as ranked percentages

Appliance	Pamodzi	Twapia
Cooker	98,8 (1)	36,0 (3)
Pressing iron	92,9 (2)	20,0 (4)
Television	84,5 (3)	44,0 (2)
Radio	83,3 (4)	65,0 (1)
Fan	17,9 (5)	13,5 (5)
Electric kettle	8,3	2,0
Freezer	4,8	3,5
Heater	4,8	2,0
Video	4,8	1,5
Battery charging	2,4	0
Sewing machine	2,4	1
Hair dryer	2,4	1,5
Shaving machine	1,2	0,5
Hammer mill	0	0,5

There are also advantages from the point of view of the utility in applying the project approach. Most prominently this is seen in the higher consumption of power, which is the main product of the utility. As seen in Table A4.8.4, consumption in Pamodzi was about two times consumption in Twapia. Payment of connection fees, although not as large as would have been the case if the normal rates had been applied, were still an order of magnitude larger than for Twapia. Finally, the total value of bills issued, as well as payment compliance with those bills, was considerably higher in the project households. All these factors may be cited in favour of applying the project principles to low-income household electrification. The utility must pay more attention to the prospective consumers, but will be rewarded with a greater return. This is the only way to achieve sustainable electrification in the long run.

Table A4.8.4 Electricity consumption and payment of bills in the project households (Pamodzi) and non-project connections (Twapia)

	Pamodzi	Twapia
Electricity consumption, kWh/month	206	87
Connection fee paid (ZMK average)	143,000	9,250
Has received bill %	77	22
Has paid the bill %	98	13

Drawbacks of the project approach to electrification
Maybe the major drawback of the project approach to electrification is the increased lead-time that is required for electrifying an area. While the whole electrification of Twapia was completed in only four months, electrification of Pamodzi took considerably longer than anticipated. While the project aimed at completing the installations in six months, after ten months barely 150 out of the planned 200 households were connected. From the point of view of logistics and costs in maintaining the operation, such an over-run is cumbersome and costly.

One reason for the long-drawn-out implementation period is probably the need experienced by participants to make a commitment of their own, and to measure their own scarce resources. On the other hand, this ensures that the households that come through and pay their dues will also be prepared for electrification to a greater extent, will have more responsibility for the installations, and will be better prepared for paying their bills. In addition, they will not come to regard electricity as a 'free for all', which may easily be the result if everybody is connected without exception.

Appendix 4.9

Brief resumé of the principal researcher and assistant researchers

Principal Researcher – O. S. Kalumiana

Oscar Sibote Kalumiana is a Deputy Director in the Department of Energy in Lusaka, Zambia. He has participated in numerous energy projects at regional and international levels. The range of projects he has been involved in includes renewable energy, biomass projects, energy and environmental policy studies. He is a principal researcher for the 'Energy Services for the Urban Poor' Theme Group.

Assistant Researcher – Charles Mulenga

Charles Mulenga holds a BA degree in Economics and currently works in the Ministry of Energy and Water Development as an economist. His duties include financial and socio-economic analysis of energy and water projects.

Assistant Researcher – Imakando P. Mubita

Imakando P. Mubita holds a BA degree in Public Administration. Having worked at a senior level for a leading regional financial institution, he is currently an entrepreneur, some of whose projects are in the energy sector.

Appendix 4.10 Selected time series data – Zambia

Year	1992	1993	1994	1995	1996	1997	1998	1999	2000	2001
National population (millions)	8.30	8.50	8.70	9.00	9.20	9.40	9.70	9.88	10.20	10.38
National population growth rate (%)	3.7	2.4	3.4	3.3	2.2	2.2	3.2	2.1	2.0	1.7
Urban population (millions)	2.4	2.4	3.5	3.5	3.6	3.7	3.8	3.9	3.9	4.0
GDP (millions US$)	2,843	2,926	2,734	2,861	2,966	3,064	3,580	3,826	3,959	4,166
GNP per capita (US$)	342	344	310	314	312	315	358	320	300	320
Total modern energy consumption (000 toe)	1,096	1,270	1,286	1,302	1,030	1,040	1,030	1,040	1,054	1,102
Modern energy consumption per capita (kgoe)	158	146	140	145	104	111	106.2	106.3	103.3	106
Modern energy production (000 toe)	1,310	1,230	1,180	1,200	1,200	1,220	1,210	1,210	1,110	1,200
National debt (US$ millions)	6,709	6,485	6,804	6,952	7,054	6,654	6,865	6,507	6,311	5,671
Merchandise exports, f.o.b. (US$ millions)	1,120	994	1,067	1,186	993	1,119	816	756	746	884
Installed capacity (MW)	1,786	1,786	1,786	1,786	1,786	1,786	1,786	1,786	1,786	1,786
Electricity generation (GWh)	6,517	8,082	8,115	7,824	7,089	7,870	7,658	7,798	8,213	9,110
Total electricity consumption (Gwh)	5,533	5,727	5,422	5,235	5,682	5,619	5,537	4,949	5,466	4,924
Electricity consumption per capita (kWh)	666.6	673.8	623.2	581.7	617.6	597.8	570.8	500.9	535.9	474.4
National electrification levels (%)	15	15	15	18	18	18	20	20	20	20
Urban electrification levels (%)	45	46	48	48	48	48				
Rural electrification levels (%)	2	2	2	2	2	2				
System losses (%)	13	14	20	22	15	15	18	15	15	27

Sources: AFREPREN/FWD, 2003; Chandi, 2003; EIU, 2001; IEA, 2003; Kalumiana, 2003; Mbewe, 2003; Phelan, 2003; UNDP, 2003; World Bank, 2003a; World Bank, 2003b

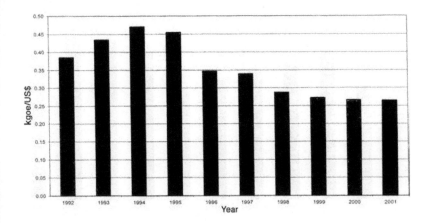

Figure A4.10.1 Zambia: Modern energy consumption (kgoe) per US$ of GDP
(US$), 1992–2001

Sources: AFREPREN/FWD, 2003; Chandi, 2003; IEA, 2003; Kalumiana, 2003; Mbewe, 2003; World Bank, 2003a; World Bank, 2003b

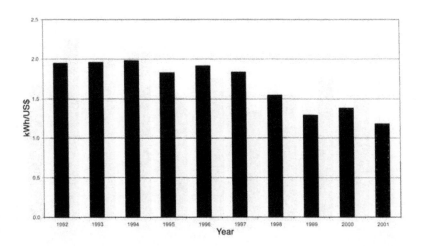

Figure A4.10.2 Zambia: Electricity consumption (kWh) per US$ of GDP (US$),
1992–2001

Sources: AFREPREN/FWD, 2003; Chandi, 2003; IEA, 2003; Kalumiana, 2003; Mbewe, 2003; World Bank, 2003a; World Bank, 2003b

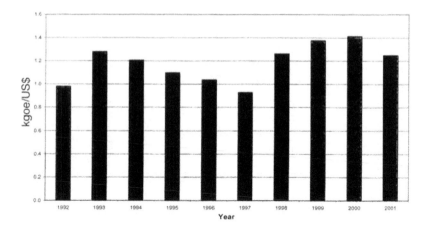

Figure A4.10.3 Zambia: Modern energy consumption (kgoe) per US$ of merchandise export (US$), 1992–2001

Sources: AFREPREN/FWD, 2003; Chandi, 2003; IEA, 2003; Kalumiana, 2003; Mbewe, 2003; World Bank, 2003a; World Bank, 2003b

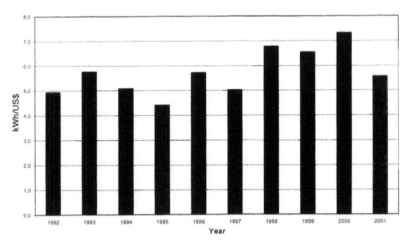

Figure A4.10.4 Zambia: Electricity consumption (kWh) per US$ of merchandise export, 1992–2001

Sources: AFREPREN/FWD, 2003; Chandi, 2003; IEA, 2003; Kalumiana, 2003; Mbewe, 2003; World Bank, 2003a; World Bank, 2003b

Part 5

ZIMBABWE

Ikhupuleng Dube

COUNTRY PROFILE
Zimbabwe

SELECTED INDICATORS

Zimbabwe

Land area (km²): 391,000
Capital city: Harare
National population (millions): 12.82 (2001)
National population growth rate (%): 1.1 (2001)
Urban population (millions): 4.2 (2001)
Urban population growth rate (%): 2.4 (2001)
Urban population as % of total population: 32.8 (2001)
GDP growth rate (%): −10.41 (2001)
GNP per capita (US$): 480 (2001)
Gini index : 56.8 (1995 Survey year)
Official exchange rate (US$: Z$): 824 (September, 2003)
Economic activities: Agriculture, forestry, commerce, mining, manufacturing
Modern energy consumption per capita (kgoe): 203 (2001)
Modern energy production (000 toe): 4,210 (2001)
Energy sources: Coal, imported petroleum, solar, biomass, hydro, coalbed methane
Installed capacity (MW): 1,961 (2001)
Electricity generation from internal sources (GWh): 11,972 (2001)
Electricity consumption *per capita* (kWh): 710 (2001)
Urban electrification rates (%): 84 (2001)
System losses (%): 14.6 (2001)

Sources: AFREPREN, 2003; Dube, 2003; IEA, 2003; Karekezi et al, 2002; Kayo, 2002; Mapako, 2003; Phelan, 2003; UNDP, 2003; World Bank, 2003a; World Bank, 2003b

10

Introduction

Rationale of the study

Despite the wide coverage of the electricity distribution network in urban areas, 20 per cent of the households are still to be connected to the grid. Urban electrification is nevertheless well-advanced compared to that of other African countries. It is also significantly higher than electrification in rural areas, where, according to the statistics of the Zimbabwe Electricity Supply Authority (ZESA, 2000f), only 20 per cent of the population had access to electricity in 2000. Figure 5.1 shows a comparison of urban and rural electrification in Zimbabwe, and how Zimbabwe compares to other selected African countries.

The steep challenge facing electricity suppliers in Zimbabwe is to ensure that both the remaining urban households, which are predominantly poor, and the majority of rural communities are connected to the national grid. This challenge is well articulated by

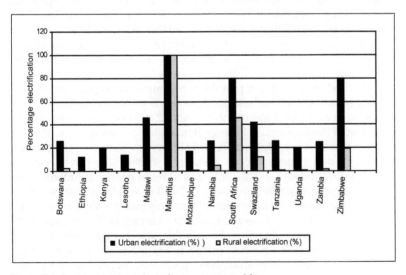

Figure 5.1 Rural and urban electrification rates in Africa

Source: AFREPREN/FWD, 2002

ZESA in its mission statement: 'We are totally committed to the total electrification of Zimbabwe at world-class standards and competitive pricing.'

The majority of the poor still do not have access to electricity. In addition, 25 per cent of those who are connected do not have adequate electricity supplies as they are supplied through load limiters instead of conventional meters (ZESA, 2000f: 15). Load limiters are miniature circuit breakers restricting the amount of electricity that can be used by a household. Households using such supplies often supplement their electricity usage with other forms of energy, such as fuelwood and kerosene. Table 5.1 shows the usage of electricity for cooking by the different households.

Table 5.1   Percentage access by households to energy sources by poverty status

Fuel used for cooking	Rural areas		Urban areas		All Zimbabwe	
	Poor	Non-poor	Poor	Non-poor	Poor	Non-poor
Electricity or LPG	0.5	5.9	47.6	80.8	11.7	38.3
Kerosene	1.0	13.5	39.7	33.7	10.2	25.4
Wood or coal	98.6	80.6	12.6	5.4	78.1	36.3

Source: CSO, 1998

The higher percentage of non-electrified households in rural areas has directed the emphasis of current government policies and ZESA's efforts to achieve total electrification towards the need to expand the distribution network to rural areas. Through the Expanded Rural Electrification Programme and Rural Electrification Agency, the government has committed massive financial investment – to the tune of Z$24 billion or US$400 million – to improving access to energy in the next five years (ZESA, 2002: 3). In urban areas no fund or agency has been established, reflecting the prevailing assumptions (1) that very little in terms of investment on infrastructure needs to be undertaken in urban areas to achieve total electrification, and (2) that the poor cannot afford the cost of modern forms of energy from an income perspective. Findings of a previous study (Dube, 2001: 4–5), however, show that the poor can afford the cost of modern forms of energy if upfront costs can be reduced.

The government's energy policy is to make energy affordable to the urban poor through the provision of blanket subsidies that benefit all income categories. The government's pricing policy on electricity offers a lifeline tariff to all domestic electricity customers. In addition to the lifeline electricity subsidies, households also benefit from subsidies because power is in any case priced below the long-run marginal cost (LRMC). The absence of initiatives specifically targeted at the poor is occurring in an environment characterized by increasing levels of poverty due to economic hardships.

Recent trends (Reserve Bank Zimbabwe, 2001) show that the formal sector is shrinking as a result of the general economic decline. Erratic fuel supplies, shortage of foreign currency, high inflation rates and shortages of basic commodities and raw materials, as a result of inappropriate economic policies and the current political crisis, have shrunk the Zimbabwean economy. This has led the urban poor to resort to the informal sector as their source of livelihood.

The role of micro-enterprises in providing incomes to urban households cannot be overemphasized. The GEMINI Survey (1998: 11) shows that 57.8 per cent of urban households have incomes or supplement their incomes from micro-enterprises and informal sector activities. The informal sector is also an important source of employment for the poor urban households. The same survey shows that 1,647,664 households, or 15 per cent of the total population, are employed in the informal sector, and that the number of people deriving their income from informal sector activities grew by 22 per cent between 1991 and 1998 (1998: 27).

Despite the importance of the informal sector as a source of income to poor urban households, it continues to receive no other preferential energy policies than those enjoyed by the rich and the formal sector. An examination of the electricity pricing structure shows that the informal sector and the power utility cross-subsidize the other formal sectors. This unfair electricity pricing policy stifles the development of the informal sector through the erosion of its profit margins.

11

Do the Urban Poor Need Subsidies
to Access Modern Energy?

Research approach

The aim of the following analysis is to determine whether without subsidies the poor households can afford modern forms of energy. The methodology used is outlined in Part 3.

Field surveys were carried out in the major cities of Zimbabwe and involved the use of close-ended and structured questionnaires. Households were asked questions verbally and interactively. From the survey, current energy use patterns and the cost of energy (inclusive of subsidies) were ascertained for various income categories. The income categories derived are all households, non-poor households and poor households. Poor households were further classified into two categories: very poor households and extremely poor households. The classification of the households into these categories was derived from the stated incomes as sorted by the poverty datum lines provided by the Central Statistics Office.

The key expenditure items identified during the survey were rent or mortgage, food, health, education, transport and travel, including vehicle maintenance costs, and other long-term committed repayments such as accounts and telephone expenditures. The non-essential expenditure included entertainment, furniture, non-essential households goods (radios, televisions, etcetera), pay television and others.

Findings

The main energy sources used by the urban household in Zimbabwe are electricity, kerosene and fuelwood. LPG and coal are marginally used. Electricity is often used in conjunction with other forms of energy such as kerosene and fuelwood. There are also various forms of electricity supplies, namely load limiters ranging from one ampère to 30 ampères, prepayment metered electricity supplies and conventional metered electricity supplies. For ease of analysis, the units for prepayment and load limiters were converted to the equivalent units of conventional meter supplies and the applicable tariff for the conventional metered supplies applied. Of the above energy sources, only electricity and kerosene are subsidized.

Electricity consumers are given a lifeline tariff and are also charged below the LRMC. Kerosene users are charged below the landed price of kerosene. Both electricity and kerosene attract levies and taxes. Electricity charges include a one per cent rural electrification levy and sales tax. Kerosene also has duties. Appendix 5.1 shows energy consumption patterns and cost of energy for the different household categories. The non-subsidized monthly energy costs were calculated by removing subsidies from the cost of subsidized energy, and the results are summarized in Table 5.2. Owing to the blanket nature of subsidies, and the fact that

Table 5.2 Comparison of the current monthly household energy cost and the monthly cost without subsidies

Household category	All	Non-poor	Poor	Very poor	Extremely poor
Kerosene					
Cost with subsidy (Z$)*	730	952	654	654	0
True cost (Z$)	682	889	611	611	0
Shortfall (Z$)	48	63	43	43	0
Electricity					
Cost with subsidy (Z$)	1,014	1,623	721	727	675
True cost (Z$)	1,695	2,285	1,333	1,393	1,202
Shortfall (Z$)	–681	–662	–600	–666	–527
Electricity and kerosene					
Cost with subsidy (Z$)	817	1,202	689	689	0
True cost (Z$)	1,323	1,802	1,131	1,131	0
Shortfall (Z$)	–506	–600	–442	–442	0
Electricity and fuelwood					
Cost with subsidy (Z$)	1,005	1,546	857	0	857
True cost (Z$)	1,450	1,960	1,277	0	1,277
Shortfall (Z$)	–445	–414	–420	0	–420
Electricity, kerosene and fuelwood					
Cost with subsidy (Z$)	1,135	1,515	995	882	714
True cost (Z$)	1,557	1,870	1,379	1,392	1,053
Shortfall (Z$)	–422	–355	–384	–510	–339
Kerosene and fuelwood					
Cost with subsidy (Z$)	959	1,235	821	871	670
True cost (Z$)	921	1,187	793	848	651
Shortfall (Z$)	38	48	28	23	19

Note: * This cost of kerosene includes the higher black market price of kerosene, Exchange rate: US$1 = ZW$55
Source: Survey by author

they are constant for all household categories, while the very poor consume less electricity in monetary and units terms than other categories, the level of subsides they capture is lower than that for other categories (Table 5.3).

The results show that although kerosene subsidies exist, most urban households of all income categories are already paying a higher cost of kerosene than the gazetted, unsubsidized price. This is because subsidized kerosene is only available at service stations. The current shortage of kerosene has resulted in its sale mainly through the black market. On the black market, street vendors sell kerosene at a significantly higher price than the subsidized price (if it was available in the formal sector). Government controls on the price of kerosene have resulted in the reluctance of the formal sector to import the product, citing viability problems. The result is that such controls have impacted negatively on the price of kerosene for the poor since they have to spend more on the black market.

Households using electricity only, or electricity with other forms of energy, were found to capture the largest share of the energy subsidies. This demonstrates the higher weight of electricity subsidies, compared to subsidies on other forms of energy. Due to the blanket nature of the electricity subsidies, there was minimal differentiation in the level of subsidies captured by different income groups.

Having ascertained the levels of subsidies by household income categories and energy sources, the next step was to ascertain the household expenditure patterns according to key household expenditure items. The difference between total consumption expenditure on key items and total income was assumed to constitute the level of disposable income devoted to non-essential expenditure (budget reserve). This could be used to partially meet additional energy costs arising from the removal of subsidies, if the households were unwilling to cut their expenditures on essential items. Appendix 5.2 shows the household consumption expenditure by key expenditure items, household income category and energy used. The level of unsubsidized energy used by different urban household income groups was compared to household energy budget shares, total income, budget reserve and the unsubsidized cost of modern energy (electricity was used as a proxy for modern energy).

If the level of non-subsidized energy was found not to be significant and not to reduce expenditures on key household items when compared to the above indicators, then this was considered to be an indication that the poor could afford the non-subsidized costs of modern energy sources. Table 5.3 shows the comparison of level of subsidies to the above affordability indicators.

The removal of electricity subsidies will result in the energy budget of the poor households increasing significantly by an average of 84 per cent. The very poor using electricity seem to be the group that would be

Table 5.3 Comparison of energy subsidies to household expenditure and income indicators

Household category	All	Non-poor	Poor	Very poor	Extremely poor
Electricity					
Subsidy as % of energy budget	67	41	84	87	77
Non-subsidized energy as % of non-subsidized electricity	100	100	100	100	100
Subsidy as % of total income	4	2	7	6	8
Subsidy as % of reserves	14	5	25	14	53
Electricity and kerosene					
Subsidy as % of energy budget	62	50	64	64	0
Non-subsidized energy as % of non-subsidized electricity	78	79	85	81	0
Subsidy as % of total income	2	1	3	3	0
Subsidy as % of reserves	3	2	10	10	0
Electricity and fuelwood					
Subsidy as % of energy budget	44	27	49	0	49
Non-subsidized energy as % of non-subsidized electricity	86	86	96	0	106
Subsidy as % of total income	3	1	6	0	6
Subsidy as % of reserves	8	3	44	0	44
Electricity, fuelwood and kerosene					
Subsidy as % of energy budget	41	42	42	5	64
Non-subsidized energy as % of non-subsidized electricity	92	82	103	100	88
Subsidy as % of total income	2	1	4	4	8
Subsidy as % of reserves	5	1	20	44	74
Kerosene					
Subsidy as % of energy budget	–7	–7	–7	–7	0
Non-subsidized energy as % of non-subsidized electricity	40	39	46	44	0
Subsidy as % of total income	0	0	0	0	0
Subsidy as % of reserves	0	0	–1	–1	0
Fuelwood and kerosene					
Subsidy as % of energy budget	–4	–4	–3	–3	–3
Non-subsidized energy as % of non-subsidized electricity	54	52	59	61	54
Subsidy as % of total income	0	0	0	0	0
Subsidy as % of reserves	0	0	–1	0	–1

Source: Survey by author

most affected by the increase in electricity charges of 87 per cent. For the extremely poor households electricity costs will increase by 77 per cent if electricity subsidies are removed. Such an increase appears to be very substantial. However, this increase is equal to 7 per cent of income for all poor households. The corresponding figures for very poor and extremely poor urban households rose by six and eight per cent respectively.

The removal of subsidies will necessitate providing an additional 25 per cent of the budget reserve of all the poor household categories to meet the additional electricity costs. The extremely poor and the very poor household categories would need to channel 53 per cent and 14 per cent of their non-essential expenditure towards meeting the additional electricity cost. The non-poor need to commit only an additional 4 per cent of their incomes towards the increased energy costs and 14 per cent of their non-essential expenditure.

The extremely poor will be the household category affected most by the removal of electricity subsidies. Their response would be to cut down on electricity usage (by resorting to other complementary energy sources) and/or cut down on essential expenditure. Other groups could cushion themselves from the impact of electricity price increases arising from the removal of subsidies by committing an insignificant portion of their non-essential expenditure towards meeting the additional electricity costs.

It can be concluded that in general subsidies are not decisive for the affordability of modern forms of energy by the non-poor, but their removal could have a much more significant effect on the incomes of the poorest segment of the urban poor. The cost of the non-subsidized, non-modern forms of energy is adequate to cover the non-subsidized cost of modern energy in the absence of subsidies. However, there may be need for subsidies to be targeted at the very vulnerable groups, instead of such subsidies being applied across all household income categories.

12

Are Subsidies for Upfront Costs
a Better Option?

Research approach

Even if they could afford monthly energy costs, households could still not afford the cost of modern energy if the upfront costs of energy are beyond their reach. The first part of the analysis therefore involves ascertaining the cost of non-subsidized connection fees. These were derived by carrying out a market survey (involving key suppliers and other service providers) to derive the true cost of materials, labour, transport and overheads needed for a household to be connected to the distribution system.

Material costs were derived from materials used in ZESA service connections and sourced from major suppliers. Labour costs were based on the ZESA outsourcing rates. These are rates ZESA charges for working on customers' installations located beyond the metering point. Transport costs were based on Automobile Association of Zimbabwe rates. There are no subsidies for the internal wiring of houses, nor for the upfront costs associated with energy derived from kerosene, LPG and fuelwood.

The methodological approach used for the next section is outlined in Part 3.

Findings

Impact of upfront costs on energy access
The impact of upfront costs was ascertained by comparing the cost of the devices to income and expenditure, and they were computed as a one-off payment, or where applicable amortized. The cost amortization took into consideration the duration given for hire purchases by retail outlets and the discount rates used by the same outlets. The amortization costs for internal wiring and compact distribution boards assumed the ZESA planning assumptions of a discount factor of 16 per cent and an amortization period of five years. The discount factor for hire purchase retail outlets is 45 per cent and the repayment period is up to two years. Table 5.4 shows the cost scenarios of the basic device and upfront costs that could be incurred by households if subsidies, including those for connection fees, are removed.

Table 5.4 Device and upfront costs of basic electrical devices

Device	Upfront costs (Z$)	Amortized monthly costs (Z$)
One-plate stove	2,700	173
Iron	895	57
4 light bulbs	240	240
Internal wiring using conventional method	11,458	278
Internal wiring using compact distribution board	2,171	53
Connection fees without subsidies	7,249	176
Total initial non-subsidized costs	24,713	977

Note: Exchange rate: US$1 = ZW$55
Source: Survey by authors

During the survey the cost of the basic kerosene devices was also ascertained. It was discovered that kerosene devices are not sold on hire purchase, as is the case with the electrical devices. Low capital cost made it unnecessary to amortize the cost of kerosene devices. Table 5.5 shows the basic kerosene prices.

Table 5.5 Cost of kerosene devices

Device	Cost (Z$)
Open wick lamp	40
One-plate stove	299
Solid iron	70
Total non-subsidized costs	409

Source: Survey by author

LPG is not widely used. However, an interview with LPG suppliers shows that since the advent of kerosene shortages, LPG users have increased by over 60 per cent. During the study, the cost of LPG and associated basic devices was ascertained and the results are given in Table 5.6.

Table 5.6 Upfront costs of LPG and associated devices

Type of cost	Cost (Z$)
Cylinder –4.5 kg	6,166
–10 kg	One-off deposit of Z$250
4.5 kg	548 /two weeks
10 kg	1,188 /month
Normal gas cooking stove	475
Gas lamp	1,785

Source: Survey by author

The amortized LPG device costs per month were found to be Z$539, while the monthly cost for LPG was Z$1,096. The device costs without amortization were Z$8,426. The study established that only 4.5 kg cylinders are sold, at a unit price of Z$6,166. Larger cylinders are generally not sold, but rented out indefinitely upon a deposit of Z$250, which has not changed over the years. LPG cylinders imported from South Africa are currently unavailable, owing to the increase in LPG users and the shortage of foreign currency.

To ascertain the ability of households to change the type of energy they use, the device and upfront costs of the potential energy source were compared to household income and the non-essential expenditure. (see Table 5.7).

Table 5.7 Comparison of upfront cost and device cost to household incomes and budget reserves

	All households	Non-poor	Poor
Electricity devices			
Costs without amortization compared to incomes (%)	155	70	260
Costs without amortization compared to budget reserve (%)	511	198	1086
Costs with amortization compared to incomes (%)	5	2	9
Costs with amortization compared to budget reserve (%)	18	7	39
Subsidies as % of income	4	2	7
Subsidies as % of budget reserve	14	5	30
Kerosene devices			
Costs without amortization compared to incomes (%)	3	1	4
Costs without amortization compared to budget reserve (%)	8	3	18
Subsidies as % of income	0	0	0
Subsidies as % of budget reserve	0	0	0
LPG			
Costs without amortization compared to incomes (%)	53	23	89
Costs without amortization compared to budget reserve (%)	174	68	370
Costs with amortization compared to incomes (%)	3	2	6
Costs with amortization compared to budget reserve (%)	11	4	24

Source: Survey by author

The results show that if electricity costs were not amortized, as is currently the norm, then the poorer households would find it difficult to change from other non-electrical energy sources to electricity. If the electricity costs are amortized, as is the case with a compact distribution board, then electricity upfront costs are within reach of poorer households. The results also show that it could be easier for households

Table 5.8 Comparison of monthly LPG recurrent cost to recurrent cost of electricity and kerosene

	All households
Electricity	
Monthly cost as proportion of income (%)	11
LPG	
Monthly cost as proportion of income (%)	7
Kerosene	
Monthly true cost as proportion of income (%)	5

Source: Survey by author

using kerosene to switch to LPG, as the impact of LPG upfront costs are significantly lower than those of electricity, even if the upfront costs are not amortized.

The comparison of the monthly recurrent cost of electricity, LPG and kerosene (each as a percentage of income) is presented in Table 5.8. The results show that the monthly energy budget share of electricity is marginally higher than that of LPG, but LPG upfront costs are lower. This indicates that poorer households currently using kerosene will find it easier to switch from kerosene to LPG than to electricity. This is in line with current observations by LPG suppliers, who have significantly expanded their customer base.

It can then be concluded that upfront electricity costs without amortization would limit the scope of fuel switching. If the costs are amortized, then the poor have the ability to use electricity. The impact of upfront costs in determining access to a particular energy form was found to be more decisive than the removal of subsidies. The results also show that LPG could be a substitute for non-electrical forms of energy, and could easily replace electricity if subsidies are removed.

Other factors affecting access to energy
The study shows that other factors, apart from energy expenditure and upfront energy cost, could affect access to different energy forms by the urban poor. The factors analyzed are availability of electrical gadgets amongst the urban poor, and the choice of energy use by consumers.

The availability of a wide range of electrical devices may tend to limit the scope of fuel switching, since some of the equipment might operate on electricity only. In addition, the availability of a large number of household energy end-use devices could present opportunities for energy savings by households or partial fuel switching. Table 5.9 shows the prevalence of electrical devices amongst the urban poor in Zimbabwe.

Table 5.9 Ownership of electrical devices by urban households

Device type	All households (%)	Non-poor (%)	Poor (%)	Very poor (%)	Extremely poor (%)
One-plate stove	18.0	8.3	21.7	13.2	25.8
Two-plate stove	35.2	22.2	40.2	50.0	35.5
Two-plate stove with oven	9.4	16.7	6.5	6.7	6.5
Four-plate stove with oven	21.9	44.4	13.0	20.0	9.7
Electric geyser	10.9	30.6	3.3	0.0	4.8
Kettle	30.5	55.6	20.7	36.7	12.9
Instant heater	14.8	30.6	8.7	13.3	6.5
Steam shower	2.3	5.6	1.1	3.3	0.0
Electric iron	71.9	83.3	67.4	83.3	59.7
Refrigerator	51.6	88.9	37.0	56.7	27.4
Radio	79.7	94.4	73.9	96.7	62.9
Television	64.8	88.9	55.4	70.0	48.4

Source: Survey by author

The results show that the majority of the poor and extremely poor urban households own one- or two-plate stoves, kettles, electric irons, radios and televisions. About 27.4 per cent of the extremely poor households were found to own refrigerators, compared to 88 per cent of the non-poor. The possession of a range of electrical devices by the poor household categories tends to limit the extent to which these households can switch to other non-electrical energy forms. The alternative for such households would be to find substitutes for electricity for purposes such as heating, and to use electricity only for purposes such as powering refrigerators, radios and televisions.

Furthermore, the existence of a wider range of electrical devices in the homes of the poor means that there could be some scope for the households to engage in energy efficiency practices. However, certain barriers would need to be addressed before households could practise energy efficiency and demand-side management effectively. The most pressing of these issues is energy pricing, according to a Southern Centre and Risø Laboratories (1994) study on the potential of energy efficiency in Zimbabwe. Other areas identified by the same study as barriers towards the efficient utilization of energy by households in Zimbabwe are:

- Availability of energy-efficient home appliances (most appliances are locally produced and do not incorporate the latest technologies for energy efficiency);

- Availability of finance for importation of energy-efficient technologies and appliances;

- Lack of energy efficiency standards and policies;

- Lack of customer information on possible energy efficiency practices and benefits.

Despite these setbacks, the RISØ study shows that about 20 per cent of the energy used by the households could be saved through energy efficiency practices. This would be more feasible if the right signals were sent to the end user – through the removal of subsidies, for example.

The study derived the percentage increase in the level of energy cost due to the removal of subsidies. It was then assumed that the removal of subsidies would increase the cost of the energy source by the same magnitude. Households were then asked the extent to which they would absorb the additional cost without significant pruning of key expenditure items. The preferential ability to pay was then compared to the cost of unsubsidized modern energy. If the level of preferred energy cost was equal to or greater than the non-subsidized cost of energy, then the poor households were considered to be able to absorb the increase in the cost of modern energy (Table 5.10).

Table 5.10 Maximum amount buyers are willing to pay for total energy compared to the true cost of energy

	All households	Non-poor	Poor	Very poor	Extremely poor
Electricity only					
Preferred expenditure limit (Z$)	1,398	2,050	1,131	1,575	938
True energy costs (Z$)	1,695	2,285	1,500	1,938	1,202
Shortfall (Z$)	297	235	369	363	264
Electricity and kerosene					
Preferred expenditure limit (Z$)	1,454	2,180	1,000	1,000	0
True energy costs (Z$)	1,885	2,530	1,183	1,183	0
Shortfall (Z$)	431	350	183	183	0
Electricity and fuelwood					
True energy costs (Z$)	2,206	3,830	1,277	0	1,277
Preferred expenditure limit (Z$)	1,991	3,500	1,129	0	1,129
Shortfall (Z$)	215	330	148	0	148
Electricity, fuelwood and kerosene					
True energy costs (Z$)	1,557	2,475	1,379	1,344	1,392
Preferred expenditure limit (Z$)	1,398	2,800	1,143	1,117	1,153
Shortfall (Z$)	159	−325	236	227	239
Kerosene and fuelwood					
True energy costs (Z$)	1,164	1,017	1,914	2,346	1,807
Preferred expenditure limit (Z$)	1,825	3,833	1,362	3,250	1,018
Shortfall (Z$)	−661	−2,816	552	−904	789
Kerosene only					
True energy costs (Z$)	682	178	1,185	1,185	0
Preferred expenditure limit (Z$)	1,000	500	1,500	1,500	0
Shortfall (Z$)	−318	−322	−315	−315	0

Note: Exchange rate: US$1 = ZW$55
Source: Survey by author

The results show that the non-poor households using electricity are willing to pay a significant portion of the subsidy. An analysis of the shortfall due to the removal of the subsidy shows that there is room for the non-poor to cut non-essential expenditures to meet the energy shortfall. Poor households will need to meet a shortfall of Z$688. They will need to draw significantly on their reserves, totalling Z$2,275. However, these reserves and other expenditure on non-essential items are still adequate to meet the shortfall. The extremely poor will need to raise an additional Z$527 from other expenditure items to meet the shortfall. Although consumption expenditure would be affected more in their case than for the other household categories, subsidies are not necessarily decisive in determining whether the extremely poor can afford electricity.

The last factor considered was preference in the use of particular energy forms by the urban poor. Households were asked to state what their preferred energy sources would be if the removal of subsidies resulted in an increase in energy to a particular level. The percentage share of the households willing to change their sources of energy and the reasons they gave were then derived. The results are shown in Table 5.11.

Table 5.11 Preferences for different energy sources (%)

	All households	Non-poor	Poor	Very poor	Extremely poor
Electricity	82.0	78.8	83.2	95.7	77.6
Affordable	21.0	7.7	26.6	25.6	25.6
Affordable upfront costs	1.0				
Clean	21.9	30.8	19.0	13.4	28.2
Easily available	28.6	42.3	24.0	21.7	25.6
Easy to use	27.6	19.2	30.4	34.5	21.5
Fuelwood	7.0	12.1	5.2	4.3	6.1
Affordable	33.3	25.0	40	100	33.3
Affordable upfront costs	22.5	25.0	20		33.3
Clean	44.4				
Easily available		50.0	40		33.4
Gas	0.8	3.0			
Easy to use	100.0	100			
Kerosene	10.2	6.1	11.6		16.3
Affordable	61.5	50	63.6		57.1
Affordable upfront costs	30.7		36.4		42.9
Easily available	7.7	50			

Source: Survey by author

The results show that the majority of the households preferred to use electricity, followed by kerosene and fuelwood. Even the poor households would prefer to use electricity, though the percentage of the extremely poor who prefer to use electricity is lower than that of the non-poor. Overall, more poor than non-poor households preferred to use electricity. Whereas the poor preferred to use electricity, followed by kerosene, the non-poor preferred to use electricity followed by fuelwood. The reason could be that the non-poor often use electricity for house warming (through fireplaces) and also that the non-poor prefer to prepare certain meals using fuelwood – in the roasting of meat and the preparation of other traditional delicacies, for example.

The majority of the households preferred to use electricity for reasons other than affordability. About 80 per cent of the households cited reasons such as cleanliness of the energy source, easier usage and availability as the main reasons for preferring electricity. The majority of kerosene users cited affordability as the main reason for their choice, while for fuelwood users availability and affordability of upfront costs were the main reasons.

From the aforegoing analysis, it can be concluded that pricing considerations are not decisive for influencing the choice of energy use. Though some households preferred to use kerosene, the fact that most households buy their kerosene at prices considerably higher than the stipulated price, seems to imply that the removal of subsidies does not affect the choice of energy use. The results seem to indicate that factors other than energy pricing influence the choice of energy use.

13

Who Captures the Subsidies?

To answer this question, the type and level of energy subsidies for electricity and kerosene were ascertained, based on the methodology outlined in Part 3.

Lifeline tariff subsidies entail the preferential pricing of domestic electricity usage for units up to 1,000kWh. The lifeline subsidy charges for the various usage blocks are given in Table 5.12.

Table 5.12 Lifeline tariff subsidy charge

Usage block (kWh)	Present charge (Z$/kWh)	Real charge (Z$/kWh)	Level of subsidy (Z$/kWh)
1–50	0.99	3.21	2.22
51–300	1.10	3.21	2.11
301–1000	3.09	3.21	0.12
Above 1000	3.21	3.21	0

Source: ZESA, 2000g

Table 5.13 Monthly lifeline tariff subsidy distribution

Consumption band (kWh)	Total no. of customers	% of customers	Annual energy consumption (kWh)	% of total	Average consumption (kWh)	Total subsidized revenue (Z$)
0–200	104,869	26.90%	12,042,406	8%	115	26,023,242
201–400	140,374	36.01%	36,899,196	26%	263	78,669,801
401–600	67,932	17.43%	32,428,309	23%	477	39,106,414
801–1000	17,815	4.57%	15,732,014	11%	883	11,123,508
1001–1200	9,530	2.44%	10,312,123	7%	1082	6,084,238
1201–1400	5,676	1.46%	7,284,306	5%	1283	3,623,729
1401–1600	3,536	0.91%	5,235,976	4%	1481	2,257,488
1601–1800	2,327	0.60%	3,921,358	3%	1685	1,485,627
1801–2000	1,672	0.43%	3,155,936	2%	1888	1,067,455
2000+	4,107	1.05%	15,691,383	11%	3821	2,622,032
TOTAL	357,838	100.00%	142,703,007	100%	12,978	172,063,534

Note: Exchange Rate: US$1 = ZW$55
Source: ZESA, 2000e

The revenue forgone by ZESA's operation of a lifeline tariff for domestic customers was calculated by first classifying the domestic customers according to usage blocks. To achieve this task a computer procedure was developed to classify all ZESA domestic customers according to usage blocks of 200kWh. The classification was made according to the number of customers in each usage block, the average household energy sold per user block, and the number of domestic customers in the same usage block. The derived level of subsidy charge (Table 5.12) was then applied to the average consumption of each usage block to derive the level of subsidized electricity for each customer. The total subsidy was derived by multiplying the subsidy to each customer by the number of customers in each usage block (Table 5.13).

The total monthly subsidy to the households through the lifeline tariff is Z$172 million per month or Z$2,064 million annually. The study also sought to ascertain the composition of this monthly subsidy according to non-poor and poor households. If poor households were considered to be those consuming less than 200 units per month, then the percentage of such users was found to be 26.9 per cent. The total amount of subsidy to these households was found to be Z$26.02 million, or a mere 15 per cent of the total lifeline tariff subsidy. This clearly shows that households other than the poor are absorbing the highest share of lifeline tariff subsidies.

Subsidies due to pricing below the LRMC for the domestic metered sector
The subsidies arising from pricing electricity below the LRMC were further ascertained. From Table 5.13 it can be observed that beyond monthly consumption of 1,000 units, customers are charged a flat rate. This flat rate is still below the LRMC. This means that instead of the utility charging Z$3.21/kWh it should have been charging Z$4.13/kWh. The additional subsidy in the flat charge is Z$0.92/kWh. This subsidy is over and above the inherent subsidy for the different consumption blocks detailed in Table 5.13.

The method adopted for calculating the total electricity subsidies due to pricing electricity below the LRMC was the same as in the previous case. It involved the classification of all the domestic customers in ZESA's billing system according to the number of customers per specific energy usage block and the total energy sales for each usage block. Taking into consideration the difference in the current tariff without lifeline subsidies and the LRMC, the subsidized unit tariff due to pricing below LRMC was derived.

The level of subsidy charge (Z$0.92/kWh) was then applied in the average consumption of each customer to derive the subsidy in monetary terms of the forgone revenue due to pricing below LRMC. The total subsidy for all the customers in each usage block was derived by multiplying the average subsidy per customer by the number of customers in each usage block.

Table 5.14 Monthly subsidies to the domestic sector due to pricing below LRMC

Consumption band (kWh)	Total no. of customers	% of customers	Annual energy consumption (kWh)	% of total consumption	Average consumption (kWh)	Total subsidized revenue (Z$)
0–200	104,869	26.90%	12,042,406	8%	115	11,079,014
201–400	140,374	36.01%	36,899,196	26%	263	33,947,260
401–600	67,932	17.43%	32,428,309	23%	477	29,834,044
601–800	31,984	8.20%	21,832,233	15%	683	20,085,654
801–1000	17,815	4.57%	15,732,014	11%	883	14,473,453
1001–1200	9,530	2.44%	10,312,123	7%	1,082	9,487,153
1201–1400	5,676	1.46%	7,284,306	5%	1,283	6,701,562
1401–1600	3,536	0.91%	5,235,976	4%	1,481	4,817,098
1601–1800	2,327	0.60%	3,921,358	3%	1,685	3,607,649
1801–2000	1,672	0.43%	3,155,936	2%	1,888	2,903,461
2000+	4,107	1.05%	15,691,383	11%	3,821	14,436,072
TOTAL	389,824	100.00%	164,535,240	115%	422	151,372,421

Note: Exchange rate: US$1 = ZW$55
Source: ZESA, 2000d

The sum of the total subsidies in each usage block resulted in the total subsidy for all domestic metered customers being derived. Table 5.14 summarizes the results of the above analysis.

The power utility subsidizes monthly domestic metered customers by up to Z$151.4 million per month or Z$1,816.8 million annually through pricing below the LRMC. Of this amount, 7.3 per cent is the subsidy to households that could be classified as poor. However, 92.7 per cent is the subsidy to non-poor households. This again shows that the pricing of electricity below the LRMC benefits the non-poor households significantly more than the poor.

Subsidies due to the costing of electricity below the LRMC for other customer categories

Unlike the domestic metered customers, other customer categories are not afforded the lifeline tariff but are still charged below their respective LRMCs. To ascertain the level of subsidy for these customer categories, the tariff per customer category is calculated. The results were compared to the expected LRMC for each category according to the results obtained by the ZESA LRMC study (2000d: 10).

The difference between the current tariff level and the LRMC for each category was assumed to be the tariff level required to reach the LRMC. The next step was to ascertain the annual energy sales to each customer category. These were derived from the ZESA C12 billing report (2000a). The multiplication of the annual sales per customer category and the tariff level required to reach the LRMC gave the total subsidized energy by customer category. The results of this analysis are shown on Table 5.15.

Table 5.15 Annual subsidies to other customer categories

Category	Tariff as in Dec. 2000 (Z$/kWh)	LRMC Z$/kWh	Difference Z$/kWh	Sales (kWh)	Total subsidy (Z$)
Load limited domestic	2.31	4.13	1.82	362,531,942	659,808,134.44
Public lighting	3.25	4.13	0.88	49,432,912	43,500,962.56
Low-voltage mining and industrial	4.90	4.13	–0.77	162,606,397	–125,206,925.69
High-voltage mining and industrial (11 kV)	2.15	3.36	1.21	1,413,203,140	1,709,975,799.40
High-voltage mining and industrial (33kV)	2.04	2.92	0.88	918,597,663	808,365,943.44
Low-voltage commercial	5.39	4.13	–1.26	1,075,385,183	–1,354,985,330.58
High-voltage commercial (11kV)	2.70	3.36	0.66	358,244,955	236,441,670.30
High-voltage commercial (33 kV)	2.37	2.92	0.55	57,244,818	31,484,649.90
Low-voltage agriculture	4.62	4.13	–0.50	878,817,766	–439,408,883
High-voltage agriculture (11kV)	1.98	3.36	1.38	116,009,782	160,093,499.16
High-voltage agriculture (33kV)	1.76	2.92	1.16	298,899,592	346,723,526.72
Subtransmission secondary	1.16	2.53	1.38	1,845,668,628	2,528,566,020.36
Subtransmission primary	0.88	2.53	1.65	968,497,090	1,598,020,198.50
TOTAL					6,203,379,265.51

Note: Exchange rate: US$1 = ZW$55
Source: ZESA, 2000d

The total subsidy due to pricing other customers below the LRMC adds up to Z$6,708 billion dollars (US$112 million) annually. However, of this amount Z$1,921 billion (US$35 million) is the cross-subsidy provided by other customer categories priced above the LRMC. Customers in the low-voltage mining, industrial, commercial and agricultural sectors (low-usage customers, most of which are small-scale enterprises) are charged above their LRMCs and are actually subsidizing other customer categories.

Large-scale users such as high-voltage industrial, mining, commercial and agricultural customers are charged below their respective LRMCs and are being subsidized by other customer categories. This means that the effective subsidy is Z$6,207.7 million. Of this total, the subsidy captured by the household category is only 10.5 per cent. The economically active sectors therefore absorb the largest proportions of the subsidies.

From the above analysis it is very clear that the largest proportion of the electricity subsidies benefit the non-poor and the economically active sectors.

14

What Is the Impact of Subsidies on Utilities and Public Finance?

Research approach

To determine the impact of subsidies on public finances the total subsidies to the electricity and kerosene sector were computed. The methodological approach of ascertaining the various components of the electricity subsidies was outlined in the a foregoing section. In addition, subsidies arising from subsidized connection fees were included.

The kerosene subsidy margin was derived from the landed price of kerosene and the pump price. From the annual statistics of the Department of Energy, the average annual kerosene consumption by households was ascertained. The multiplication of the subsidy margin and sales of kerosene to households gave the amount of kerosene subsidies. The analysis did not take into consideration the filtering of domestic subsidies to other sectors, since these are supposed to pay the landed price of kerosene. In practice there are loopholes that can be used to buy subsidized kerosene by other categories. Data on such sales are lacking.

Adding up the two subsidies on electricity and petroleum products provided an indication of the magnitude of the total national energy subsidy. To ascertain whether current energy subsidies are too great a burden on public sector finances, the following indicators were then derived:

- current annual electricity subsidies compared to ZESA revenue;
- current annual electricity subsidies compared to the ZESA debt;
- potential number of domestic customers that could be connected utilizing the current electricity subsidies;
- current annual kerosene subsidies compared to NOCZIM revenue;
- current annual kerosene subsidies compared to NOCZIM debt;
- total energy subsidies compared to government expenditure;
- total subsidies as a percentage of government deficit;
- total subsidies as a percentage of the gross domestic product.

Subsidies were considered too great a burden if the above indicators were significantly high.

Findings

The electricity subsidies were derived using the methodology outlined above. Additional subsidies are incurred by ZESA in charging service connections fees to the domestic households below the true cost. ZESA annually connects an average of 21,839 domestic customers (Table 5.16). The service fee per customer is Z$1,600, compared to the true connection fee of Z$7,612. The total annual revenue from connection fees was found to be on average Z$34.9 million. If ZESA was charging the true connection fee, it would accrue an annual revenue of Z$166.2 million. This means that in connecting domestic customers below the true cost, ZESA forgoes annually revenue totalling Z$131.3 million. Other customer categories are charged on a cost-recovery basis.

Table 5.16 Service fee connection subsidy

Average annual number of connections	21,839
Subsidized connection fee	Z$1,600
Subsidized revenue from connection fees	Z$34,942,400
True connection fee	Z$7,612
True revenue from connection fees	Z$166,238,468
Annual connection fee subsidy	Z$131,296,068

Note: Exchange rate: US$1 = ZW$55
Source: Survey by author

Kerosene for the domestic sector is charged at a pump price of Z$50 per litre. Energy statistics from the Department of Energy (2000) show that the average total annual consumption level of kerosene by households is 56,750,000 litres. The landed price of kerosene is estimated to be Z$59 per litre. Assuming the above average annual consumption of kerosene by households, the annual revenue NOCZIM loses by subsidizing kerosene is ZW$510.75 million (Table 5.17).

Table 5.17 Kerosene subsidies

Amount of kerosene used by households	56,750,000 litres
Subsidized kerosene price	Z$50
Revenue from subsidized kerosene price	Z$2,837,500,000
True kerosene price	Z$59
Revenue from true kerosene price	Z$ 3,348,250,000
Annual kerosene subsidy	Z$ 510,750,000

Source: Survey by author and NOCZIM, 2001

Comparison of the level of subsidies to energy utilities and government's key financial indicators
Table 5.18 shows the comparison of the energy subsidies to a selection of public and utility indicators.

Table 5.18 Comparison of energy subsidies to public sector finances

Total annual electricity subsidies (Z$)	10,220,265,092
ZESA revenue (1999) (Z$)	19,100,000,000
ZESA debt (1999) (Z$)	10,564,685,000
True connection fee (Z$)	7612
Electricity subsidies as % of ZESA revenue (2000)	53.51
Electricity subsidies as % of ZESA debt (2000)	96.74
Possible connections through subsidies	1,342,652
Total annual kerosene subsidies (Z$)	510,750,000
NOCZIM revenue (2000) (Z$)	26,400,000,000
NOCZIM debt (2000) (Z$)	18,000,000,000
Kerosene subsidies as % of NOCZIM revenue (2000)	1.93
Kerosene subsidies as % of NOCZIM debt (2000)	2.84
Total annual subsidies (Z$)	10,731,015,092
Government expenditure (2000) (Z$)	164,592,573,000
GDP (2000) (Z$)	457,985,000,000
Government deficit (2000) (Z$)	74,367,388,000
Total annual subsidies as % of government expenditure (2000)	6.52
Total annual subsidies as % of GDP	2.34
Total annual subsidies as % of government deficit (2000)	59.62

Note: Exchange rate: US$1 = ZW$55
Source: Survey by author

From a financial analysis point of view, subsidies could be considered a burden on ZESA's finances. However, it is often argued that the impact of electricity subsidies should not be judged only on financial terms. There are envisaged economic benefits to society. Some of the benefits often stated are:

- attraction of investment;
- lowering of production cost and boosting of competitiveness of Zimbabwean goods on domestic, regional and international markets;
- employment creation;
- improvement of the quality of life and standard of living through the provision of affordable electricity.

If the above factors are taken into consideration, electricity subsidies might not be a burden on ZESA's finances but could be contributing to the country's economic and social development. However, due to resource and time constraints, the impact of subsidies on the social and economic aspects could not be ascertained. If only financial benefits are considered, then electricity subsidies are a burden on ZESA's finances.

As an additional indicator of the impact of subsidies on ZESA's finances, the number of domestic customers that could be connected using the annual electricity subsidies was considered. If the true connection fee of Z$7,612 is assumed, then the number of domestic customers that could be connected from the same subsidy is 1,342,652. This is four times the number of ZESA's domestic customers. However, the calculation does not take into consideration the infrastructure that would be needed to connect such a number of customers. Without considering other network expansion costs, the annual electricity subsidies are adequate to connect most urban households.

The impact of connecting those households could not be ascertained. The connection of a large number of households without other mechanisms for substituting or partially substituting the required subsidies might result in the worsening of ZESA's finances, as ZESA might be required to subsidize these additional customers.

The level of annual kerosene subsidies was found to be Z$681 million, amounting to 1.9 per cent of NOCZIM's total revenue of Z$26.4 billion, and to 2.8 per cent of NOCZIM's total debt of Z$18 billion. It can be concluded that kerosene subsidies are not too great a burden on NOCZIM's finances. As is the case for electricity, additional benefits accruing through the existence of kerosene subsidies (such as reduction in deforestation) or additional problems associated with kerosene usage (such as environmental pollution and energy-related problems) could not be ascertained within the scope of this study. The possible negative effects would arise from the increase in kerosene usage due to the existence of subsidies.

From a macroeconomic perspective, it was found that energy subsidies constitute 6.21 per cent of the annual government expenditure of Z$164.6 billion dollars. Total annual energy subsidies amount to 2.23

Table 5.19 GDP growth and inflation rates forecasts for some SADC countries

	Real GDP growth (%)			Inflation rates (%)		
	2000	2001	2002	2000	2001	2002
Angola	3.8	3.0	0.0	357.5	150.0	70.0
Botswana	7.5	4.0	6.5	6.5	5.5	5.0
Malawi	3.4	4.1	4.2	51.4	30.0	30.0
Mozambique	4.5	7.0	6.0	11.4	8.0	5.0
Namibia	3.5	3.5	3.2	6.0	5.8	4.0
South Africa	3.1	3.5	3.5	7.7	6.0	5.5
Zambia	3.0	4.0	4.0	30.1	17.5	15.0
Zimbabwe	−10.0	−10.0	−5.0	55.9	90.0	100.0

Sources: AFREPREN/FWD, 2003; EIU, 2003a; EIU 2003b

per cent of GDP and 14.43 per cent of the government deficit. These figures are very significant as far as government financial indicators are concerned. Zimbabwe's current GDP growth rate is estimated at −10 per cent. This means that subsidies could have reduced the negative GDP growth rate by a magnitude of 2.23 per cent. Table 5.19 shows current and projected GDP growth rates in Southern Africa.

The table shows that with a projected negative GDP growth rate, subsidies totalling 2.23 per cent are a burden on Zimbabwe's economic growth. However, with very high inflation rates, one would assume that subsidies are needed to cushion the poor. Nevertheless, results of this study show that the poor can afford the cost of non-subsidized modern energy, and also that the poor do not benefit from the subsidy.

Given the above fiscal indicators, an economic analysis was undertaken to ascertain to what extent the level of subsidies could have been used to meet government's expenses in terms of Zimbabwe's budget allocations to a selection of ministries (Table 5.20).

Table 5.20 Comparison of government expenditure and the level of subsidies

Ministry	Vote allocation Z$	Subsidy as % of vote allocation
Public Service, Labour and Social Welfare	5, 791,183,000	185.3
Defence	34,403,332,000	31.2
Finance and Economic Development	34,340,703,000	31.2
Industry and International Trade	1,440,780,000	744.8
Rural Resources and Water Development	5,370,034,000	199.8
Lands, Agriculture and Rural Resettlement	16,943,090,000	63.3
Mines and Energy	812,283,000	1,321.1
Environment and Tourism	969,762,000	1,106.6
Transport and Communication	6,109,162,000	175.7
Local Government, Public Works and National Housing	8,963,508,000	119.7
Health and Child Welfare	22,459,863,000	47.8
Education, Sport and Culture	50,395,134,000	21.3
Youth Development, Gender and Employment	1,605,364,000	668.4

Note: Exchange rate: US$1 = ZW$55
Source: Ministry of Finance and Economic Development, 2001

From the table, it is clear that the level of the current energy subsidies is significantly greater than the annual budget allocation of key government ministries, and could cover half the financial resources needed for the annual expenditure of the Ministry of Health and Child Welfare. Subsidies could cover the budget of the Ministry of Industry and Trade by a factor of seven, Mines and Energy by a factor of 13 and Tourism and Environment by a factor of 11. It should be noted that industry, mining, tourism and agriculture are the mainstay elements in the Zimbabwean economy. The current energy subsidies constitute 63 per cent of the budget share of the Agriculture and Resettlement Ministry. Agriculture and resettlement activities are the current core economic initiatives being implemented by the government under its fast-track land reform programme. Subsidies account for 21 per cent of the Ministry of Education budget and 185 per cent of the Ministry of Social Welfare budget.

15

What are the Implications of Subsidies on the Informal Sector?

As a first step in addressing this issue, secondary data sources, particularly the GEMINI Survey (1998) were used to determine the nature of activities by small and micro-enterprises (SMEs). This was used to ascertain the group in which micro-enterprises belong in the ZESA tariff categories. The ZESA categorization is dependent on the nature of the activity and the location of the micro-enterprise.

To find out if the current electricity tariff was stifling the growth of micro-enterprises, the current electricity unit charges for various economic activities were ascertained. This charge was compared to the LRMC. If such a unit charge is above that of other categories, or above the LRMC, then the current electricity tariff was assumed to impact negatively on the operations of the micro-enterprises compared to other economic activities.

The Gemini Survey (1998: 11, 21) showed that there were 860,392 manufacturing, commercial and service SMEs in Zimbabwe, which provided employment to 1.65 million persons. Of these SMEs, 69 per

Table 5.21 Sectoral distributions of small and micro-enterprises

Sector	Percentage of SMEs
Manufacturing	**42.3**
– Food and beverages	5.3
– Textiles	20.1
– Wood and wood products	9.4
– Chemicals and plastics	0.4
– Non-metallic minerals processing	1.3
– Fabrication (metal)	2.6
– Other manufacturing	3.3
Construction	**1.0**
Trade	**45.2**
– Retail trade	44.6
– Restaurants, hotels and bars	0.6
Transport	**0.6**
Renting rooms and flats	**6.8**
Services	**4.0**
All sectors	**100.0**

Source: GEMINI Survey, 1998

cent are home-based and as a result constitute energy for household use (*ibid.*: 32).

Unfavourable pricing of energy for this sector has a negative impact on the operators of such activities, who are essentially poor, and on women in particular as the larger gender group (57.1 per cent) involved in informal sector activities (*ibid.*: 34).

To analyze the impact of electricity pricing on SMEs, the nature of their activities and their location were ascertained. Table 5.21 shows that SMEs in the energy-intensive manufacturing sector (42.3 per cent) and in the trade sector (45.2 per cent) dominate the informal sector in Zimbabwe. Their operations are carried out in various locations (*ibid.*: 32) as shown in Table 5.22. As has been mentioned, 69 per cent of SMEs are located in homes. This means that their energy usage patterns and pricing will be determined by the pricing formula of the residential sector. Those operating outside the home will be priced as low-capacity

Table 5.22 Location of SMEs

Location	% of small and micro-enterprises
Home	69.0
Commercial district	12.1
Roadside	8.8
Mobile	4.2
Market	3.7
Industrial area	0.7
Other	1.5
Total	100.0

Source: GEMINI Survey, 1998

Table 5.23 ZESA classification of small and micro-enterprises using electricity

Description of small and micro-enterprises	Customer category
Food and beverages preparation	Low-voltage commercial
Textiles and leather processing and production	Low-voltage industrial
Paper, printing and publishing	Low-voltage industrial
Chemicals and plastics	Low-voltage industrial
Non-metallic mineral processing	Low-voltage industrial
Fabricated metal production	Low-voltage industrial
Other manufacturing	Low-voltage industrial
Construction	Low-voltage commercial
Retail trade	Low-voltage commercial
Wholesale trade	Low-voltage commercial
Restaurants, hotels and bars	Low-voltage commercial
Finance, real estate and business services	Low-voltage commercial
Other services	Low-voltage commercial

Source: ZESA, 1999.

operations in the industrial, commercial or farming sectors, according to the ZESA customer classification. Urban-based SMEs operating outside the home and using electricity are classified by ZESA as shown in Table 5.23. Most SMEs using electricity fall under low-voltage categories, either industrial or commercial.

Table 5.24 shows comparisons of the unit charges of the different tariff classes, the number of customers in each class and the LRMC of each tariff class. The SMEs are classified in the low-voltage classification of each customer category. The results show that 301,217 customers in the domestic sector are charged at 5.8 US cents/kWh compared to their LRMC of 7.5 US cents /kWh. This means that domestic metered customers are charged 22.67 per cent below the LRMC, and so are SMEs falling under the domestic sector. Based on this finding, the domestic sector (including home-based SMEs) could be considered to be beneficiaries of the subsidy policy. However, the unit charge paid in the domestic sector is still higher than the unit charges of the larger industrial, mining and farming consumers – and so the pricing of home-based SMEs is unfavourable compared to the pricing of large formal economic

Table 5.24 Comparison of unit charges for the different customer categories

Customer category	No. of customers	Unit charge USc/kWh	Long-run marginal cost USc/kWh	% difference
Domestic conventional	301,217	5.8	7.5	22.67
Domestic load limited	121,820	4.2	7.5	44.00
Low-voltage industrial and mining	1,919	8.9	7.5	−18.67
High-voltage mining and industrial (11kV)	408	3.9	6.1	36.07
High-voltage mining and industrial (33kV)	71	3.7	5.3	30.19
Low-voltage commercial	42,038	9.8	7.5	−33.67
High-voltage commercial (11kV)	244	4.9	6.1	19.67
High-voltage commercial (33kV)	25	4.3	5.3	18.87
Low-voltage agriculture	11,726	8.4	7.5	−12.00
High-voltage agriculture (11kV)	99	3.6	6.1	41.00
High-voltage agriculture (33kV)	76	3.2	5.3	40.00
Subtransmission secondary (industrial and mining)	4	2.1	4.6	54.35
Subtransmission primary (industrial and mining)	3	1.6	4.6	65.22

Source: Survey by author

activities.

Domestic customers with load limiter supplies are charged at 4.2 US cents/kWh, or 44 per cent below an LRMC of 7.5 US cents/kWh for the sector. Although charged lower than the LRMC, such customers are not likely to benefit from such a pricing mechanism, as they are likely to supplement their energy requirements with other forms of energy.

The 1,919 low-voltage industrial and mining consumers are charged at 8.9 US cents/kWh compared to the LRMC of 7.5 US cents/kWh. Since their charge is 18.67 per cent above the LRMC, they are actually cross-subsidizing other consumer categories. Most SMEs operating outside the home base are in this category, subject to highly unfavourable pricing.

High-voltage industrial and mining consumers supplied at 11 kV are charged at 3.7 US cents/kWh, 36.07 per cent below an LRMC of 6.1 US cents. Currently there are 408 consumers in this tariff class, which excludes SMEs and clearly benefits from the current pricing mechanism.

Large-scale industrial and mining customers are fed at 33 kV. Currently there are 71 such customers, a tariff class by definition exclusive of SMEs. The formal enterprises in this customer category are charged a unit price of 3.7 US cents/kWh, 30.19 per cent below an LRMC of 5.3 US cents/kWh. These customers are therefore beneficiaries of the current pricing mechanism.

Low-voltage commercial customers, including a high proportion of trade-related SMEs, are charged a unit price of 9.8 US cents/kWh, 23.47 per cent more than an LRMC of 7.5 US cents/kWh. There are 42,038 customers in this category, who are cross-subsidizing the other customer categories and do not benefit from the current pricing mechanism.

The 244 high-voltage commercial customers are charged at 4.9 US cents/kWh, 19.67 per cent below an LRMC of 6.1 USc/kWh. These beneficiaries of the current pricing mechanism are mainly large-scale construction companies, hospitals and large hotels, and therefore exclusive of SMEs.

The 25 very large-scale commercial customers are charged a unit price of 4.3 US cents/kWh, 18.87 per cent below an LRMC of 5.3 US cents/kWh, so they too benefit from the current pricing structure.

Low-voltage agricultural customers are charged at 12 per cent above the LRMC. Customers falling under this category are 11,726 mainly small-scale farming customers. Agriculturally based SMEs fall into this category and are cross-subsidizing other large-scale farming operations. Large-scale farming operations have either 11 kV supplies or 33 kV supplies. These are charged at 41 and 40 per cent below the LRMC respectively, to benefit substantially from the subsidies policy.

Finally, the large-scale industrial customers, numbering 7, are charged at 46 per cent below the LRMC, enjoying substantial benefit from the ZESA pricing policy.

It can thus be concluded that the current electricity policy benefits large-scale economic activities at the expense of SMEs.

16

Policy Options and Recommendations

The results show that the poor could afford the cost of modern energy without subsidies. The need for subsidies also differs considerably across household income categories. In addition, the study shows that the largest share of subsidies is absorbed by the non-deserving cases. This has resulted in energy subsidies being a burden on public finances. This section of the report presents policy initiatives that could be implemented in place of subsidies or to ensure that subsidies:

- are targeted to deserving cases only;
- provide one-off start-up capital and seed money for recommended policy initiatives;
- are not a burden on public finances.

Furthermore, the proposed policy options are assessed for their feasibility in Zimbabwe's context by considering the following factors:

- institutional and management capability;
- legal framework;
- economic and financial viability;
- existing human resources and technical capacity.

Impact of subsidies on affordability of modern forms of energy by the poor

The core issues identified by the study on the impact of subsidies on affordability of modern energy by the poor are:

- Some poor urban households can afford the non-subsidized cost of modern energy.
- The majority of kerosene users do not benefit from the existing subsidies due to distribution problems.
- The upfront cost of energy limits the ability of households to access modern forms of energy.

- The potential exists for energy saving through energy-efficient practices if implementation barriers are addressed.

- LPG could be used to replace some non-modern forms of energy.

To address the above issues the following policy options could be considered:

- Restructure the pricing regime to ensure that only deserving household categories benefit from subsidies.

- Amortize the upfront cost of energy to ensure easier access to modern energy.

- Carry out studies on technologies that could reduce the upfront cost of electricity.

- Reduce the amount of energy use through the promotion of energy efficiency practices.

- Improve kerosene distribution structures and practices.

- Promote the widespread usage of LPG through mechanisms that address the current distribution problems.

Restructure the pricing regime to ensure that only deserving household categories benefit from subsidies
The objective of this policy option is to redesign the existing electricity tariff structure, so as to ensure that subsidies are not indiscriminate, but targeted only at deserving cases.

INSTITUTIONAL AND MANAGEMENT CAPACITY
Currently electricity tariffs are designed and implemented by ZESA. However, the Minister of Mines and Energy approves the applicable tariff before it is implemented. Under this policy option, ZESA could redesign the tariff in such a way that the lifeline tariff benefits only the deserving cases. The problem that would be faced by ZESA is the determination of deserving households. ZESA could consider only the poor households that have been vetted by the Ministry of Labour and Social Welfare as poor. The Ministry has indeed been vetting and registering individuals and households deemed to be poor. Such households could benefit from social services such as free education and health, and energy pricing should be a part of this broader picture.

The design of the tariff would be the responsibility of ZESA, as is the current practice. The new tariff will need cabinet approval, as is currently the norm. After the planned unbundling of ZESA, the supply companies (SUPCOs) could implement the tariff design and the proposed Office of the Regulator would handle the approval process in line with its proposed mandate of tariff approval.

LEGAL FRAMEWORK
There are no legal barriers constraining the review of tariffs. However, the tariff level would need cabinet approval or the approval of the Regulator, once such an office is put in place. The new Electricity Act mandates suppliers to review tariffs. Government approval might be required to use the Department of Social Welfare for vetting purposes.

FINANCIAL AND ECONOMIC VIABILITY
The review of the tariff structure by ZESA is an ongoing exercise that imposes no additional costs on ZESA. The vetting of deserving cases by the Ministry of Labour and Social Welfare is also an ongoing process, with finance for the purpose provided by the state.

HUMAN RESOURCES AND TECHNICAL CAPACITY
All the institutions involved have adequate human resources and technical capacity to carry out their recommended tasks. The Office of the Regulator is not yet in existence, but is supposed to recruit its core personnel from existing ZESA departments with the requisite skills.

Reduce the amount of energy use through the promotion of energy efficiency practices
One way of making households afford energy in the absence of subsidies is for them to reduce wastage on energy use. The findings show that energy consumption levels are high, possibly driven up by the existence of subsidies. The results further show that the removal of subsidies will impact negatively on electricity users more than on users of other energy forms. It is recommended that electrical energy-saving practices be implemented to ensure the optimum use of energy at least cost. Apart from making energy relatively cheaper, energy efficiency could result in the reduction of domestic electricity use, currently accounting for 21 per cent of total electricity sales. This is in an environment characterized by power imports of up to 50 per cent and chronic foreign currency shortages.

A study carried out by ZESA (1992) identified the following zero-cost or low-cost initiatives, which could be implemented to save energy in Zimbabwe's households:

- household loss reduction (switching off inessential devices);
- use of new-generation fluorescent lamps;
- use of domestic solar water heaters;
- use of compact fluorescent lamps in place of incandescent lamps;
- improved seals for refrigerators and freezers;
- use of water heater time switches;
- lowering of water heater thermostat temperature settings.

INSTITUTIONAL AND MANAGEMENT CAPACITY

Institutions that need to be mobilized to achieve the efficient usage of domestic electrical energy are ZESA, the government and the private sector. The role of the government would be to formulate policies, through the existing section in the Department of Energy, that promote energy efficiency and investments in energy efficiency. Such policies are enshrined in the new draft energy policy document. The government and ZESA are also currently involved in a pilot project to promote the usage of timer switches to reduce the level of energy consumption by electrical water heaters in the domestic sector. Furthermore, through the Ministry of Education and Technology and the existing educational places of higher learning, the government can introduce courses to address such relevant subjects as energy management. ZESA's role would be:

- to enhance the provision of energy efficiency information to its customers;

- to pursue investments in energy efficiency;

- to offer to the private sector and to individuals training skills in energy efficiency and demand-side management (DSM);

- to introduce an appropriate tariff mechanism that promotes the efficient utilization of energy;

- to facilitate entry points for private sector investment in energy efficiency and DSM.

The role of the private sector would be to mobilize resources to invest in DSM, produce energy efficiency equipment and provide energy efficiency services. Currently, a number of private companies are engaged in the promotion of energy efficiency in Zimbabwe. They could be encouraged to create and operate energy service companies.

LEGAL FRAMEWORK

The existing legal framework is not a barrier to the promotion of energy efficiency in Zimbabwe and the current Electricity Act specifies ZESA's role. One of the objectives of ZESA's Research Section is to promote and coordinate energy efficiency activities amongst ZESA's different stakeholders.

FINANCIAL AND ECONOMIC VIABILITY

The envisaged energy efficiency initiatives are low- or zero-cost options, which require little in terms of capital investment. The financial resources needed are minimal and can be afforded by the identified institutions. The removal of subsidies might result in better opportunities for energy efficiency and investment. They would also result in the reduction of power imports, in an environment characterized by foreign currency shortages. Energy-saving practices would also enable ZESA to defer or reduce the level of capital investment and thereby the required LRMCs and subsidy levels. And customers would get value for money by paying only for energy they actually use.

HUMAN RESOURCES AND TECHNICAL CAPACITY

Skills to implement energy efficiency initiatives are available in ZESA and the private sector. The Department of Energy has reasonable skills in policy formulation.

Amortize the upfront cost of energy to ensure easier access to modern forms of energy

Under this policy option electrical energy suppliers will amortize the costs of the internal wiring of houses over a period of time such as five years.

INSTITUTIONAL AND MANAGEMENT CAPACITY

Institutionally, this will involve the electrical energy suppliers paying for the costs of internal wiring and recovering their costs from the sales of energy. The key players will be the energy suppliers, local contractors and the households. The energy suppliers will provide funds for the internal wiring of the houses of the poor in the same way that they currently finance other power projects in the areas where the poor normally reside. They could recoup their investment from sale of electricity. Local contractors can carry out the internal wiring and be paid for the work done by energy suppliers. Households would use the energy and pay monthly bills.

In South Africa municipalities such as the Durban Municipality in conjunction with ESKOM are successfully amortizing the access cost of electricity in formerly marginalized townships. In Zimbabwe, before the amalgamation of power suppliers into ZESA, municipalities were actively involved in the wiring of new houses. They even introduced schemes such as load limiters to poor households. Municipalities which amortized the upfront electricity costs, such as the Bulawayo City Council, have the highest electrification rates in the country (99 per cent) (CSO, 1992).

LEGAL FRAMEWORK

There are no legal barriers to such a proposal and it is permissible under the current Electricity Act and Companies Act. The procedure would be the one ZESA is currently using for its projects.

HUMAN RESOURCES AND TECHNICAL CAPACITY

There would be no need for additional skills other than those that are currently available in-house.

FINANCIAL AND ECONOMIC VIABILITY

The main question is whether the poor could afford to repay the initial capital costs. A financial analysis was undertaken to determine the feasibility of such a proposal. ZESA would have to amortize the initial internal wiring costs of Z$11,423 over five years. This time is short given the fact that ZESA is currently investing in projects with long lead times. For small projects ZESA assumes operational and maintenance costs of 1.5 per cent of the investment cost, and a discount rate of 34 per cent for the financial appraisal of projects. With an internal rate of return of 107 per cent, the project is viable. The net present value is calculated to be Z$3,642, which is a very good return on investment. The benefit–cost ratio is 1.5 and, with a payback period of less than two years, this policy option is viable.

Carry out studies on technologies that could reduce the upfront cost of electricity

Currently there are a number of technologies that could be implemented to lower distribution costs and also the cost of internal wiring. Technologies such as compact distribution boards, used in limited quantities in Zimbabwe and much more extensively in South Africa, have resulted in significant reduction of the upfront cost of electricity. Aerial bundled conductors, another technological innovation, have reduced the cost of distribution networks by as much as 15 per cent in Zimbabwe (Dube, 2000: 5).

The objective of the study would be to review current practices employed in distribution and internal wiring and to recommend technological improvements so as to lower costs. The current wiring rules in Zimbabwe were designed in the 1950s and have not been reviewed since then, despite technological advances. However, care should be taken to ensure that change in engineering standards would not compromise safety, system reliability or stability.

INSTITUTIONAL AND MANAGEMENT CAPACITY

The principal player in the supply of modern forms of energy to the urban poor is ZESA. ZESA should carry out studies on the improvement in distribution and internal wiring practices. ESKOM in South Africa is currently spearheading such research work. In Zimbabwe, universities and the Scientific and Industrial Research Development Corporation could also undertake such studies. The latter has an Energy Institute that is mandated to look at energy issues, including technologies. The Standards Association of Zimbabwe would need to be a player in such an initiative, to ensure that new technological practices are adopted, documented and enforced in line with current practices. Other regional research organizations such as AFREPREN could initiate studies on the subject matter and be instrumental in regional dissemination, a role it has undertaken successfully in addressing other energy–technological issues in the past. The private sector, especially equipment manufacturers, would need to be involved, too.

LEGAL FRAMEWORK
Existing legal barriers pertain to licences and intellectual property rights.

FINANCIAL AND ECONOMIC VIABILITY
The local organizations identified are currently adequately funded by government, and in the case of ZESA have adequate financial resources to undertake the envisaged task. Regional research organizations would need external support to carry out the study. The availability of foreign currency to pay for licences could be a problem.

HUMAN RESOURCES AND TECHNICAL CAPACITY
Basic skills and human resources are available. External specialized skills would be needed.

Improve kerosene distribution structures and practices
The results of the study show that the intermediary suppliers are capturing the largest share of kerosene subsidies. The identified reasons for this state of affairs are that large-scale kerosene suppliers are reluctant to sell kerosene because of the low profit margins realized. The second reason is the absence of kerosene distribution facilities in the proximity of urban poor residential areas. Thus two issues need to be addressed. First, there is a need to engage the large suppliers in a dialogue to ascertain their concerns and their problems, and to agree on reasonable rates of return on the sale of kerosene – possibly the same rate of returns they derive from selling other petroleum products. Second, the licensing mechanism should be used to ensure that new investments and players also cover the areas mostly populated by the poor.

INSTITUTIONAL AND MANAGEMENT CAPACITY
The central player should be the government. The government should engage in a dialogue and agree on reasonable levels of profit margins realized by the suppliers. The suppliers are service station operators who are represented by the Motor Trade Association of Zimbabwe (MTAZ). The government through its licensing policies should also ensure that the neighbourhoods populated by the majority of the poor are covered by new licenses.

LEGAL FRAMEWORK
There are no legal barriers.

FINANCIAL AND ECONOMIC VIABILITY
It should be possible to jump-start the process without encountering financial barriers. The only financial issue that needs to be addressed is

maintaining fairness in the kerosene pricing mechanism as it applies to both investors and customers.

HUMAN RESOURCES AND TECHNICAL CAPACITY
Most of the necessary personnel and skills needed to implement the policy option are available.

Promote the widespread usage of LPG through mechanisms that address the current distribution problems
The results of the study show that LPG could partially or wholly substitute non-modern forms of energy. However, some distribution problems need to be addressed before LPG could be widely used.

INSTITUTIONAL AND MANAGEMENT CAPACITY
LPG is imported by NOCZIM and its distribution is mandated to private oil companies. However, these companies have limited distribution points, despite the fact that currently many more companies have been registered to distribute petroleum products. Most of them are also involved in massive expansion of their facilities. They need to be encouraged either through incentives or through the licensing process to incorporate LPG selling points at their existing and new distribution facilities.

LEGAL FRAMEWORK
Some distribution companies are currently selling LPG in Zimbabwe. There are no legal or regulatory requirements barring oil companies from distributing LPG.

FINANCIAL AND ECONOMIC VIABILITY
The biggest constraint is the foreign currency needed by companies manufacturing 4.5 kg cylinders and for the importation of larger cylinders. The Reserve Bank of Zimbabwe will need to be lobbied to extend the foreign currency allocation preferences currently extended to ZESA and NOCZIM to companies trading in LPG.

HUMAN RESOURCES AND TECHNICAL CAPACITY
Most of the requisite skills are locally available.

Distribution of subsidies amongst different income groups and their impact on public finances

The results of the study show that the non-poor households and the large-scale electricity users are the largest beneficiaries of the subsidy policy. This is largely due to the blanket nature of the subsidies. It is recommended that the tariff structure be redesigned to ensure that only intended target groups benefit from subsidies. The study also shows that subsidies seem to be a burden on public finances from a financial point of view. However the social and economic benefits arising from the presence of the subsidies could not be ascertained. It is therefore recommended that the following policy initiatives be considered:

- Redesign the electricity tariff to ensure that only the intended beneficiaries benefit from the subsidy.

- Carry out studies to ascertain the economic benefits of the energy subsidies.

Redesign the electricity tariff to ensure that only the intended beneficiaries benefit from the subsidy

INSTITUTIONAL AND MANAGEMENT CAPACITY
ZESA is currently responsible for setting out of tariffs, which are then approved by government. They are therefore no institutional and management problems in implementing this policy option.

LEGAL FRAMEWORK
There are currently no legal impediments to implementing the policy option. The tariff review is covered by both existing and proposed power sector legislation.

FINANCIAL AND ECONOMIC VIABILITY
The tariff review is an ongoing exercise. No additional financing is needed for the task.

HUMAN RESOURCES AND TECHNICAL CAPACITY
There is enough in-house capacity to design tariffs.

Carry out studies to ascertain the economic benefits of the energy subsidies
The study shows that, from a financial point of view, subsidies are a burden on ZESA's finances. However, if the societal benefits are factored in, subsidies might not seem so burdensome. It is recommended that studies be carried out to ascertain the social costs and benefits emanating from the existence of subsidies.

INSTITUTIONAL AND MANAGEMENT CAPACITY
The principal player in the supply of electricity is ZESA, through its subsidiaries. These could carry out surveys to ascertain the true economic value of the electricity subsidies to society. This will result in a better understanding of whether the subsidies that they are offering are really of benefit to society or simply a financial burden.

LEGAL FRAMEWORK
There are no legal barriers with regards to this policy option.

FINANCIAL AND ECONOMIC VIABILITY
Only minimum resources are needed to carry out such studies. Given the importance attached to subsidies and the forgone revenue because of subsidies, the cost of carrying out such a study is negligible.

HUMAN RESOURCES AND TECHNICAL CAPACITY
ZESA has adequate in-house capacity to carry out the proposed study.

Pricing of electricity to small and micro-enterprises

A favourable pricing of electricity supplies to SMEs can be achieved through the restructuring of the price regime to ensure equity. Such a pricing formula should be based on the cost of supply to the respective tariff class, not on the ability to pass on the cost to the consumer, as is currently the case. ZESA should utilize its abundant in-house skills to revisit its pricing formula. There are no barriers to effect this option.

From the analysis above, it is evident that there are several policy intervention options that could be adopted by policy makers in addressing the constraints discussed in the study on energy services for the urban poor and micro-enterprises. Some of the options are limited by the present situation in the country in the areas of institutional and management capacity, legal framework, financial and economic feasibility and the availability of skills. Table 5.25 summarizes the discussion on the feasibility of the policy options with respect to the five aspects.

The table shows that the redesign of tariffs would address a large range of issues such as better targeting of subsidies and their gradual removal. The table also shows that the redesigning of subsidies is a viable option. This policy option is thus recommended and should be accompanied by other viable options. These are:

- Improve kerosene distribution structures and practices.

- Promote the widespread usage of LPG through mechanisms that address the current distribution problems.

- Carry out studies to ascertain the economic benefits of the energy subsidies.

- Amortize the upfront cost of energy to ensure easier access to modern energy.

- Reduce the amount of energy use through the promotion of energy efficiency practices.

Table 5.25 Filtering of draft policy options

Draft policy option	Institutional & management capacity	Legal framework	Financial and economic viability	Human and technical resources	Viability
Impact of subsidies on affordability of modern forms of energy					
Restructure the pricing regime to ensure that only deserving household categories benefit from subsidies	No barriers	No barriers	No barriers	No barriers	Viable
Reduce the amount of energy use through energy efficiency practices	No barriers	No barriers	No barriers	Available	Viable
Carry out studies on technologies that could reduce the upfront cost of electricity	No barriers	No barriers	Some barriers	Available	Partially viable
Amortize the upfront cost of energy to ensure easier access to modern energy	No barriers	No barriers	No barriers	Available	Viable
Improve kerosene distribution structures and practices	No barriers	No barriers	No barriers	Available	Viable
Promote the widespread usage of LPG through mechanisms that address the current distribution problems	No barriers	No barriers	No barriers	Available	Viable
Distribution of subsidies and their impact on public finances					
Redesign tariff structure to ensure that subsidies do not go to the non-targeted groups	No barriers	No barriers	No barriers	Available	Viable
Carry out studies to ascertain the economic benefits of subsidies	No barriers	No barriers	No barriers	Available	Viable
Unfavourable pricing of small and micro-enterprises					
Redesign the tariff structure to ensure equity	No barriers	No barriers	No barriers	Available	Viable

Part 5 • References

AFREPREN/FWD, 2002. *African Energy Data Handbook*, Nairobi: AFRE-PREN/ FWD.

——, 2003. *African Energy Data Handbook*, Nairobi: AFREPREN/ FWD.

CSO, 1992. *Census 1992*, Harare: Central Statistics Office.

——, 1998. *Poverty in Zimbabwe* Harare: Central Statistics Office.

Department of Energy, 2000. *Annual Energy Bulletin and Balance*, Harare: Ministry of Energy and Power Development.

Dube, I., 1999. *Feasibility Study for the Utilisation of Aerial Bundled Conductors*, Harare: Zimbabwe Electricity Supply Authority (ZESA).

——, 2000. 'Energy Services for the Urban Poor in Zimbabwe', Energy Services for the Urban Poor Theme Group, Nairobi: AFREPREN/FWD.

——, 2001. 'Energy Services for the Urban Poor in Uganda', short-term study report for the AFREPREN Theme Group on 'Energy Services for the Urban Poor', Nairobi: AFREPREN/ FWD.

——, 2003. 'Country Data Validation: Zimbabwe', unpublished, Nairobi: AFREPREN/ FWD.

EIU, 2003a. *Country Profile – Angola*, London: Economist Intelligent Unit.

——, 2003b. *Country Profile – Botswana*, London: Economist Intelligent Unit.

ESMAP, 1992. 'Zimbabwe Integrated Energy Strategy', Evaluation Report No. 8768 ZIM, Washington, DC: World Bank.

GEMINI, 1998. 'Zimbabwe: a Third National Survey of Macro and Small Enterprises', final report, survey by Price Waterhouse Coopers, Harare: US Agency for International Development, pp. 3, 11, 21, 27, 32, 34.

Government Printers, 2000. *Urban Councils Act*, Harare: Government Printers, Chapter 29: 15.

GTZ, 1995. *Cooking Patterns and Domestics Fuel Use in Masvingo Province: an Analysis and Possible Options for Decreasing Fuel Consumption*, Masvingo: Gesellschaft für Technische Zusammenarbeit.

IEA, 2003. *Energy Balances of Non-OECD Countries 2000–2001*, Paris: International Energy Agency.

Karekezi, S., J. Kimani, L. Majoro and W. Kithyoma, 2002. *African Energy Data and Terminology Handbook*, AFREPREN Occasional Paper No. 13, Nairobi: AFREPREN/ FWD.

Kayo, D., 2002. 'Country Data Validation: Zimbabwe', unpublished, Nairobi: AFREPREN/FWD.

Kebede, B., A. Bekele, and E. Kedir, 2002 'Affordability of Modern Fuels and

Patterns of Energy Demand in Urban Ethiopia', Working Paper No. 295, Nairobi: AFREPREN/ FWD.

Mapako, M., 2003. 'Country Data Validation: Zimbabwe', unpublished, Nairobi: AFREPREN/ FWD.

Ministry of Finance and Economic Development, 2001. *Budget Statements Presented to the Parliament of Zimbabwe*, Harare: Ministry of Finance and Economic Development.

NOCZIM, 2001. *Kerosene Pricing Database*, Harare: National Oil Company of Zimbabwe.

Phelan, J. (ed.), 2003. *African Review Journal*, 39, 8 (London: Alain Charles Publishing Ltd).

Qase, N. and A. Wendy, 1999. *Energy Provision for the Urban Poor: South African Country Case Study*, Cape Town: Energy and Development Research Center, University of Cape Town.

Ranninger, H. M., 1999. *A Key Role For Service Meters in the Social Policy for Low Income Customers at EDM [Electricidade de Mozambique]*, Paris: Electricité de France.

Reserve Bank of Zimbabwe, 2001. *Quarterly Economic and Statistical Review*, 24, 1/4 (Harare: Reserve Bank of Zimbabwe).

Southern Centre for Energy and Environment and Risø Laboratories, 1994. *Domestic Energy Consumption and its Impact on the Environment*, Harare: Southern Centre for Energy and Environment.

The Herald, 2001. 'NOCZIM's Financial Woes Deepen', 15 June 2001, Harare.

UNDP, 2003. *Human Development Report, 2003*, Oxford and New York: Oxford University Press and United Nations Development Programme.

Van der Merwe, A. J., 1999. *Challenges Facing Distributors Supplying the Domestic Sector: the Way Forward*, Bloemfontein: Bloemfontein Electricity.

WAPCOS (India), 1991. Evaluation Report on the 1980–1988 Electrification Master Plan Zimbabwe: Policy and Planning for Electrification in Rural Areas, Harare: Ministry of Energy and Power Development.

Wienand R. F., 1999. *Domestic Time of Use Tariff. The Durban Experience*, Durban: Durban Metro Electricity.

Weymann A. and A. Massing, 1999. *Access to Energy for the Urban Poor: the Malian Case*, Eichborn: GTZ–HEP.

World Bank, 2000. *Entering the 21st Century: World Development Report 1999/2000*, Washington, DC: World Bank.

——, 2003a. *African Development Indicators, 2003*, Washington, DC: World Bank.

——, 2003b. *World Development Indicators, 2003*, Washington, DC: World Bank.

ZESA, 1992. *Survey on Domestic Energy Use,* Harare: Zimbabwe Electricity Supply Authority

——, 1995a. *Technical and Socio-Economical Characteristics of the Rural Areas: the ZESA Solar Project*, Harare: Zimbabwe Electricity Supply Authority.

——, 1995b. *Customer Charter*, Harare: Zimbabwe Electricity Supply

Authority, p. 1.

——, 1996. *Household Energy Use Questionnaire*, Harare: Zimbabwe Electricity Supply Authority.

——, 1999. *Household Energy Use Questionnaire*, Harare: Zimbabwe Electricity Supply Authority.

——, 2000a. 'C12 Billing Report', Harare: Zimbabwe Electricity Supply Authority, pp. 1–5.

——, 2000b. *Project Appraisal Manual*, Harare: Zimbabwe Electricity Supply Authority.

——, 2000c. *Customer Quotation Guidelines*, Harare: Zimbabwe Electricity Supply Authority.

——, 2000d. *Long Run Marginal Cost Study*, Harare: Zimbabwe Electricity Supply Authority.

——, 2000e. *Tariff Review Study*, Harare: Zimbabwe Electricity Supply Authority.

——, 2000f. 'Consumer Services Department, December 2000 Monthly Report', Harare: Zimbabwe Electricity Supply Authority, p. 15.

——, 2000g. 'Billing Sheet', Harare: Zimbabwe Electricity Supply Authority.

——, 2002. *Rural Electrification Marketing Brochure*, Harare: Zimbabwe Electricity Supply Authority, p. 3.

Part 5 • Appendices

Appendix 5.1 Energy consumption patterns and costs for the urban households by source of energy

	Kerosene only	Electricity only	Electricity & kerosene	Electricity & fuelwood	Electricity, kerosene & fuelwood	Kerosene & fuelwood
ALL HOUSEHOLDS						
Average electricity units (kWh)	0	426	264	276	288	0
Average electricity cost (Z$)	0	1,014	626	654	696	0
Average fuelwood amount (kg)	0	0	0	160	72.7	167
Average fuelwood cost (Z$)	0	0	0	351	138	388
Average kerosene amount (l)	11.5	0	4.6	0	4.6	9
Average kerosene cost (Z$)	730	0	191	0	301	571
Total energy cost (Z$)	730	1,014	817	1,005	1,135	959
Average monthly income (Z$)	18,000	15,979	27,862	15,371.8	17,257	15,971
NON-POOR						
Average electricity units (kWh)	0	574	344	351	370	0
Average electricity cost (Z$)	0	1,623	964	983	1,036	0
Average fuelwood amount (Kg)	0	0	0	275	100	170
Average fuelwood cost (Z$)	0	0	0	563	172	416
Average kerosene amount (l)	15	0	7.3	0	3.8	13
Average kerosene cost (Z$)	952	0	238	0	307	819
Total energy cost (Z$)	952	1,623	1202	1,546	1,515	1,235
Average monthly income (Z$)	21,000	35,518	43,166.7	29,112.5	59,046.8	43,750
POOR						
Average electricity units (kWh)	0	335	250	263	242	0
Average electricity cost (Z$)	0	812	538	627.28	564	0
Average fuelwood amount (Kg)	0	0	0	94	67.2	150

Average fuelwood cost (Z$)	0	0	0	230	131	349
Average kerosene amount (l)	10.3	0	2.3	0	4.8	7.5
Average kerosene cost (Z$)	654	0	150	0	300	472
Total energy cost (Z$)	654	721	689	857	995	821
Average monthly income (Z$)	15,000	9,466.45	14,743	7,520	8,899	7,423

VERY POOR

Average electricity units (kWh)	0	335	250	0	266	0
Average electricity cost (Z$)	0	727	538	0	525	0
Average fuelwood amount (Kg)	0	0	0	0	49	160
Average fuelwood cost (Z$)	0	0	0	0	84	493
Average kerosene amount (l)	10.3	0	2.3	0	4.2	6
Average kerosene cost (Z$)	654	0	150	0	273	378
Total energy cost (Z$)	654	727	689	0	882	871
Average monthly income (Z$)	15,000	13,841	14,743	0	14,429	13,500

EXTREMELY POOR

Average electricity units (kWh)	0	302	0	263	181	0
Average electricity cost (Z$)	0	675	0	627	357	0
Average fuelwood amount (Kg)	0	0	0	94	49	145
Average fuelwood cost (Z$)	0	0	0	230	84	355
Average kerosene amount (l)	0	0	0	0	4.2	5
Average kerosene cost (Z$)	0	0	0	0	273	315
Total energy cost (Z$)	0	675	0	857	714	670
Average monthly income (Z$)	0	6,492	0	7,520	6,748	6,318

Exchange rate: US$1 = ZW$55
Source: Survey by author

Appendix 5.2 Household consumption expenditure by key items

Expenditure (Z$)	Energy	Rent	Food	Water	Service rate	Health	School fees	Transport	Accounts	Other	Total	Income
All households												
Electricity	1,014	1,199	4,430	222	129	393	536	1,059	1,706	454	11,142	15,979
Electricity-kerosene	817	781	5,115	287	204	735	1,844	977	1,569	715	13,044	27,862
Electricity- fuelwood	1,005	815	3,591	485	359	473	858	927	1,278	273	10,064	15,372
Keros.- electr.- fuelwood	1,135	1,027	3,982	316	146	472	1,271	752	1,087	132	10,320	18,707
Kerosene- fuelwood	959	222	3,206	66	57	552	782	1,078	353	29	7,304	15,971
Kerosene	730	350	2,750	125	100	850	423	1,450	0	0	6,778	18,000
Non-Poor												
Electricity	1,623	1,240	7,714	319	239	771	1,334	2,221	5,881	1,714	23,056	35,518
Electricity-kerosene	1,202	308	5,667	292	196	1,019	3,700	1,008	2,667	550	16,609	43,167
Electricity-fuelwood	1,546	753	5,125	900	725	500	2,096	1,550	2,515	750	16,460	29,113
Keros.-electr.-fuelwood	1,515	1,433	7,350	528	269	1,230	5,414	1,725	3,667	500	23,631	58,039
Kerosene- fuelwood	1,235	206	5,625	144	63	1,400	1,848	1,700	875	0	13,096	43,750
Kerosene	952	400	2,500	250	200	700	525	500	0	0	6,027	21,000
Poor												
Electricity	721	1,197	3,368	194	77	273	253	688	308	34	7,113	9,490
Electricity-kerosene	689	1,186	4,643	283	211	491	254	950	629	857	10,193	14,743
Electricity- fuelwood	857	850	2,714	249	150	457	150	571	571	0	6,569	7,520
Keros.-electr.-fuelwood	995	926	3,140	263	116	283	235	508	442	40	6,948	8,874
Kerosene- fuelwood	821	227	2,462	42	55	291	454	886	192	38	5,468	7,423
Kerosene	654	300	3,000	0	0	1,000	320	2,400	0	0	7,674	15,000

Very poor												
Electricity	727	1,273	4,553	322	175	420	504	1,073	461	0	0	14,353
Electricity-kerosene	689	1,186	4,643	283	211	491	254	950	629	857	9,508	14,743
Electricity- fuelwood	0	0	0	0	0	0	0	0	0	0	10,193	0
Keros. -electr. -fuelwood	882	729	3,629	3629	529	75	291	214	829	1,029	11,836	13,500
Kerosene- fuelwood	871	150	3,500	25	0	500	475	2,100	0	0	7,621	13,500
Kerosene	654	300	3,000	0	0	1,000	320	2,400	0	0	7,674	15,000
Extremely poor												
Electricity	675	1,153	2,683	120	21	188	108	465	219	54	5,686	6,684
Electricity-kerosene		0	0	0	0	0	0	0	0	0	0	0
Electricity- fuelwood	857	850	2,714	249	150	457	150	571	571	0	6,569	7,520
Keros.-electr.-fuelwood	714	1,007	2,939	154	132	279	244	376	200	56	6,101	6,557
Kerosene- fuelwood	670	241	2,273	45	65	253	450	665	227	45	4,934	6,318

Source: Survey by author

Appendix 5.3 Selected time series data – Zimbabwe

Year	1992	1993	1994	1995	1996	1997	1998	1999	2000	2001
National population (millions)	10.40	10.80	11.20	11.50	11.50	11.50	11.70	11.90	12.10	12.82
National population growth rate (per cent)	3.0	1.9	2.9	1.9	1.8	2.7	1.7	1.7	1.9	1.1
Urban population (millions)	3.1	3.2	3.4	3.5	3.7	3.8	3.9	4.0	4.1	4.2
GDP (US$ millions)	7,156	7,280	7,690	7,610	8,260	8,475	6,500	8,240	7,838	7,172
GNP per capita (US$)	688	674	687	662	718	737	556	504	688	480
Total modern energy consumption (000 toe)	4,713	4,381	4,722	4,673	3,160	3,110	3,110	3,740	3,314	2,596
Modern energy consumption per capita (kgoe)	450	471	432	424	282	270	265.8	263.0	273.9	203
Modern energy production (000 toe)	5,060	4,750	4,610	4,730	4,700	4,540	4,680	4,680	4,630	4,210
National debt (US$ millions)	4,060	4,285	4,524	5,007	4,976	4,919	4,707	4,566	4,244	3,780
Merchandise exports, f.o.b (US$ millions)	1,530	1,610	1,947	2,216	2,496	2,424	1,925	1,924	1,791	1,715
Installed capacity (MW)	1,961	1,961	1,961	1,961	1,961	1,961	1,961	1,961	1,961	1,961
Electricity generation (GWh)	10,282	8,760	9,544	10,123	10,495	11,311	11,891	12,363	12,090	11,972
Total electricity consumption (GWh)	8,850	9,115	9,094	9,488	8,591	8,119	8,085	6,938	9,196	9,102
Electricity consumption per capita (kWh)	851	844	812	825	747	706	691	583	760	710
National electrification levels (per cent)	28	29	31	32	34	35	36	39	40	40
Urban electrification levels (per cent)	69	67	69	72	70	74	78	80	84	84
Rural electrification levels (per cent)	11	14	15	14	17	16	15	18	18	19
System losses (per cent)	8.6	11.0	12.1	11.0	11.0	10.8	10.7	13.2	13.0	14.6

Sources: AFREPREN, 2003; Dube, 2003; IEA, 2003; Karekezi et al., 2002; Kayo, 2002; Mapako, 2003; Phelan, 2003; UNDP, 2003; World Bank, 2003a; World Bank, 2003b

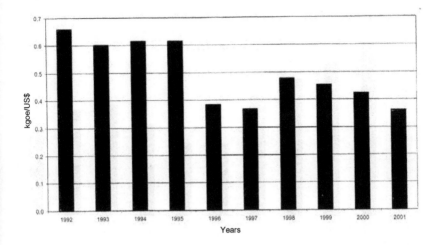

Figure A5.3.1 Zimbabwe: Modern energy consumption (kgoe) per US$ of GDP, 1992–2001

Sources: AFREPREN, 2003; Dube, 2003; IEA, 2003; Kayo, 2002; Mapako, 2003; World Bank, 2003a; World Bank, 2003b

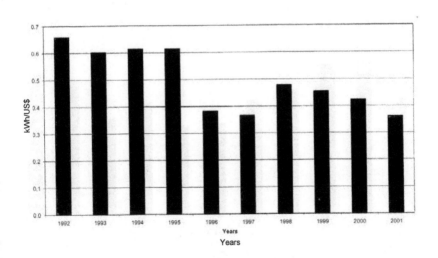

Figure A5.3.2 Zimbabwe: Electricity consumption (kWh) per US$ of GDP, 1992–2001

Sources: AFREPREN, 2003; Dube, 2003; IEA, 2003; Kayo, 2002; Mapako, 2003; World Bank, 2003a; World Bank, 2003b

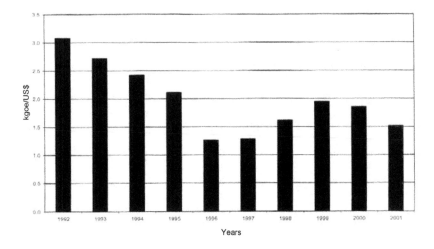

Figure A5.3.3 Zimbabwe: Modern energy consumption (kgoe) per US$ of merchandise export, 1992–2001

Sources: AFREPREN, 2003; Dube, 2003; IEA, 2003; Kayo, 2002; Mapako, 2003; World Bank, 2003a; World Bank, 2003b

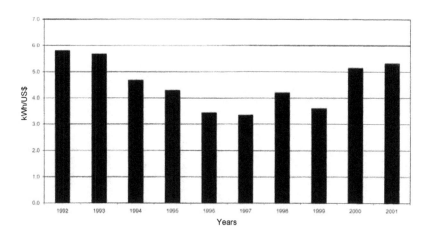

Figure A5.3.4 Zimbabwe: Electricity consumption (kWh) per US$ of merchandise export, 1992–2001

Sources: AFREPREN, 2003; Dube, 2003; IEA, 2003; Kayo, 2002; Mapako, 2003; World Bank, 2003a; World Bank, 2003b

Part 6

ETHIOPIA

Bereket Kebede

with

Elias Kedir, Aselefech Abera and Solomon Tesfaye

COUNTRY PROFILE
Ethiopia

SELECTED INDICATORS

Land area (km²): 1,097,000
Capital city: Addis Ababa
National population (millions): 65.4 (2001)
National population growth rate (%): 2.3 (2001)
Urban population (millions): 9.9 (2001)
Urban population growth rate (%): 4.2 (2001)
Urban population as % of national population: 15.1 (2001)
GDP growth rate (%): 6.47 (2001)
GNP *per capita* **(US$):** 100 (2001)
Gini index : 48.6 (2000 survey year)
Official exchange rate (US$: Birr): 8.55 (September 2003)
Economic activities: Agriculture, fishing, forestry, mining, manufacturing
Modern energy consumption *per capita* **(kgoe):** 19.3 (2001)
Modern energy production (000 toe): 1,320 (2001)
Energy sources: Biomass, natural gas, hydropower, imported oil, dung
Installed capacity (MW): 493 (2001)
Electricity generation (GWh): 1,812 (2001)
Electricity consumption *per capita* **(kWh):** 17.2 (2001)
Urban electrification rates (%): 13.00 (2001)
System losses (%): 22 (2001)

Sources: AFREPREN, 2003; IEA, 2003; Karekezi et al., 2002; Kebede, 2003; Teferra, 2003; Phelan, 2003; UNDP, 2003; Wolde Ghiorgis, 2003; World Bank, 2003a; World Bank, 2003b

17

Introduction

Rationale of the study

Subsidies in general and energy subsidies in particular are widespread in developing countries. Estimated total government energy subsidies in developing countries in 1992 amounted to over US$ 50 billion (Goldemberg and Johannson, 1995)[1] – more than the Official Development Assistance (ODA) to the same countries. Given the importance of subsidies in general and energy subsidies in particular in most developing countries, a focus on these issues is clearly important.

Making energy affordable to the poor is a widely cited reason for subsidies. Whether subsidies really achieve this objective should be examined. In Part 6, the significance of kerosene and electricity subsidies to Ethiopian urban households is examined in the context of household purchasing power.

Following the lead of the World Bank, poverty reduction has become a centrepiece of policy in developing countries; this has focused attention on the transfer of resources to the poor. How much of the subsidies non-targeted groups capture, and whether there are more efficient ways of applying subsidies will be important elements in this policy debate. If the social costs of energy subsidies (in the form of leakages to the non-poor, for example) are high, they should be either abolished or redesigned. Other more efficient ways of using the same resources should be considered. These constitute the second set of issues addressed in Part 6.

The economic reforms sweeping through most of the developing countries have also pushed the issue of subsidy to the forefront of the policy debate because of its impact on public finance. On one hand, subsidies imply increases in government expenditures (or reductions in revenue). This has a direct impact on one of the objectives of structural adjustment programmes: reducing government budget deficit to arrest increases in aggregate demand. Part 6 also assesses the impact of energy subsidies on Ethiopian public finance.

The lack of rapid growth in the formal and large-scale modern sector in many developing countries has led to the increased importance of the informal sector constituted by the small and micro-enterprises (SMEs). This implies that the performance of SMEs will have a significant impact on the welfare of the urban poor. Examining whether the electricity tariff in Ethiopia is supportive of the activities of SMEs can shed light on the problems of energy supply to the sector.

Before we turn to this and other issues, the next section presents an overall description of urban energy demand in Ethiopia.

The pattern of urban energy demand in Ethiopia[2]

Urban households in Ethiopia expend around a tenth of their income on energy. The budget share of total energy expenditure falls as income rises when the whole sample is considered. While the mean energy budget share of the poor is 10 per cent, that for non-poor households decreases to 7 per cent (although the non-poor expend more in absolute terms). Energy budget share consistently decreases with *per capita* expenditures, declining from 11 per cent to 5 per cent when moving from the lowest to the highest deciles. But this consistent decline in the budget share of energy is observed only for five of the urban centres out of the eleven when the data are disaggregated. There are many instances where the energy budget shares increase in the middle deciles. Hence, the widely observed empirical regularity of declining energy budget shares with higher incomes does not seem to hold at lower levels of aggregation.

Energy use patterns significantly vary between urban areas. In Jimma and Harar, firewood is the most important fuel for all income groups. In Gondar and Nazret, charcoal plays a similar role, except for the lowest deciles that depend on firewood. In Mekele and Bahr Dar, while firewood is the most important fuel for most income groups, charcoal takes over for the richest. In Harar and Dire Dawa, higher-income groups shift from firewood to kerosene, and in Addis Ababa the most important fuel changes from kerosene to electricity with higher incomes.

The dependence of households on biomass fuels also significantly decreases with income on the aggregate level. The lowest *per capita* expenditure decile expends 70 per cent of its energy budget on biomass fuels but the corresponding figure for the richest decile is 42 per cent. While firewood is the most important single fuel for nine deciles, electricity becomes the most important only for the richest decile, followed by kerosene, with firewood dropping to third place.

The expenditure on firewood is the most important – 38 per cent of the households' energy budget – followed by electricity (20 per cent) and kerosene (19 per cent). Charcoal accounts for 17 per cent and dung cakes for 5 per cent of the household energy budget. Butane gas and sawdust are the least important, accounting for only 1 per cent or less of energy expenditures. The combined percentage share of firewood, charcoal and dung cakes is 60 per cent, showing heavy dependence on biomass fuels, on one hand, and a tremendous potential for increasing the demand for modern fuels on the other.

The dependence on biomass fuels in the urban centres varies widely. The shares of biomass fuels range from 26 per cent (Addis Ababa) to 85 per cent (Gondar). The next urban centre with the least dependence on biomass fuels after Addis Ababa is Dire Dawa with 46 per cent. Addis Ababa is the only urban centre without heavy dependence on biomass fuels. Variations in kerosene and electricity budget shares across the urban centres are also significant; the shares for kerosene vary between 3 per cent (Gondar) and 35 per cent (Addis Ababa), and those for electricity between 10 per cent and 36 per cent (Addis Ababa). Addis Ababa is on top for all three modern forms of energy – kerosene, butane gas and electricity.

The observed consistent increase in the use of modern fuels (or the decline of biomass fuels) as income rises on the aggregate level does not hold for all individual urban areas. Econometric tests indicate that this pattern does not exist at least for some urban areas. The explanatory power of the 'energy ladder' hypothesis is weakened at lower levels of aggregation.

Budget elasticities are all positive, indicating that no fuel is an inferior good – an increase in the income of households increases the demand for all types of fuels. Positive budget elasticity for traditional fuels is symptomatic of a lower level in terms of 'energy transition'. This is in contrast to some findings in African countries – for example, for charcoal in Zambia (see Mulenga, 2000). The positive income elasticity for traditional fuels in urban areas of Ethiopia is one reason on the demand side that can slow down the expansion of modern fuels. Income elasticities indicate that while firewood and kerosene are basic fuels, households tend to use more charcoal and electricity with rising income. This is not a neat transition as predicted by the 'energy ladder' hypothesis.

Own-price elasticities of firewood and charcoal are high, implying that the demand for them will decline significantly with a rise in their prices. On the other hand, the demand for electricity is less sensitive to changes in prices. In the light of the recent increase in the electricity tariff towards its long-run marginal cost, the second result is comforting; the rise in electricity price is not expected to reduce the demand for electricity drastically.

When we look at cross-price elasticities, the following picture emerges. An increase in the price of firewood increases the demand for charcoal, dung cakes and electricity. Since the budget share like the elasticity of charcoal is relatively high, the results suggest that when the price of firewood increases households mainly shift towards charcoal. The elasticities also indicate that the effects on the two modern fuels, kerosene and electricity, are opposite; an increase in the price of firewood encourages the consumption of electricity but discourages the use of kerosene.

An increase in the price of charcoal reduces the consumption of firewood and dung cakes while increasing that of kerosene; the consumption of electricity is not affected. When charcoal becomes more expensive, households mainly shift towards kerosene. Due to the high cross-price elasticity with respect to dung cakes and the importance of firewood in household energy budgets, the fall in the mean household expenditures on the two is also relatively high.

An increase in the price of dung cakes increases the consumption of charcoal and electricity while reducing that of firewood and kerosene. A rise in the price of dung cakes mainly shifts households towards charcoal.

Increase in the price of kerosene reduces the consumption of charcoal, dung cakes and electricity and increases that of firewood; households move mainly towards firewood. A removal or reduction of the kerosene subsidy as part of the economic reform in Ethiopia implies an increased demand mainly for firewood. The argument for keeping the subsidy on kerosene to arrest deforestation by suppressing demand for firewood makes sense in this context if it is true that the increased demand for firewood leads to deforestation.[3] But a rise in the price of kerosene will depress the demand for electricity.

An increase in the price of electricity increases the demand for firewood and dung cakes, while depressing that for charcoal and kerosene. In terms of the absolute magnitudes of the effects, kerosene will be most affected. The recent increase in electricity tariff probably reduced the consumption of kerosene while increasing that of traditional fuels – particularly dung cakes and firewood.

In general, while dung cakes/electricity and firewood/electricity are substitutes for each other, kerosene/dung cakes and kerosene/electricity are complements. The cross-price elasticity estimates match with the energy end-use patterns of urban households. The substitution between electricity and dung cakes and firewood is mainly explained by fuel used for *injera*[4] preparation. With recent expansion in the use of electric devices to bake *injera*, electricity has become a substitute for dung cakes and firewood. Kerosene is a complement to electricity and dung cakes because they are used for different purposes. Apart from lighting, electricity is mainly used for *injera* baking – and so are dung cakes. But kerosene is used for cooking and preparing tea/coffee and not for *injera* preparation.

An increase in the price of traditional fuels is usually considered an important factor pushing households towards the use of modern fuels. Cross-price elasticity estimates indicate that this is true in the case of electricity: increases in the prices of firewood and dung cakes increase the demand for electricity, while demand is not affected by a higher charcoal price. But the effect of an increase in the price of traditional fuels on the demand for kerosene is ambiguous: an increase in the prices of firewood and dung cakes *reduces* the demand for kerosene. On the other hand, an increase in the price of charcoal increases mean household kerosene expenditure. This result tallies with the end use pattern of households, since kerosene is mainly a substitute for charcoal.

With a unit increase in income, the highest rises in energy expenditures are on firewood and electricity for the poor and non-poor respectively.

These results give us an idea of how different types of economic growth affect energy demand. If economic growth is pro-poor – increasing the income of the poor relatively more than that of the non-poor – a significant aggregate increase in the demand for firewood is expected. On the other hand, if it is not pro-poor a significant increase in the demand for electricity is expected. In terms of satisfying the energy needs of the urban poor in the short run, policy issues related to biomass fuels are important.

More options exist in urban areas – even for the poor – as compared to their rural counterparts. For instance, while the budget share of electricity is second for the non-poor after firewood, charcoal and kerosene are the second most important fuels for poor households. Policy may have to take charcoal – a more efficient source of heat than firewood – as an important energy source for the urban poor in the short run. In addition, that poor households expend the same amount of their energy budget on kerosene as on charcoal underscores the fact that kerosene is a realistic substitute for biomass fuels, even for the poor in urban areas.

The next chapter focuses on the relationship between costs of energy and the purchasing power of the urban poor in Ethiopia.

18

Expenditures of the Urban Poor
and Costs of Energy

Can poor urban households in Ethiopia afford modern fuels – particularly kerosene and electricity? Among other reasons, governments subsidize kerosene and electricity in particular and energy in general to make them affordable to the poor. Whether subsidies have helped to accomplish this objective is rarely examined. This chapter will address the issue by comparing estimates of fuel costs with the purchasing power of Ethiopian households.

First, the amount of subsidy on each unit of kerosene and electricity has to be identified. Then kerosene and electricity costs are adjusted upwards to reflect the increase in costs if the subsidies were to be abolished. These adjusted costs are then compared to estimates of the purchasing power of different categories of households. Mean energy expenditures are used as proxies for purchasing power.

Data from the Central Statistical Authorities (CSA) 1995/6 Household Income, Consumption and Expenditures Survey are used. Three categories of energy expenditures are identified (CSA, 1998):

- The first category consists of items recorded under 'fuel and power' and includes expenditures on firewood, charcoal, sawdust, dung cakes, kerosene, electricity, matches, candles, butane gas, dry cells and others. We refer to this category as Fuel 1.

- The second category includes Fuel 1 plus transport fuel, motor oil and greases (probably used by households with automobiles). This is categorized as Fuel 2.

- Households also expend money on energy appliances in addition to the expenditures included in Fuel 2. The appliances include, *mtad*,[5] charcoal stoves (both earthen and metal ware), charcoal iron, frying pan, cooking pan, kettles and jugs, *biretmtad, mekuya, etanmachesha*,[6] stove holder, kerosene lamp and lamp, flash/torch light, gas stove, electric bulb, thermos flask, electric wire, adapters and distributors, plugs and sockets. Fuel 2 plus expenditures on these appliances are categorized as Fuel 3.

Table 6.1 Mean annual energy consumption of all households converted into kerosene

Fuel	Unit fuel used	Mean content	Energy (MJ per unit)	Gross energy use (MJ)	Typical efficiency	Useful energy in MJ	Kerosene equivalent (litre)
Firewood	kg	462.08	15.5	7162.24	0.1	716.22	20.46
Charcoal	kg	87.31	29.0	2531.99	0.2	506.39	14.47
Dung cakes	kg	22.50	15.5	348.75	0.1	34.88	1.00
Sawdust	kg	2.13	15.5	33.02	0.1	3.30	0.09
Kerosene	litre	77.37	35.0	2707.95	0.3	812.36	23.21
Electricity	kWh	175.07	3.6	630.25	0.65	409.65	11.70
Butane gas	kg	3.70	45.5	168.35	0.45	75.84	2.17
Total				13582.55		2558.64	73.10
Gross total							243.68

Note: Energy content and typical efficiency from Hosier and Kipondya (1993). Dung cakes and sawdust are assumed to have the same energy content as firewood.
Source: Survey by author

To estimate the costs of using kerosene or electricity, average fuel amounts used by certain categories of households have to be identified. As described in Part 3, this is done by converting the total energy use of households into kerosene or electricity equivalents. Tables 6.1 and 6.2 present the mean annual energy consumption of all households converted into equivalent amounts of kerosene and electricity.

The third columns in the respective tables give us the average physical amounts of fuels used by households; for example, on the average urban households use 462 kg of firewood and 87 kg of charcoal in a year. If we multiply these amounts by the energy content of the fuels (given in column four), the average gross energy use of households is identified (column five). To arrive at useful energy (column seven), the gross figures have to be scaled down by typical efficiencies (column six). If useful energy is divided by the energy content of kerosene or electricity, the corresponding equivalent amounts of the respective fuels giving the same amounts of useful energy can be known. For example, the average urban household in Ethiopia uses a total amount of useful energy from all fuels that is equivalent to 73 litres of kerosene or 711 kilowatt hours of electricity. But in order to get this amount of useful energy a larger amount of kerosene and electricity has to be used, depending on the efficiency of kerosene and electricity use. Hence, in order to get the above-mentioned amounts of useful energy, 244 litres of kerosene or 1,093 kilowatt hours of electricity have to be used.

A similar conversion of energy consumption into kerosene and electricity equivalents for poor and non-poor households – for households located in different urban areas and in different *per capita*

Table 6.2 Mean annual energy consumption of all households converted into electricity

Fuel	Unit	Mean fuel used	Energy content (MJ per unit)	Gross energy use (MJ)	Typical efficiency	Useful energy (KWh)
Firewood	kg	462.08	15.5	7162.24	0.1	198.95
Charcoal	kg	87.31	29	2531.99	0.2	140.66
Dung cakes	kg	22.50	15.5	348.75	0.1	9.69
Sawdust	kg	2.13	15.5	33.02	0.1	0.92
Kerosene	litre	77.37	35	2707.95	0.3	225.68
Electricity	kWh	175.07	3.6	630.25	0.65	113.80
Butane gas	kg	3.70	45.5	168.35	0.45	21.05
Total				13582.55		710.79

Note: Energy content and typical efficiency from Hosier and Kipondya (1993). Dung cakes and sawdust are assumed to have the same energy content as firewood.
Source: Survey by author

expenditure deciles – is done. Energy use of households across all the three classifications varies significantly. The average energy use of non-poor households is 2.3 times than that of poor households; while the kerosene and electricity equivalents of poor households are 133 litres and 592 kilowatt hours respectively, the corresponding figures for non-poor households are 298 litres and 1,335 kilowatt hours. The inter-city variation is also large; the highest average household energy consumption (in Addis Ababa) is more than twice that of the lowest (Debre Zeit). While mean household kerosene and electricity consumption totals in Debre Zeit are 166 litres and 745 kilowatt hours of electricity, in Addis Ababa they are 346 litres and 1,552 kilowatt hours respectively. Average household energy consumption consistently increases with *per capita* expenditure deciles. The mean energy consumption of the richest decile of households is 2.8 times than that of the poorest. While the kerosene and electricity equivalents are 131 litres and 586 kilowatt hours for the poorest decile, the corresponding figures for the richest are 365 litres and 1,636 kilowatt hours. As expected, richer households use a larger amount of total energy than poorer households.

To identify the effect of the subsidy on the cost of using kerosene, the subsidy on each litre has to be identified. Tadesse (1996) indicates that the retail price of kerosene as calculated should have been Birr 1.54 per litre, but the government decided to keep the price at Birr 1.25 per litre; the subsidy was 19 per cent of total final price. The subsidy on each litre of kerosene was Birr 0.293, at the time roughly corresponding to the 1995/6 CSA survey. Birr 0.293 is added to the current price of kerosene in the computation of costs to identify how much cost would have increased if there were no subsidy.

Since households can use kerosene either only for cooking or for both cooking and lighting, two estimates for the costs of kerosene use are made. The cost needed to buy kerosene and stove is designated as Cost A and the cost for the purchase of kerosene, stove and lamp as Cost B. The kerosene equivalents derived above are included in computing these costs.

Table 6.3 presents the cost estimates (with and without subsidy) and the average energy expenditures for (1) all, (2) poor and (3) non-poor households. Note the significant variation between cost estimates for the poor and non-poor, reflecting the differences in the amount of energy used by the two groups of households. Similarly, the average energy expenditures of the non-poor are significantly higher than those of the poor. In addition, the same mean values for Fuel 1 and 2 in the case of poor households indicate that no automobiles are owned by the poor: remember that the difference between the two is made up of transport fuel, motor oil and greases.

The last six rows of Table 6.3 give ratios between different cost estimates and mean energy expenditures. Ratios less than one indicate affordability, since energy expenditures are higher than cost estimates. Since Cost A (cooking only) is the cheapest alternative and Fuel 3 the highest energy expenditure, the ratios of the two are the lowest. Similarly, since Cost B (cooking and lighting) is the most expensive estimate and Fuel 1 the least energy expenditure, the ratios of the two are the highest. For all, for poor and for non-poor households, ratios between costs and energy expenditures are less than one when the subsidy is considered. In the case where subsidies are excluded (and costs thus increase by the amount of the subsidy), while all ratios between Cost A and Fuel 1 are less than one, they are greater or equal to one for the ratio between Cost B and Fuel 1. Probably the more relevant ratios are those with Fuel 3; this is because the cost estimates include equipment (stove and lamp) and the corresponding energy expenditure that contains costs of equipment is Fuel 3. All the ratios with Fuel 3 are less than one except for poor households without subsidy for Cost B; in the case of Cost A, even without subsidy, the cost is marginally lower than energy expenditure (a ratio of 0.99). The ratio for poor households without subsidy for Cost B is only 8 per cent greater than one. Hence, even though a removal of subsidy may marginally affect poor households in accessing the more expensive energy alternative (with both stove and lamp), the effect seems to be small. These results indicate that the removal of the kerosene subsidy probably would not make much difference to the affordability of the fuel even for poor households. The difference between urban areas, in addition to that between poor and non-poor households, is important. Depending on differences in income/expenditure and the prices of equipment and kerosene, both purchasing power and kerosene costs vary. Appendix 6.1 presents information on these inter-city variations. As in Table 6.3, ratios of costs and energy expenditures (for all households) with and without

Table 6.3 Costs of using kerosene and energy expenditures of all poor and non-poor households

Costs of kerosene	All urban areas	Poor	Non-poor
Cost A (stove)(with subsidy)(Birr)	448.24	261.75	538.23
Cost B (stove + lamp)(with subsidy)(Birr)	474.08	287.59	564.07
Cost A (stove)(without subsidy)(Birr)	519.63	300.43	625.42
Cost B (stove + lamp)(without subsidy)(Birr)	545.47	326.27	651.26
Fuel & power 1 (Birr)	533.05	292.19	649.28
Fuel & power 2 (Birr)	557.35	292.19	685.30
Fuel & power 3 (Birr)	617.94	303.29	769.76
Cost A/Fuel 3 (with subsidy)	0.73	0.86	0.70
Cost B/Fuel 3 (with subsidy)	0.77	0.95	0.73
Cost B/Fuel 1 (with subsidy)	0.89	0.98	0.87
Cost A/Fuel 3 (without subsidy)	0.84	0.99	0.81
Cost B/Fuel 3 (without subsidy)	0.88	1.08	0.85
Cost B/Fuel 1 (without subsidy)	1.02	1.12	1.00

Note: The Birr–US$1 exchange rate was around 6.50 in 1996.
Source: Survey by author

subsidy are given. All ratios, except those for the town of Gondar, are less than one. The higher energy consumption per household (only second to Addis Ababa) and the low energy expenditure of Gondar explains the high ratios. But even in the case of Gondar, the highest ratio is 30 per cent higher than one (without subsidy). The more relevant ratios of costs with Fuel 3 (without subsidy) are 1.22 (Cost A) and 1.27 (Cost B). These figures also underscore the conclusion we arrived at earlier: kerosene subsidies do not seem to be hugely important in improving the affordability of kerosene to the average household in most urban areas.

The classification into only two groups, poor and non-poor, may gloss over finer variations in affordability among households. To get a more detailed picture, energy expenditures and the cost of using kerosene are computed for *per capita* expenditure deciles (Appendix 6.2). All cost to expenditure ratios (with subsidy) are less than one, indicating that for all *per capita* expenditure deciles (including the poorest) kerosene is affordable. When subsidies are excluded, only 25 per cent of the ratios are greater than one. Most of the ratios that are greater than one are concentrated among the three lowest *per capita* expenditure deciles that correspond to poor households. The highest ratio in these groups is 1.11; costs are 11 per cent higher than energy expenditures. If we focus on the ratios of costs (A and B) to Fuel 3, only two out of six are greater than one and for these costs are only 4 per cent and 7 per cent higher than energy expenditures. For example, for the poorest *per capita* expenditure decile, Cost B is higher than energy expenditure by 7 per cent; the same ratio drops below one as early as the third *per capita* expenditure decile in the sequence linking poorest and richest households. These results, in addition to showing that the removal of subsidy does not significantly affect affordability for the poor as whole, indicate that its effect even on the poorest of the poor is not extreme.

In the computation of costs of kerosene, the total costs of stove and lamp are included. This information is important since it gives an idea of the total upfront cost households have to bear in order to use kerosene, and generally households pay the cost as a lump sum. But since annual costs are calculated, this procedure implicitly assumes that the stoves and lamps are used only for one year, even though they actually are used for longer periods. We did not bother to compute costs of kerosene that take depreciation into account, because spreading the fixed costs over the lifespan of the equipment will further reduce the costs and increase energy expenditures (expenditures for more than a year are considered) and the conclusions will be strengthened. Hence, those cost-to-expenditure ratios marginally higher than one will be less than one.

All the results above indicate that the kerosene subsidy does not play an important role in making kerosene affordable to the poor. Now let us turn to electricity. In the case of electricity, the subsidy can take two forms. First, the lifeline tariff is deliberately kept low in the expectation that most poor households will use an amount of electricity below the lifeline level. Second, even tariffs above the lifeline level are below the LRMC. To approximate the amounts of electricity subsidy captured by each household, the difference between the average tariff in 1996 and the LRMC is taken as an estimate of the subsidy on each kilowatt hour of electricity. While the average tariff in 1996 was Birr 0.20, the LRMC, as determined in 1994, was Birr 0.3707. The difference between the two, Birr 0.1707, is the average subsidy on each kilowatt hour. In other words, the electricity subsidy was around 46 per cent of the LRMC.

Eight different combinations of appliances are considered in estimating the various alternative costs of using electricity. The main utensils used with electricity are the *mtad* and the stove. In addition to the costs of purchasing the two, connection fees, costs of wiring, bulbs and electric bills are considered. The eight combinations are:

1 *Mtad*, stove and internal wiring with electric pole (designated as Cost A);
2 *Mtad* and internal wiring with service pole (Cost B);
3 Stove and internal wiring with service pole (Cost C);
4 Internal wiring with electric pole without *mtad* and stove (Cost D);
5 *Mtad*, stove and internal wiring without service pole (Cost E);
6 *Mtad* and internal wiring without service pole (Cost F);
7 Stove and internal wiring without service pole (Cost G);
8 Internal wiring without *mtad*, stove and service pole (Cost H).

While Cost A is the most expensive combination, Cost H is the cheapest. The computation of the costs of these alternatives is done both with and without subsidy; in the latter case, the LRMC is used instead of

Table 6.4 Costs of using electricity and energy expenditures of all poor and non-poor households

Costs of electricity (in Birr)		All households	Poor	Non-poor
With *mtad*, stove and pole (with subsidy)	Cost A	2,344.22	2,244.00	2,392.58
With *mtad* and pole (with subsidy)	Cost B	1,777.47	1,677.25	1,825.83
With stove and pole (with subsidy)	Cost C	1,891.88	1,791.66	1,940.24
Without *mtad* and stove, but with pole (with subsidy)	Cost D	1,325.13	1,224.91	1,373.49
With *mtad* and stove but without pole (with subsidy)	Cost E	1,975.22	1,875.00	2,023.58
With *mtad*, without pole (with subsidy)	Cost F	1,408.47	1,308.25	1,456.83
With stove, without pole (with subsidy)	Cost G	1,522.88	1,422.66	1,571.24
Without *mtad*, stove and pole (with subsidy)	Cost H	956.13	855.91	1,004.49
With *mtad*, stove and pole (without subsidy)	Cost A	2,530.87	2,345.12	2,620.50
With *mtad* and pole (without subsidy)	Cost B	1,964.12	1,778.37	2,053.75
With stove and pole (without subsidy)	Cost C	2,078.53	1,892.78	2,168.16
Without *mtad* and stove, but with pole (without subsidy)	Cost D	1,511.78	1,326.03	1,601.41
With *mtad* and stove but without pole (without subsidy)	Cost E	2,161.87	1,976.12	2,251.50
With *mtad*, without pole (without subsidy)	Cost F	1,595.12	1,409.37	1,684.75
With stove, without pole (without subsidy)	Cost G	1,709.53	1,523.78	1,799.16
Without *mtad*, stove and pole (without subsidy)	Cost H	1,142.78	957.03	1,232.41
Fuel & power 1	Fuel 1	533.05	292.19	649.28
Fuel & power 2	Fuel 2	557.35	292.19	685.30
Fuel & power 3	Fuel 3	617.94	303.29	769.76
Cost A/Fuel 1 (with subsidy)		4.40	7.68	3.68
Cost H/Fuel 3 (with subsidy)		1.55	2.82	1.30
Cost A/Fuel 1 (without subsidy)		4.75	8.03	4.04
Cost H/Fuel 3 (without subsidy)		1.85	3.16	1.60

Source: Survey by author

the average electricity tariff at the period to value the amount of electricity equivalent for total energy use. Table 6.4 presents the costs of electricity use (with and without subsidy) and energy expenditures for all, poor and non-poor households.

The cost figures in the table indicate significant differences in the alternatives considered. For example, Cost A (the most expensive alternative) is around 2.5 times Cost H (the least expensive) without subsidy. Instead of presenting all the cost to energy expenditure ratios (which add up to 24), Table 6.4 presents the highest and lowest values. While the ratio of Cost A to Fuel 1 is the highest (most expensive cost alternative divided by the least energy expenditure) the ratio of Cost H to Fuel 3 is the lowest; all other ratios are between the two. All the ratios reported in the table are more than one. Even the lowest ratios are significantly higher than one, particularly for the poor. The least-cost alternative with subsidy is 182 per cent higher than energy expenditures; this increases to 216 per cent without subsidy. These figures underscore the fact that electricity is too expensive for the average household and especially for poor households. In addition to indicating that electricity in general is too expensive, the results also emphasize that subsidy does not crucially change the situation of the poor. Even the situation of non-poor households is not that good (costs being 30–60 per cent higher than purchasing power).

To examine conditions in different urban contexts, the same exercise is repeated for urban areas (Appendix 6.3). All urban areas face a similar situation: the ratios of costs to energy expenditures are greater than one for all urban areas and for all alternatives considered, with and without subsidy. These results show that the electricity subsidy does not play a crucial role. But this does not mean that there are no variations across the urban areas: for example, the ratios for Cost A to Fuel 1 (with subsidy) range between 1.13 for Mekele and 5.23 for Dire Dawa.

On the average, electricity seems to be too expensive for both poor and non-poor households. To examine the possible differences within poor and non-poor households, ratios of costs to energy expenditures are computed for *per capita* expenditure deciles. Except in a single case, as expected all ratios are greater than one: only the richest *per capita* expenditure decile has a ratio less that one. Particularly, the ratios for poor households (belonging to the three lowest *per capita* expenditure deciles) are significantly higher than one, ranging from 2 to 8. These figures, in addition to showing that electricity is too expensive for the poor, again emphasize that subsidies do not play a crucial role in making it affordable. In addition, the fact that only one ratio (for the richest decile) is less than one indicates that electricity seems to be expensive even for the relatively well-to-do.

In the case of kerosene, depreciation and amortization of fixed costs (costs of stove and lamp) were neglected because they are relatively less important and only reinforce the conclusions already reached. In the case of electricity, however, fixed costs are substantial, and spreading the fixed costs over the lifespan of equipment can change the conclusion derived.

The fixed elements in the estimation of the cost of electricity include internal wiring with or without electric pole, electric *mtad* and electric stove. We assume that each has a lifespan of ten years and that all depreciate at a constant and uniform rate. In other words, the annual depreciation of these fixed components is one tenth of their total value.

In addition to specifying the lifespan of equipment and the rate of depreciation, an interest rate is required to discount future values, since costs and energy expenditures are now supposed to be made over a ten-year period. The minimum deposit interest rate fixed by the National

Bank of Ethiopia (the central bank) was 6 per cent by the beginning of 1998 (*Addis Tribune*, 1998). Future costs and expenditures are discounted to their present value using this 6 per cent interest rate.

Table 6.5 Ratios of total present value of costs to expenditures for poor households

Cost to expenditure ratios	With subsidy	Without subsidy
Cost A/Fuel 1	1.25	1.59
Cost A/Fuel 2	1.25	1.59
Cost A/Fuel 3	1.20	1.54
Cost H/Fuel 1	0.77	1.12
Cost H/Fuel 2	0.77	1.12
Cost H/Fuel 3	0.74	1.08

Source: Survey by author

Appendix 6.5 contains the present values of the mean energy expenditures of poor households and electricity costs A and H, with and without subsidy. Since a ten-year lifespan and uniform depreciation rate are assumed, the values for each year are one-tenth of the total values. In the second part of Appendix 6.5, current values are discounted into present values by using the 6 per cent interest rate. The relevant figures to see in the table are the total present values of energy expenditures (fuels 1, 2 and 3) and total present values of costs (costs A and H), with and without subsidy (these have been italicized). Table 6.5 presents cost–energy expenditure ratios in terms of their present values derived from the figures in Appendix 6.5.

The ratios in Table 6.5 are significantly lower than those in Table 6.4. For example the ratio of Cost A to Fuel 1 plunges from 7.68 to 1.25 (with subsidy) and from 8.03 to only 1.59 (without subsidy). Similarly, the ratio of Cost H to Fuel 3 falls from 2.82 to 0.74 (with subsidy) and from 3.16 to 1.08 (without subsidy). In other terms, if amortization is ignored, the purchasing power of poor households is short of the unsubsidized cost of acquiring the least-cost alternative by around 216 per cent. On the other hand, if costs and energy expenditures are amortized and computed in terms of present values, this difference drops to a mere 8 per cent, even for the case without subsidy. The implication of these results is that poor households most likely do not have the purchasing power in question, if they are required to cover the upfront costs of electricity all at once. But if the costs are spread over longer periods of time, even poor households, it seems, can afford to pay for electricity supplied without subsidy. The most important obstacle for poor households in accessing electricity seems to be that costs are incurred in a lump-sum fashion.

The above results have important policy implications. First, the subsidies on tariff do not seem to play an important role in affecting affordability of electricity to poor households; the overall changes in the cost–expenditure ratios are not hugely significant, with or without subsidy. Hence, the objective of improving the accessibility of electricity to poor households does not seem to be fulfilled by subsidies on tariff. Second, given a mechanism that can spread costs over relatively long periods of time, it would seem that poor households (probably with a marginal shortfall) can afford electricity even when supplied without subsidy.

Fixed costs can be spread over longer periods of time in two ways. The first is through long-term contracts with electricity and equipment suppliers that enable households to pay the costs (including interest payments) over longer periods of time. This will spread costs to households as well as enabling suppliers to recover costs. But this requires a stable relationship between suppliers and consumers. The second mechanism to spread costs is credit. If credit is available to the poor, they can cover the upfront costs and pay their debt over longer periods of time. The results indicate that, given long-term credit, poor households on the average seem to be capable of settling their debts. In other terms, if a mechanism that enables households to bring their future income to the present is created, they can afford unsubsidized electricity. Thus credit institutions in general and/or specialized creditors targeting households with a demand for electricity connection can help improve the situation.

Classification of households into the finer groups of *per capita* expenditure deciles reinforces the above conclusion; Appendix 6.6 presents the cost–expenditure ratios on this basis. The ratios for all *per capita* expenditure deciles except the poorest are less than one. These figures are in stark contrast to those in Table 6.5, where depreciation/amortization is ignored and all the ratios are significantly greater than one. With amortization, only in three cases out of eight are the values greater than one for the poorest *per capita* expenditure decile. In addition, these are only marginally higher than one: the highest ratio indicates that costs are 14 per cent higher than the purchasing power of households. These results reiterate the two previous conclusions. First, subsidies on electricity tariffs are playing a minimal role in improving affordability to the poor. Second, even poor households seem to have the purchasing power to access unsubsidized electricity if a mechanism to spread costs over longer periods of time is available. The fact that the ratios for the second and third *per capita* expenditure deciles are all less than one, while some of those for the poorest decile are greater than one, indicates differences in the purchasing power of the extreme poor relative to the other poor.

In our computation of the present value of costs and energy expenditures so far, we have assumed that prices and income (energy expenditures) of households do not change over the time period considered. But if there is inflation and economic growth/decline, costs and expenditures will not remain the same. Let us incorporate some aspects of these changes in the analysis.

Since the Ethiopian economy is characterized by low inflation, a 2 per cent inflation rate is assumed; accordingly, let us suppose that all costs in our case increase by 2 per cent every year. With the exception of the periods during the border conflict between Ethiopia and Eritrea and some drought years, the economy grew relatively fast after 1991, and so we assume a growth rate of 5 per cent. Energy expenditures are also assumed to grow at the same rate as income.

Table 6.6 Ratios of total present value of costs to expenditures for poor households (2% inflation and 5% income growth)

Cost–expenditure ratios	With subsidy	Without subsidy
Cost A/Fuel 1	1.10	1.33
Cost A/Fuel 2	1.10	1.33
Cost A/Fuel 3	1.06	1.28
Cost H/Fuel 1	0.68	0.91
Cost H/Fuel 2	0.68	0.91
Cost H/Fuel 3	0.66	0.88

Source: Survey by author

The current and discounted present values of mean energy expenditures of poor households and electricity costs, with and without subsidy, are given in Appendix 6.7. The relevant ratios of costs to energy expenditures are given in Table 6.6. The results are similar to those in Table 6.5, where no inflation and income growth is assumed. The exclusion of subsidy seems to affect the affordability of electricity only marginally and the cheaper options seem to be affordable to the poor.

To summarize, the results in this section indicate that subsidies on kerosene and electricity do not seem to play a crucial role. The majority of the urban population, it would appear, can afford unsubsidized kerosene and electricity if arrangements for the spread of fixed costs, particularly those for electricity, are provided. Given the relatively high rates of subsidies, these conclusions may be surprising. For example, if kerosene and electricity subsidies were abolished, on average the respective prices of the fuels would increase by 23 per cent and 85 per cent![7] What is shown in the analysis of this section is that these large increases in the prices of kerosene and electricity implied by subsidy removal do not significantly change the overall costs *vis-à-vis* the purchasing power of households as captured by energy expenditures. Particularly in the case of electricity, the more important obstacles for poor households is their inability to spread fixed costs or get access to long-term credit.

The next chapter will examine the distribution of kerosene and electricity subsidies.

19

Who Captures Energy Subsidies?

Methodology

The previous section compares costs of kerosene and electricity with the purchasing power of households to examine if they have made significant differences. Another related issue with subsidies is to identify who captures them. One of the main objectives of subsidies is to help the poor. Most of the subsidy will not reach the poor if richer households in urban areas use most of the kerosene and electricity.

To identify the amount of subsidies captured by each household, the quantity of kerosene and electricity consumed is multiplied by the average subsidy per unit. First, the mean amount of subsidies captured by different categories of poor/non-poor households, for *per capita* expenditure deciles and individual urban areas, is computed. This helps to identify the income groups that capture most of the subsidies on energy.

Second, by regressing the amounts of subsidies each household captures on total household expenditure, household size and dummy variables for the urban areas, the relationship between income and subsidies can be examined further in a multivariate framework. Controlling for all the variables on which we have information is a clear advantage of this framework. A positive and significant coefficient on total expenditure, controlling for other variables, indicates that subsidies increase with household income (expenditures); richer households capture more subsidies, indicating a large leakage. The regression analysis on the aggregate level will also be extended to individual urban areas. This helps to identify regional variations. The next section presents the empirical results.

Empirical results

This section analyzes the distribution of subsidies. First, it examines the amounts of subsidies captured by households at different levels of income. Second, the regional variations as reflected in the amounts of subsidies captured by households located in different urban areas are analyzed.

As indicated above, to estimate the kerosene subsidies captured by each household, the subsidy per litre of kerosene is multiplied by the

Table 6.7 Total and mean kerosene and electricity subsidies for poor and non-poor households (in Birr)

	Mean kerosene subsidy per household	Total kerosene subsidy	Mean electricity subsidy per household	Total electricity subsidy	Mean expenditure per household
Non-poor	28.92	94398.04	39.88	130155.30	10346.64
Poor	9.71	15295.91	9.18	14451.67	2994.21
All	22.67	109693.95	29.88	144606.97	7953.57

Note: The Birr–US$1 exchange rate was around 6.50 in 1996.
Source: Survey by author

quantity of kerosene consumed. In the case of electricity, the difference between the average tariff and the LRMC is taken as an estimate of the subsidy on each kilowatt hour of electricity. The amount of electricity consumed by each household is multiplied by the subsidy per kilowatt hour to get estimates of the electricity subsidy captured by each household.

Table 6.7 gives the mean and total kerosene and electricity subsidies captured by poor and non-poor households. The figures in the table clearly show that non-poor households get most of the subsidies; 86 per cent of kerosene and 90 per cent of electricity subsidies go to non-poor households. This is also illustrated by mean kerosene and electricity subsidies per household; mean household kerosene and electricity subsidies of the non-poor are respectively 2.98 and 4.34 times those of the poor.

Table 6.8 Total and mean kerosene and electricity subsidies for per capita expenditure deciles (in Birr)

Per capita expenditure deciles	Mean kerosene subsidy per household	Total kerosene subsidy	Mean electricity subsidy per household	Total electricity subsidy	Mean expenditure per household
Poorest	8.95	4321.33	10.47	5055.04	2905.94
2	15.65	7576.31	15.58	7540.78	4252.40
3	15.74	7620.73	18.48	8943.72	5019.22
4	19.96	9642.55	22.22	10733.82	5853.70
5	20.62	9982.09	25.87	12520.23	6727.05
6	23.02	11143.59	28.79	13936.70	7651.52
7	27.31	13189.25	32.64	15767.35	8910.31
8	26.45	12800.41	36.64	17731.36	10199.24
9	31.21	15104.44	44.68	21624.34	11798.75
Richest	37.56	18139.22	63.36	30603.71	16020.89

Note: The Birr–US$1 exchange rate was around 6.50 in 1996.
Source: Survey by author

Table 6.9 Quantile (median) regressions of kerosene and electricity subsidies on total household expenditures and household size

Number of observations =   4839
Raw sum of deviations 96457.45 (about 11.18088)
Min sum of deviations 61545.72; Pseudo R² = 0.3619

Kerosene	Coefficient	Std. Err.	t	P>|t|	[95% Conf. Interval]	
Expenditure	0.0010337	0.0000244	42.32	0.000	0.0009858	0.0010816
H'hold size	0.0497361	0.0582557	0.85	0.393	-0.0644717	0.1639438
Mekele	6.083083	0.6382880	9.53	0.000	4.831747	7.334418
Bahr Dar	-3.326336	0.6385636	-5.21	0.000	-4.578211	-2.07446
Gondar	-3.690308	0.6383031	-5.78	0.000	-4.941673	2.438943
Dessie	24.97649	0.6448922	38.73	0.000	23.71221	26.24077
Jimma	-3.02052	0.6387289	-4.73	0.000	-4.27272	-1.76832
Nazret	7.197915	0.5644546	12.75	0.000	6.091327	8.304503
Debre Zeit	14.91348	0.6387098	23.35	0.000	13.66132	16.16564
Harar	13.25117	0.6393628	20.73	0.000	11.99773	14.50461
Addis Ababa	35.81055	0.3617429	98.99	0.000	35.10137	36.51973
Dire Dawa	21.95438	0.5645963	38.89	0.000	20.84751	23.06124
Constant	-0.8966398	0.3323659	-2.70	0.007	-1.548228	-0.2450512

Number of observations = 4839
Raw sum of deviations 129220.7 (about 9.8323202)
Min sum of deviations 101906.8; Pseudo R2 = 0.2114

Variable	Coefficient	Std. Err.	t	P>|t|	[95% Conf. Interval]	
Expenditure	0.0016411	0.0000340	48.21	0.000	0.0015744	0.0017078
H'hold size	0.1050429	0.0813043	1.29	0.196	-0.0543505	0.2644363
Mekele	1.8163900	0.8899701	2.04	0.041	0.0716433	3.561137
Bahr Dar	2.0005320	0.8886595	2.25	0.024	0.2583541	3.742709
Gondar	32.924740	0.8900186	36.99	0.000	31.1799	34.66958
Dessie	10.153140	0.8991911	11.29	0.000	8.390316	11.91596
Jimma	2.9281910	0.8906342	3.29	0.001	1.182142	4.674239
Nazret	4.5588100	0.7870469	5.79	0.000	3.015839	6.10178
Debre Zeit	6.4006460	0.8905339	7.19	0.000	4.654794	8.146499
Harar	1.9977850	0.8914537	2.24	0.025	0.2501294	3.74544
Addis Ababa	36.144500	0.5045159	71.64	0.000	35.15542	37.13359
Dire Dawa	3.0137560	0.7872424	3.83	0.000	1.470403	4.55711
Constant	-4.9232410	0.4634400	-10.62	0.000	-5.831794	-4.014687

Source: Survey by author

To examine further the relationship between subsidies and household income, Table 6.8 presents the mean and total kerosene and electricity subsidies captured by *per capita* expenditure deciles. This can reveal more information since the classification is finer than dividing households into only two groups, poor and non-poor. The figures show that both mean per household as well as total subsidies consistently increase with the *per capita* expenditure deciles. Mean kerosene and electricity subsidies per household for the richest decile are respectively 4.2 and 6.1 times those of the poorest decile. The results for *per capita* expenditure deciles confirm those from the classification of households into poor and non-poor; higher-income households capture most of the kerosene and electricity subsidies.

Next, as we have mentioned, the distribution of subsidies can be examined further by regression analysis. This approach enables us to examine the relationship by controlling for additional variables (like household size and location). Subsidies captured by households are regressed on total household expenditure, household size and dummy variables for urban areas. Table 6.9 presents the results from a quantile regression. Quantile (median) regression is used instead of OLS (ordinary least squares) to minimize the influence of outliers.

Controlling for household size and location (represented by the urban dummies), the amounts of both subsidies are significantly and positively related to household expenditure. An increase of household expenditure by one Birr increases kerosene and electricity subsidies by 0.10 and 0.16 Ethiopian cents, and both coefficients are highly significant. These results reiterate our previous findings that relatively well-to-do households capture most of the subsidies. In both regressions, the coefficients on household size are insignificant; the consumption of kerosene and electricity, and correspondingly the subsidies captured by households, are not statistically affected by household size.

An important feature of the results from the regression analysis is that in both cases all urban dummies are highly significant at conventional levels; significant regional variations exist in the distribution of subsidies. In the case of kerosene, compared to 'Other' urban areas (which is the excluded urban dummy), Bahr Dar, Gondar and Jimma get smaller and all the others higher amounts of subsidies. In the case of electricity, all urban areas get higher amounts of subsidies as compared to 'Other' urban areas. The significant variations between the urban areas point to the need to incorporate this regional dimension into our analysis.

Table 6.10 gives mean and total kerosene and electricity subsidies and *per capita* expenditures by urban areas, revealing some important patterns. Compared to mean expenditure per household, the amounts of subsidies captured by households are small, as a result of the small budget share of the fuels. For example, in Addis Ababa kerosene and electricity subsidies together are 1.13 per cent of mean household expenditure. Hence, the impact of kerosene and electricity subsidies on the overall welfare of urban households should not be exaggerated.

Addis Ababa has the highest figures by far for both kerosene and electricity subsidies (mean as well as total values). While the mean subsidy per household for Addis Ababa is around Birr 49 and Birr 77 for kerosene and electricity respectively, the second-highest figure for kerosene is Birr 35 (Dessie) and for electricity Birr 59 (Gondar).

Table 6.10 Total and mean kerosene and electricity subsidies by urban centres (in Birr)

Town	Mean kerosene subsidy per household	Total kerosene subsidy	Mean electricity subsidy per household	Total electricity subsidy	Mean expenditure per household
Mekele	18.44	4149.14	13.04	2933.10	7210.93
Bahr Dar	4.75	1068.81	10.57	2378.19	6334.95
Gondar	1.42	319.31	59.21	13322.79	6527.76
Dessie	35.25	7789.45	23.84	5268.28	5352.24
Jimma	5.56	1250.51	11.76	2646.74	7564.80
Nazret	18.70	5609.91	15.22	4567.11	6833.607
Debre Zeit	21.94	4936.62	20.86	4693.70	6042.28
Harar	24.08	5418.75	15.24	3429.02	8895.71
Addis Ababa	49.52	55713.94	76.57	86136.04	11144.50
Dire Dawa	29.97	8992.22	16.73	5018.17	7644.40
Others	9.36	14445.30	9.21	14213.85	7027.75

Note: The Birr–US$1 exchange rate was around 6.50 in 1996.
Source: Survey by author

Significant differences in mean subsidy per household exist between the urban areas for both kerosene and electricity use. For kerosene the values range between Birr 1.42 (Gondar) and 49.52 (Addis Ababa), and for electricity between Birr 9.21 (Others) and Birr 76.57 (Addis Ababa). This has implications for regional equity: given the federal structure of the government, this issue is politically sensitive in the current period.

Reflecting the regional variation in the use of kerosene and electricity, the ranking of the towns by mean household energy expenditures is not the same for the two fuels. For example, Gondar is last in terms of kerosene subsidies but second after Addis Ababa when we consider electricity use. Thus regional variation depends on fuel type.

In the cases of both kerosene and electricity, household incomes/expenditures are significantly and positively correlated to subsidies after controlling for the urban dummies. Does this positive relationship between subsidies and incomes hold for each urban area? Do richer households in each urban area capture more of the subsidies? How much do these coefficients differ across the urban areas? Quantile regressions, similar to the previous ones, for each urban area are estimated separately to address these questions. The kerosene or electricity subsidies captured by households are regressed on total household expenditure and household size for each urban area. The coefficients of the regressions with the corresponding t-values are given in Table 6.11.

All the coefficients for both kerosene and electricity subsidies on household expenditure are highly significant and positive, except one.

Table 6.11 Coefficients of quantile regressions for kerosene and electricity subsidies on expenditure and household size

Towns	Kerosene subsidies			Electricity subsidies		
	Constant	Expenditure	H'hold size	Constant	Expenditure	H'hold size
Mekele	−7.2617	.0022	1.1528	−1.6952	.0014.	0812
	(−3.84)**	(10.46)**	(2.86)**	(−1.33)	(9.42)**	(0.30)
Bahr Dar	−.0956	.0001.	0024−	1.6967	.0006	.7098
	(−1.16)	(5.10)**	(0.13)	(−2.04)*	(5.75)**	(3.93)**
Gondar	.6131	−.0000	.0102	16.4342	.0031	.8768
	(2.86)**	(−1.14)	(0.21)	(4.70)**	(7.24)**	(1.11)
Dessie	−4.2125	.0066	.4213	−4.1466	.0040	.1416
	(−1.33)	(14.50)**	(0.60)	(−2.15)*	(14.80)**	(0.33)
Jimma	.0890	.0003	−.0595	3.3756	.0004	.3946
	(0.25)	(8.42)**	(−0.74)	(2.88)**	(4.31)**	(1.54)
Nazret	−2.8441	.0029	−.3733	−.7618	.0010	.9679
	(−1.30)	(12.05)**	(−0.76)	(−0.55)	(6.30)**	(3.18)**
Debre Zeit	11.5536	.0016	−.0581	−6.4178	.0034	4709
	(2.52)*	(3.21)**	(−0.07)	(−2.47)*	(12.11)**	(0.94)
Harar	5.4883	.0024	−.8496	3.8102	.0009	−.3882
	(1.64)	(8.02)**	(−1.25)	(2.97)**	(7.96)**	(−1.52)
Addis Ababa	21.8106	.0015	1.7885	−7.7703	.0045	3.1774
	(11.28)**	(14.52)**	(5.50)**	(−2.10)*	(22.87)**	(5.09)**
Dire Dawa	11.5928	.0020	.4316	−.1799	.0015	−.1479
	(2.96)**	(4.49)**	(0.55)	(−0.14)	(10.32)**	(−0.57)
'Others'	1.4230	.0004	.1209	−1.4677	.0010	−.1066
	(5.70)**	(16.04)**	(2.10)*	(−8.12)**	(52.00)**	(−2.57)**

Note: T-values are given in brackets. ** Significant at 1%. * Significant at 5%.
Source: Survey by author

The exception is that of Gondar for kerosene subsidies; in addition to being statistically insignificant the value of the coefficient is zero (rounded to four decimal places). The results emphasize that just as in the aggregate case, both kerosene and electricity subsidies increase with household income for each urban area. But the regional variations are reflected by the spread of the coefficients. For example, a Birr 100 increase in household expenditure does not affect kerosene subsidy in Gondar but increases it by as much as Birr 0.66 for Dessie; the others are found in between. A similar change in expenditure increases electricity subsidies between Birr 0.04 (Jimma) and Birr 0.45 (Addis Ababa).[8]

All the results so far strongly indicate that both kerosene and electricity subsidies are mostly captured by the well-to-do; the higher the expenditure of households, the larger the subsidy captured by them. This implies that if the subsidies are removed most of the cost will be born by richer urban households. With the recent policy shift towards an emphasis on poverty alleviation in developing countries in general and Ethiopia in particular (following the lead of the World Bank) the weight given to costs borne by relatively richer households is considered to be small; the social cost of subsidy removal is not high.

Three important effects have not been incorporated into our discussions so far. First, subsidy removal increases government revenue; this increases social welfare, as long as a positive weight is attached to government revenue. The increase in social welfare with the decrease in government expenditure further reduces the social costs of subsidy removal. Second, with the removal of subsidy and the increase in price, household demand for kerosene and electricity is expected to adjust downwards correspondingly, if other factors remain constant. The resulting contraction in the consumption of modern fuels can be taken as social cost as long as the expansion of modern fuels is considered socially useful. Third, depending on cross-price effects, the change in prices following subsidy removals will change the demand for other fuels. Detailed examination of all these effects is beyond the scope of the current research.

The next chapter examines the role of kerosene and electricity subsidies in public sector finance.

20

Energy Subsidies
and Public Finance

Subsidies increase government expenditures or reduce revenues affecting public finance negatively. Structural adjustment programmes that are undertaken in many developing countries – including Ethiopia – are attempting to reduce government budget deficits and one of the ways of doing that is removing subsidies. This section examines the importance of kerosene and electricity subsidies in Ethiopian public finance.

In the case of Ethiopia, the kerosene subsidy is financed by additional taxes collected from other fuels, mainly from gasoline – this is a case of cross-subsidization. For instance, in 1996 the kerosene subsidy was financed by taxes collected from gasoline (56.7 per cent), automotive diesel oil (29.2 per cent), industrial fuel oil (10.1 per cent) and asphalt (4.0 per cent) (Tadesse, 1996). This means that the direct effect of the kerosene subsidy on government finances is zero, since this subsidy is recovered by the additional taxes on other fuels. But there are indirect effects that may be transmitted through price changes. For example, because of the additional taxes imposed on the other fuels – gasoline, automotive diesel oil, industrial fuel oil and asphalt – their demand declines, indirectly reducing the taxes that can be collected from them. To identify those effects, demand elasticity and other feedback effects have to be identified; but that is beyond the scope of this chapter.

The case of electricity is different, since no explicit cross-subsidization occurs. The tariff rates and subsidies for 1995/6 are used for the analysis because household-level information is available from the CSA's income and expenditure survey of 1995/6. Two electricity tariff revisions – in 1997 and 1998 – increased rates and correspondingly reduced subsidies. Table 6.12 presents the tariff rates between 1994 and 1998 and the LRMCs.

Before 1994 the Ethiopian Electric Power Corporation (EEPCO) had two different tariff rates for the Interconnected (ICS) and the Self-contained (SCS) systems. Tariff rates and service charges for the SCS were higher than for the ICS, reflecting higher marginal costs in the former. But the rates were unified in 1994 – this is why the tariff rates shown in Table 6.12 are the same, while the marginal costs are significantly different from each other.

The tariff rates for all types of customers – except for street lighting – as well as for all electricity blocks have significantly and consistently

Table 6.12 Tariff rates between 1994 and 1998 and marginal costs in 1994

Consumption (kWh/month)	Tariff rate (Birr/kWh) April 1998	Tariff rate (Birr/kWh) April 1997	Tariff rate (Birr/kWh) Oct. 1994	Marginal costs (1994) ICS	SCS
1 Domestic					
Equivalent flat rate	0.3897	0.2809	0.1772	0.3707	1.1425
0–50	0.2730	0.2109	0.1540		
50–100	0.2921	0.2235	0.1600		
100–200	0.4093	0.2930	0.1819		
200–300	0.4508	0.3165	0.1873		
300–400	0.4644	0.3255	0.1917		
400–500	0.4820	0.3371	0.1973		
>500	0.5691	0.3657	0.2113		
2 General/commercial					
Equivalent flat rate	0.5511	0.4301	0.3653	0.3461	1.1098
0–50	0.4990	0.3890			
>50	0.5691	0.4443			
0–25			0.3096		
25–100			0.3522		
100–10003			0.3666		
>1000			0.3727		
3 Low-voltage time-of-day industrial					
Equivalent flat rate	0.4736	0.3690	0.2563	0.2936	1.0638
Peak	0.6087	0.4755	0.2842		
Off–peak	0.4455	0.3469	0.2407		
4 High-voltage time-of-day industrial 15KV					
Equivalent flat rate	0.3349	0.2597	0.2341	0.2225	
Peak	0.4168	0.3243	0.2530		
Off–peak	0.3224	0.2499	0.2230		
5 High-voltage time-of-day industrial 132 KV					
Equivalent flat rate	0.3119	0.2416		0.2225	
Peak	0.3882	0.3017			
Off–peak	0.3003	0.2325			
6 Street lighting					
Equivalent flat rate	0.3970 .	0.3087	0.3333		

Note: ICS and SCS are the Interconnected (grid) and Self–contained systems respectively.
Source: EEPCO, 1994

increased between 1994 and 1998. For instance, while the equivalent flat rate for the domestic sector increased by 120 per cent between 1994 and 1998, the corresponding percentages for commercial, low-voltage (LV) industrial, high-voltage (HV) industrial (15 KV) and street lighting were 51, 85, 43 and 19 per cent respectively. The increases for the tariff rates of particular electricity blocks are even higher. For example, the domestic sector tariff for consumption higher than 500 kWh increased by 169 per cent during the same period, while all tariff rates for domestic sector blocks above 100 kWh increased by at least 125 per cent. The LV industrial tariff (peak hour) increased by 114 per cent. Even comparing the tariff rates of 1998 to those of 1997 – a period of only one year – reveals significant increases. Tariff rates for the different consumption blocks of

Table 6.13 Electricity subsidies per kWh between 1994 and 1998 (in Birr)

Consumption (kWh/month)	Subsidy per kWh April 1998		Subsidy per kWh April 1997		Subsidy per kWh Oct. 1994	
	ICS	SCS	ICS	SCS	ICS	SCS
			1 Domestic			
0–50	0.0977	0.8695	0.1598	0.9316	0.2167	0.9885
50–100	0.0786	0.8504	0.1472	0.9190	0.2107	0.9825
100–200	−0.0386	0.7332	0.0777	0.8495	0.1888	0.9606
200–300	−0.0801	0.6917	0.0542	0.8260	0.1834	0.9552
300–400	−0.0937	0.6781	0.0452	0.8170	0.1790	0.9508
400–500	−0.1113	0.6605	0.0336	0.8054	0.1734	0.9452
>500	−0.1984	0.5734	0.0050	0.7768	0.1594	0.9312 2.
			2 General/commercial			
0–50	−0.1529	0.6108	−0.0429	0.7208		
>50	−0.2230	0.5407	−0.0982	0.6655		
0–25					0.0365	0.8002
25–100					−0.0061	0.7576
100–1000					−0.0205	0.7432
>1000					−0.0266	0.7371
			3 Low-voltage industrial			
Peak	−0.3151	0.4551	−0.1819	0.5883	0.0094	0.7796
Off–peak	−0.1519	0.6183	−0.0533	0.7169	0.0529	0.8231
			4 High-voltage industrial (32 KV)			
Peak	−0.1943		−0.1018		−0.0305	
Off–peak	−0.0999		−0.0274		−0.0005	
			5 High-voltage industrial (132 KV)			
Peak	−0.1657		−0.0792			
Off–peak	−0.0778		−0.0100			

Source: EEPCO, 1994

electricity increased by at least 28 per cent (commercial and LV industrial). As in the 1994–8 period, the highest increase (56 per cent) was for the domestic sector +500 kWh consumption block. The above figures indicate that the government has significantly increased the tariff rates for all sectors and electricity blocks. This measure is in line with the overall reform programme of the government, which aims to reduce or abolish subsidies.

Deducting the tariff rates from the LRMCs gives estimates of the electricity subsidies per kWh for the different sectors and for various consumption blocks of electricity (Table 6.13). Because of the substantially higher marginal cost of the SCS as compared to the ICS and the unification of the two tariff rates, in all three years all customers from the SCS enjoyed positive amounts of subsidy. In addition, the subsidies to SCS customers are substantially higher than those received by ICS customers. Yet for all electricity consumption blocks and categories of customer, the SCS subsidy per kWh has declined consistently over the years.

Though SCS customers are enjoying a positive – if declining – amount of subsidy per KWh even in 1998, the experience of ICS customers is different. In 1994 only the commercial and HV industrial sectors were paying tariffs higher than the marginal cost. By 1998 all sectors and electricity consumption blocks (with the exception of those in the domestic sector consuming between zero and 100 kWh) were paying tariffs higher than the marginal cost. In other words, with only two exceptions subsidies were negative.

The overall trend captured by the figures in Table 6.13 indicates the following:

1   Subsidies for all sectors as well as electricity consumption blocks have significantly declined or been removed altogether.

2   Customers from the SCS are still substantially subsidized.

3   Except for the lifeline tariff for the domestic sector consuming below 100 kWh, all other sectors and electricity blocks are paying more than the marginal cost.

Table 6.13 shows subsidies per kWh. Total amounts of subsidies have to be computed in order to gain an idea of the overall magnitude. Although complete information on the amounts of electricity consumed per consumption blocks for all sectors is unavailable, data on the number of domestic and commercial customers classified by electricity blocks for the period of August 2000 to July 2001 were used to get estimates of the total amounts of electricity subsidies for the domestic and commercial sectors. The midpoints of the electricity blocks are used as estimates of actual consumption. For instance, 75 kWh is the estimated consumption of each customer in the block between 50 and 100 kWh.[9] Multiplying the mid-points by the subsidies per kWh corresponding to the electricity

Table 6.14 Total subsidies in Birr by electricity blocks and by sector (August 2000–July 2001)

	kWh<50	50–100	100–200	200–300	300–400	400–500	>500	Total
Domestic (ICS)	7418889	2890176	6791557	260180	–731624	–761210	–2143906	13724062
Domestic (SCS)	5761916	3277533	2744160	837648	317754	201873	365990	13506874
Commercial (ICS)	–1627942	–1852928	–3800470	–2854615	–2223603	–1928571	–10467246	–24755375
Commercial (SCS)	713674	645090	851515	427412	287005	234479	969468	4128643
TOTAL	12266537	4959871	6586762	–1329375	–2350468	–2253429	–11275694	6604204

Note: The Birr–US$1 exchange rate was around 8.00 in 2001.
Source: EEPCO, 1994

blocks – given in Table 6.13 – and then by the number of customers in that block gives an estimate of the total subsidy to households in that block. The monthly figures are then converted to annual figures (Table 6.14).

The overall annual electricity subsidy to the domestic and commercial sectors was around Birr 6.6 million. But this overall figure glosses over many variations between the sectors and electricity blocks.

1 The domestic sector gets a subsidy of more than Birr 26 million. Half of the subsidy to the domestic sector is in the self-contained system (SCS), even though the interconnected system (ICS) serves 17 times more customers; the numbers of domestic customers from the ICS and SCS in July 2001 were 497,711 and 29,152 respectively. The heavy subsidy of the SCS is a reflection of the deliberate policy of supporting small town/rural electrification.

2 The commercial sector using ICS pays around Birr 25 million above marginal costs. In addition, commercial customers in all the electricity blocks pay tariffs higher than marginal costs. For instance, commercial customers using less than 50 kWh of electricity pay around Birr 1.6 million above marginal costs.

3 Both domestic and commercial customers for all blocks using electricity from SCS get subsidy, and thus all pay below marginal costs. The total amount of subsidy to the SCS is around Birr 17.6 million.

4 Even though the lifeline tariff for the domestic sector is 100 kWh, customers using as much as 300 kWh are getting subsidy. Customers using between 100 and 300 kWh of electricity get around Birr 7 million in subsidy. This is because of the subsidy they get on the first 100 kWh of electricity.

In addition to the net subsidy coming from the government (amounting to Birr 6.6 million), a lot of cross-subsidization occurs. On one hand, customers from the ICS are subsidizing those using SCS. On the other hand, the commercial and domestic ICS customers using more than 300 kWh are subsidizing the rest. If there was no cross-subsidization, then the total amount of subsidies to be covered by the government would have been Birr 35 million. Since the net subsidy provided by the government is Birr 6.6 million, around 81 per cent of the subsidies in the electricity sector are collected from the sector itself.

Even though the data used do not include the industrial sector, the same pattern is expected to hold. In the first place, the industrial sector using SCS electricity is subsidized, like the other sectors using this source, while industrial ICS customers pay more than the marginal cost (Table 6.13). Second, the trend in the decline of subsidies over time is also observed for the industrial sector between 1994 and 1998.

The existence of cross-subsidization means that the impact of electricity subsidies on public finance is minimal. For example, the estimated revenue of the government in 1998/9 was Birr 9,330 million (IMF, 1999). As a percentage of the total revenue of the government, the net subsidies are a mere 0.07 per cent. Currently, the issue should probably focus on whether cross-subsidization is justifiable or not. But the examination of this issue is beyond the scope of this study.

The next section examines the electricity tariff paid by small and micro-enterprises compared to other sectors.

21

Electricity Tariffs
and Informal Sector Enterprises

Tariff rates for domestic, commercial and low- or high-voltage industrial users vary. This chapter starts by comparing the electricity tariffs for informal sector enterprises with those for other sectors of the economy. In addition, the importance of electricity bills as an element in the total cost of operating small and micro-enterprises is analyzed.

The Central Statistical Authority (CSA) of Ethiopia uses the following criteria to identify informal sector operators:

1   At least one member of the household is engaged in productive activity.

2   Employment status: the owner of the activity is either an employer or self-employed;

3   The establishment/activity is not a corporate type of enterprise.

4   The establishment/activity does not keep a complete book of accounts.

5   The number of persons engaged – if any – is less than 10, including the operator.

6   The establishment/activity is not registered by any licensing authority.

No information on tariff rates that are particularly relevant for informal sector enterprises using electricity is available, and so direct knowledge of whether SMEs get electricity subsidies is unobtainable. As long as they are home-based enterprises, the likely tariff they face is that for the domestic sector. If informal enterprises are consuming more than 100 kWh they are paying more than the marginal cost for the higher consumption above 100 kWh. But since they benefit from the subsidies for the first 100 kWh of electricity, they receive a net subsidy even if their consumption reaches as high as 260 kWh. Even though the objective of maintaining a lifeline tariff is to supply electricity at cheaper rates for lower-income groups, this tariff also subsidizes home-based enterprises using less than 260 kWh.

The informal enterprises not classified under the domestic sector can fall under either the commercial or low-voltage (LV) industrial tariffs. In terms of tariffs per kWh, the highest rates (in equivalent flat rates) for all the three years is commercial, followed by LV industrial (Table 6.12). Tariff levels for HV industrial are the lowest in all the three years.

Table 6.15   Tariff–marginal cost ratios by customer categories and electricity blocks (1994–8)

| | Tariff–marginal cost ratios | | | | | |
| | ICS | | | SCS | | |
	1998	1997	1994	1998	1997	1994
	Domestic					
Equivalent flat rate	1.0513	0.7578	0.4780	0.3411	0.2459	0.1551
0–50	0.7364	0.5689	0.4154	0.2389	0.1846	0.1348
50–100	0.7880	0.6029	0.4316	0.2557	0.1956	0.1400
100–200	1.1041	0.7904	0.4907	0.3582	0.2565	0.1592
200–300	1.2161	0.8538	0.5053	0.3946	0.2770	0.1639
300–400	1.2528	0.8781	0.5171	0.4065	0.2849	0.1678
400–500	1.3002	0.9094	0.5322	0.4219	0.2951	0.1727
>500	1.5352	0.9865	0.5700	0.4981	0.3201	0.1849
	Commercial					
Equivalent flat rate	1.5923	1.2427	1.0555	0.4966	0.3875	0.3292
0–50	1.4418	1.1240		0.4496	0.3505	
>50	1.6443	1.2837		0.5128	0.4003	
	LV industrial					
Equivalent flat rate	1.6131	1.3283	0.8730	0.4452	0.3666	0.2409
Peak	2.0732	1.6196	0.9680	0.5722	0.4470	0.2672
Off–peak	1.5174	1.1815	0.8198	0.4188	0.3261	0.2263
	HV industrial 15 KV					
Equivalent flat rate	1.5052	1.1672	1.0521			
Peak	1.8733	1.4575	1.1371			
Off–peak	1.4490	1.1231	1.0022			
	HV industrial 132 KV					
Equivalent flat rate	1.4018	1.0858				
Peak	1.7447	1.3560				
Off–peak	1.3497	1.0449				

Source: EEPCO, 1994

But the direct comparison of tariff rates for different sectors probably does not tell us much, as the rates may reflect the underlying marginal costs of supplying them. To examine tariff rates in relation to the marginal costs, tariff–marginal cost ratios are given for both for the ICS and SCS in Table 6.15.

Tariff–marginal cost ratios for all three years in SCS are less than one, indicating that customers getting electricity from that type of supply are subsidized. But the ratios consistently increase over the years, indicating that the level of subsidies has been decreasing. In the SCS sector the ratios are highest for the commercial sector, followed by the LV industrial sector.

Subsidies are presumably directed towards consumption rather than production units.

In the case of ICS, all ratios for the equivalent flat rates are higher than one in 1998; the highest ratio is for LV industrial – in 1998 and 1997 – followed by the commercial sector. Indeed in 1994, despite being subsidized, LV industrial had the third-highest ratio. The tariff structure shows clear bias against LV industrial (SMEs). Even when individual tariff rates for particular electricity blocks are considered, the ratios for LV industrial are usually the highest.

The above findings indicate that the electricity subsidy in Ethiopia is aimed at subsidizing consumption rather than production. Since some of the informal sector enterprises are located inside households, it is likely that this policy has also subsidized them as long as their consumption of electricity remains relatively low. But the figures also show that relatively high tariffs (taking marginal costs into account) are found in the low-voltage industrial and commercial sectors. In both sectors, significant numbers of SMEs exist. The figures also indicate that the bias against SMEs has been increasing over time between 1994 and 1998.

The effect of electricity tariffs also depends on the significance of electricity in the overall energy input of SMEs. Enterprises that are heavily dependent on electricity will face a correspondingly higher cost of production due to higher tariff rates.

To demonstrate the importance of electricity tariffs in SME operations, Table 6.16 presents the average monthly value of energy and other costs of informal sector enterprises, categorized by sectors. There is a very wide variation in the energy intensity – ratio of energy cost to total cost – of different sectors in the informal economy. For example, while the construction sector expends only 1.07 per cent of its costs on energy the corresponding figure for manufacturing is 35.29 per cent. Similarly, the importance of electricity in overall costs is also very variable, ranging from 0 per cent for mining and quarrying to 5.96 per cent for manufacturing (Figure 6.1).

The variation in terms of dependence on electricity as a source of energy is also very high. At one extreme one finds the mining and quarrying sector and, at the other, manufacturing: while the mining and quarrying sector does not use *any* electricity, the construction sector depends *only* on electricity as its source of power. Sectors with a heavy dependence on electricity will be hardest hit by the current tariff structure: they include construction, transport, community and personal services, agriculture, forestry, hunting and fishing.

To establish a rough estimate of how much the differential tariff rates have affected costs of production in informal sector enterprises, take the equivalent flat rates for the domestic and commercial sectors in 1994 (since the data for informal sector enterprises are for 1996, the relevant tariffs are those of 1994). The tariff for the domestic sector was 48.51 per cent of that of the commercial sector. Assuming that informal sector

Table 6.16 Estimate of average monthly value (in Birr) of energy expenses of informal sector establishments by industry type, 1996

Sector	Type of energy source		Other expenses	Total
	Electricity	Wood, charcoal & others		
Agriculture, Forestry, Hunting & Fishing	24,429	30,580	2,997,881	3,052,890
Mining & Quarrying		6,861	89,659	96,520
Manufacturing	1,188,892	5,855,677	12,915,292	19,959,861
Construction	7,311		674,330	681,641
Trade, Hotels & Restaurants	555,452	1,299,309	105,805,473	107,660,234
Transport	1,306	995	246,546	248,847
Community & Personal Services	113,797	92,857	1,804,764	2,011,418
TOTAL	1,891,187	7,286,279	124,533,945	133,711,411

Source: CSA, 1996

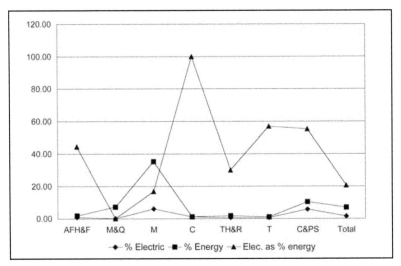

Figure 6.1 Share of electricity and energy from total cost of informal sector monthly expenses

Legend: % Electric = % of electricity cost from total cost; % Energy = % of energy cost from total cost; Elec % energy = % of electricity from energy costs; AFH&F = Agriculture, Forestry, Hunting and Fishing; M&Q = Mining & Quarrying; M = Manufacturing; C = Construction; TH&R = Trade, Hotels and Restaurants; T=Transport; C&PS=Catering and Personal Services
Source: CSA, 1996

enterprises were paying the commercial sector tariff in 1996, the amount they should have paid if the domestic tariff rates were applied can be estimated. This would have saved more than half of their electricity costs. For all informal sector enterprises, the savings would add up to more than Birr 900,000; this is around 7 per cent of total costs for the industry as a whole. Most of the savings – around Birr 577,000 – would have been in the manufacturing sector. The tariff rates that are higher than marginal costs have inflated the costs of producers, particularly those heavily dependent on electricity – like manufacturers.

The above findings imply that the current tariff structure is not favourable to informal sector enterprises.

22

Policy Options

This chapter discusses some policy options related to the findings reported in the previous sections. To begin with the kerosene subsidy, its abolition is probably the advisable policy. In the first place, as the empirical findings showed, leakage to non-poor households is high and the social cost of kerosene subsidy removal is low. In addition, the kerosene subsidy does not play an important role in improving affordability to the poor. Since subsidies for kerosene are raised by higher taxes from other fuels, the abolition of subsidies will have the added advantage of reducing the burden on the consumers of those other fuels.

Poor households are probably capable of accessing non-subsidized electricity if fixed costs are amortized over longer periods, or if credit is provided. Hence, if government gives priority to the dissemination of electricity among the poor it seems advisable to focus on the issue of spreading fixed costs over longer periods of time.

A component part of the fixed cost of electricity that is directly under the control of the government is connection fees, since electricity supply is monopolized by EEPCO, a government-owned utility. Spreading connection fees by incorporating them in electricity bills minimizes the down-payment households have to make to access electricity without increasing the financial burden on the utility, as the full cost is to be recovered. While the risk of customers defaulting on payments is greater – since bills will increase by the amortized amount of connection fees – as long as EEPCO supplies the electricity it will have the means to enforce con-tractual obligations.

In addition to connection fees, the fixed costs of electricity include the purchase of electrical equipment. Directly subsidizing the purchase of electrical equipment by poor households is one policy option. The practical implementation of this option will be difficult as the private sector supplies electrical equipment to households. Alternatively, the government can establish a fund to which poor households can apply when seeking to purchase electrical equipment. It can also enter into an arrangement whereby suppliers are compensated for the sale of their equipment at lower prices to poor households. In addition to creating a strain on government resources, these options are very difficult to put into practice, as they need an efficient targeting system that identifies the poor and avoids corruption. In addition, if poor households can purchase electrical equipment at subsidized prices a secondary market could develop where the poor sell on the equipment at a higher market value.

The government can also use tax or similar incentives for private sector suppliers of equipment either to extend credit or spread fixed costs. But the administration and monitoring of these operations is probably difficult.

Other innovative arrangements by the government and NGOs should also be tried. In most government- and NGO-sponsored welfare programmes, energy is not considered as a priority in the livelihood of the poor. Integrating energy as an essential element of the livelihood of the poor can be helpful, as when targeted micro-credit programmes are directed towards covering the fixed costs of electricity.

In the long run, falling prices of electricity and electrical equipment are the best guarantee of making them accessible to all segments of the population. Improvements in efficiency and higher levels of competition in electric generation and distribution, as well as in the marketing of electrical equipment, are required. Improvements in efficiency reduce marginal costs, and as long as the pricing principle of equating marginal cost with marginal revenues is maintained in the sector, this pulls electricity tariffs down. EEPCO's monopoly in generation and distribution of electricity may have to be terminated in the interests of increasing competition. A regulatory institutional framework that maintains competitive conditions in the electricity sector will also be required.

The empirical findings show that non-poor households capture most of the kerosene subsidies. And in the above discussion the abolition of kerosene subsidies is suggested as a preferred policy option. Can other, more efficient forms of targeting be used? For instance, giving out kerosene coupons to poor/targeted households is one option. This is administratively demanding. First, identifying the poor is usually difficult. Mistakes of inclusion (including the non-poor) and exclusion (excluding the poor) occur. Second, the administrative cost of identification and the distribution of coupons can be large. Third, there is potential for corruption. Finally, we have seen that a second market for coupons can develop.

For customers of electricity from the ICS, all tariff rates are higher than marginal costs except for consumption levels of up to 100 kWh for the domestic sector. This means, in effect, that the government has abolished all electricity subsidies except for the lifeline tariff. The lifeline seems to be set at too high a level (100 kWh). For example, of the total number of domestic customers in the month of August 2001, 74 per cent were consuming less than the lifeline tariff (EEPCO). In other words, the lifeline tariff was subsidizing 74 per cent of the customers. The empirical findings also indicate that non-poor households consume most of the electricity in urban areas. Hence, most of the 74 per cent of customers that are subsidized by the lifeline tariff are non-targeted groups. This leakage to non-targeted groups can be minimized by reducing the lifeline tariff to a level that realistically approximates the consumption level of poor households.

A related problem is that households consuming more than the lifeline tariff will enjoy the subsidy for the first 100 kWh they use. For example, those households that consume as much as 262 kWh are subsidized.[10] Even though they pay tariff rates higher than the marginal cost when their consumption exceeds 100 kWh, the subsidy they get on the first 100 kWh compensates for that. This is another form of leakage to non-targeted groups. In addition to reducing the level of the lifeline tariff, it is necessary to redesign it to pinpoint the target group. A variable tariff rate can help to do that. All households consuming more than the lifeline threshold can be made to pay a higher tariff even for the first units of electricity within the lifeline range. To avoid sudden jumps in payment for those who are consuming just above the lifeline threshold, a smoothing procedure that slowly increases the rate at the threshold can be introduced.

The current revisions in the tariff rates in Ethiopia have substantially reduced electricity subsidies. Overall the burden on public finance due to electricity subsidy is very small. But this is achieved through substantial cross-subsidization within the electricity sector. First, customers using the ICS in general subsidize those using the SCS. Second, mainly commercial and productive sectors subsidize domestic customers using less than 200 kWh.

The government's objective of promoting the welfare of people in small towns and rural areas is probably the main reason for the subsidization of customers from the SCS. Whether their subsidization at the expense of ICS customers, particularly commercial and industrial, is justifiable is an issue that needs to be discussed. Some of the issues are: Should customers from the SCS be subsidized at all? If there is a need for subsidy, should the commercial and industrial sectors in the ICS pay for it? Or should the government look for an alternative source? The social costs and benefits of each should be analyzed.

Similarly, the advisability of cross-subsidizing domestic consumers at the expense of commercial and productive ones should be re-examined. This seems to be a reflection of the overall feature of government policy that emphasizes the welfare – rather than the productive – aspects of poverty reduction. Lifeline tariffs are supposed to improve the welfare of poor households directly rather than indirectly increasing it by maximizing growth in the economy. Commercial and productive sectors are made to pay tariff rates greater than marginal costs. Revising rates towards eliminating the excess of tariff over marginal costs seems necessary. Since tariff rates are biased against the commercial and industrial sectors, changes to correct these biases seem advisable. This could reduce energy costs substantially, particularly for those heavily dependent on electricity.

Finally, there is a need to re-examine the method used to determine the LRMC of electricity. The current practice probably inflates the LRMC since actual costs of utilities are considered. Possible inefficiencies in electricity production and distribution mean that actual costs are expected to be higher than efficiency costs. The computation of LRMC must be based on best practice.

The main policy recommendations can be summarized in the following list:

- Abolish kerosene subsidies.

- EEPCO should spread out connection fees over electricity bills.

- Encourage innovative ways of integrating energy programmes into welfare programmes.

- Reduce the ceiling for the lifeline tariff.

- Implement a variable tariff rate for the lifeline tariff.

- Re-examine the advisability of subsidizing customers of the SCS as compared to those of the ICS.

- Eliminate the bias against commercial and productive electricity customers.

- Change the method of determining LRMC to one based on best practice.

Part 6 • Notes and References

Notes

1 Current amounts of subsidies are probably lower after structural adjustment programmes in the developing countries in the 1990s.
2 This is mainly drawn from Kebede *et al.* (2001) and Kebede *et al.* (2002).
3 Since most firewood used as fuel is in the form of leaves and twigs this may not directly lead to the felling of trees as in the case of other end uses (construction, furniture, etcetera). And if the firewood is supplied from well-managed sources its use may not necessarily lead to deforestation.
4 *Injera* is a pancake-like food prepared from cereals.
5 *Mtad* is a clay utensil used to bake *injera*.
6 *Biretmtad* is a large metal pan used to roast cereals. *Mekuya* is a smller pan usually used to roast coffee. *Etanmachesha* is an incense burner.
7 After 1996 the government commenced a staged reduction of the subsidy on kerosene and electricity.
8 Like the regressions on the aggregate level, most of the coefficients on household size are not significant.
9 In the case of the highest electricity block (>500 kWh), since we do not have a maximum value, 550 kWh is taken as the average.
10 Using the figures given in Table 6.13, the amount of total subsidy captured by households consuming certain quantities of electricity can be computed. A household using just 100 kWh gets a subsidy of Birr 8.82 ((50*0.0977) + (50*0.0786)). The next 100kWh reduces total subsidy to Birr 4.96; the tariff rate is 3.86 more than marginal cost in this range. To reduce this subsidy to zero, the household must use an additional 62 kWh of electricity from the next block (200–300 kWh) (4.96/0.0801 = 61.9). This means households consuming as much as 262 kWh still get a net subsidy as a result of the lifeline tariff.

References

AFREPREN/FWD, 2003. *African Energy Data Handbook*, Nairobi: AFRE-PREN/FWD.
Addis Tribune, 1998. 'NBE Reduced Minimum Deposit Interest Rate and Frees Lending Rates', 16 January 1998, Addis Ababa.
CSA, 1996. *Urban Informal Sector Sample Survey*. Addis Ababa: Central Statistical Authority.

——, 1997. Report on Monthly and Annual Average Retail Prices of Goods and Services by Urban Centres, Addis Ababa: CSA.

——, 1998. Revised Report on the 1995/6 Household Income, Consumption and Expenditure Survey, Addis Ababa: CSA.

Deaton, A., 1997. *The Analysis of Household Surveys: a Micro-econometric Approach to Development Policy*, Baltimore and London: Johns Hopkins University Press, for World Bank.

EEPCO, 1994. Tariff Structure, 1952–90 EFY (1960–98 GC), mimeograph, Addis Ababa: Ethiopian Electric Power Corporation.

Goldemberg, J. and T. B. Johansson, 1995. 'Overview: Energy as an Instrument for Socio-Economic Development', in J. Goldemberg and T. B. Johansson (eds.), *Energy as an Instrument for Socio-Economic Development*, New York: United Nations Development Programme.

Hosier, R. H. and W. Kipondya, 1993. 'Urban Household Energy Use in Tanzania: Prices, Substitutes and Poverty', *Energy Policy*, 21, 5, May, Oxford: Elsevier Science Ltd.

IMF, 1999. *Ethiopia: Recent Economic Development*. Washington, DC: International Monetary Fund.

Kebede, B., 2003. 'Country Data Validation: Ethiopia', unpublished, Nairobi: AFREPREN/FWD.

Kebede, B., B. Almaz and K. Elias, 2001. 'Affordability of Modern Fuels and Patterns of Energy Demand in Urban Ethiopia', final report for the 'Energy for the Urban Poor' Theme Group, Nairobi: AFREPREN/FWD.

——, 2002. 'Can the Urban Poor Afford Modern Energy? The Case of Ethiopia', *Energy Policy*, 30, 11–12, Oxford: Elsevier Science Ltd.

Mulenga, S. B. 2000. 'The Demand for Wood Fuel and Substitution Possibilities in Urban Zambia', in *Opportunities for Africa: Micro-evidence from Households and Firms*, Oxford: Centre for the Study of African Economies (CSAE).

Phelan, J. (ed.), 2003. *African Review Journal*, 39, 8, London: Alain Charles Publishing Ltd.

Tadesse, H., 1996. 'Petroleum Products Pricing: the Case of Ethiopia', project submitted to the College of Petroleum and Energy Studies (CPES), Oxford University.

Teferra, M., 2003. 'Country Data Validation: Ethiopia', unpublished, Nairobi: AFREPREN.

UNDP, 2003. *Human Development Report, 2003*, Oxford and New York: United Nations Development Programme.

Wolde-Ghiorgis, W., 2003. 'Country Data Validation: Ethiopia', unpublished, Nairobi: AFREPREN.

World Bank, 2000. *Entering the 21ˢᵗ Century: World Development Report 1999/2000*, Washington, DC: World Bank.

——, 2003a. *African Development Indicators 2003*, Washington, DC: World Bank.

——, 2003b. *World Development Indicators 2003*, Washington, DC: World Bank.

Appendix 6.1 Cost of kerosene use with and without subsidy and mean energy expenditures of households by urban areas

Cost of using kerosene with subsidy by urban areas

Item		Mekele	Bahir Dar	Dessie	Gondar	Debre Zeit	Jimma	Nazret	Harar	Addis Ababa	Dire Dawa	Other towns
Kerosene + stove	Cost A	560.61	352.09	420.49	563.46	279.55	342.89	366.28	382.86	490.23	334.79	376.29
Kero. + stove + lamp	Cost B	586.58	376.33	444.43	593.00	319.66	359.42	389.95	417.05	512.98	361.06	402.13
Fuel & power 1 (all)	Fuel 1	718.06	475.53	552.77	526.63	441.99	495.05	473.41	496.28	633.86	468.25	487.46
Fuel & power 2 (all)	Fuel 2	731.63	481.13	552.77	526.63	487.35	498.25	514.71	503.75	707.61	469.85	490.59
Fuel & power 3 (all)	Fuel 3	829.19	521.56	573.68	539.24	531.11	610.13	564.91	565.12	790.05	506.58	546.97
Cost A/Fuel 1		0.78	0.74	0.76	1.07	0.63	0.69	0.77	0.77	0.77	0.71	0.77
Cost A/Fuel 2		0.77	0.73	0.76	1.07	0.57	0.69	0.71	0.76	0.69	0.71	0.77
Cost A/Fuel 3		0.68	0.68	0.73	1.04	0.53	0.56	0.65	0.68	0.62	0.66	0.69
Cost B/Fuel 1		0.82	0.79	0.80	1.13	0.72	0.73	0.82	0.84	0.81	0.77	0.82
Cost B/Fuel 2		0.80	0.78	0.80	1.13	0.66	0.72	0.76	0.83	0.72	0.77	0.82
Cost B/Fuel 3		0.71	0.72	0.77	1.10	0.60	0.59	0.69	0.74	0.65	0.71	0.74

Cost of using kerosene without subsidy by urban areas

Item		Mekele	Bahir Dar	Dessie	Gondar	Debre Zeit	Jimma	Nazret	Harar	Addis Ababa	Dire Dawa	Other towns
Kerosene + stove	Cost A	643.11	415.59	486.47	655.82	328.18	406.13	423.29	441.77	591.60	391.56	435.07
Kero. + stove + lamp	Cost B	669.08	439.83	510.41	685.36	368.29	422.66	446.96	475.96	614.35	417.83	460.91
Cost A/Fuel 1		0.90	0.87	0.88	1.25	0.74	0.82	0.89	0.89	0.93	0.84	0.89
Cost A/Fuel 2		0.88	0.86	0.88	1.25	0.67	0.82	0.82	0.88	0.84	0.83	0.89
Cost A/Fuel 3		0.78	0.80	0.85	1.22	0.62	0.67	0.75	0.78	0.75	0.77	0.80
Cost B/Fuel 1		0.93	0.92	0.92	1.30	0.83	0.85	0.94	0.96	0.97	0.89	0.95
Cost B/Fuel 2		0.91	0.91	0.92	1.30	0.76	0.85	0.87	0.94	0.87	0.89	0.94
Cost B/Fuel 3		0.81	0.84	0.89	1.27	0.69	0.69	0.79	0.84	0.78	0.82	0.84

Source: Author's survey

Appendix 6.2 Cost of kerosene use with and without subsidy and mean energy expenditures by *per capita* expenditure deciles

Cost of using kerosene with subsidy by expenditure deciles

		Poorest	2.00	3.00	4.00	5.00	6.00	7.00	8.00	9.00	Richest
Kerosene + stove	Cost A	259.34	342.22	353.68	394.11	434.39	459.59	510.13	519.41	558.67	650.11
Kerosene + stove + lamp	Cost B	285.18	368.06	379.52	419.95	460.23	485.43	535.97	545.25	584.51	675.95
Fuel & power 1	Fuel 1	292.18	386.48	432.96	472.13	530.87	560.45	599.18	643.37	687.34	724.71
Fuel & power 2	Fuel 2	292.18	386.48	435.07	472.13	533.31	564.16	604.05	664.73	757.66	863.13
Fuel & power 3	Fuel 3	302.12	403.76	453.38	506.64	565.64	601.01	667.72	738.47	849.96	1082.03
Cost A/Fuel 1		0.89	0.89	0.82	0.83	0.82	0.82	0.85	0.81	0.81	0.90
Cost A/Fuel 2		0.89	0.89	0.81	0.83	0.81	0.81	0.84	0.78	0.74	0.75
Cost A/Fuel 3		0.86	0.85	0.78	0.78	0.77	0.76	0.76	0.70	0.66	0.60
Cost B/Fuel 1		0.98	0.95	0.88	0.89	0.87	0.87	0.89	0.85	0.85	0.93
Cost B/Fuel 2		0.98	0.95	0.87	0.89	0.86	0.86	0.89	0.82	0.77	0.78
Cost B/Fuel 3		0.94	0.91	0.84	0.83	0.81	0.81	0.80	0.74	0.69	0.62

Cost of using kerosene without subsidy by expenditure deciles

		Poorest	2.00	3.00	4.00	5.00	6.00	7.00	8.00	9.00	Richest
Kerosene + stove	Cost A	297.60	395.02	408.49	456.01	503.36	532.98	592.38	603.30	649.45	756.92
Kerosene + stove + lamp	Cost B	323.44	420.86	434.33	481.85	529.20	558.82	618.22	629.14	675.29	782.76
Cost A/Fuel 1		1.02	1.02	0.94	0.97	0.95	0.95	0.99	0.94	0.94	1.04
Cost A/Fuel 2		1.02	1.02	0.94	0.97	0.94	0.94	0.98	0.91	0.86	0.88
Cost A/Fuel 3		0.99	0.98	0.90	0.90	0.89	0.89	0.89	0.82	0.76	0.70
Cost B/Fuel 1		1.11	1.09	1.00	1.02	1.00	1.00	1.03	0.98	0.98	1.08
Cost B/Fuel 2		1.11	1.09	1.00	1.02	0.99	0.99	1.02	0.95	0.89	0.91
Cost B/Fuel 3		1.07	1.04	0.96	0.95	0.94	0.93	0.93	0.85	0.79	0.72

Source: Author's survey

Appendix 6.3 Costs of electricity use with and without subsidy and mean energy expenditures of households by urban areas

Item	Cost	Mekele	Bahir Dar	Dessie	Gondar	Debre Zeit	Jimma	Nazret	Harar	Addis Ababa	Dire Dawa	Other towns
Costs with subsidy												
With mtad, stove and pole	A	2,266.18	2,044.31	2,248.51	2,360.01	2,167.36	2,261.88	2,148.73	2,289.20	2,571.87	2,450.44	2,305.55
With mtad and pole	B	1,699.43	1,884.31	1,681.76	1,793.26	1,600.61	1,695.13	1,581.98	1,722.45	2,005.12	1,748.11	1,738.80
With stove and pole	C	1,873.91	1,594.93	1,847.64	1,898.07	1,784.86	1,836.88	1,797.06	1,812.84	1,989.06	1,940.02	1,853.21
Without mtad and stove, but with pole	D	1,873.91	1,594.93	1,847.64	1,898.07	1,784.86	1,836.88	1,797.06	1,812.84	1,989.06	1,940.02	1,853.21
With mtad and stove, but without pole	E	1,897.18	1,675.31	1,879.51	1,991.01	1,798.36	1,892.88	1,779.73	1,920.20	2,202.87	2,081.44	1,936.55
With mtad, without pole	F	1,330.43	1,515.31	1,312.76	1,424.26	1,231.61	1,326.13	1,212.98	1,353.45	1,636.12	1,379.11	1,369.80
With stove, without pole	G	1,504.91	1,225.93	1,478.64	1,529.07	1,415.86	1,467.88	1,428.06	1,443.84	1,620.06	1,571.02	1,484.21
Without mtad, stove and pole	H	938.16	1,065.93	911.89	962.32	849.11	901.13	861.31	877.09	1,053.31	868.69	917.46
Costs without subsidy												
With mtad, stove and pole	A	2,532.40	2,074.17	2,441.22	2,658.03	2,324.22	2,456.26	2,341.41	2,488.33	2,836.85	2,642.32	2,459.20
With mtad and pole	B	1,965.65	1,914.17	1,874.47	2,091.28	1,757.47	1,889.51	1,774.66	1,921.58	2,270.10	1,939.99	1,892.45
With stove and pole	C	2,140.13	1,624.79	2,040.35	2,196.09	1,941.72	2,031.26	1,989.74	2,011.97	2,254.04	2,131.90	2,006.86
Without mtad and stove, but with pole	D	1,573.38	1,464.79	1,473.60	1,629.34	1,374.97	1,464.51	1,422.99	1,445.22	1,687.29	1,429.57	1,440.11
With mtad and stove, but without pole	E	2,163.40	1,705.17	2,072.22	2,289.03	1,955.22	2,087.26	1,972.41	2,119.33	2,467.85	2,273.32	2,090.20
With mtad without pole	F	1,596.65	1,545.17	1,505.47	1,722.28	1,388.47	1,520.51	1,405.66	1,552.58	1,901.10	1,570.99	1,523.45
With stove without pole	G	1,771.13	1,255.79	1,671.35	1,827.09	1,572.72	1,662.26	1,620.74	1,642.97	1,885.04	1,762.90	1,637.86
Without mtad, stove and pole	H	1,204.38	1,095.79	1,104.60	1,260.34	1,005.97	1,095.51	1,053.99	1,076.22	1,318.29	1,060.57	1,071.11
Fuel & power 1 (all)	1	718.06	475.53	552.77	526.63	441.99	495.05	473.41	496.28	633.86	468.25	487.46
Fuel & power 2 (all)	2	731.63	481.13	552.77	526.63	487.35	498.25	514.71	503.75	707.61	469.85	490.59
Fuel & power 3 (all)	3	829.19	521.56	573.68	539.24	531.11	610.13	564.91	565.12	790.05	506.58	546.97
Cost A/Fuel 1 (with subsidy)		3.16	4.30	4.07	4.48	4.90	4.57	4.54	4.61	4.06	5.23	4.73
Cost H/Fuel 3 (with subsidy)		1.13	2.04	1.59	1.78	1.60	1.48	1.52	1.55	1.33	1.71	1.68
Cost A/Fuel 1 (without subsidy)		3.53	4.36	4.42	5.05	5.26	4.96	4.95	5.01	4.48	5.64	5.04
Cost H/Fuel 3 (without subsidy)		1.45	2.10	1.93	2.34	1.89	1.80	1.87	1.90	1.67	2.09	1.96

Source: Author's survey

Appendix 6.4 Costs of electricity with and without subsidy and energy expenditures of *per capita* expenditure deciles

		Poorest	2	3	4	5	6	7	8	9	Richest
Costs with subsidy											
With *mtad*, stove and pole	Cost A	2,242.71	2,287.24	2,293.41	2,315.13	2,336.78	2,350.32	2,377.47	2,382.47	2,403.56	2,452.70
With *mtad* and pole	Cost B	1,675.96	1,720.49	1,726.66	1,748.38	1,770.03	1,783.57	1,810.72	1,815.72	1,836.81	1,885.95
With stove and pole	Cost C	1,790.37	1,834.90	1,841.07	1,862.79	1,884.44	1,897.98	1,925.13	1,930.13	1,951.22	2,000.36
Without *mtad* & stove, but with pole	Cost D	1,223.62	1,268.15	1,274.32	1,296.04	1,317.69	1,331.23	1,358.38	1,363.38	1,384.47	1,433.61
With *mtad* & stove, but without pole	Cost E	1,873.71	1,918.24	1,924.41	1,946.13	1,967.78	1,981.32	2,008.47	2,013.47	2,034.56	2,083.70
With *mtad*, without pole	Cost F	1,306.96	1,351.49	1,357.66	1,379.38	1,401.03	1,414.57	1,441.72	1,446.72	1,467.81	1,516.95
With stove, without pole	Cost G	1,421.37	1,465.90	1,472.07	1,493.79	1,515.44	1,528.98	1,556.13	1,561.13	1,582.22	1,631.36
Without *mtad*, stove and pole	Cost H	854.62	899.15	905.32	927.04	948.69	962.23	989.38	994.38	1,015.47	1,064.61
Costs without subsidy											
With *mtad*, stove and pole	Cost A	2,342.72	2,425.27	2,436.69	2,476.96	2,517.08	2,542.18	2,592.50	2,601.77	2,640.87	2,731.93
With *mtad* and pole	Cost B	1,775.97	1,858.52	1,869.94	1,910.21	1,950.33	1,975.43	2,025.75	2,035.02	2,074.12	2,165.18
With stove and pole	Cost C	1,890.38	1,972.93	1,984.35	2,024.62	2,064.74	2,089.84	2,140.16	2,149.43	2,188.53	2,279.59
Without *mtad* & stove, but with pole	Cost D	1,323.63	1,406.18	1,417.60	1,457.87	1,497.99	1,523.09	1,573.41	1,582.68	1,621.78	1,712.84
With *mtad* & stove, but without pole	Cost E	1,973.72	2,056.27	2,067.69	2,107.96	2,148.08	2,173.18	2,223.50	2,232.77	2,271.87	2,362.93
With *mtad*, without pole	Cost F	1,406.97	1,489.52	1,500.94	1,541.21	1,581.33	1,606.43	1,656.75	1,666.02	1,705.12	1,796.18
With stove, without pole	Cost G	1,521.38	1,603.93	1,615.35	1,655.62	1,695.74	1,720.84	1,771.16	1,780.43	1,819.53	1,910.59
Without *mtad*, stove and pole	Cost H	954.63	1,037.18	1,048.60	1,088.87	1,128.99	1,154.09	1,204.41	1,213.68	1,252.78	1,343.84
Fuel & power 1	Fuel 1	292.18	386.48	432.96	472.13	530.87	560.45	599.18	643.37	687.34	724.71
Fuel & power 2	Fuel 2	292.18	386.48	435.07	472.13	533.31	564.16	604.05	664.73	757.66	863.13
Fuel & power 3	Fuel 3	302.12	403.76	453.38	506.64	565.64	601.01	667.72	738.47	849.96	1082.03
Cost A/Fuel 1 (with subsidy)		7.68	5.92	5.30	4.90	4.40	4.19	3.97	3.70	3.50	3.38
Cost H/Fuel 3 (with subsidy)		2.83	2.23	2.00	1.83	1.68	1.60	1.48	1.35	1.19	0.98
Cost A/Fuel 1 (without subsidy)		8.02	6.28	5.63	5.25	4.74	4.54	4.33	4.04	3.84	3.77
Cost H/Fuel 3 (without subsidy)		3.16	2.57	2.31	2.15	2.00	1.92	1.80	1.64	1.47	1.24

Appendix 6.5 Present value of costs of electricity and energy expenditure of poor households with and without subsidy (6% interest rate)

Items in current value	Year 1	Year 2	Year 3	Year 4	Year 5	Year 6	Year 7	Year 8	Year 9	Year 10
Electricity bill (with subsidy)	118.472	118.472	118.472	118.472	118.472	118.472	118.472	118.472	118.472	118.472
12 electric bulbs	37.44	37.44	37.44	37.44	37.44	37.44	37.44	37.44	37.44	37.44
Connection fee (30 m) including pole	106.90	106.90	106.90	106.90	106.90	106.90	106.90	106.90	106.90	106.90
Connection fee (30 m) excluding pole	70.00	70.00	70.00	70.00	70.00	70.00	70.00	70.00	70.00	70.00
Electric mtad (aluminium)	45.23	45.23	45.23	45.23	45.23	45.23	45.23	45.23	45.23	45.23
Electric 3-plate stove (Ariston)	56.68	56.68	56.68	56.68	56.68	56.68	56.68	56.68	56.68	56.68
Fuel 1 (poor)	292.19	292.19	292.19	292.19	292.19	292.19	292.19	292.19	292.19	292.19
Fuel 2 (poor)	292.19	292.19	292.19	292.19	292.19	292.19	292.19	292.19	292.19	292.19
Fuel 3 (poor)	303.29	303.29	303.29	303.29	303.29	303.29	303.29	303.29	303.29	303.29
Electricity bill (without subsidy)	219.59	219.59	219.59	219.59	219.59	219.59	219.59	219.59	219.59	219.59

Items in present value ($r=0.06$)	Year 1	Year 2	Year 3	Year 4	Year 5	Year 6	Year 7	Year 8	Year 9	Year 10	Total
Electricity bill (with subsidy)	118.47	111.77	105.44	99.47	93.84	88.53	83.52	78.79	74.33	70.12	924.28
12 electric bulbs	37.44	35.32	33.32	31.44	29.66	27.98	26.39	24.90	23.49	22.16	292.10
Connection fee (30 m) including pole	106.90	100.85	95.14	89.76	84.67	79.88	75.36	71.09	67.07	63.27	833.99
Connection fee (30 m) excluding pole	70.00	66.04	62.30	58.77	55.45	52.31	49.35	46.55	43.92	41.43	546.12
Electric mtad (aluminium)	45.23	42.67	40.26	37.98	35.83	33.80	31.89	30.08	28.38	26.77	352.89
Electric 3-plate stove (Ariston)	56.68	53.47	50.44	47.59	44.89	42.35	39.95	37.69	35.56	33.55	442.17
Fuel 1 (poor)	292.19	275.65	260.05	245.33	231.44	218.34	205.98	194.32	183.32	172.95	2279.57
Fuel 2 (poor)	292.19	275.65	260.05	245.33	231.44	218.34	205.98	194.32	183.32	172.95	2279.57
Fuel 3 (poor)	303.29	286.12	269.93	254.65	240.23	226.64	213.81	201.71	190.29	179.52	2366.19
Present value of Cost A (with subsidy)	364.72	344.08	324.60	306.23	288.89	272.54	257.11	242.56	228.83	215.88	2845.44
Present value of Cost H (with subsidy)	225.91	213.12	201.06	189.68	178.94	168.81	159.26	150.24	141.74	133.72	1762.48
Electricity bill (without subsidy)	219.59	207.16	195.43	184.37	173.93	164.09	154.80	146.04	137.77	129.97	1713.15
Present value of Cost A (without subsidy)	465.84	439.47	414.59	391.13	368.99	348.10	328.40	309.81	292.27	275.73	3634.33
Present value of Cost H (without subsidy)	327.03	308.52	291.05	274.58	259.04	244.37	230.54	217.49	205.18	193.57	2551.37

Source: Author's survey

Appendix 6.6 Current and discounted present values of electricity costs with and without subsidy and energy expenditures, by per capita expenditure deciles (6% interest rate)

	Poorest	2.00	3.00	4.00	5.00	6.00	7.00	8.00	9.00	Richest
Current energy expenditure for per capita expenditure deciles										
Fuel 1	292.18	386.48	432.96	472.13	530.87	560.45	599.18	643.37	687.34	724.71
Fuel 2	292.18	386.48	435.07	472.13	533.31	564.16	604.05	664.73	757.66	863.13
Fuel 3	302.12	403.76	453.38	506.64	565.64	601.01	667.72	738.47	849.96	1082.03
Energy expenditure in present value (10 yrs)										
Fuel 1	2279.50	3015.20	3377.82	3683.41	4141.68	4372.46	4674.62	5019.37	5362.42	5653.96
Fuel 2	2279.50	3015.20	3394.28	3683.41	4160.72	4401.40	4712.61	5186.02	5911.03	6733.87
Fuel 3	2357.05	3150.01	3537.13	3952.65	4412.95	4688.90	5209.35	5761.32	6631.13	8441.67
Present value of Cost A (with subsidy)	2360.33	2465.45	2480.00	2531.28	2582.37	2614.33	2678.42	2690.22	2740.01	2855.98
Present value of Cost H (with subsidy)	1185.73	1290.85	1305.40	1356.68	1407.78	1439.74	1503.82	1515.62	1565.41	1681.38
Present value of Cost A (without subsidy)	2595.42	2789.90	2816.81	2911.68	3006.20	3065.33	3183.89	3205.71	3297.82	3512.36
Present value of Cost H (without subsidy)	1420.82	1615.30	1642.21	1737.08	1831.60	1890.73	2009.29	2031.12	2123.23	2337.77
Cost A/Fuel 1 (with subsidy)	1.04	0.82	0.73	0.69	0.62	0.60	0.57	0.54	0.51	0.51
Cost H/Fuel 1 (with subsidy)	0.52	0.43	0.39	0.37	0.34	0.33	0.32	0.30	0.29	0.30
Cost A/Fuel 1 (without subsidy)	1.14	0.93	0.83	0.79	0.73	0.70	0.68	0.64	0.61	0.62
Cost H/Fuel 1 (without subsidy)	0.62	0.54	0.49	0.47	0.44	0.43	0.43	0.40	0.40	0.41
Cost A/Fuel 3 (with subsidy)	1.00	0.78	0.70	0.64	0.59	0.56	0.51	0.47	0.41	0.34
Cost H/Fuel 3 (with subsidy)	0.50	0.41	0.37	0.34	0.32	0.31	0.29	0.26	0.24	0.20
Cost A/Fuel 3 (without subsidy)	1.10	0.89	0.80	0.74	0.68	0.65	0.61	0.56	0.50	0.42
Cost H/Fuel 3 (without subsidy)	0.60	0.51	0.46	0.44	0.42	0.40	0.39	0.35	0.32	0.28

Source: Author's survey

Appendix 6.7 Current and discounted present values of electricity costs with and without subsidy and energy expenditures of poor households (average for all towns; 6% interest rate; 2% inflation; 5% income growth)

Items in current value	Year 1	Year 2	Year 3	Year 4	Year 5	Year 6	Year 7	Year 8	Year 9	Year 10	Total
Electricity bill (with subsidy)	118.47	120.84	123.26	125.72	128.24	130.80	133.42	136.09	138.81	141.59	1297.24
12 electric bulbs	37.44	38.19	38.95	39.73	40.53	41.34	42.16	43.01	43.87	44.74	409.96
Connection fee (30 m) including pole	106.90	109.04	111.22	113.44	115.71	118.03	120.39	122.79	125.25	127.76	1170.53
Connection fee (30 m) excluding pole	70.00	71.40	72.83	74.28	75.77	77.29	78.83	80.41	82.02	83.66	766.49
Electric mtad (aluminium)	45.23	46.14	47.06	48.00	48.96	49.94	50.94	51.96	53.00	54.06	495.30
Electric 3-plate stove (Ariston)	56.68	57.81	58.96	60.14	61.35	62.57	63.83	65.10	66.40	67.73	620.57
Fuel 1	292.189	306.80	322.14	338.25	355.16	372.92	391.56	411.14	431.70	453.28	3675.14
Fuel 2	292.189	306.80	322.14	338.25	355.16	372.92	391.56	411.14	431.70	453.28	3675.14
Fuel 3	303.288	318.45	334.38	351.09	368.65	387.08	406.44	426.76	448.09	470.50	3814.73
Electricity bill (without subsidy)	219.59	223.98	228.46	233.03	237.69	242.44	247.29	252.24	257.28	262.43	2404.43
Items in present value (r=0.6)	Year 1	Year 2	Year 3	Year 4	Year 5	Year 6	Year 7	Year 8	Year 9	Year 10	Total
Electricity bill (with subsidy)	118.47	114.00	109.70	105.56	101.58	97.74	94.05	90.51	87.09	83.80	1002.50
12 electric bulbs	37.44	36.03	34.67	33.36	32.10	30.89	29.72	28.60	27.52	26.48	316.81
Connection fee (30 m) including pole	106.90	102.87	98.98	95.25	91.65	88.20	84.87	81.67	78.58	75.62	904.59
Connection fee (30 m) excluding pole	70.00	67.36	64.82	62.37	60.02	57.75	55.57	53.48	51.46	49.52	592.35
Electric mtad (aluminium)	45.23	43.53	41.88	40.30	38.78	37.32	35.91	34.56	33.25	32.00	382.76
Electric 3-plate stove (Ariston)	56.68	54.54	52.48	50.50	48.59	46.76	44.99	43.30	41.66	40.09	479.59
Fuel 1	292.19	289.43	286.70	284.00	281.32	278.66	276.04	273.43	270.85	268.30	2800.92
Fuel 2	292.19	289.43	286.70	284.00	281.32	278.66	276.04	273.43	270.85	268.30	2800.92
Fuel 3	303.29	300.43	297.59	294.79	292.00	289.25	286.52	283.82	281.14	278.49	2907.32
Present value of Cost A (with subsidy)	364.72	350.96	337.71	324.97	312.71	300.91	289.55	278.63	268.11	257.99	3086.26
Present value of Cost H (with subsidy)	225.91	217.39	209.18	201.29	193.69	186.38	179.35	172.58	166.07	159.80	1911.64
Electricity bill (without subsidy)	219.59	211.30	203.33	195.66	188.27	73.04	174.33	167.75	161.42	49.60	1644.29
Present value of Cost A (without subsidy)	465.84	448.26	431.34	415.07	399.40	276.20	369.83	355.87	342.44	223.79	3728.04
Present value of Cost H (without subsidy)	327.03	314.69	302.81	291.39	280.39	161.68	259.63	249.83	240.40	125.60	2553.45

Source: Author's survey

Appendix 6.8 Selected time series data – Ethiopia

Year	1992	1993	1994	1995	1996	1997	1998	1999	2000	2001
National population (millions)	50.20	51.60	53.10	54.60	56.40	58.10	59.90	61.70	63.50	65.40
National population growth rate (%)	-2.5	-2.7	3.0	2.9	3.0	2.7	2.5	2.4	2.4	2.3
Urban population (millions)	7.0	7.2	7.3	7.5	8.0	8.4	8.8	9.2	9.5	9.9
GDP (US$ millions)	5,197	5,300	4,545	5,800	6,400	5,875	6,028	7,067	7,451	7,933
GNP per capita (US$)	110	120	110	110	110	110	115	100	100	100
Total modern energy consumption ('000 toe)	590	730	850	950	1,020	1,090	1,150	1,150	1,200	1,265
Modern energy consumption per capita (kgoe)	10.8	13.7	15.5	16.8	17.5	18.2	18.8	18.3	19.1	19.3
Modern energy production ('000 toe)	680	850	970	1,090	1,170	1,150	1,190	1,210	1,310	1,320
National debt (US$ millions)	9,341	9,703	10,067	10,310	10,077	10,079	10,352	5,544	5,481	5,697
Merchandise exports, f.o.b (US$ millions)	154	222	280	454	412	599	602	485	486	441
Installed capacity (MW)	381	384	390	417	417	417	417	424	424	493
Electricity generation (GWh)	1,147	1,278	1,389	1,470	1,554	1,604	1,610	1,650	1,722	1,812
Total electricity consumption (Gwh)	853.4	835.9	903.2	973.0	1,017.6	1,095.8	1,157.3	1,177.9	1,212.2	1,122.3
Electricity consumption per capita (KWh)	17.0	16.2	17.0	17.8	18.0	18.9	19.3	19.1	19.1	17.2
National electrification levels (%)	1.6	1.6	1.6	1.6	1.7	1.8	1.9	2.0	2.1	2.1
Urban electrification levels (%)	10.41	10.68	10.94	11.41	11.76	12.08	12.36	12.70	12.83	13.00
Rural electrification levels (%)	0.13	0.14	0.16	0.19	0.18	0.16	0.16	0.17	0.17	0.20
System losses (%)	15	19	19	19	18	18	16	17	17	22

Sources: AFREPREN, 2003; IEA, 2003; Karekezi et al, 2002; Kebede, 2003; Teferra, 2003; Phelan, 2003; UNDP, 2003; Wolde Ghiorgis, 2003; World Bank, 2003a; World Bank, 2003b

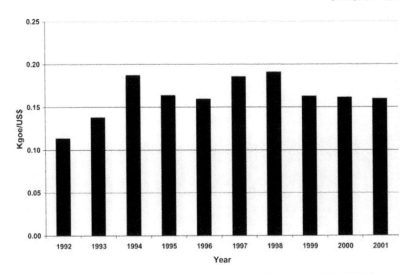

Figure A6.8.1 Ethiopia: modern energy consumption (kgoe) per US$ of GDP, 1992–2001

Sources: AFREPREN, 2003; Chandi, 2003; IEA, 2003; Kalumiana, 2003; Mbewe, 2003; World Bank, 2003a; World Bank, 2003b

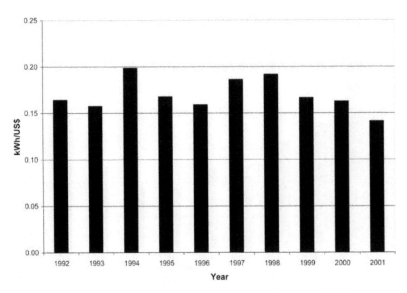

Figure A6.8.2 Ethiopia: Electricity consumption (kWh) per US$ of GDP, 1992–2001

Sources: AFREPREN, 2003; Chandi, 2003; IEA, 2003; Kalumiana, 2003; Mbewe, 2003; World Bank, 2003a; World Bank, 2003b

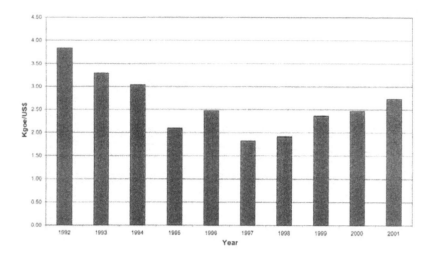

Figure A6.8.3 Ethiopia: modern energy consumption (kgoe) per US$ of merchandise export, 1992–2001

Sources: AFREPREN, 2003; Chandi, 2003; IEA, 2003; Kalumiana, 2003; Mbewe, 2003; World Bank, 2003a; World Bank, 2003b

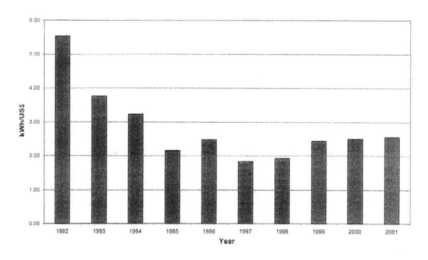

Figure A6.8.4 Ethiopia: Electricity consumption (kWh) per US$ of merchandise export, 1992–2001

Sources: AFREPREN, 2003; Chandi, 2003; IEA, 2003; Kalumiana, 2003; Mbewe, 2003; World Bank, 2003a; World Bank, 2003b

Part 7

TANZANIA

Maneno J. J. Katyega
with
Norbert Kahyoza

COUNTRY PROFILE
Tanzania

SELECTED INDICATORS

Land area: 883,749 km^2
Capital city: Dar-es-Salaam
National population (millions): 34.55 (2001)
National population growth rate (%): 2.1 (2001)
Urban population (millions): 11.8 (2001)
Urban population growth rate (%): 8.7 (2001)
Urban population as a % of national population: 34.2 (2001)
GDP growth rate (%): 5.69 (2001)
GNP per capita (US$): 270 (2001)
Gini index: 38.2 (1993 survey year)
Official exchange rate (US$: TShs): 1,055.50 (September, 2003)
Economic activities: Agriculture, mining, commerce, construction, tourism
Modern energy consumption per capita (kgoe): 20 (2000)
Modern energy production (000 toe): 990 (2000)
Energy sources: Hydro, natural gas, coal, biomass, imported petroleum, solar
Installed capacity (MW): 863 (2001)
Electricity generation (GWh): 2,770 (2001)
Electricity consumption per capita (kWh): 58 (2001)
Urban electrification rates (%): 39 (2001)
System losses (%): 28 (2001)

Sources: AFREPREN/FWD, 2003; IEA, 2003; Karekezi et al., 2002; Katyega, 2003; Marandu, 2003; Phelan, 2003; UNDP, 2003; World Bank, 2003a; World Bank, 2003b

23

Tanzania is located in East Africa (1.0–11.5°S and 29.5–40.5°E) with a surface area of 883,749 square kilometres and a population of 34.6 million in the year 2002. The country has access to the lakes of Victoria, Tanganyika and Nyasa. Its economy is predominantly rural and agricultural. The contribution of mining and tourism to GDP is rising fast. The *per capita* income of Tanzania in 2002 was TShs256,490 or US$262 (Ofisi ya Rais 2003). The average daily income of a Tanzanian is less than a dollar: the country is among the poorest countries of the world.

Tanzania's energy consumption *per capita* is low, estimated at 0.5 toe. Primary energy consumption is roughly 92 per cent biomass, 7 per cent petroleum products and the balance hydroelectricity and coal (Marandu *et al.*, 1999). Yet the country has abundant and diversified energy resources including hydropower, coal, natural gas and fossil fuels.

Past energy initiatives aimed at the poor, like kerosene and LPG subsidies, were removed in 1998. The only energy subsidy available is the lifeline electricity tariff. Currently, no other energy sources, traditional or modern, used by the poor are subsidized.

This study investigates the impact of subsidies on energy utilities and public finance. In addition, the amount of electricity subsidies is estimated and who captures them is investigated. The lack of relevant data prevents us from comparing estimates of purchasing power with costs of energy to examine the effect of subsidies on affordability, a standard procedure in the other country studies.

24

What is the Impact of Subsidies
on Utilities and Public Finance?

First, the magnitude of electricity subsidies is established. The next step is to clarify whether the subsidies are internal (cross-subsidies) or are shouldered by the government or the energy utility. Initially, the magnitude of subsidies is investigated for each fuel and energy unit consumed. Next, the level of subsidies by energy source is aggregated to obtain an indication of the total amount of energy subsidies. This approach does not, however, capture the following types of subsidies:

- waived duties on equipment for major power and petroleum projects;
- other tax holidays enjoyed by investors in both the electricity and petroleum subsectors;
- favourable duties imposed on imported electricity-generating equipment.

Table 7.1 provides a summary of the current uniform tariff in the country and compares prevailing tariffs to long-run marginal costs. As shown in the table, the current tariff departs markedly from the LRMC. For example, to reach the LRMC levels, a tariff increase of nearly 200 per cent is required for the 0–100 kWh range. Such significant deviations

Table 7.1 Current tariff levels compared to long-run marginal cost, 2000

Tariff class	Energy/capacity range	Tariff USc/ kWh	LRMC USc/ kWh	Required % increase to LRMC	Demand charge US$/kVA	Service charge US$/month
1 General	0-100 kWh	3.0	8.9	+197	0.0	0.3
	101-500 kWh	4.8	8.9	+85	0.0	0.9
	501-2,500 kWh	11	18.9	−19.8	0.0	2.5
	2501-7,500 kWh	20.7	8.9	−57	0.0	2.5
2 Low voltage	>7,500 kWh, < 50 kVA	8.8	8.9	+1.1	9.6	5.0
3 High voltage	11/33 kV	8.4	7.7	8.3	7.4	−5.0
4 Public	kWh	3.5	8.9	+154	0.0	0.0
5 Zanzibar	132 kV	2.7	7.2	+167	4.2	5.0
Levy (VAT):	20%					

Source: TANESCO

from the LRMC send the wrong signals to consumers and service providers. For consumers, very low tariffs encourage wasteful consumption For service providers, the incentive to provide electricity is undermined.

The first 100 kWh electricity block constitutes the lifeline tariff. The next block of 400 KWh is still subsidized but at a lower rate; both tariff blocks are below the LRMC. Tariff rates above 500 kWh in the 'general' category are higher than the LRMC. But both public lighting and bulk supply to Zanzibar are below the LRMC, while Tariff 3 (high voltage) pays more than the LRMC and hence is not subsidized.

Tables 7.2 and 7.3 summarize subsidized consumption in terms of energy and monetary value respectively for the year 2000. Table 7.2 indicates that the number of consumers in subsidized energy consumption steps (Tariff 1, steps 1 and 2, Tariff 4 and Tariff 5) constitute about 86 per cent of all consumers – all Tariff 1 consumers enjoy the lifeline tariff. Of the 2,313 GWh of electricity supplied in the year 2000, 1,048 GWh, or approximately 45 per cent, was subsidized. In monetary terms, energy subsidies were about 23 per cent of the expected revenue if electricity was supplied at the LRMC (Table 7.3). In absolute terms, energy subsidies were estimated at US$45.1 million out of the expected LRMC energy revenue of US$198.1 million. Capacity (kVA) subsidies were about US$3.1 million out of an expected revenue of US$28.3 million.[1]

But apart from the subsidies incorporated in electricity tariffs, the government has also subsidized electricity-related projects. One of these projects is rural electrification. As part of its development budget, the government, through the Ministry of Energy and Minerals has been providing funds for rural electrification projects along with donors and the energy utility. The funds have been used to extend electricity services rather than for operation and maintenance (see Table 7.4). For the period 1995–2000, the government and TANESCO contributed TShs 0.42 billion and TShs 9.96 billion respectively. A further TShs 25.28 billion was contributed by foreign donations, aid and soft loans. The total contribution for the period was TShs 35.66 billion, or an annual capital subsidy of TShs 7.132 billion.

In addition to the subsidies incorporated in electricity tariffs and the financing of rural electrification, customer service line connections are also subsidized. For single- and three-phase connections, customers contribute TShs105,000 (US$131) and TShs288,000 (US$360) respectively. The respective true costs of these connections are TShs188,000 (US$235) and TShs488,000 (US$610). There are roughly 24,000 single-phase and 1,000 three-phase connections every year. Hence, an estimate of the annual service line subsidy is in the region of US$2.75 million.[2]

Total capital-related subsidies in 2000 were to the tune of US$9.65 million, including US$6.90 million in electrification subsidies and US$2.75 million in service line connection subsidies. By adding this sum to the energy and capacity subsidies of US$48.2 million, we reach a total figure of US$57.85 million.

Table 7.2 Electricity subsidies and leakage in energy terms, 2000

1 Tariff	2 Steps in kWh	3 No. consumers	4 % of consumers	5 Energy consumption in GWh/a	6 % of total GWh	7 Energy tariff US¢/kWh Current	8 Energy tariff US¢/kWh LRMC	9 LRMC GWh exp. rev US$m/a	10 Step 1 0–100 kwh	11 Step 2 101–500 kwh	12 Step 3 501–2500 kwh	13 Step 4 >2500 kwh	14 Energy subsidy GWh/a	15 Non-subsidised GWh/a	16 Energy leakage GWh/a	17 Capacity consumption in GVA/a	18 Capacity tariff US$/kVA Current	19 Capacity tariff US$/kVA LRMC	20 LRMC GVA exp. rev US$ m/a
1	0–100	146754	35.9	107.325	4.6	3	8.9	9.552	107.325				107.325	0.000	0.000	0	0.00	0.0	0
	101–500	203344	49.7	466.485	20.2	4.8	8.9	41.517	244.013	222.472			466.485	0.000	466.485	0	0.00	0.0	0
	501–2500	49056	12.0	430.417	18.6	11.1	8.9	38.307	58.867	235.469	136.081		294.336	136.081	294.336	0	0.00	0.0	0
	>2501	7902	1.9	364.360	15.8	20.6	8.9	32.428	9.482	37.930	189.648	127.300	47.412	316.948	47.412	0	0.00	0.0	0
	Total T1	407056	99.5	1368.587	59.2														
2	kWh	1139	0.3	343.169	14.8	8.8	8.9	30.542				343.169	0.000	343.169	0.000	1.463	9.60	10.71	15.672
	kVA																		
3	kWh	144	0.0	469.115	20.3	8.4	7.7	36.122				469.115	0.000	469.115	0.000	1.427	7.40	6.86	9.784
	kVA																		
4	kWh	528	0.1	6.408	0.3	3.5	8.9	0.570		6.408			6.408	0.000	6.408				
5	kWh	1	0.0	125.915	5.4	2.7	7.2	9.066		125.915			125.915	0.000	125.915	0.316	4.20	8.86	2.794
	kVA																		
	Total 2–5	1812	0.4	944.607	40.8														
	Total 1–5	408868	100.0	2313.194	100.0			198.104	419.687	628.194	325.729	939.584	1047.881	1265.313	940.556	3.206			28.250

Percentage of total energy in GWh — 45.30 / 54.70

Energy subsidy by tariff steps in energy terms (GWh) — 419.687 / 628.194

Total energy subsidy in energy terms (GWh) — 1047.881 / 40.66

Total energy leakage in energy terms (GWh) — 940.556

Source: TANESCO

Table 7.3 Electricity subsidies and leakage in monetary terms, 2000

1 Tariff	2 Steps in kWh	3 No. consumers	4 % of consumption GWh/a	5 Energy tariff USc/kWh Current	6 Energy tariff USc/kWh LRMC	7 Capacity GVA	8 Capacity tariff USc/kWh Current	9 Capacity tariff USc/kWh LRMC	10 LRMC revenue US$m/a	11 Consumption Step 1 0-100 kWh	12 Consumption Step 2 101-500 kWh	13 Consumption Step 3 501-2500 kWh	14 Consumption Step 4 >2500 kWh	15 Energy subsidy Step 1 0-100 kWh	16 Energy subsidy Step 2 101-500 kWh	17 Energy subsidy Step 3 501-2500 kWh	18 Energy subsidy Step 4 >2500 kWh	19 Capacity subsidy US$m/a	20 Net revenue by the utility US$m/a
1	0-100	146754	107.325	3	8.9	0	0.00	0.00	9.552	107.325				6.332				0.00	-6.332
	101-500	203344	466.485	4.8	8.9	0	0.00	0.00	41.517	244.013	222.472			14.397	9.121			0.00	-23.518
	501-2500	49056	430.417	11.1	8.9	0	0.00	0.00	38.307	58.867	235.469	136.081		3.473	9.654	0.00		0.00	-10.134
	>2501	7902	364.360	20.6	8.9	0	0.00	0.00	32.428	9.482	37.930	189.648	127.300	0.559	1.555	0.00	0.00	0.00	16.952
	Total T1	407056	1368.587						121.804										-23.032
2	kWh	1139	343.169	8.8	8.9		9.60	10.71	30.542				343.169						-0.343
	kVA					1.463			15.672									1.630	-1.630
3	kWh	144	469.115	8.4	7.7		7.40	6.86	36.122				469.115						3.284
	kVA					1.427			9.784										0.775
4	kWh	528	6.408	3.5	8.9				0.570		6.408				0.346				-0.346
5	kWh	1	125.915	2.7	7.2				9.066		125.915				5.666				-5.666
	kVA					0.315	4.20	8.86	2.794									1.469	-1.469
	Total 2-5	1812	944.607																
	Total 1-5	408868	2313.194																

LRMC revenue (US$m/a):
- Capacity: 28.250
- Energy: 132.80
- Energy + capacity: 254.604

Energy subsidy (LRMC revenue deficit) by steps in US$ m/a:
- Step 1: 24.762
- Step 2: 20.331
- Step 3: 0.00
- Step 4: 0.00

Capacity subsidy: 3.099

	Step totals		Net revenue
Capacity	0.00	3.099	-2.325
Energy	45.092		-7.72
Energy + capacity	48.191		-30.752

Energy by step and capacity subsidies value: 24.762 20.331 0.00 0.00 / 3.099
Total energy subsidy monetary value: 45.092
Total energy and capacity subsidy monetary value: 48.191
Leakage (energy) monetary value by step: 18.429 20.331
Total leakage (energy) monetary value: 38.760
Direct utility subsidy in monetary value: -30.752

Source: TANESCO

Table 7.4 Expenditures on rural electrification programmes, 1995–2000 (in million TShs)

SN	Electrification project	1995			1996			1997			1998			1999			2000			TOTAL		
		F	G	T	F	G	T	F	G	T	F	G	T	F	G	T	F	G	T	F	G	T
1	Tukuyu/Mwakaleli						19.28			0.20										0.00	0.00	19.48
2	Shinyanga agro-based		19.00	2.32															0.00	0.00	19.00	2.32
3	Mahenge						9.45			20.41			24.84			54.35			1.92	0.00	0.00	110.97
4	Mafinga/Mufindi			9.14																0.00	0.00	9.14
5	Chunya		1.50	87.78			45.14			89.95			168.69			153.36				0.00	1.50	544.92
6	Mpanda			0.20																0.00	0.00	0.20
7	Kyela			11.20			0.35						0.91			4.56				0.00	0.00	17.02
8	Mbozi			61.90			71.61			232.72			0.74							0.00	0.00	366.97
9	Mbinga			4.42			4.58			0.54										0.00	0.00	9.54
10	Ileje			0.81			4.97			6.49			65.75		132.50	302.25			16.32	0.00	132.50	396.59
11	Makete		6.00	47.50			180.09			147.22			21.75			57.31			23.71	0.00	6.00	477.58
12	Lugoba			69.63			2.15			40.78			45.43			57.13			0.61	0.00	0.00	215.73
13	Urambo			12.35			11.74			0.02						0.25				0.00	0.00	24.36
14	Power IV			0.18			116.18	785.19		3.61	10399.93		783.98	10822.62	265.00	1213.50	3271.00		1389.97	25278.74	265.00	3507.42
15	Chitipa			100.99			67.54			2.42						1.27			0.55	0.00	0.00	172.22
16	Kilimanjaro						32.77			129.02			6.35			58.55				0.00	0.00	226.69
17	Lupembe						5.49			21.10			30.13			60.41				0.00	0.00	117.68
18	Sengerema/Bunda									497.75			1073.19			489.89			588.44	0.00	0.00	2649.27
19	Chomachankola												2.70			17.91			1.92	0.00	0.00	22.53
20	Manyoni												3.90			345.33			14.93	0.00	0.00	364.16
21	Kiomboi												3.60			224.68			22.68	0.00	0.00	250.96
22	Tandahimba																		8.90	0.00	0.00	8.90
23	Igunga															6.07			23.03	0.00	0.00	29.10
24	Ruangwa																		19.43	0.00	0.00	19.43
25	Geita															1.00			11.33	0.00	0.00	12.33
26	Meatu															9.96			29.67	0.00	0.00	39.63
27	Nassa																		7.79	0.00	0.00	7.79
28	Kibakwe																		19.66	0.00	0.00	19.66
29	Kanyigo															253.41			48.81	0.00	0.00	302.22
30	Gairo															0.14			21.23	0.00	0.00	21.37
	Total expenditure	0	26.50	408.42	0	0	571.34	785.19	0	192.23	10399.93	0	2231.96	10822.62	397.50	3311.33	3271.00	0	2250.90	25278.74	424.00	9966.18

Notes: F = Foreign, G = Government, T = TANESCO. Total funding TSh billion: F=25.28, G=0.42, T=9.97. Funding (%): F=70.9, G=1.2, T=27.9.

Source: TANESCO

Government expenditure for the year 2000 was TShs1,236.907 billion (about US$1,547.50 million). As indicated above, electricity subsidies for year 2000 are estimated at US$57.85 million, accounting for 3.74 per cent of government expenditure (see Table 7.5). In 1997 energy subsidies were 3.65 per cent of government expenditure. In comparison to the burden of subsidies on public finance found for some other sub-Saharan African countries,[3] this is not very large.

A question arises as to who shouldered the indicated energy and capital subsidies in Tanzania. To appreciate the problem, one needs to investigate the nature of both types of subsidies. Up to the year 1985, government used to subsidize energy – specifically, the operation and maintenance of certain rural electrification branches (Meta Systems, 1985). During the period from 1985 to the end of 2001, electricity energy subsidies in Tanzania did not involve the flow of resources from government to the utility. Instead it involved cross-subsidies among consumer groups (London Economics *et al.*, 1993; Katyega *et al.*, 1998; and Tables 7.3 and 7.4).[4] An important question, therefore, is whether cross-subsidies in 2000 had any negative financial implications for the utility.

Based on Table 7.3 (column 20), net revenue for the utility in the year 2000 was –US$30.75 million. This negative amount corresponds to the subsidy the energy utility shouldered.[5] As total computed energy and capacity subsidy in the year totalled US$48.2 million, large consumers cross-subsidized the difference (US$17.45 million). Therefore, the utility shouldered about 66 per cent, or two thirds of the subsidies. Repeating the analysis for year 1997, the utility shouldered about 37 per cent of the subsidies (see Table 7.5).

Table 7.5 Impact of electricity subsidies on public finances (US$ million)

Type of subsidy	Year 2000	Year 1997
Capital subsidies		
. Government (rural electrification)	0.00	0.00
. Foreign/donor (rural electrification)*	4.09	1.26
. TANESCO (rural electrification)	2.81	1.91
. TANESCO (service line)	2.75	2.75
Energy subsidies**		
. Government	0.00	0.00
. X-subsidies large consumers	19.76	29.26
. X-subsidies TANESCO	28.43	11.11
Total subsidies	57.84	46.29
TANESCO total subsidies	38.08	17.03
TANESCO LRMC revenue	226.35	172.59
Government expenditure***	1,547.50	1,269.64
TANESCO subsidies as a proportion of total subsidies (%)	65.83	36.79

Notes: * Assumed on-loaned to TANESCO and ignoring interest; ** Includes capacity-related charges
        ***Source: President's Office, Planning and Privatisation, 2002
Source: TANESCO, 2002.

Moreover, government has been considering underwriting all the previous rural electrification grants and soft loans made to Tanzania and on-loaned to the national utility at higher interest rates.[6] These include most of the foreign funds, which for the period 1995 – 2000 totalled about TShs 9.96 billion. Even if interest charges for the borrowed funds are ignored, the utility's capital subsidies are quite substantial.

The necessary conclusion is that electricity subsidies are a great burden to the utility and large commercial and industrial electricity consumers, rather than the exchequer.

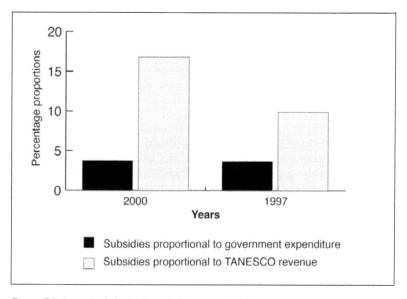

Figure 7.1 Impact of electricity subsidies on public finance
Source: TANESCO.

25

Who Captures the Subsidies?

The electricity consumption in the country by tariff category and blocks or steps is used to estimate the amounts of subsidies captured by different consumers. The amount of subsidy captured by electricity customers consuming above the lifeline block is used as a proxy for energy captured by non-poor. In other words, customers using electricity below the lifeline threshold are assumed to be poor. Note that customers using an amount of electricity above the lifeline threshold get subsidy first because they pay the lifeline tariff for the first 100 kWh, and second because even tariff rates above 100 kWh are less than the LRMC.

For the year 2000 data (Tables 7.6–7.7), electricity subsidies are available to consumers in General Tariff 1 (step 1 and 2), public lighting (Tariff 4) and bulk supply to Zanzibar (Tariff 5). General Tariff 1 is for residential, light commercial and light industrial consumers. All Tariff 1 consumers obtain 100 kWh (step 1/lifeline) and 400 kWh (step 2) subsidies. As lifeline consumption is a proxy for consumption by the poor, consumption of it by non-lifeline consumers constitutes electricity subsidy leakage. Table 7.6 shows the extent of subsidies leakage to the non-poor in the General Tariff 1 category. From the table it can be seen that subsidized lifeline consumption by the poor constitutes about 12 per cent of all Tariff 1 subsidies. The extent of the leakage to the non-poor amounts to 808 out of 916 GWh.

Moreover, subsidizing customers using up to 500 kWh appears inconsistent with supporting the consumption of the poor. Therefore the revised tariff introduced at the beginning of May 2002 reduced the subsidy from 500 kWh per month to only 100 kWh (see Table 7.7). However, the new tariff still offers 100 kWh energy subsidies to both poor and non-poor (those using more than 100 kWh) Tariff 1 customers. Using the year 2000 figures and restricting subsidies to the 100 kWh level, our analysis tells us that leakage of 312 GWh still results, so that the associated reduction in leakage is 61 per cent. Extending the analysis to cover tariffs 1–5, total leakage in the year 2000 was 940.6 GWh and constituted about 40.7 per cent of all energy consumed. In monetary value, it was about US$38.76 million and roughly 17 per cent of the total LRMC expected revenue (Tables 7.7 and 7.8). The leakage is huge.

However, the above analysis has some shortcomings. The general tariff caters for households, light commercial and light industrial enterprises.

Table 7.6 Extent of electricity leakage to the non-poor in 2000

Tariff	Steps in kWh	Number of consumers	Total consumption GWh	500 kWh subsidy Subsidy GWh	500 kWh subsidy Leakage GWh	100 kWh subsidy Subsidy GWh	100 kWh subsidy Leakage GWh
I	0–100	146,754	107.325	107.325	0	107.325	0
	101–500	203,344	466.485	466.485	466.485	244.013	244.013
	501–2,500	49,056	430.417	294.336	294.336	58.867	58.867
	>2,500	7,902	364.360	47.412	47.412	9.482	9.482
	Totals	407,056	1,368.587	915.558	808.233	419.687	312.362

Source: TANESCO

Table 7.7 Electricity tariffs in Tanzania, May 2002–June 2003

Tariff	Type	Range	Energy TShs/kWh	Energy USc/kWh	Capacity TShs/kVA	Capacity US$/kVA	Service charge TShs/mo.	Service charge US$/mo.
I	General	0-100 kWh	25.90	2.6	0.00	0.00	200.00	0.20
		101-7,500 kWh	90.00	9.0	0.00	0.00	1,500.00	1.50
2	Low voltage	>7,500 kWh; <50 kVA	58.50	5.9	6,220.00	6.22	6,000.00	6.00
3	High voltage	11/33 kV	55.50	5.6	6,050.00	6.05	6,000.00	6.00
4	Zanzibar	132 kV	54.15	5.4	7,343.50	7.34	10,507.00	10.51

Source: TANESCO

Households are the majority. It is therefore not fair to generalize that all general tariff consumers constitute households. Should light industrial and light commercial consumers (in General Tariff 1) also benefit from lifeline subsidies? Another complication of this type of analysis is that some of the general tariff consumers share a meter. This is common in some of the rented houses. Where several poor households share a meter, the implication is that they have access to less subsidized energy than they would if they had separate meters. However, it is not in the financial interest of the utility to install several conventional energy meters in such houses. This creates difficulties in targeting energy subsidies to the poor.

To conclude, it is mainly the non-poor who benefit from electricity subsidies. The subsidy leakage is huge. A portion of the saved subsidies could be retargeted as a customer connection initiative involving service lines and internal wiring costs. Redesigning tariff structures for targeting the poor is a priority.

26

Subsidies and the Informal Sector

The extent of current electricity tariff structures and subsidies relevant to income-generating activities of the urban poor are assessed in this chapter. The cost of current energy for home-based micro-enterprises is compared to their income. The chapter also investigates the extent to which energy subsidies reach home-based micro enterprises.

To get the necessary data and tackle the above-mentioned issues, a mini-survey was undertaken during August 2001. This involved home-based micro-enterprises and the informal sector. The survey was undertaken in Sinza, Mwenge and Ubungo areas. A total of 20 informal enterprises were surveyed. Owing to the small-scale nature of the survey and the unavailability of a sampling frame, the information gathered is not representative of informal sector enterprises in Dar-es-Salaam. A simple questionnaire was used.

The data from the survey indicate that food vendors, beer brewers and tinsmiths do not use electricity (see Table 7.8); all their activities are undertaken during daytime. Auto-repair, carpentry, beauty salon and tailoring activities consume between 100 and 500 kWh per month. None of the activities surveyed fell within the lifeline tariff block consumption level. Grain-milling and Internet café enterprises consumed more than 500 kWh per month. We can conclude that many home-based and informal sector enterprises benefit from electricity subsidies, and that this is inherent in the tariff structure.

We also investigated the cost implication for home-based micro-enterprises of using the prevailing as compared with the true-cost electricity tariffs. There were difficulties in determining the total amount of subsidies enjoyed by the multitude of home-based micro-enterprises. TANESCO records do not include such information; nor do previous informal sector surveys. However, the consumption of most of the home-based micro-enterprises falls under Tariff 1, steps 1 to 3. Under the 2000 tariff, all consumers enjoyed subsidies up to 500 kWh per month, but, as we have seen, such subsidies have been reduced to only 100 kWh since 1 May 2002. For most electricity-consuming micro-enterprises, the cost of electricity as a proportion of income or total cost would double if electricity was priced at the LRMC. Another observation is that the micro-enterprises are profitable even if electricity is priced at the LRMC. In other words, even though energy subsidies increase the profits of

Table 7.8 Home-based micro-enterprise energy consumption and cost patterns in 2001

Micro-enterprise of cost	Number surveyed	Charcoal		Kerosene		Electricity		Cost at current electricity tariff		Cost at true cost electricity tariff	
		% Using	Average (kg)	% using	Average (litres)	% using	Average kWh	% of income	% of net total cost	% of net income	% total
Food vending	4	100	123	0	0	0	0	0	0	0	0
Beer brewing	1	100	84	100	42	0	0	0	0	0	0
Auto-repair	2	0	0	0	0	100	260.7	6.5	6.0	13.7	11.1
Carpentry	2	0	0	0	0	100	317.8	40.8	9.6	102.2	16.4
Grain mills	2	0	0	0	0	100	971.0	133.3	34.7	282.6	34.8
Tinsmith	2	50	210	50	12	0	0	0	0	0	0
Beauty Salon	4	0	0	0	0	100	158.0	6.5	2.5	16.0	5.2
Tailoring	2	50	18	0	0	100	101.6	14.0	10.4	40.0	19.8
Internet café	1	0	0	0	0	100	933.7	23.5	12.9	25.8	13.8

Source: Survey by author

informal sector enterprises, they would still be profitable if electricity was priced at the LRMC. In view of this fact, subsidies may well appear unnecessary for informal sector enterprises.

Our conclusions can therefore be summarized as follows:

- Micro-enterprises benefit from the existing electricity pricing structure.

- Subsidies beef up their business profits.

- Nevertheless, subsidies could be removed without reversing the profitability of the micro-enterprises – even though reduced profits would ensue.

27

Policy Options

The findings of Part 7 indicate the need to rationalize electricity subsidies by limiting their levels. The lifeline tariff threshold should preferably be set at 50 kWh per month (or not more than 100 kWh). In addition, subsidies for those consuming above the lifeline tariff should be removed. Those above the lifeline threshold should pay the full or more than the full cost of electricity (the latter to cross-subsidize lifeline consumption).

An electricity utility exists and is able to implement the redesigning and/or gradual phasing-out of subsidies. In the absence of a regulatory body in the country, the Ministry of Energy is expected to continue playing this role, unimpeded by institutional or legal barriers. The energy utility's financial situation is expected to improve, too, while reduced subsidies will help to plug subsidy leakage.

Regular reviews of tariff rates, structures and consumer segmentation are necessary to guarantee that lifeline tariff levels benefit only the poor.

Table 7.9 A suggestion on year 2003 tariff structure segmentation

Tariff		Energy step	Energy USc/kWh	Capacity US$/kVA/ month	Service US$/ month
Low-voltage supply					
1a	Residential/public lighting	0–50 kWh	2.6	0	0.2
		51–7500 kWh	9.0	0	1.5
1b	Light commercial	0–50 kWh	2.6	0	0.2
		51–7500 kWh	9.0	0	1.5
1c	Light industrial	0–50 kWh	2.6	0	0.2
		51–7500 kWh	9.0	0	1.5
2a	Commercial	>7,500 kWh, <50 kVA	5.9	6.2	6.0
2b	Industrial	>7,500 kWh, <50 kVA	5.9	6.2	6.0
High-voltage supply					
3a	Agricultural	11/33 kV	5.5	6.1	6.0
3b	Cooperatives	11/33 kV	5.5	6.1	6.0
3c	Heavy industries	11/33 kV	5.5	6.1	6.0
3d	Mining	11/33 kV	5.5	6.1	6.0
4	Zanzibar	132 kV	5.4	7.3	10.5

Notes: Energy prices for tariffs 2, 3 and 4 can be lowered from suggested reductions in subsidies in Tariff 1. Also, possibilities for time-of-day tariffs for Tariff 3 could be investigated.
Source: TANESCO.

Lifeline subsidies should be limited; 50 kWh per month is suggested. Further, segmentation of Tariff 1 and the introduction of agricultural and cooperative tariffs is suggested. Segmentation of Tariff 1 into residential/ public lighting, light commercial and light industrial is suggested. Similarly, the introduction of a mining tariff appears to be important given the tax incentives presently offered to mining investors. Some suggestions for a 2003 tariff structure are given in Table 7.9. Actual tariff formulation would obviously require a tariff study.

No specific electricity subsidies are targeted at micro-enterprises, but most informal sector activities already benefit from the existing lifeline electricity subsidies. As the informal sector activities can afford electricity at prevailing and true energy costs, energy subsidies appear not to be necessary for them. Since most of the urban poor find their employment in the informal sector, one way to fight poverty is by supporting income-generating activities, including home-based ones with access to electricity. This can be done through favourable connection strategies, via soft loans and innovative financing of electrification. Subsidies could be used to meet upfront electricity costs, rather than energy consumption.

Notes

1 However, the above analysis does not capture distortional effects caused by energy subsidies: for example, infrastructure overloading and poor power quality due to induced over-consumption of subsidized energy; or the effect of inter-fuel domestic substitution. Data for these distortional effects could not be obtained.
2 This is computed by using the information given above: 24,000 (235–131) + 1,000 (610–360) = US$2.75 million.
3 See, particularly, results for Uganda and Zimbabwe in this volume.
4 Following commercial operation of the IPTL plant (a 100 MW independent power producer) from January 2002, government is providing monthly electricity energy subsidies to the utility so that it can meet its power purchase obligations.
5 Poor revenue collections can exaggerate the extent of the subsidies.
6 The annual interest rate is 7–10 per cent, depending on the source of funds.

References

AFREPREN/FWD, 2003. *African Energy Data Handbook*, updated, Occasional Paper No. 13, Nairobi: AFREPREN/FWD.

Bureau of Statistics, 1991. *Household Budget Survey 1990/91*, Vol. 1, Dar-es-Salaam: Government Printer.

——, 2000. *Baseline Poverty Monitoring Report*, Dar-es-Salaam: Government Printer.

——, 2002. *Household Budget Survey 2000/01*, Dar-es-Salaam: Government Printer.

Dube, I. 2001. 'Energy Services for the Urban Poor in Zimbabwe,' medium-term study report, Nairobi: AFREPREN/FWD.

ESMAP (Energy Sector Management Assistance Programme), 1988. 'Tanzania Woodfuel/Forestry Project: Main Report and Annexes,' World Bank Energy Unit, Industry and Energy Department, Washington DC: World Bank.

Hosier, R. H. and W. Kipondya, 1993. 'Urban Household Energy Use in Tanzania: Prices, Substitutes and Poverty', *Energy Policy*, 21, 5 (May).

Hosier, R. H. 1994. *Informal Sector Energy Use in Tanzania: Efficiency Employment Potential*, Stockholm: Stockholm Environment Institute.

IEA, 2003. *Energy Balances of Non-OECD Countries, 2000–2001*, Paris:

International Energy Agency.

Karekezi, S., M. Mapako and M. Teferra (eds) 2002, 'Africa: Improving Modern Energy Services for the Poor', *Energy Policy Journal*, special issue, Vol. 30, No. 11-12, Oxford: Elsevier Science.

Kebede, B. 2002. 'Energy Subsidies and the Urban Poor in Ethiopia: the Case of Kerosene and Electricity', medium-term study report, Nairobi: AFREPREN/FWD.

Kalumiana O. S. 2002. 'Energy Services for the Urban Poor in Zambia,' third draft, Nairobi: AFREPREN/FWD.

Katyega, M., 2003. 'Country Data Validation: Tanzania', unpublished, Nairobi: AFREPREN/FWD.

Katyega, M., E. E. Marandu and I. L. Masalla, 1998. 'Management and Efficiency of the Power Sector in Tanzania,' mimeo, Nairobi: AFREPREN/ FWD.

Katyega, M. J. J., B. Naimani and N. Kahyoza, 2001. 'Special Household Energy Survey, Dar-es-Salaam,' mimeo, Nairobi: AFREPREN/FWD.

Katyega, M. J .J., N. Kahyoza, M. Mtepa and A. Wilson, 2003. 'Energy Services for the Urban Poor in Tanzania', revised third draft, Nairobi: AFREPREN/ FWD.

Kyokutamba, J. 2002. *Energy Services for the Urban Poor in Uganda*, Nairobi: AFREPREN/FWD.

London Economics Limited, Kennedy and Donkin Power Limited and LE Energy, 1993. 'Electricity Tariff Study', Final Report, Vol. 2, London: Overseas Development Assistance (ODA), November.

Marandu, E., 2003. 'Country Data Validation: Tanzania', unpublished, Nairobi: AFREPREN/FWD.

Marandu, E., M. Katyega, J. Mnzava and I. L. Masalla, 1999. 'Tanzania,' in M. R. Bhagavan (ed.), *Reforming the Power Sector in Africa,* London: Zed Books.

Meta Systems, 1985. 'Tanzania Tariff Study', 1911 N. Fort Meyer Drive, Suite 907, Arlington VA.

Ofisi ya Rais – Mipango na Ubinafsishaji, 2003. 'Hali ya uchumi wa Taifa katika mwaka 2002', Dar es Salaam: Mpiga Chapa Mkuu wa Serikali.

Phelan, J. (ed.), 2003. *African Review Journal*, 39, 8, London: Alain Charles.

President's Office, Planning and Privatization, 2002. *The Economic Survey 2001*, Dar-es-Salaam: Government Printer.

Vice-President's Office, 1999. *Poverty Eradication Strategy*, Dar-es-Salaam: Government Printer.

——, 2000. 'Poverty Reduction Paper', Dar-es-Salaam: Government Printer.

UNDP, 2003. *Human Development Report, 2003*, Oxford and New York: Oxford University Press and United Nations Development Programme.

Wolde Ghiorgis, W., 2003. 'Country Data Validation: Ethiopia', unpublished, Nairobi: AFREPREN/FWD.

World Bank, 2000. *Entering the 21st Century: World Development Report 1999/2000*, Washington DC: World Bank.

——, 2003a. *African Development Indicators 2003*, Washington DC: World Bank.

——, 2003b. *World Development Indicators 2003*, Washington DC: World Bank.

Appendix 7.1 Selected time series data – Tanzania

Year	1992	1993	1994	1995	1996	1997	1998	1999	2000	2001
National population (millions)	27.10	27.90	28.80	29.60	30.50	31.30	32.10	32.92	33.70	34.55
National population growth rate (%)	3.0	3.0	3.2	2.8	3.0	2.6	2.6	2.6	2.6	2.1
Urban population (millions)	5.6	6.4	6.7	7.2	7.8	8.5	9.2	10.0	10.9	11.8
GDP (US$ millions)	4,900	5,000	5,100	5,300	5,500	5,700	5,900	6,109	6,419	6,784
GNP per capita (US$)	170	170	160	160	190	210	240	260	280	270
Total modern energy consumption (000 toe)	650	610	610	620	620	620	630	650	682	
Modern energy consumption per capita (kgoe)	24	22	21	21	20	20	20	20	20	
Modern energy production (000 toe)	830	860	850	860	880	860	910	950	990	
National debt (US$ millions)	6,678	6,798	7,235	7,406	7,362	7,129	7,633	8,052	7,440	6,676
Merchandise exports, f.o.b (US$ millions)	414	411	486	593	696	794	577	563	663	776
Installed capacity (MW)	482	482	575	655	655	655	655	655	835	863
Electricity generation (GWh)	1,918	1,879	1,803	1,878	2,022	1,979	2,195	2,340	2,465	2,770
Total electricity consumption (GWh)	1,435	1,417	1,460	1,631	1,829	1,701	1,710	1,914	2,036	
2015Electricity consumption per capita (kWh)	59	59	58	58	63	58	57	62	64	58
National electrification levels (%)	7	7	7	7	7	7	7	7	7	10
Urban electrification levels (%)					26.4					39
Rural electrification levels (%)					1	1	1	1	1	2
System losses (%)	25	24	19	14	11	17	22	24	25	28

Sources: AFREPREN, 2003; IEA, 2003; Karekezi et al, 2002; Katyega, 2003; Marandu, 2003; Phelan, 2003; UNDP, 2003; World Bank, 2003a; World Bank 2003b

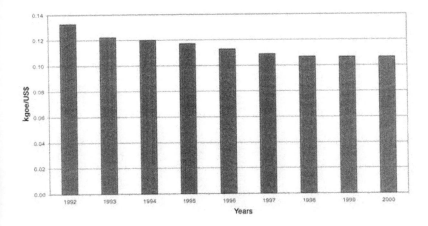

Figure A7.1.1 Tanzania: modern energy consumption (kgoe) per US$ of GDP, 1992–2000

Sources: AFREPREN, 2003; IEA, 2003; Katyega, 2003; Marandu, 2003; World Bank, 2003a; World Bank 2003b

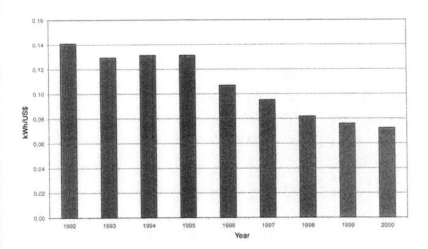

Figure A7.1.2 Tanzania: Electricity consumption (kWh) per US$ of GDP, 1992–2000

Sources: AFREPREN, 2003; IEA, 2003; Katyega, 2003; Marandu, 2003; World Bank, 2003a; World Bank 2003b

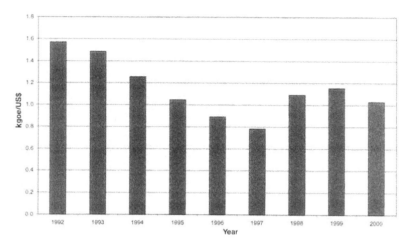

Figure A7.1.3 Tanzania: Modern energy consumption (kgoe) per US$ of
merchandise export, 1992–2000
Sources: AFREPREN, 2003; IEA, 2003; Katyega, 2003; Marandu, 2003; World Bank, 2003a; World Bank, 2003b

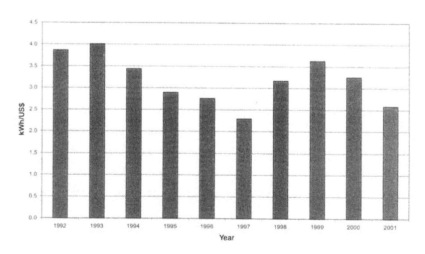

Figure A7.1.4 Tanzania: Electricty consumption (kWh) per US$ of merchandise
export, 1992–2001
Sources: AFREPREN, 2003; IEA, 2003; Katyega, 2003; Marandu, 2003; World Bank, 2003a; World Bank, 2003b

Part 8

UGANDA

Joan Kyokutamba

COUNTRY PROFILE
Uganda

SELECTED INDICATORS

Land area (km²): 197,097
Capital city: Kampala
National population (millions): 22.79 (2001)
National population growth rate (%): 2.6 (2001)
Urban population (millions): 3.79 (2001)
Urban population growth rate (%): 6.16 (2002)
GDP growth rate (%): 4.6 (2001)
GNP *per capita* **(US$): 260 (2001)**
Modern energy consumption *per capita* **(kgoe):** 24 (2001)
Modern energy production (000 toe): 840 (2001)
Official exchange rate (US$: UShs): 1,974.25 (September, 2003)
Economic activities: Agriculture, mining and semi-processing, manufacturing, construction, forestry, fishing, commerce
Energy sources: Hydro, biomass, petroleum
Installed capacity (MW): 263 (2001)
Electricity generation (GWh): 1,577 (2001)
Electricity consumption *per capita* **(kWh):** 57.9 (2000)
Urban electrification rates (%): 23.65 (2001)
System losses (%): 36.0 (2001)
Gini coefficient : 37.4 (1993 survey year)

Sources: AFREPREN/FWD, 2003; EIU, 1995–2003; Engorait, 2001; IEA, 2003; Karekezi et al., 2002; Kyokutamba, 2003; Phelan, 2003; UNDP, 2003; World Bank, 2003a; World Bank, 2003b

28

Introduction

Rationale of the study

Most urban households and small business enterprises involved in the informal sector do not have access to modern energy services. This is despite the importance of adequate energy as input for the success of their businesses and household operations. Low-income earners in Ugandan urban centres experience many forms of socio-economic challenge that could be relieved by the provision of improved access to non-traditional forms of energy. Table 8.1 shows the national energy balance over the past three years, and demonstrates the predominance of traditional energy.

Table 8.1 Energy consumption situations in Uganda, 1999–2001

Year	Energy consumption per capita (Kgoe)	Commercial energy consumption per capita (Kgoe)	Composition (%)		
			Biomass	Oil Products	Electricity
1999	315.1	23.8	92.3	6.7	1.0
2000	307.9	22.6	92.7	6.2	1.1
2001	308.4	22.3	92.8	6.1	1.1

Source: GoU, 2003

In a bid to promote electricity access through the national utility, the Uganda Electricity Board (UEB), the Ugandan government operated a heavily subsidized domestic tariff. The tariff reviewed by this study was in effect between 1993 and 2001. The electricity subsidies were effected by:

- setting a lifeline tariff;
- setting part of the tariff below the long-run marginal cost for households and industrial consumers;
- Setting a 79 per cent subsidy on electricity connection to domestic premises.

233

The study evaluated the impact of the above subsidies in enabling the urban poor to access modern energy. The study focused on urban areas because the basic infrastructure for the distribution network and generation capacity already exists, unlike in rural areas.

Lack of access to modern energy by the poor not only limits their share of social welfare but also impacts negatively on their income generation activities. Unlike in the rural areas, where people engage in agriculture, households in urban areas derive their incomes from small-scale or micro-enterprises.

The study is based on household energy consumption data derived from the Uganda Bureau of Statistics (UBOS), and the Uganda National Household Survey (UNHS), which was conducted between 1992 and 2000. The number of households covered by the survey was 10,000, selected from the four regions of Uganda and made up of all income categories from the survey.

Like the other main sections of this volume, Part 8 addresses the following questions:

1 Do the urban poor need subsidies to access modern energy?

2 Are subsidies for upfront costs a better option?

3 Who captures the subsidies?

4 What is the impact of subsidies on utilities and public finance?

5 What are the implications of subsidies for the informal sector?

29

Do the Urban Poor Need Subsidies
to Access Modern Energy?

To answer this question, data on types and quantities of energy consumed by households were assessed and the total expenditure on energy derived. Then, using the energy budget as a proxy for affordability, levels of affordability were assessed – with and without subsidies. The assessment involved converting different energy sources used by the poor into a single energy source, using energy efficiencies and the absolute energy content of each energy source.

Households were classified into extremely poor (with incomes up to UShs50,000), very poor (with incomes of UShs50,000–100,000) and moderately poor (with incomes of UShs100,000–150,000). For commercial energy sources like electricity, the level of subsidy included in each energy source was computed. A level of subsidy significantly higher than the energy budget meant that the current energy expenditure of the poor would be insufficient to cover the non-subsidized cost of electricity.[1]

Affordability of energy by the urban poor – with subsidies

The UEB provided the subsidies listed in Table 8.2 to domestic consumers.

Table 8.2 Categories of electricity subsidies

Category	Amount of power offered	Percentage subsidized
Level 1	1–30 kWh	79
Level 2	31–200 kWh	30
Other subsidy	Upfront cost of household connection	79

Source: UEB, 1993

According to the UNHS (1999/2000), 50 per cent of urban households were classified as poor; these are households falling below the national poverty line. Out of this total 14 per cent were classified as *moderately poor*, 24 per cent as *very poor* and 12 per cent as *extremely poor*.

From the household data, the total energy expenditures by households were derived. The results are tabulated in Table 8.3.

Table 8.3 Household energy expenditure by income group

Household category	Average expenditure on energy (UShs)
Extremely poor	5,525
Very Poor	10,170
Moderately poor	12,800
All poor	11,880

Source: UBOS, 2001

Table 8.4 Mean monthly energy expenditure for average households converted to buy various energy sources

Energy item	Energy units	Cost of fuel (UShs)	Mean energy used	Energy content (MJ per unit)	Typical efficiency	Useful energy (MJ)	Useful energy (kWh)
Electricity (1)	kWh	100	118.8	3.6	0.65	278	77.2
Electricity (2)	kWh	168	70.7	3.6	0.65	165.4	45.9
Kerosene	Litres	1120	10.6	35.0	0.30	111.3	30.9
Charcoal	Kg	165	71.5	29.0	0.20	414.7	115.2
Firewood	Kg	200	59.4	15.5	0.10	92.1	25.6
Others	Kg	100	1188	15.5	0.10	184.1	51.1

Note: Electricity (1) = 1993 tariff, applicable at time of survey. Electricity (2) = September 2002 tariff. For charcoal, energy expenditure is based on an ordinary (i.e., not an improved) metallic stove.
Source: Hosier and Kipondya, 1993

The ability of households to afford various types of energy sources based on their monthly expenditure was then examined. This involved converting the various energy sources into a single energy source (electricity). Table 8.4 shows the energy sources converted into equivalent electricity. Households that used charcoal were found to obtain a higher measure of useful energy units from their energy expenditure than households that used other sources. Nonetheless, since charcoal could not be used for all household energy purposes, other energy sources have to be sought for lighting. If households used their expenditure on firewood, they obtained lower amounts of useful energy units than from any other source.

On the basis of the 1993 tariff – 'Electricity (1)' in Table 8.4 – the energy expenditure of an average household was only enough to purchase 77 kWh of electricity. After the tariff review of September 2002 – 'Electricity (2)' – the same energy expenditure could purchase only 46 kWh of electricity. The implication of the price change was that the reduction in subsidies diminished the power of households to purchase electricity. The useful energy expenditure of the poor, moderately poor, very poor and extremely poor households converted into electricity equivalents is presented in Table 8.5.

Table 8.5 Mean annual energy expenditure for all poor, moderately poor, very poor and extremely poor households converted into electricity

Energy item	Useful energy in kWh			
	Poor	Moderately poor	Very poor	Extremely poor
Electricity (1)	77.2	83.2	66.0	35.9
Electricity (2)	45.9	49.5	39.3	21.3
Kerosene	30.9	33.3	26.4	14.3
Charcoal	115.3	103.3	82.1	44.6
Firewood	25.5	27.5	21.8	11.9
Others	51.1	55.1	43.8	23.8

Source: Kyokutamba, 2001; UBOS, 2001

Results from Table 8.5 indicate the differential ability among poor households to afford the cost of modern energy. Using the 1993 tariff, the energy expenditure of *moderately poor* households was equivalent to 83 kWh per month while that of *extremely poor* households was only 36 kWh per month. After the second tariff change in 2002, the same energy expenditure in both cases could only purchase 50 kWh and 21 kWh respectively.

Affordability of energy by the urban poor – without subsidies

To obtain the amount of subsidy in the energy consumption bills of each household category, the consumption levels given in Table 8.6 are used.

Table 8.6 Level of subsidy available for domestic electricity consumers

True Tariff	Consumption level (kWh)	Unit cost (UShs)	Level of subsidy contained (as a percentage of true cost)
Ushs100	0–30	20	80.0
	31–170	70	30.0
Ushs168	0–30	50	29.8

Source: UEDCL, 2001

In the 1993 tariff, the non-subsidized tariff that was charged for each kilowatt hour (kWh) for domestic electricity consumers was Ushs100. This cost was only applicable to households that consumed electricity in excess of 200 kWh. Depending on the level of consumption, all domestic electricity consumption that did not add up to 200 KWh was charged at a unit rate of either Ushs20 (equivalent to an 80 per cent subsidy) or Ushs70 (equivalent to 30 per cent subsidy). The electricity tariff was then revised first in June 2001 and again in September 2002. In both cases, the principle of a subsidy on the initial 30 kWh was maintained, but the charge on both occasions rose to 50 shillings.

The equivalent amounts of electricity households could buy without subsidy are given in Table 8.7.

Table 8.7 Household ability to purchase electricity at non-subsidized prices

Household category	Equivalent amount of electricity (1) that households could buy without subsidy (kWh)	Equivalent amount of electricity (2) households could buy without subsidy (kWh)
Extremely poor	36	18
Very poor	66	33
Moderately poor	83	41.5
Average poor household	72	38.6

Source: UBOS, 2001

Up to June 2001, all urban poor households had the financial ability to pay for unsubsidized costs of 'Electricity (1)' offered within the 30 kWh bracket. After the tariff change, the financial ability of households (especially the extremely poor) had been reduced so significantly that they could hardly afford the prices of 'Electricity (2)'. After the change in tariff, the expenditure of poor households on 'Electricity (2)' was inadequate to meet the purchasing power of the unsubsidized energy, rendering subsidies decisive in the ability of extremely poor households to afford

Table 8.8 Projection of basic costs of using electricity in a typical urban poor household

Activity	Appliance	No of items	No. of hrs per day	Estimated units required	Total cost (a) @ UShs100	Total cost (b) @ UShs168
Lighting	60w bulbs	3	4	21.6 kWh	2,160	3,628.8
Entertainment	15w radio	1	10	4.5 kWh	450	756
Ironing	1000w flat iron	1	0.5	15 kWh	1,500	2,520
Cooking	2000w hot plate	1	3	180 kWh	18,000	30,240
Cooking	With improved charcoal stove	1	4	2.5kg	415	415
Grand total with electricity only				221.1 kWh	22,110	37,144.8
Grand total with electricity for lighting and charcoal for cooking				3.5	4,525	7,320

Source: Survey by author

energy. The *moderately poor*, whose energy expenditure was the highest among the poor, could only obtain an equivalent of about 41 kWh with the changed tariff. From their energy budget, the *very poor* category could only obtain about 33 kWh, and the *extremely poor* only 18 kWh.

In addition to the above analysis, the study made an assessment of the basic energy requirements of a typical poor household, aiming to measure the adequacy of the 30 kWh of electricity offered at the lifeline tariff. An assessment of the energy requirements for households was derived by tabulating household energy use per item, and the period that electricity could be required for each activity, per day, for one month. The results are shown in Table 8.8.

The cost of electricity was initially computed using the unsubsidized prices and the 1993 tariff (see column 6). The 2002 tariff (column 7) was used for comparison. According to the table, the basic amount of electricity that a household with two rooms would need for cooking would be more than 220 kWh. However, if charcoal was used for cooking instead of electricity, the household would need at least 41 kWh of electricity. The basic electricity requirement therefore surpasses the amount of 30 kWh provided by the subsidy.[2]

The next chapter examines the relationship between subsidies and upfront costs.

30

Are Subsidies for Upfront Costs
a Better Option?

Apart from the subsidy embedded in energy consumption, the study also looked at the impact of upfront costs in affecting the access to energy by the urban poor. The rationale was that upfront energy costs might hinder access to modern forms of energy by the poor. The current low-voltage electricity distribution policy stipulates that individual households are expected to meet the cost of connection from the nearest service point. Two issues are involved, the cost of house wiring by individual households and upfront costs payable to the utility for connection to the grid.

Market surveys were used to estimate wiring materials and labour costs needed for a two-roomed house requiring the erection of only one pole to effect connection. The cost of equipment and materials used for connecting households to the grid was derived from the records of the Uganda Electricity Distribution Company Limited (UEDCL)[3] (see Appendices 8.2 and 8.3). The materials provided by the UEDCL remain the property of the company.

The cost of materials was used as a proxy for connection fees required by the utility for electricity connection. By comparing annual household energy expenditure to the unsubsidized cost of connection for the shortest possible distance, the affordability levels for the poor were derived. The analysis considered both lump sum and amortized upfront energy costs.

Throughout the period in which the 1993 tariff was applicable, the UEB policy for domestic consumers offered a 79 per cent subsidy on connection fees to all households. The subsidy would be effective if the premises were located within a one-pole distance (about 30 metres) from the nearest point of access. A review of the connections made by the UEB during the period under review indicated that more than 90 per cent of the new connections carried out were according to that specification. The subsidy didn't cover the cost of internal house wiring, however: that remained a household responsibility. Thus households had to cater for upfront costs comprising house wiring charges, utility connection fees and the cost of electrical equipment like bulbs, a flat iron and other devices (see Appendices 8.4–8.6).

In many cases, upfront costs of electricity have been the major deterrent factor to households wishing to access electricity. Although the UEDCL maintained the capital cost contribution subsidy at 79 per cent after revising the tariff in 2001 and 2002 (Appendices 8.2 and 8.3), the effectiveness of this subsidy has still to be demonstrated for poor households. The financial decision to be made about switching from non-commercial traditional means of energy to electricity is also dependent on various circumstances.

If the premises are self-owned, the following different scenarios in the costs incurred should be compared:

* Subsidized connection fees + cost of house wiring + cost of equipment + subsidized monthly cost of electricity (Cost 1); or

* Subsidized connection fees + cost of house wiring + cost of equipment + non-subsidized monthly cost of electricity (Cost 2); or

* Non-subsidized connection fees + cost of house wiring + cost of equipment + non-subsidized monthly cost of electricity (Cost 3); or

* Non-subsidized connection fees + cost of house wiring + cost of equipment + subsidized monthly cost of electricity (Cost 4).

If the premises are rented, the first two costs of connection fees and house wiring may not be incurred. And if wiring of the premises has already been done, the only financial requirement would be either:

* Cost of equipment + subsidized monthly cost of electricity (Cost 5); or

* Cost of equipment + non-subsidized monthly cost of electricity (Cost 6).

Table 8.9 The cost of switching from other sources of energy to electricity, and its effect on annual energy budgets for poor urban households

Range of costs to be incurred		Moderately poor	Very poor	Extremely poor
Cost 1	SF + 135,000 + 197,000 + 48,600 =	534,200	502,640	446,912
Cost 2	NSF + 135,000 + 197,000 + 48,600 =	615,608	567,321	482,057
Cost 3	SF + 135,000 + 389,492 + 48,600 =	726,692	695,132	639,404
Cost 4	NSF + 135,000 + 389,492 + 48,600 =	808,100	759,813	674,549
Cost 5	NSF + 48,600 =	283,608	235,321	150,057
Cost 6	SF + 48,600 =	202,200	170,640	114,912
	Affordability ratios			
Cost 1		3.48	4.11	6.73
Cost 2		4.00	4.64	7.26
Cost 3		4.73	5.69	9.64
Cost 4		5.26	6.22	10.17
Cost 5		1.84	1.92	2.26
Cost 6		1.31	1.39	1.7

Notes: Cost SF represents subsidized fuel costs and Cost NSF represents the cost of non-subsidized fuel. The already known cost of electricity subsidy was removed from the total energy cost for NSF. Household energy expenditure and the cost of equipment take into consideration both lighting and cooking.[4]
Source: Survey by author

These costs comprise market prices for materials needed to install electricity in a two-roomed house, the cost of basic energy appliances and other costs for connecting to the grid. The detailed list of these items can be found in Appendices 8.4–8.6. The cost of fuel was based on the electricity tariff prevailing in 1999 and the average household energy expenditure for each category per month was derived from the National Household Survey of 1999/2000. The computations used for the above cost combinations are summarized in Table 8.9.

In all the six scenarios of cost combinations, standard minimum costs for each item were maintained in arriving at estimates to cover house wiring, connection fees and basic electrical equipment for a poor household. The main variation across the household categories was the annual household expenditure on energy, which comprised the cost of fuel. Current expenditure on energy was built into all fixed costs (1–6) in order to provide a clear illustration of the total cost that a household would incur in switching from other forms of fuel to electricity.

The two costs common to both self-owned and rented households were the minimum costs for wiring and the cost of basic electrical equipment. It is possible that different tastes and knowledge of the market could influence choices of equipment for households. Some households would probably spend more than others on the same items. However, the same is not true for wiring standards, which have to meet the strict specifications of the Ministry of Works and Housing. Equipment considered as not basic for households was left out of the estimated computation of the total cost.

The analysis indicated that the cost of house wiring comprised a substantial part of fixed upfront costs. The rigidity of wiring standards demanded by the Ministry of Works and Housing could be considered to be higher than the basic requirements of simple households. The total cost of wiring alone could be considered rather unfair to poor urban households, who may in practice not need the same level of sophistication. It could be proposed that, without compromising safety, the cost of wiring be greatly reduced and made more affordable to households by the use of fewer materials than those indicated by the Ministry of Works and Housing. This is because poor urban households use electricity mainly for lighting. A different ensemble of wiring equipment – requiring smaller and relatively cheaper transformers, cables and other insulated equipment – could be utilized. This would be less costly to the utility and the consumer. A cheaper option of Single Wire Earth Return (SWER), as indicated in Table 8.10, could be a solution to reduce upfront costs for poor households whose overall usage of electricity need not demand heavy investment. The same mechanism has been field-tested in countries like Australia, Brazil, Botswana, Côte d'Ivoire, Gabon, Morocco and South Africa, and is adjudged to have made a tremendous difference. Estimates for a typical poor household unit of two rooms are presented in Table 8.10.

Table 8.10 Cost of wiring a two-roomed house by SWER

Material	No.	Cost in Ushs@	Total
13A gang flush socket[1]	2	3500	7000
5A 1-gang 1-way flush switch[2]	2	2500	5000
40w incandescent lamp or equivalent lamp holder pendant (screw-type)[3]	2	2000	4000
Ceiling roses[4]	2	500	1,000
Wire lighting points in 1.5 mm PVC insulated in-fill conduit	12 meters	550	6600
Wire for socket power point in 2.5 mm PVC insulated cable in-fill conduit in concealed metallic box	8 meters	700	5600
Consumer unit[5]	1	25,000	25,000
5A MCB[6]	2	15,000	30,000
Labour costs			15,000
Total cost			99,200

Notes: 1 Normal wall socket outlet; 2 Normal 1-way light wall switch; 3 A bulb holder that is fixed on the ceiling or wall. Mainly used in bathrooms; 4 A bulb holder that is suspended from the ceiling by the electrical cable; 5 Main junction box that contains the circuit breakers; 6 Miniature circuit breaker
Source: Da Silva and Kyokutamba, 2002

The cost of SWER would only be 73.7 per cent of the conventional wiring of the same two-roomed house and it is more affordable for low-income households. In areas where 3-phase machinery is needed, booster converters would be used at a lower cost than 3-phase wiring. The adoption of the SWER mechanism would be subject, however, to current standards for Medium Tension, Low Tension and house wiring as set and maintained by law. After being studied and reviewed by stakeholders and found suitable by the custodians of standards, the SWER mechanism could be adopted so that households would use cheaper material to access electricity.

In addition to the possible reduced cost of wiring, awareness of energy efficiency methods and practices by households could reduce the final cost of energy consumption. Such practices would encourage the adoption of demand-side mechanisms like using energy-efficient devices for lighting and heating. As a result, electricity usage per unit cost would be reduced, resulting in lower electricity bills.

This study assumed that capital support would continue to be available for the foreseeable future. It based the possibility of policy intervention for poor households on estimates of the total cost of house wiring and connection that would be financed through loans to willing consumers.

If the electricity distribution company has enough funds, it could choose to finance the project and recover the loans through monthly bills, in addition to supporting connection costs to premises. Alternatively, the utility could approach a bank to finance the project and manage the loans on its behalf. In addition, other credit institutions could be encouraged to participate in granting loan schemes. The repayment period for individual borrowers would depend on the prevailing commercial terms given by the lending institution, which should be tailored to suit household energy expenditure trends.

Households wishing to access the electricity connection loan could be given an opportunity to utilize their energy budgets upfront and would have to commit themselves to paying a small interest fee for the loan. The method of loan recovery could be based on amortized costs of house wiring, connection to the grid, basic electrical equipment and monthly electricity bills. The difference in the value of the loan to various household categories would be reflected in the component of monthly energy consumption bills. Table 8.11 presents a projection of the loan repayment schedule.

Table 8.11 Loan repayment schedule for household electricity connection

Household category	Loan amount	Loan period	Principal cost	Premium
Moderately poor	534,200	Five years	745,794	12,430
Very poor	502,640	Seven years	791,236	9420
Extremely poor	446,915	> Sixteen years	>1 million	5844

Source: Survey by author

Moderately poor households (using 1999 income levels) would be able to pay back the loan within five years at an interest rate of 14 per cent by paying UShs12,430 per month. By the end of the fifth year, the household would have paid UShs745,794. The other figures can also be interpreted in the same fashion. Using only their energy expenditure budgets the extremely poor category of households would need a much longer payback period. The extremely poor households would pay back their loans within a period of about 16 years.

The utility could test this new idea through a pilot project to bring interested households to appreciate the method of loan recovery and amortized billing. In order to ensure that households included in the initial pilot project actually pay back the loans, it is proposed that only households engaged in some income-generating activity be connected at first. To manage the loan in the initial stage as a pilot project and guarantee that members pay back the loan when it is due, the money could be placed in a revolving fund so that other households would benefit.

The loan module can be operated in the same manner that the utility manages loans taken by the government for energy projects. Currently, the government incurs interest rates of less than 5 per cent when borrowing money from international finance institutions. The loans, initially lent to UEB before being transferred to successor companies of UEB for various power projects, carry interest rates of 7.5–10 per cent for periods of seven to ten years.[5]

On the same basis, the distribution company could borrow funds for extending power connection to poor households for a medium-term repayment period of ten to twelve or fifteen years. The rates would be based on Bank of Uganda marginal rates for onlending purposes. If the scheme were to be supported directly by commercial banks, current lending rates are in the range of 13–15 per cent for long-term development projects. These rates provide a competitive financial environment for households that have some income generation activities. Assuming that inflation maintains its current trend, the cost of the loan would be competitive.

The current energy subsidies are supposed to improve the access of the poor to energy services. But whether this objective is attained or not depends on whether the subsidies are properly targeted towards the poor. The next chapter examines who captures the energy subsidies.

31

Who Captures the Subsidies?

In the study poor households who used electricity were derived from the total number of electricity consumers billed by the utility in 1999. The maximum amount of electricity consumed by different income groups and the level of subsidy inherent in each consumption block or level per month were computed. The computation was then used to derive the equivalent amount of energy consumed without subsidies for each tariff level and income group. The different types of subsidies considered are:

- the lifeline tariff;
- electricity tariffs below the long-run marginal cost;
- subsidies in the form of connection fees for domestic premises.

The analysis considered only recurrent energy consumption and did not include subsidies offered to meet upfront energy costs, owing to lack of data on the number of connections and the level of subsidies.

The number of households connected to electricity nationally in 1999 is tabulated in Table 8.12.

Table. 8.12 Number of households connected to grid electricity in 1999

Expenditure group (000 UShs)	No. of urban households	No. of rural households	Total no. of households
0–50	768	186	954
50–100	10,862	2866	13,728
100–150	26,323	3076	29,396
150–250	40,908	5792	46,700
250–400	35,265	3687	38,952
400–600	20,939	2876	23,817
600 plus	44,982	4301	49,283
TOTAL	180,047	22,784	202,830

Source: UBOS, 2001

From the records collected, far less than 1 per cent of the households in the *extremely poor* category had electricity connection. Five and 13 per cent of the *very poor* and *moderately* poor categories households had electricity. This implies that poor urban households together comprised

19 per cent of all households with electricity from UEB in 1999. Poor households had notably fewer electricity connections than non-poor households. Consequently, the benefit of subsidized electricity was enjoyed by a much lesser percentage of consumers among poor than among non-poor households.

After categorizing electricity consumers, the next step was to compute and establish the actual quantity of subsidized units consumed by each group of households. The UEB tariff schedule (1993) for domestic consumers stipulated the levels of consumption and subsidized units of electricity offered. The computation of the financial implication at each consumption level revealed the impact created by each level of subsidy as displayed in Table 8.13.

Table 8.13 Summary of the domestic electricity tariff, true cost and subsidy (1993)

Total units of electricity subsidized (kWh)	Unit cost in UShs	Subsidized cost of energy in UShs	Cost of subsidy in UShs	Effect of VAT and service charge in UShs	Total cost including subsidy in UShs	Total cost without subsidy in UShs
30	20	600	2400	1272	1872	4272
170	70	11,900	5100	3193	15,093	20,193
200	70	12,500	7500	3295	15,795	23,295

Note: Value Added Tax for the service was 17% and the service charge was UShs 1000
Source: UEB, 1993

In Table 8.13, the subsidy on each consumption level is identified as the difference between the actual total cost incurred by consumers and what should have been payable. The maximum subsidy that can be captured on a household's energy expenditure is presented in the fourth column of the table. However, the specific level of subsidy captured depends on the actual energy expenditure of individual households.

Table 8.14 assumes that the entire energy expenditure of poor households with an electricity connection is applied to purchasing

Table 8.14 Urban poor household expenditure on energy converted to electricity and level of subsidy captured relative to the total subsidy offered (1993 tariff)

Household category	Amount spent on electricity in UShs	Number of units consumed (kWh)	Maximum subsidy captured in UShs	Percentage of total subsidy captured
Non-poor	> 15,795	200+	7,500	100.0
Moderately poor	12,800	161	6,330	84.4
Very poor	10,170	130	5,400	72.0
Extremely poor	5,525	75	3,750	50.0
Average poor h'hold	11,880	150	6,000	80.0

Source: Survey by author; UEB, 1993

electricity and shows the possible equivalent amount of electricity accessed by each category. It also portrays the cost and implications of the subsidy on the energy expenditure of each household category.

The non-poor households, who can afford to purchase more than 200 units (the maximum amount of subsidy), enjoy a 100 per cent subsidy benefit on electricity. The *moderately poor*, however, can only capture 84 per cent of the subsidy, the *very poor* only obtain 72 per cent, and the *extremely poor* only 50 per cent.

Tables 8.13 and 8.14 show that non-poor households with incomes above UShs150,000 are able to capture a higher percentage of the subsidy offered on electricity than poor households. The limitation of this analysis is that, in practice, none of the households use all their energy expenditure on electricity. Nevertheless, poor urban households do not benefit from the electricity subsidy as much as the non-poor. This is not only because few poor households are connected to the grid but also because those connected consume fewer units of electricity than the total number of units to which the subsidy applies.

Resources for energy subsidies come either from the energy utility or from the government. Impacts on these two sources are analyzed in the next chapter.

32

What is the Impact of Subsidies
on Utilities and Public Finance?

Using the detailed UEB tariff schedule for 1993 (Table 8.15), the study assumes that the long-run marginal cost reflects the true cost of supplying electricity. Thus all tariff determinants like bulk sales, time-of-day use and cost of distribution are held constant and all tariff charges priced below the LRMC for any of the UEB tariff codes are considered subsidized. The assumption implies that the only unsubsidized tariffs in the whole schedule are the two tariffs set above the LRMC:

- those relating to energy sold on Code 2 for commercial and small industrial supplies up to 50kVA; and

- energy sold on Code 5 for streetlights.

Subsidies from setting the tariff below the LRMC

In the report of the final study conducted by Price Waterhouse and UEB in 1990, it was stated that the LRMC was the main principle used for designing the 1993 electricity tariffs. As a long-term load management tool, the LRMC was to ensure adequate supply for a system facing severe supply constraints in the areas of generation, transmission and distribution. The report specified that the LRMC concept was preferred because it carried provisions for sufficient pricing and proper signals to discourage wasteful consumption. The UEB tariff schedule designed during that time is shown on Table 8.15.

According to the tariff design, domestic consumers were the primary determinants of the system peak, occurring at 6–8 am in the morning and 7–11 pm in the evenings, when most household activities were in progress. The LRMC-based cost rate assigned user responsibility for the capacity during peak hours in such a way that most of the usage levels in the tariff and energy rate were set to equal the LRMC at the distribution level.

In application however, whereas the LRMC measured additional costs as a result of each additional output, prices set on the LRMC alone were inadequate. LRMC prices alone could not ably guarantee the revenue requirements of the electricity system to ensure its sustainability. Revenue requirements were therefore based on the cost of depreciation,

Table 8.15 The UEB tariff schedule (1993)

Code	Amount covered	Tariff since 1993 (UShs/kWh)	Required percentage to reach the average tariff (level of subsidy)
Code 1 Domestic (a) (b) (c)	1–30 units 31–200 units Above 200 units Standing service fee	UShs20 per unit UShs70 per unit UShs100 per unit UShs1000	80 30 0
Code 2 Commercial/small industrial	Low-voltage supplies up to 50 kVA Unit charge Standing service fee	UShs115 per unit UShs4000 per month	−15
Code 3.1 Large industrial/commercial	High-voltage tariff (with maximum demand of 500kVA and over, taken at 11,000/33,000 volts. Minimum MD charge 500 kVA 1st 2000 kVA All over 2000 kVA Unit charge Standing service fee	UShs10,000 per kVA UShs8000 per kVA UShs70 per unit Ushs15,000/month	30
Code 3.2 Large industrial/commercial	High-voltage off-peak tariff. For consumers on Code 3.1, an off-peak rate is available for supplies taken and separately metered between 11 pm and 6 am daily. Subject to special arrangement. Unit charge	UShs50 per unit	50
Code 4.1 General tariff (commercial and industrial)	Low-voltage supplies in excess of 50 kVA up to 500 kVA Minimum MD charge 50 kVA per month All kVA Unit charge Standing service fee	UShs10,000 per KVA UShs75 per unit UShs10,000 per month	25

Table 8.15 cont.

Code	Amount covered	Tariff since 1993 (UShs/kWh)	Required percentage to reach the average tariff (level of subsidy)
Code 4.2 General tariff (commercial and industrial) off-peak	For consumers on Code 4.1, an off-peak rate is available for supplies taken and separately metered between 11 pm and 6 am daily. Subject to special agreement. Unit charge	UShs55 per unit	45
Code 5 Street lighting	Unit charge Standing service fee	UShs125 per unit Ushs4000 per month	−25

Code 6 Time-of-day tariff	Energy costs	Demand charges
On-peak rate (6 pm–11 pm)	UShs130 per kVA	UShs10,000 per kVA per month
Off-peak rate (11 pm –5 am)	UShs65 per kVA	UShs5000 per kVA per month
Shoulder rate (5 am–6 pm)	UShs94 per kVA	UShs10,000 per kVA per month

Source: UEB, 1993

average incremental efficiency of the plant and the economic cost of investment. In that regard, although the LRMC that was used to establish the electricity tariff was UShs94, what was considered the optimum price of electricity was the average tariff of UShs100 per unit, as charged under Code 1c.

The percentage required to reach the average tariff of electricity in each setting was considered to be equivalent to the level of subsidy offered on that tariff. The optimum tariff of UShs100 per unit was used to determine the subsidy offered by UEB to consumers for each tariff. The percentage subsidy varied from 80 per cent, in the case of the lifeline domestic tariff, to 30 per cent on the next domestic tariff. For the domestic supply, no subsidy at all was offered for units in excess of 200 kWh, for which the optimum tariff for power was charged. In other cases, like commercial and small industrial enterprises and street lights, the tariffs were set higher than the average tariff by 15 and 25 per cent respectively, implying that proceeds from those categories could have been used to cross-subsidize other utility consumers. The financial impact of the subsidy on the utility was computed by quantifying the total sum of the subsidy from annual energy sales, using the information in the next section.

The subsidy on electricity consumption bills

In order to test whether or not electricity subsidies placed too great a burden on public sector finances, the total amount of electricity sold by the utility at subsidized prices was examined. Data regarding energy sales and revenue for the year 1999 were obtained from the Consumer Billing Department of the UEB. The level of subsidy offered was computed using the electricity bill frequency. By considering the billed quantity in each tariff category and multiplying it by the current tariff, which included the subsidy, it was possible to derive the total revenue obtained from each tariff range. Table 8.16 reveals the actual billing made in each tariff code and the expected revenue.

Table 8.16 Tariff frequency analysis for subsidized energy for the year 1999

	Billing quantity (kWh)	Total revenue at subsidized prices (UShs)	Expected revenue without subsidies	Gross subsidy (UShs)	Subsidy as percentage of tariff
Class code 1					
(a) 1-30 kWh	39,437,571	788,751,420	3,943,757,100	3,155,005,680	80
(b) 31-200 kWh	152,341,353	10,663,894,710	15,234,135,300	4,570,240,590	30
6.1 (For Diplomats)	78,324	5,482,680	7,832,400	2,349,720	30
Subtotal	191,857,248	11,458,128,810	19,185,724,800	7,727,595,990	40.3
Code 3.1-3.2					
Regular tariff	58,757,958	4,111,057,083	5,875,795,800	1,764,738,717	30
Off peak	142,850,066	7,142,503,298	14,285,006,600	7,142,503,302	50
Subtotal	201,608,024	11,253,560,381	20,160,802,400	8,907,242,019	44.2
Code 4.1, 4.2 & 6.4					
Regular tariff	133,249,218	9,993,691,346	13,324,921,800	3,331,230,454	25
Off-peak	18,773,796	1,032,558,771	1,877,379,600	844,820,829	45
Subtotal	152,023,014	11,026,250,117	15,202,301,400	4,176,051,283	27.5
Grand total		33,737,939,308	54,548,828,600	20,810,889,292	38.2

Source: UEB, 1999

The tariff given in each code in Table 8.15 was used to derive the current price of electricity for Table 8.16. By taking the total billed energy in kWh and multiplying it by the optimum tariff of UShs100 in all cases, the total subsidy in each tariff category was derived. The subsidy thus obtained from the billing was presented as a percentage of the optimum amount of revenue that ought to have been received had electricity been sold at the optimum price (expected revenue).

The total subsidy on domestic consumption represented by codes 1a, 1b and 6.1 was about 46 per cent of the true cost of electricity. The table indicates a high subsidy of 80 per cent at the lifeline level (Code 1a). However, the low level of electricity sales sold in that category had a correspondingly small effect on the total subsidy accruing to consumers. Yet in Code 1b, where the subsidy contribution of 30 per cent was lower, a higher level of energy consumed was billed and this had a relatively higher impact. Non-domestic codes 3.1, 3.2, 4.1 and 6.4 were billed below the average tariff, and carried subsidies in the range 27–44 per cent. The total volume of electricity sales in all codes sold to UEB consumers in 1999 carried subsidies up to 38 per cent of what the revenue might have been.

This study attempted to relate the level of subsidy to the national economic situation and to the public financial burden. An outline of the whole scope of electricity subsidies to consumers was analyzed first. The gross subsidy obtained was then compared to the GDP and the national budget deficit for the financial year 1999/2000. The GDP and national budget support figures used to assess the effect of the subsidy were derived from a government document, the *Background to the Budget, (1999/2000)*.

Detailed data on electricity sold and revenue realized, derived from Table 8.16, were used to examine the financial effect of the subsidy. The actual amount spent, and the level of subsidy to electricity consumers, is presented in Table 8.17.

Table 8.17 Amount of electricity subsidy in each tariff code

Code	Amount subsidized (UShs)	Level of subsidy as percentage
1a	3,155,005,680	15.16
1b	4,570,240,590	21.96
6.1	2,349,720	0.01
3.1	1,764,738,717	8.48
3.2	7,142,503,302	34.32
4.1	3,331,230,454	16.01
4.2	844,820,829	4.06
All codes	20,810,889,292	100.00

Source: UEB, 2000; GoU, 1999

During the financial year 1999/2000, GDP was UShs363,645 billion, whilst the budget deficit for which support was sought externally in the same period was UShs96,738 billion (GoU, 1999). When compared with

Table 8.18 Summary of the effect of subsidies on public finances

Tariff code	Gross subsidy – revenue forgone by UEB (UShs)	Subsidy as a percentage of GDP (UShs363,645,000,000)	Subsidy as a percentage of national budget deficit (UShs96,738,000,000).
Code 1 & 6.1	7,727,595,990	2.13	7.99
Code 3	8,907,242,019	2.45	9.21
Code 4 & 6.4	4,176,051,283	1.15	4.32
Total subsidy on energy sales	20,810,889,292	5.73	21.52

Source: GoU, 2000; UEB, 2000

GDP alone, the total electricity subsidy was about 6 per cent; and the subsidy compared to the budget deficit was about 22 per cent. Table 8.18 summarizes the financial comparison of the consumer price subsidy to GDP and the national budget deficit.

The subsidy offered to electricity consumers in the three tariff codes was compared. The level of subsidy offered in codes 1 and 6.1 for domestic bills only was 2 and 8 per cent respectively of GDP and the budget deficit for the financial year 1999/2000. Electricity sold under other tariff codes (3,4 and 6.4) was billed below the LRMC. The revenue obtained from codes 3.4 and 6.4 was less than the optimum figure. Subsidized revenue was 4 per cent of GDP and 14 per cent of the national budget deficit for the period 1999/2000. The sum of these ratios gives us the inclusive result (6 per cent of GDP, 22 per cent of the budget deficit) mentioned above.

Senior members of the utility have argued that electricity subsidies are often used as a critical tool to attract investment into an economy, and that Uganda has needed to do this given the current low level of industrialization. The technocrats added that there is a growing need to create jobs through increased production. Low tariffs are therefore necessary to enhance low production costs and to make product prices competitive. Large consumers are also cheap to serve because they use bulk power, which is cheap to transport and maintain. Such consumers, they argued, pay more in actual terms because of the consolidated charge they pay on each kilovolt ampère (kVA) installed, rather than on the level of usage. From this perspective, too, subsidized tariffs could be desirable and should not be perceived simply as a burden on the public sector.

While analyzing the high level of subsidization of consumer tariffs, and contemplating how best subsidies could benefit the economy, national data on grid connections were examined. It was indicated that the total number of household consumers with access to electricity at the time was less than 4 per cent. The subsidy was then compared with the number of households that would have been served had the same amount of money been used to connect households instead. This analysis was combined with another regarding the subsidy on capital cost contribution and its possible effects. The impact of the subsidy on public finance was also examined and presented.

The subsidy on capital cost contribution (upfront costs)

As indicated elsewhere in this study, all new grid electricity consumers were expected to pay a capital cost contribution for the connection of power to their premises. As part of the policy targeted to encourage domestic electricity consumers, the 1993 UEB tariff design included a subsidy of 79 per cent on that initial cost of service. The UEDCL retained this subsidy after the tariff was changed in June 2001. The subsidy is on the full cost of materials, accessories, labour and overhead costs for service to a domestic scheme within an 80-metre distance that requires no new pole to be erected. All schemes constructed for a distance exceeding one pole are normally excluded from the subsidy and the full cost of the scheme is paid. Where the subsidy is applicable, the utility has costs indicated for the unsubsidized cost of the service and what client should pay at subsidized rates.

The initial capital requirement for a new electricity installation was given as UShs389,492 in 1999. However, with the 79 per cent subsidy, the cost of the service to consumers was only UShs80,000. For purposes of analysing the issue, it was estimated that 90 per cent of all schemes connected in 1999 were subsidized. The average cost of connection was taken to be a standard proxy to represent the unsubsidized cost of each new connection. A similar cost was used to estimate the revenue forgone by the utility in the process of connecting 90 per cent of the 4,200 new schemes, instead of charging the full cost for the service.[6]

The total cost of subsidy extended to domestic consumers towards capital contribution was determined by computing the forgone revenue to the utility through the financing of the schemes. To ascertain the cost of forgone revenue, the true capital cost of the scheme that should have accrued to UEB in 1999 was computed by multiplying the unsubsidized cost of the scheme by 90 per cent of all the schemes constructed by the utility. The total subsidized revenue from the same number of schemes was computed by multiplying the result by the subsidized cost of each scheme. The forgone revenue to the utility was derived when the two results were compared.

If each of the 3,780 new schemes extended to domestic consumers had been charged at the unsubsidized cost of UShs389,492, instead of UShs80,000, the utility would have received UShs1,472 million as revenue. However, the same number of schemes connected and charged at UShs80,000 each earned revenue of only UShs302 million for the utility. The reduced earnings from the service imply that subsidizing the schemes cost the utility and government a total of UShs1,170 million. The forgone revenue comprised the cost of subsidy incurred by the utility for connecting domestic consumers. The utility's forgone revenue was compared to public finances, and to the GDP and the budget deficit for the financial year 1999/2000.

Effect of capital cost contribution subsidy on GDP

The GDP for the financial period 1999/2000 was UShs363,645 million. The forgone revenue carried in subsidies to capital cost contribution for new schemes was UShs1,170 million. The subsidy on capital cost contribution as a percentage of GDP was approximately 0.3 per cent.

Capital cost contribution towards the installation of electricity in a household could be considered as a development fund towards the expansion of the national grid. With the current low level of national connection, a contribution of 0.3 per cent of GDP in a year was significantly low. Analysis of the impact of the subsidy compared to the need for accelerated electrification suggests that the capital cost contribution needs to be subsidized further, so as to enable more consumers to access the grid.

Considering the small number of households that have benefited from the subsidy, it is easy to conclude that either the current level of subsidy attached to capital cost contribution is very low and inadequate; or that the total upfront cost of connection is too high for most households. On the other hand, the fact that very few households are able to get access to electricity means that most households cannot benefit from the increased power generation capacity that UEB has developed over the years.

Given that higher capacity, the government may realize that it needs to change the current marketing strategy so as to provide electricity to the growing number of potential local domestic consumers of electricity before focusing on the export market. Increased support for households to afford the capital cost contribution could be one of the dynamic ways to market electricity by targeting local demand.

Effect of capital cost contribution subsidy on budget deficit

The budget deficit for the financial year 1999/2000 was Ushs96,738 million. In the previous section, the subsidy on capital cost contribution during the year 1999 was shown to have been UShs1,170 million. When the above cost was compared to total capital requirement for connections made to domestic premises at UShs1,472 million, the ratio was less than one. The effect of the subsidy on capital cost contribution to total budget support requirement was only 1 per cent.

This study has assumed that power extension to households is an investment meant to improve people's welfare, like investment in education, water or health. It has also been assumed that it would be in the national interest if as many households as possible had access to such a service. From that perspective, a 1 per cent equivalent of the national budget support requirement could be regarded as an insignificant cost, given the low level of electrification (less than 5 per cent) in the country as a whole. Considering the purpose to which capital cost contribution was directed, the subsidy was not a burden on public finances at all. Rather, the equivalent of 1 per cent could be considered a very inadequate contribution to the welfare of households.

Compared to other forms of electricity subsidies that were in force at that time, capital cost contribution ought to have received a higher proportion of the subsidy than was the case. Table 8.19 presents a summary of the financial implications of the three electricity subsidies: the lifeline tariff, the tariffs charged below the LRMC and the subsidy on capital cost contribution. The subsidies are then compared to economic indicators for 1999/2000.

The level of subsidy offered in the form of the lifeline tariff (0–30 kWh) was almost 1 per cent of the GDP in 1999/2000 and more than 3 per cent of the cost of the budget deficit during the same period. Although the utility would not regard the tariffs set below the LRMC as subsidies, even if they had the same effect, the type of subsidy they carried was the highest of them all: 5 per cent of GDP and 18 per cent of the budget deficit for the year 1999/2000. Capital cost contribution was the least of all, with 0.03 per cent of GDP and 1 per cent of the budget deficit. If the total subsidy on electricity was used to finance new schemes, about 56,429 new domestic schemes would be connected to the grid in one year. Given the same cost rate it should have taken only three years for the utility to double the number of domestic consumers in the year 1999.

This study has limited itself to costs incurred by households and the power distributor, but system planners should note that expansion of the customer base could call for up-rating of the subtransmission system.

Table 8.19 The effect of electricity subsidies on the national budget in 1999/2000

Type of subsidy	Annual cost of subsidized electricity (UShs)	Cost of electricity without subsidies (UShs)	Revenue forgone by UEB (cost of subsidy) in UShs	Cost of subsidy as % of GDP	Cost of subsidy as a %of national budget deficit
Life line tariff	788,751,420	3,943,757,100	3,155,005,680	0.87	3.26
All electricity tariffs set below the LRMC	32,951,187,888	50,605,071,500	17,653,883,612	4.85	18.25
Capital cost contribution	302,400,000	1,472,279,760	1,169,879,760	0.32	1.21
Total electricity subsidy (UShs.)	34,042,339,308	56,021,108,360	21,978,769,052	6.04	22.72
Total electricity subsidy (US $)	19,452,765	32,012,062	12,559,297		

Source: UEB, 1999; GoU, 1999

Table 8.20 Selected performance indicators for the Uganda Electricity Board, 1999–2000 (in millions of UShs)

Year	Current assets	Current liabilities	Monthly sales	Equity/ retained earnings	Long-term debt	Debt service coverage ratio
1991	15,606.9	20,997.0	746.8	224,675.4	62,914.2	0.28
1992	21,968.0	28,727.6	1,738.0	267,819.9	52,198.9	0.19
1993	37,382.9	26,388.2	2,420.3	513,584.5	76,423.8	0.15
1994	46,898.3	28,816.6	3,843.9	525,666.8	90,852.9	0.17
1995	56,588.9	32,752.8	4,002.5	537,502.4	138,148.2	0.26
1996	77,076.0	46,026.0	4,658.3	471,732.4	157,658.9	0.33
1997	81,769.4	63,193.0	5,154.6	357,832.0	189,034.9	0.53
1998	82,504.2	67,488.2	5,193.8	333,047.2	277,347.7	0.83
1999	96,667.0	80,268.1	5,458.5	324,162.1	512,758.1	1.58
2000	128,209.3	76,954.3	6,666.9	350,361.3	620,332.0	1.77

Source: UEB, 2000

Effect of subsidies on the long-term debt of the UEB

The UEB is a government parastatal established by the Electricity Act of parliament in 1964 and revised by the Electricity Act, 1999. All annual reports of the Board testify to the fact that, as a government parastatal, the UEB's programmes and projects were wholly financed by public capital in the form of either power sales or government-guaranteed loans sourced from bilateral and multilateral partners. Government would on-lend these loans to the UEB at low rates set by the Central Bank (Mugyenzi, 1999).

For a long time after the formation of the utility, the level of household electrification remained very low and tariffs were heavily subsidized to encourage industrial and household consumers (Kyokutamba, 2001). One of the consequences of low consumer tariffs was that the utility was often unable to conduct profitable commercial business with its clients. In order to manage its electrification programmes, the parastatal sought external financial assistance. Unfortunately, financial inability was compounded by other inherent inefficiencies caused by the monopolistic operations of the utility (Mugyenzi, 1999). Structural and performance problems weakened the financial structure and the pricing policy could not be contained.

Table 8.20 shows some financial indicators for the UEB (1991–2000), revealing an annual growth of current assets thanks to external financing through loans. New capital was also realized in improved monthly sales and increased equity and retained earnings each year. As the UEB continued to charge tariffs set below the LRMC, however, its ability to service debt diminished as the ratio steadily increased.

Although government had ceased to finance parastatals from the treasury and was promoting the policy of commercialization, the UEB was not able to adapt fully to the new demands. Failure to commercialize was based on the poor self-financing mechanisms of the utility and a tariff principle that was contrary to commercial practices (although this problem should not overshadow the fact that the majority of Ugandans still found the electricity tariff very high). Unless subsidized pricing was terminated, the low tariff design was bound to push the utility and the government into more serious financing problems. This was because the rate of growth of retained earnings was too low and would never grow to match the demands and effects that had been set by long-term debt.

The national external debt totals recorded in the years 1998, 1999 and 2000 were US$3,631.6 million, US$3,499.6 million and US$3,612.7 million respectively. Although the contribution of electricity to the national debt was more than 80 per cent in 1999, this represented a minimal contribution to the level of electrification in the country. Unfortunately, the level of indebtedness that was being experienced in the electricity sector, as given by the debt service ratio, had reached the most unbearable proportions.

The informal sectors in the urban areas of sub-Saharan African countries have become important providers of employment. Since at least some informal sector enterprises use electricity, the tariff rates affect their operations. The next chapter examines how subsidies incorporated in electricity tariffs affect the operations of informal sector enterprises.

33

What Are the Implications of Subsidies for the Informal Sector?

Research approach

During the study, two informal sector energy surveys were carried out and data collected on the types of enterprises operated by the urban poor, the types of energy sources and appliances used by small and micro-enterprises (SMEs), and the level of energy used. The important role of non-commercial energy sources like firewood and charcoal was noted by the study. While all energy types were addressed in order to appreciate the various energy sources used for production, however, more emphasis was placed on electricity.

The study appraised the basic rationale of energy subsidies, especially on electricity, and the extent to which subsidies facilitate reduced costs of production. All tariff codes that include subsidies were identified and used to test the extent to which the tariff setting facilitated production or enhanced equity. The extent to which initiatives improve access to commercial energy for SMEs was highlighted and assessed.

The scope of the study covered the domestic tariff, applicable to home-based enterprises, and the commercial tariffs, including those applicable to SMEs. For the analysis, data collection on the cost of electricity was based on the electricity tariff structure of 1993 and comparisons with the June 2001 and September 2002 tariffs.

Findings

There is anecdotal evidence that in Uganda, as in most African economies, the informal sector is the fastest-growing economic sector. Although it may not enjoy robust policy support, it has in many ways replaced government as the largest single employer. In the absence of reliable documentation on the type of industry and production enterprises operated by the informal sector, the research team carried out a couple of small-scale energy surveys in 2001.

The enterprises surveyed differ in size but were employing one to ten people. They were randomly selected from the poorer parts of Kampala. Reference was made to Kyokutamba (2001) for a list of common enterprises found in the informal sector and the energy types they use for production.

Other outdoor enterprises were also visited and interviewed. Although all energy sources were investigated, only electricity and charcoal were analyzed. The following issues were identified and investigated during the energy surveys:

- energy sources available;

- patterns of energy use and quantities utilized;

- cost of energy used for production;

- effect of tariffs on energy cost for enterprises using electricity;

- effect of different tariff rates for electricity in different sectors, consumption levels and consumption blocks;

- type of machinery used for production.

The enterprises investigated were mainly retail businesses and those that deal in small-scale manufacturing and fabrication: grain millers, food and beverages processing, wood workshops, foundry and metal fabrication workshops, hairdressing, secretarial/printing, bakeries, laundry places (*dhobi*), motor vehicle garages, restaurants, bars, fast-food outlets and tailors. It should be noted that even though the UEB tariff schedule used in the survey has been reviewed twice since the original survey, (June 2001 and September 2002), data on which the principal ideas were investigated remained unchanged. It was the contention of the research team that the information in the report remained applicable.

Extent of electricity use and the tariff implication
The findings indicated that very few urban poor households use electricity in home-based enterprises of the type being investigated. As a matter of fact, almost none of the enterprises where electricity was used – like hair salons and barbers, radio and electronic workshops, and some beer-selling enterprises – were operated in households. (This finding was confirmed by data from the national census, 2002). Most households that prepared food to be sold in restaurants used other energy forms like charcoal and firewood for cooking, even when they had access to electricity. What was disturbing, however, was that the level of activity of such enterprises and consequently their energy consumption seemed not to match their receipted bills from UEB. Tampering with the energy supply and metering installations could not be ruled out.

Many SMEs did not benefit from the subsidized tariff because they had no access to electricity at all. Worse still, with the reviews of June 2001 and September 2002 tariffs had been raised by 53 per cent since the year 2000, making a large hole in the profits of small business enterprises. Some households also revealed that they specifically avoid using electricity because of the poor distribution network. They reported experiencing dim lights in the early hours of the evening when they were busy and needed light most. They also argued that the utility's bills were higher than they should be, and that the light they paid for was not only dim but also unpredictable.

The implication was that, in the circumstances, 200 kWh of subsidized energy would not be sufficient to operate an enterprise successfully. A number of household-based enterprises indicated that, wherever possible, they supplemented electricity with other energy sources like kerosene to light their business premises at night, in case of power outages.

In order to get the broader view of electricity costs for enterprises, specific costs on the tariff code were examined. On the 1993 electricity tariff, Code 1 for households had three parts and two phases of subsidies below the LRMC. The optimum tariff was UShs100, but was not meant for business enterprises. Code 2 was for 'Commercial and small-scale industries'. On the 1993 tariff, this code was related to small-scale enterprises, especially those located outside the household. This same code was redesigned and merged with the household tariff to comprise 'Low-voltage supply for small general service'. The new codes were named 10.1 and 10.2, and retained in 2002.

Data from the UEB indicate that the 2001 tariff review equated the 'household tariff' with the 'small-scale commercial users' tariff' to form the 'low-voltage supply for small general service tariff'. From this tariff the difference in the financial requirement for upfront capital contribution was omitted. The consumption tariff that 'small-scale/ commercial enterprises' had to pay on Code 2 was UShs115 per kWh on the 1993 schedule. The tariff became UShs189 per kWh in 2001 and was adjusted to UShs168 in 2002. Forty per cent of the respondents who used electricity for production claimed that the tariff comprised a major part of their production expenses, and was burdensome.

Code 3.1 (see Appendices 8.13 and 8.14 for details of different codes) was for 'commercial and large industrial enterprises' on the 1993 tariff and became Code 20 for 'low-voltage supply for medium-scale industries' in the tariff changes of 2001 and 2002. Tariff charges on this code in the 1993 tariff schedule were only UShs70 per kWh; they were adjusted to UShs171.60 in 2001 and then to UShs152.40 in 2002.

Code 3.2 was another code for 'low-voltage supply for medium-scale consumers', labelled Code 22 after the tariff review. This tariff code was meant for maximum-demand consumers with a capacity of 50kVA who consumed power between 11 pm and 6 am. Power consumed during that time would cost only UShs50 per kWh. This charge was adjusted to UShs96.60 per kVA in 2001, and to UShs80.60 per kVA in 2002. Since the study was limited to SMEs, no respondents using this tariff code had been identified for the survey.

Differentiated energy consumption tariffs signified that the proportion of energy in the production cost was much higher for small commercial enterprises than it was for medium and large industrial/commercial enterprises. Tariff schedules showed that they were revised downwards in September 2002 after the hike in 2001 – but low-voltage users and commercial enterprises still had to pay more for the energy they consumed for production than their counterparts.

Although the tariffs for low-voltage medium industries and high-voltage large industrial users had the unique maximum-demand charge per installation, the extra ratings were realistically built in the tariff. Sources from the utility indicated that consumers are encouraged to use more power at night so as to smooth out the daily peak. Utility sources argued that since there are other cost-related issues in operating night shifts, utilities generally offer lower tariffs during this period. This provision could be interpreted to mean a favourable consideration of the production conditions. Unlike the cost of low-voltage supply on the small general service tariff, which seems so high for enterprises, the tariffs for industrial users were set to support enterprise production.

It should be noted that the main principle in tariff design has since changed from that of the LRMC, as used for the 1993 tariff, to 'full cost recovery plus profit for energy sold'. Unfortunately, the discriminatory principle that targeted profit from the tariff on small commercial users, while charging other consumers rather fairly, was maintained. Even after the tariff review, electricity used by small commercial enterprises was being charged at a higher tariff relative to other enterprises. Could it be true that the effect of the tariff on production might indicate that high commercial electricity tariffs would discourage production and the growth of enterprise?

Information obtained from members of the Gatsby Trust[7] on electricity consumption in typical production enterprises gave some insight into monthly energy bills (Table 8.21). Energy costs were the basic indicators of impact on production costs and the profitability of enterprises. The table reflects the very high monthly cost of electricity for small-scale manufacturers. The data were later used as benchmarks for related enterprise performance. Enterprise response to requests for information on related costs like business profitability and the percentage contribution of energy to the total cost of production was not forthcoming. Entrepreneurs clearly regarded business information as top secret!

Table 8.21 Typical power consumption in enterprises

Sector	Power rating	Monthly power bill
Maize mill	2 motors 60 KW	900,000–1,200,000
Carpentry	2 motors 7.5 KW	200,000
Foundry	3.75–5.25 KW	200,000
Metal fabrication	10 kVA	50,000–100,000
Secretarial/printing	5 kVA	100,000
Leather	4 kVA	30,000

Source: Uganda Gatsby Trust, 2002

In comparison with data from members of the Gatsby Trust, findings of the energy survey revealed the energy consumption data from commercial enterprises shown in Table 8.22. What the table reveals, first, is that the enterprises surveyed reported incredibly low levels of energy consumption, especially for electricity. The highest energy expenditure was for petroleum products and charcoal. Second, very few enterprises, if any, used grid electricity exclusively. If they had, they would probably have lost a lot of time without significant production activity at all, given the erratic and unreliable power supply experienced in the areas where their businesses were located. Consequently, enterprises had to have alternative sources of energy on standby, just in case the power went off.

Table 8.22 Energy usage in commercial enterprises

Energy type	No. of enterprises	Response percentage	Average expenditure on energy per enterprise	Average total amount spent per month
Electricity	28	40.0	10,714	300,000
Kerosene	12	17.1	5658	67,900
Petrol/diesel	3	4.3	183,500	550,500
Charcoal	23	32.9	34,348	790,000
Firewood	2	2.9	4000	8000
Candles	2	2.9	1025	2050
Total	70	100.0	–	

Source: Survey by author

Small-scale enterprises could be discouraged from using electricity for production, especially, if the increase in production implies higher bills. Another problem could arise from the knowledge that they are unable to price their commodities higher than the current level if they wish to remain competitive. Could it be possible that enterprises deliberately limit production so as to maintain specific energy costs? It would be interesting to interpret the following data for the Kampala area, captured from a frequency data analysis in 1995.

The UEB Kampala area – comprising service and revenue collection centres at Kampala Metropolitan, Wandegeya, Nakulabye, Natete, Najja-nankumbi, Kabalagala, Kitintale, Banda, Mpigi and Entebbe – was home to more than 60 per cent of the 18,031 small enterprises billed in 1999 (UEB, 1999). The average monthly energy billing for all commercial enterprises in Kampala for 1999 was 3,789,514 kWh, implying that, on average, the billing for each enterprise was not more than 350 kWh of electricity.

It should be appreciated that consumption data did not consider the type of business being operated, the type of equipment, or the number of hours per month during which it was in use. However, the average of 350 kWh per month for commercial enterprises was far too low and rather strange! On the other hand, if that consumption record was true, then something must be wrong. After the refurbishment of the generation plant at Owen Falls Power Station (Nalubaale), there was more power available and less load shedding for all consumers. Could the level of production per enterprise have been kept low deliberately to avoid the high and unfavourable tariffs? Or was it bad record keeping?

Power usage was probably adequate for those enterprises that had installed appropriate equipment with correct ratings to give energy-efficient production. However, during the survey, enterprises were found to have installed machinery that was rated higher than optimal for the efficient operation of the relevant enterprise. Such enterprises would greatly benefit from technical advice on the correct machinery to install, complete with guidance on maintenance and machine servicing.

From another perspective, most entrepreneurs interviewed during the survey were operating from rented premises to which they had connected electricity for running their businesses. With the high capital cost contribution paid for powerful three-phase installations, tenants felt cheated if for any reason they had to move from those premises and again had to pay for installations elsewhere, since the utility has no provision for transferring such equipment. Enterprises regard such a transfer as a great financial loss, and look to the power utility for a policy to provide for such a contingency. A policy guideline on the transfer of such equipment, the relevant charges and the time within which the transfer can be made would ease problems for renting enterprises when they have to change premises.

Given the competitive environment in which SMEs operate, the level of electricity tariffs applicable to them was unfavourable and does not support enterprise development. Energy costs bring about high operational costs that eat deeply into profits. High costs make small businesses unprofitable, and yet that is the sector in which most people are employed. As one of the possible strategies of poverty alleviation in the society, the electricity tariff for commercial business enterprises should be revised downwards to make enterprises profitable. Second, there was little evidence of energy efficiency awareness among SMEs that employ poorly rated equipment leading to inefficient operation and high energy bills. Sensitization programmes aimed at developing strategies of energy efficiency need to be conducted for energy equipment sellers and users. In this way the small-scale business community can educate users on appropriate equipment to install and how to operate it optimally.

Enterprises using charcoal

The Uganda energy balance indicated that biomass sources of energy constituted more than 95 per cent of the energy used in households and for commercial purposes (GoU, 2003). Before that, the ESMAP study (1996) had reported extensive use of charcoal in hotels, restaurants and other commercial enterprises. The energy survey revealed that at least 33 per cent of the enterprises investigated use charcoal for production. The average monthly expenditure on energy was established as about UShs35,000, and can be compared to five full sacks (200kgs) of charcoal.

The survey found that almost all enterprises that use charcoal – mainly restaurants and food processers – cook on ordinary metallic charcoal stoves of all types and sizes. These stoves consume energy wastefully and contribute to soaring energy bills. The use of improved, energy-saving charcoal stoves was not known among the commercial users of charcoal that we visited. The concern of the study was that many commercial enterprises dependent on charcoal could remain so for the foreseeable future. It would be in the interest of these enterprises to switch to improved charcoal stoves that consume less charcoal and reduce the cost of energy.

The last chapter in Part 8 – and in this book – discusses Uganda's policy options and our recommendations.

34

Policy Options and Recommendations

In this chapter, the feasibility of draft policy recommendations in the specific context of Uganda are filtered by considering these constraints:

* institutional and management capability;

* legal framework;

* economic and financial viability;

* existing human resources and technical capacity.

The institutional, legal, economic and human capital requirements of each recommendation are assessed in order to identify final recommendations that are feasible in Uganda.

1: Initiate and promote appropriate demand-side management (DSM) and energy efficiency mechanisms

Lack of implementation of demand-side mechanisms among SME consumers led to high energy consumption levels and bills. At the same time, the urban community seemed to lack awareness of energy-efficient methods. The use of energy-saving bulbs and properly rated electricity tools and equipment would reduce energy consumption for low-income consumers. Increased use of DSM and energy efficiency tools would also make it possible for more households and SMEs to access and consume better-quality energy at affordable prices.

Currently, due to the liberal nature of the economy, there is no restriction on the import of electrical equipment. A lot of poorly-rated equipment from various European countries floods the market. The Ministry of Trade and Industry needs to promote policies to encourage the importation of energy-efficient equipment, possibly by reducing the taxes on such items and other market-related incentives. After setting the required standards, the Ministry of Energy and Mineral Development should work closely with the Bureau of Standards and the Revenue Authority to maintain and ensure monitoring of the importation of properly rated equipment for households and SMEs.

There is need for the utility to review the actual basis of tariff design and establish who exactly contributes to the peak period. This enquiry became necessary following the study's findings that most of the households with electricity do not use electricity for cooking. As noted by Williams (1993), 'The management of domestic demand is vital if its influence on the peak system demand is to be reduced.' It has been established that access to the 'rightly delivered' type of electricity reduces user costs for households, because users tend to carry out the necessary planning required for energy. Comparison of the current energy expenditure of households and the cost of electricity has established that the difference in units obtained would not be significantly high, and that the poor can actually afford to use electricity.

Various stakeholders need to work together to make this recommendation effective. The Ministry of Finance, Planning and Economic Development and the National Chamber of Commerce need to enact policy enabling commercial banks and other finance companies to support energy businesses. The Ministry of Energy and Mineral Development and the National Chamber of Commerce should prioritize DSM and energy efficiency in their budgets, so as to support appropriate technology transfers. Enabling policies could also provide incentives for traders and dealers in such equipment. Financial encouragement could also be offered by waiving import tariffs on certain commodities, to enable such equipment to compete favourably against other, less-efficient products. At consumer level, employers could use the availability of such financial support to encourage their staff to purchase energy-efficient equipment.

It may not be necessary to regulate energy use in households and small-scale enterprises further because the Electricity Act (1964 and 1999) provides basic governing principles. The detailed methods of electricity delivery may need ratification by the UEDCL and the Bureau of Standards, but the efficient delivery of electricity may not require any legislative procedures. The institution that takes responsibility for initiating and marketing DSMs would need to prepare staff to do so. The promotion of DSM and energy efficiency pose a serious challenge, especially in a country where illegal power connections and unconventional wiring are common. As part of the coordination strategy, the Ministry of Energy needs to identify stakeholder partners to facilitate these programmes. Stakeholders who would benefit from ministerial support could include the Uganda Small Scale Industries Association (USSIA), the Gatsby Trust, the UEDCL and interested educational institutions.

2: Increase the lifeline tariff to at least 40 kWh to satisfy the basic minimum energy required by poor households

The UEDCL should redesign the low-voltage supply tariff for small general service consumers. Increasing the amount of power offered at the lifeline tariff would be a way of enabling small taxpayers to access adequate electric power for domestic lighting. The ministries of Energy and Mineral

Development and Finance, Planning and Economic Development should ensure that the UEDCL provides for this without an undue increase in overall tariffs.

It would be prudent for the government to consider financing access to household electricity under the same funding mechanism accorded to clean water, basic health and universal primary education. However, the proposed change of policy on the lifeline tariff has significant economic and financial implications. During the review period, the UEB was never compensated for the subsidized electricity it provided. Consequently, the UEB made losses instead of profits out of the electricity business. There is therefore a need to find funding or budget support to pay the UEDCL for the equivalent of 40 kWh of electricity per household at the current rate.

The legal aspect is that the proposal needs to be agreed upon by the national legislators so that the ministries of Energy and Finance can include funds to cover the subsidy in their budgets. The proposal would depend on the political will of the legislators, who will need to commit themselves on how the funding is to be effected. The policy may have to overcome government inability to finance its cost from within, at a time when almost 50 per cent of the national budget is met by donor countries.

The implementation of the proposal may not require additional UEDCL staff to handle it, requiring only an adjustment in the billing to cover 40 kWh instead of 30 kWh per month.

3: Amortize upfront costs of electricity with monthly bills

Despite the colossal amounts that government has spent on subsidies for capital cost contribution to households and small business enterprises, very few households have electricity. Since the 1993 tariff schedule became operational, the financial contribution that government has made towards the capital cost has not had a significant impact for poor households, who still cannot access electricity because of the unaffordable upfront costs of the service.

In the past, various methods were used by the UEB to increase access to electricity by households, but without much success. Crucially, households need to be sensitized to utilize the policy. Alternatively, financing institutions could be encouraged to support the electricity distribution service by offering loans to potential consumers.

Amortization of electricity bills would enable urban poor households to use their current energy expenditure to pay for electricity connections and bills over a longer period of time. The proposal to amortize costs was based on financial modules that tested the ability of poor households to meet the requisite cost of house wiring, connection charges and basic equipment for household use while paying monthly consumption bills. The idea behind amortization was that whereas poor households may not be able to pay the total cost at once, they can pay back the full cost incurred after some set period of time.

If the distribution company itself could afford it, full connection of electricity service could be extended to household consumers and the full cost recovered with interest through amortized monthly bills. Lending money to domestic consumers and recovering it through amortized costs could also guarantee the power supplier with long-term consumers. The investment would be more viable if the interest chargeable to consumers complied with the conditions of the credit institution at the time of lending. Alternatively, commercial banks and micro-financial institutions could be interested in supporting consumers interested in such services. However, accessing loans would probably require the involvement of the local village council. As a form of collateral, a local community organization could represent households and guarantee their involvement, for example by recommending the character and financial track record of the interested beneficiary.

The Electricity Act may need to be reviewed and amended to provide conditions for regulating the proposed amortization of upfront costs. Suitable by-laws would have to be enacted regarding the applicability of the amortized bills.

Although the technical staff within the distribution company are competent to carry out the current range of duties, new staff may have to be recruited to carry out aspects of the proposal. The existing billing and revenue collection systems may also need to be programmed adequately to ensure that amortized bills can be accommodated within the system.

4: Increase support to the Sustainable Energy Use in Households and Industries (SEUHI) programme for the promotion of improved charcoal stoves

The study revealed that Ugandans who spend substantial amounts of their disposable incomes on other energy sources – those more convenient for reasons of price and availability – may perhaps be unwilling to switch to electricity, even after the payment of upfront costs is amortized. This proposal recognizes the central role of biomass as an energy source for most Ugandan households and commercial enterprises. The research team sought energy solutions for such households in line with the ideals of the Sustainable Energy Use in Households and Industries (SEUHI) programme, which is based in the Ministry of Energy and Mineral Development. National energy consumption of biomass in all its forms stands at more than 94 per cent. While advocating the use of electricity, this study noted that household consumption of that energy source amounts to less than 5 per cent. The SEUHI programme, on the other hand, was a continuation of the Household Energy Project Programme (HEPP) of 1990, in which tests for energy-saving charcoal stoves and improved cookstoves for both households and commercial institutions were carried out. The ideal would be to develop a general energy access and improvement programme for all households.

No amending legislation or new law-making initiative is required for this policy option.

Lack of awareness of the qualities and performance of the improved charcoal stove, on one hand, and the high cost of the stove on the other could be one major reason why most households and commercial businesses do not own an improved charcoal stove. The performance of the improved charcoal stove was confirmed to be 25–40 per cent efficient compared to the ordinary charcoal stove, which is less than 24 per cent efficient. Other tested economic benefits indicate that the actual saving in the purchase of charcoal and durability of the equipment that can be realized by using the improved charcoal stove are 0.69 per kg per person compared to only 0.39 per kg per person for an ordinary stove. Given the necessary public awareness, households would realize that the real benefits to be accrued are encouraging enough to switch to improved charcoal stoves (Karekezi and Ranja, 1997).

The SEUHI programme was initiated to redress the limited success of the HEPP project, which had overemphasized technical aspects without due sensitivity to the requirements of the beneficiaries, who had not been involved, as owners of the programme, in ensuring its sustainability. But the SEUHI programme itself needs to develop a stronger stakeholder strategy by targeting women. As the main users of cookstoves, it is women who need to appreciate the technology. For commercial enterprises, biomass-based energy-saving equipment should be directly targeted at the entrepreneurs who would realize the shortest payback periods.

Although the proposal to amortize costs of electricity connection and consumption would be the best intervention for poor urban households, it may not be compatible with the current thrust of privatizing the power utility. In future, however, the initiative could be adopted by government as a single project to electrify urban poor settlements. A similar project is currently installed to provide rural electrification, with financial assistance from the World Bank. Since the proposal for poor urban households requires the targeting of households engaged in income-generating activities, its sustainability can be guaranteed.

5: Review wiring standards and other service connections by promoting Single Wire Earth Return (SWER)

The study observed that current house-wiring standards set by the Ministry of Works and Housing are rather rigid and too stringent relative to the technical requirement that can be fully utilized by urban poor households. It cannot be overemphasized that high upfront costs prohibit most urban poor households from accessing electricity.

The cost of wiring equipment at both medium- and low-tension levels of the distribution network and within households tends to be inflated by rigid standards. As a result, technical specifications followed by the utility and the rules and regulations of the ministries of Energy and Housing for wiring a small two-roomed house are indeed too demanding (and thus expensive) for the urban poor. Given the level of energy utilization of most household consumers, such high standards are inappropriate for most poor households. A cheaper option of Single Wire Earth Return (SWER) could be the solution to reducing upfront costs for poor households. The proposed wiring system would be appropriate because most urban poor households do not use heavy electric equipment. In areas where three-phase machinery would be needed, booster converters would be used at a lower cost compared to conventional three-phase wiring.

The Ministry of Energy in collaboration with the Institute of Profess-ional Engineers (UIPE) and the Uganda Bureau of Standards needs to formulate the appropriate standards for the SWER system to be applied. When the technical specifications have been formulated, the distribution company or private contractors on its behalf would carry out the actual construction of the power lines. This proposal would be supported by the science and technology institutions, who would spearhead research and development.

Smaller and cheaper transformers, on one hand, and cheaper cables and other conveniently insulated equipment on the other could be utilized. Such equipment is less costly for both the utility and the consumer. Some countries that have sought to relax the standards without compromising safety – like Brazil, Côte d'Ivoire, Gabon, Morocco and South Africa – and have used the SWER technology, have recorded tremendous electrification rates.

The current standards for medium- and low-tension distribution networks and house wiring are governed by law. The stakeholders con-cerned with standards – UEDCL, the Electricity Regulatory Authority (ERA), the Ministry of Housing, Works and Communications, UIPE, and the Bureau of Standards – need to review current standards to give build-ings constructed with cheaper materials access to conventional electricity.

The institutions listed above have the technical/human resource capa-city to carry out the necessary review of the wiring problem. SWER is a single-phase system of wiring that has a neutral side connected to the earth with no single conductor between the sources. It reduces the cost of both materials and labour for installation. The cost of SWER is only 60 per cent of the conventional wiring cost of a two-roomed low-income house-hold. For safety and reliability, however, the SWER system may be more easily adaptable in rural areas where households have enough space between them than in urban areas where they are crowded together.

6: Reform the metering system and enable consumers to purchase the power they can pay for at full cost recovery

The UEB maintains an energy metering system whereby each housing unit is supplied with electricity through a conventional meter box. Since the country's economic situation started improving in the early 1990s the demand for more power has become critical, resulting in load shedding and power rationing. Even when government made efforts to increase power supply by the commissioning of Kiira Power Station (Owen Falls Extension Project), there were no efforts to utilize other metering technologies to enable households to use the additional capacity.

If this policy recommendation is to be realized, the distribution company should purchase and install the appropriate meters. UEB had conceived a load management system based on prepayment metering, aimed at reducing peak power consumption. The equipment was to be installed as part of the system and was to enable the logging of energy demand by customers through remote control. Among its several advantages, it was to enable consumers to access only the amount of power for which they could conveniently afford to pay. As soon as the custoner's credit was exhausted, the system was supposed to disconnect the service automatically. The system was also designed to effect the disconnection by remote control of consumers who fraudulently atempted to bypass their meters. The project failed to take off owing to financing problems.

The prepayment and load management programme happened to be outside the scope of the main financier at the time, the World Bank. The Ministry of Finance was unable to guarantee alternative financing for the project. After the unbundling of the UEB, the government's immediate solution to the tariff problem was to increase the general tariffs, especially the domestic tariff, which previously had been highly subsidized. This focus, however, has not addressed other alternatives for serving customers through improved energy metering.

The new Electricity Act of 1999 gives ERA the authority to regulate the power sector. All costs to be included in the tariff are cleared with the regulator, to justify the tariff setting. The proposal for launching prepayment meters will only be adopted if the impact of its financial cost falls within the 'acceptable' impact of the tariff.

The capacity to make adjustments in adopting the new meters would probably need some training of technical staff to acquaint them with the new technology. Basically, the present distribution company has well-trained technical staff who can handle the technology competently. If the need arises, the staff could be given on-the-job training.

7: Design tariffs to ensure equitable tariff rates for SMEs

The study findings showed that, while large-scale manufacturers and bulk-industrial consumers were afforded electricity tariffs conducive to production, the tariff applicable to SMEs needed to be redesigned because it was high, unfair and consumer-unfriendly. The 1993 tariff setting was based on the assumption that electricity consumers engaged in business activities could afford to pay the high cost of the service – the underlying rationale being that such activities are price-elastic enough to absorb the charges. However, given the scope of the businessesss that most SMEs operate and the type of market that they serve, most have reached saturation point and are not as profitable as they appear. The overhead costs and the cost of electricity and other operations tend to be too costly for the businesses, and absorb most of the profits.

The main assumption made by the research team was that a reasonable tariff charge could be be paid easily, while a high tariff charge could lead to possible resistance, including power theft; and that whereas a reasonable tariff setting would provide the basis for a good balance sheet and ensure returns sufficient to meet the system's expansion requirements, a higher tariff charge could lead to diminishing returns since most commercial consumers would opt to use alternative sources of energy.

The new tariff design would have to be communicated to the public to make it effective, but there are no major legal obstacles to the implementation of the recommendation.

Competent professional staff within the distribution company and ERA would be able to compute estimates for economically realistic proposals within an equitable tariff design.

Thus, after a filtering process that has taken into account institutional and management capability, the legal framework, economic and financial viability and existing human resource and technical capacity, the following recommendations are deemed to be viable:

- Government should ensure that appropriate DSM and energy efficiency mechanisms are initiated and promoted in order to increase the ability of the poor to access electricity.

- The Ministry of Energy and Mineral Development should increase support to the SEUHI programme in order to promote the dissemination of improved charcoal stoves for households and commercial institutions.

- The distribution company should reform the electricity metering system and install meters that enable consumers to purchase the amount of power they can afford.

- The distribution company should design energy user tariffs to ensure equitable charges in order to encourage SMEs.

Notes

1   For a detailed description of the methodology – used in all the major sections of this book – please refer to Part 3.
2   The level of subsidy offered as the lifeline tariff has since been reduced to 15 kWh in the 2002 tariff.
3   UEDCL was originally part of the former power utility, UEB, which was unbundled into the Uganda Electricity Distribution Company Limited (UEDCL), Uganda Electricity Transmission Company Limited (UETCL) and Uganda Electricity Generation Company Limited (UEGCL).
4   To be more realistic the cost scenarios should have carried combinations in which electricity is used for lighting and charcoal or firewood for cooking, as is the conventional practice. However, this was not done because available data were not segregated enough to permit the exercise.
5   UEB project information was obtained from the Project office, Uganda Electricity Board.
6   The total number of schemes extended that year were derived from the difference between households connected in 1998 and 1999 (UEB, 2000).
7   The Gatsby Trust is a club through which the Faculty of Technology of Makerere University provides technical support to small-scale manu-facturers.

References

AFREPREN/FWD, 2003. *African Energy Data Handbook*, Nairobi: AFREPREN/FWD.

Barnes, D. and J. Halpern, 2000. 'The Role of Energy Subsidies', in World Bank, *Energy Services for the World's Poor – the Energy Development Report*, Washington, DC: World Bank, p.60.

DfID, 2002. *Energy Services for the Poor: a Consultative Document*, London: Department for International Development, May, p. 3.

da Silva, I. and J. Kyokutamba, 2002. 'Government Policies and Grid Exten-sion as Solutions for Availing Energy Services for the Urban Poor', *Proceedings of the Tenth Conference on The Domestic Use Of Energy: Towards Sustainable Energy Solutions for the Developing World*, 2–3 April 2002, Cape Town: Cape Technicon, pp. 55–8.

Dube, I., 2002. *The Impact of Energy Subsidies on Energy Consumption and Public Finance in Zimbabwe*, Nairobi: AFREPREN/FWD.

EIU, 1995. *Country Profiles 1995: Uganda*, London: Economic Intelligence Unit.

——, 1996. *Country Profiles 1996: Uganda*, London: Economic Intelligence Unit.

——, 1997. *Country Profiles 1997: Uganda*, London: Economic Intelligence Unit.

——, 1998. *Country Profiles 1998: Uganda*, London: Economic Intelligence Unit.

——, 1999. *Country Profiles 1999: Uganda*, London: Economic Intelligence Unit.

——, 2000. *Country Profiles 2000: Uganda*, London: Economic Intelligence Unit.

——, 2001. *Country Profiles 2001: Uganda*, London: Economic Intelligence Unit.

——, 2002. *Country Profiles 2002: Uganda*, London: Economic Intelligence Unit.

——, 2003. *Country Profiles 2003: Uganda*, London: Economic Intelligence Unit.

EDF, 2000, *Uganda Load Forecast Review: Update 2000*, Paris: Electricité de France.

Engorait, S., 2001. 'Country Data Validation: Uganda', unpublished, Nairobi: AFREPREN/FWD.

ESMAP, 1996, *Uganda Energy Assessment*, Washington DC: Energy Sector Management Assistance Programme, World Bank.

——, 2001, *Peri-Urban Electricity Consumers – a Forgotten but Important Group: What Can We Do to Electrify Them?*, Washington DC: Energy Sector Management Assistance Programme, World Bank.

GoU, 1998. *Policy Paper on Micro- and Small Enterprise Development*. Kampala: Government of Uganda.

——, 1999. *Background to the Budget 1999/2000. The Challenges of Poverty Eradication and Private Sector Development*, Kampala: Ministry of Finance, Planning and Economic Development of Uganda.

——, 2000. *Background to the Budget, 2000/2001. Increasing Efficiency in Poverty Reduction Service Delivery through Output-Oriented Budgeting*, Kampala: Ministry of Finance, Planning and Economic Development, Government of Uganda.

——, 2003. *Uganda Energy Balance*, Ministry Of Energy and Mineral Development, *www.energyandminerals.go.ug*.

Hosier, R. H. and W. Kipondya, 1993. 'Urban Households Energy Use in Tanzania: Prices, Substitutes and Poverty', *Energy Policy*, 21, 5, Oxford: Elsevier Science Ltd.

IEA, 2003. *Energy Balances of Non-OECD Countries, 2000–2001*, Paris: International Energy Agency.

Kalumiana, O., 2002. 'Energy Services for the Urban Poor: the Case of Zambia', medium-term study report for the AFREPREN Theme Group on 'Energy Services for the Urban Poor'. Nairobi: AFREPREN/FWD.

Karekezi, S. and T. Ranja, 1997. *Renewable Energy Technologies in Africa*, London and New York: Zed Books and AFREPREN.

Karekezi, S., M. Mapako and M. Teferra (eds) 2002, 'Africa: Improving Modern Energy Services for the Poor', *Energy Policy Journal*, special issue, Vol. 30, No. 11–12, Oxford: Elsevier Science.

Kebede, B., 2002. 'Energy Subsidies and the Urban Poor in Ethiopia: the Case of Kerosene and Electricity', medium-term study report for the "Energy Services for the Urban Poor" Theme Group, Nairobi: AFREPREN/FWD.

Kyokutamba J., 2001. *Energy Services for the Urban Poor: the Case of Uganda*, Nairobi: AFREPREN/FWD.

——, 2003. 'Country Data Validation: Uganda', unpublished, Nairobi: AFREPREN/FWD.

Mugyenzi, J., 1999. 'The Present Institutional Scene in Uganda's Power Sector', in M. Bhagavan (ed.), *Reforming the Power Sector in Africa*, London: Zed Books Ltd.

Phelan, J. (ed.), 2003. *African Review Journal*, 39, 8, London: Alain Charles.

Price Waterhouse, 1990. *Uganda Electricity Board, Tariff Report: Final Report, August 1990*, Nairobi: Price Waterhouse Africa.

Smith, N, 1998. *Low Cost Household Electrification*, London: Intermediate Technology Publications.

UBOS, 1993, *Uganda National Household Survey, 1992. Report on the Socio-Economic Survey*, Entebbe: Uganda Bureau of Statistics.

——, 1994. *Uganda National Household Survey, 1993/1994. Report on the Socio-Economic Survey*, Entebbe: Uganda Bureau of Statistics.

——, 1995. *Uganda National Household Survey, 1994/1995. Report on the Socio-Economic Survey*, Entebbe: Uganda Bureau of Statistics.

——, 1996. *Uganda National Household Survey, 1995/1996. Report on the Socio-Economic Survey*, Entebbe: Uganda Bureau of Statistics.

——, 1998. *Uganda National Household Survey, 1997. Report on the Socio-Economic Survey*, Entebbe: Uganda Bureau of Statistics.

——, 2001. *Uganda National Household Survey, 1999/2000. Report on the Socio-Economic Survey*, Entebbe: Uganda Bureau of Statistics.

UEB, 1993. *Tariff Review Summary*, Kampala: Uganda Electricity Board.

——, 1998. *Uganda Electricity Board, Report and Accounts of 1997*, Kampala: Muyanja and Lwanga, Certified Public Accountants.

——, 1999. *The Principles of Tariff Design in the Uganda Electricity Board*, Kampala: Uganda Electricity Board.

——, 2000. *Uganda Electricity Board, Report and Accounts of 1999*, Kampala: New Vision Printing and Publishing Company.

UEDCL, 2001. *Update on the Debate on the New Electricity Tariffs Effective 1st June 2001*, Kampala: Uganda Electricity Distribution Company Limited/Uganda Electricity Board.

Uganda Gatsby Trust, 2002. 'Energy for the Small-Scale Enterprise Sector in Uganda: The Challenges', in *Energy Services for Small-Scale Enterprises in Uganda – Proceedings of a National Policy Seminar*, AFREPREN Occasional Paper No. 18. Nairobi: AFREPREN, .

UNDP, 2003. *Human Development Report, 2003*, Oxford and New York: Oxford University Press and United Nations Development Programme.

Williams, A., 1993. *Energy Supply Options for Low-Income Urban Households*, Rondebosch: EDRC, University of Cape Town.

World Bank, 2000. *Entering the 21st Century: World Development Report 1999/2000*, Washington, DC: World Bank.

——, 2003a. *African Development Indicators 2003*, Washington, DC: World Bank.

——, 2003b. *World Development Indicators 2003*, Washington, DC: World Bank.

Appendix 8.1 Average monthly energy expenditure for the three categories of urban poor households (in UShs)

Item	Moderately poor	Poor	Extremely poor
Electricity	14,988	6683	N/A
Kerosene	6813	4523	2068
Charcoal	8750	5843	2662
Firewood	13,525	10,582	5665
Others	–	3788	–

Source: Kyokutamba, 2001; UBOS, 2001

Appendix 8.2 Capital contribution (1993)

Number of poles	I		I		I	I
Conductor type			25mm² SCA	25mm² SCA	50mm² SCA	50mm² SCA
Length (metres)	0	0	135	135	135	135
Solidal length (metres)	30	35	30	35	30	35
Cost (UShs) of:						
Accessories	276,915	293,730	923,012	942,827	1,017,242	1,037,057
Labour	43,588	43,588	87,176	87,176	87,176	87,176
Transport	25,000	25,000	65,000	65,000	65,000	65,000
Overhead costs	25,688	27,174	80,639	82,125	87,706	89,192
Total cost	371,191	389,492	1,155,827	1,177,128	1,257,124	1,278,425
Customer contribution	80,000	80,000	276,000	276,000	276,000	276,000
Subsidy to customer	288,191	309,492	879,827	901,129	981,125	1,002,426
% subsidy	78	79	76	77	78	78

Note: All costs are subject to 17% VAT
Source: UEB Planning Office for Schemes and Projects

Appendix 8.3 Revised scheme costing schedules, Dec. 2001

Number of poles			I	I	I	I
Conductor type			25mm^2 SCA	25mm^2 SCA	50mm^2 SCA	50mm^2 SCA
Length	0	0	135	135	135	135
Solidal Length	30	35	30	35	30	35
Cost of:						
Accessories	267,970	287,356	742,838	762,224	836,977	856,363
Labour	34,720	34,720	76,384	76,384	76,384	76,384
Transport	18,750	18,750	41,250	41,250	41,250	41,250
Overhead costs	24,108	25,562	64,535	65,989	71,596	73,050
TOTAL COST	345,548	366,388	925,007	945,847	1,026,207	1,047,047
Customer contribution	80,000	80,000	276,000	276,000	276,000	276,000
Subsidy to customer	265,548	286,388	649,007	669,847	750,207	771,047
% subsidy	76.85	78.17	70.16	70.82	73.10	73.64

Source: UEB Planning Office for Schemes and Projects

Appendix 8.4 Materials needed for wiring a two-roomed house

Material	Required number	@ UShs	Total
Conduits	I	2500	2500
Earthing electrode	I	7500	7500
Meter box	I	7500	7500
Switches	2	3700	7400
Socket outlets	I	3500	3500
Ceiling roses	2	500	1000
Lamp holders	2	750	1500
Junction box	I	18,500	18,500
2.5 mm^2 cable	10 meters	1000	10,000
1.5 mm^2 cable	10 meters	700	7000
Clips	30	30	900
Split unit	I	36,250	36,250
Total			103,550
Contingency and labour costs		30% of total	31,065
Grand total			134,615

Source: Survey by author (data from a wireman)

Appendix 8.5 Upfront costs of electricity for a new house

Item	Cost in UShs	Cost in US$
Wiring	134,615	76.92
Connection fees (to UEB)	97, 000	55.4
Security deposit (to UEB)	50,000	28.6
Total	281,615	160.92

Source: Survey by author

Appendix 8.6 Market prices for energy appliances

Energy source	Item	Cost in UShs	Cost in US$
1 Electricity	40 W bulbs (3)	3600	2.1
	One-plate electric cooker	20,000	11.40
	One flat iron	25,000	14.3
Total for electricity equipment:		48,600	27.8
2 Kerosene	Lantern (small)	4500	2.6
	Wick stove (small)	4500	2.6
	Wicks (bundle)	800	0.45
	One iron box	6500	3.7
	2 pairs of batteries	2000	1.13
Total for kerosene equipment:		18,300	10.48
3 Gas	Gas cylinder 7 kg	50,000	28.60
	Gas only	14,500	8.3
	Grill	14,000	8
	Burner	14,500	8.3
	Adapter	12,000	6.9
	Gas lantern	45,000	25.7
	One iron box	6500	3.7
	2 pairs of batteries	2000	1.13
Total for LPG equipment:		158,500	90.6

Source: Survey by author

Amortized electricity bills (Appendices 8.7–8.10)

Note: Results of testing amortized power billing after connecting poor households. The following formula could be adopted for facilitating a loan scheme for amortized upfront costs of electricity.
$A = C (1-(1/1+i/n) n) / (i/n)$.
Where: A = Amortized cost
C = Capital costs (upfront cost, device cost and compounded monthly bills)
i = interest rate chargeable
N = duration of the cost (time in years)

Appendix 8.7 Loan repayment schedule: A

R	14%		
M	12	UShs	
Loan amount		534,200.00	
Loan Repay period (Years)	PVAF	Monthly payment amounts (in UShs)	Total pay at end (in UShs)
1	11.1374552	47,964.28	575,571.34
2	20.82774314	25,648.48	615,563.57
3	29.25890435	18,257.69	657,276.83
4	36.59454596	14,597.80	700,694.58
5	42.97701647	12,429.90	745,793.98
6	48.53016806	11,007.59	792,546.19
7	53.36175991	10,010.91	840,916.79
8	57.56554932	9279.86	890,866.16
9	61.22311104	8725.46	942,350.02
10	64.40542025	8294.33	995,319.96

Source: Survey by author

Appendix 8.8 Loan repayment schedule: B

R	14%		
M	12	UShs	
Loan amount		502,640.00	
N Repay period (Years)	PVAF	Monthly payment amounts (in UShs)	Total pay at end (in UShs)
1	11.1374552	45,130.60	541,567.16
2	20.82774314	24,133.20	579,196.70
3	29.25890435	17,179.04	618,445.58
4	36.59454596	13,735.38	659,298.25
5	42.97701647	11,695.55	701,733.22
6	48.53016806	10,357.27	745,723.36
7	53.36175991	9419.48	791,236.27
8	57.56554932	8731.61	838,234.68
9	61.22311104	8209.97	886,676.93
10	64.40542025	7804.31	936,517.45

Source: Survey by author

Appendix 8.9 Loan repayment schedule: C

R	14%		
M	12	UShs	
Loan amount		502,640.00	
N			
Repay period (Years)	PVAF	Monthly payment amounts (in UShs)	Total pay at end (in Ushs)
1	11.1374552	40,127.21	481,526.52
2	20.82774314	21,457.68	514,984.27
3	29.25890435	15,274.50	549,881.83
4	36.59454596	12,212.61	586,205.39
5	42.97701647	10,398.93	623,935.82
6	48.53016806	9209.01	663,049.01
7	53.36175991	8375.19	703,516.15
8	57.56554932	7763.58	745,304.10
9	61.22311104	7299.78	788,375.81
10	64.40542025	6939.09	832,690.79
11	67.17422982	6653.07	878,205.53
12	69.58326864	6422.74	924,874.06
13	71.67928424	6234.93	972,648.38
14	73.50294991	6080.23	1,021,479.00
15	75.08965398	5951.75	1,071,315.36
16	76.47018651	5844.30	1,122,106.33

Source: Survey by author

Appendix 8.10 Loan repayment schedule: D

R	14%		
M	12	UShs	
Loan amount		502,640.00	
N			
Repay period (Years)	PVAF	Monthly payment amounts (in UShs)	Total pay at end (in UShs)
1	11.25507747	39,707.59	476,491.08
2	21.24338726	21,037.70	504,904.79
3	30.10750504	14,843.87	534,379.45
4	37.97395949	11,768.91	564,907.54
5	44.95503841	9941.31	596,478.64
6	51.15039148	8737.22	629,079.53
7	56.64845276	7889.22	662,694.32
8	61.52770299	7263.59	697,304.63
9	65.85778983	6786.02	732,889.70
10	69.70052203	6411.89	769,426.66
11	73.11075175	6112.81	806,890.68
12	76.13715747	5869.83	845,255.20
13	78.82293889	5669.82	884,492.17
14	81.20643352	5503.41	924,572.26
15	83.32166399	5363.70	965,465.12
16	85.19882363	5245.52	1,007,139.54
17	86.8647075	5144.92	1,049,563.75

Source: Survey by author

Appendix 8.11 Activities of micro-enterprises and energy technology used

Type of activity	Energy technology used	Energy consumed (%)
Food vendors	Charcoal/kerosene	77, 22
Food processers	Electricity/Charcoal/Firewood	63.6, 27.2,9
Restaurants	Electricity/Gas/Charcoal/F/wood	50, 12.5, 12.5, 25
Retail shops	Electricity/Kerosene lanterns	100
Hair salons/barbers	Electricity	100
Grain millers	Electricity/Diesel	100
Bakeries	Electricity /Firewood	100
Metal workshops	Electricity/Gas	85.7, 14.3
Wood workshops	Electricity	100
Motor vehicle garages	Electricity/Gas	50, 50
Video halls	Electricity	100
Butcheries	Electricity	100
Tailoring	Electricity	100
Beer halls	Electricity/Charcoal	30, 70
Electrical workshops	Electricity	100
Pork roasting	Electricity/Charcoal/Firewood	50, 25, 25
Dhobi/laundry	Electricity/Kerosene	66.7, 33.3

Of the 15 respondents in the micro-enterprise survey, all used charcoal as the main energy for heating and 12 used firewood in addition to charcoal. All used electricity for lighting. Only one enterprise used gas for production. None of the enterprises used kerosene in the main production although some said they used it as a supplement during load outages.

The respondents revealed their expenditure on energy for production; but it was difficult to establish what percentage that expenditure was of their total income. Listed below are the percentage contributions of each of the fuel sources to production in micro-enterprises:

Electricity	72.09
Kerosene	1.16
Gas	5.81
Petrol	1.16
Charcoal	17.44
Firewood	2.33
Total	**100.00**

Appendix 8.12 Informal sector activities that provide income for the urban poor (home-based micro-enterprises and other small enterprises)

Activity	Energy technology
Food preparation /vendors /restaurants	Biomass/kerosene/electricity
Shops	Lanterns/rechargeable lamps
Hair salons / barber shops	Electricity
Grain millers	Diesel engines/electricity
Bakeries	Biomass ovens
Food processers	Biomass/solar
Metal workshops	Gas welding tools
Wood workshops	Hand tools/lanterns/electricity
Motor vehicle garages	Gas
Video halls	Electricity/diesel generators
Butcheries	Lantern/rechargeable lamp
Tailoring	Lanterns/electricity
Beer halls	Lanterns/electricity
Electrical workshops	Electricity
Telephone services	Electricity
Bicycle repairs	Gas

Appendix 8.13 Uganda Electricity Distribution Company Ltd

ELECTRICITY RETAIL TARIFFS FOR SUPPLY OF ELECTRICITY IN UGANDA. EFFECTIVE 1 JUNE 2001

Preamble:

The Uganda Electricity Distribution Company Limited (UEDCL), has, with the approval of the Electricity Regulatory Authority (ERA) given under section 11 (f) and (g) of the Electricity Act, 1999, set the following schedule of tariffs prescribing the codes and retail tariff unit charges applicable to consumers in Uganda, effective 1 June 2001.

CODE 10.1: LOW-VOLTAGE SUPPLY FOR SMALL GENERAL SERVICE
For electricity supplies to residential houses, small shops, kiosks, etcetera, metered at low-voltage single-phase retail tariff unit charge

The first 30 kWh	UShs50.00 per kWh
Above 30 kWh	UShs189.80 per kWh
Fixed monthly fee per customer	UShs1000.00 per month

CODE 10.2: LOW-VOLTAGE SUPPLY FOR SMALL GENERAL SERVICE
For electricity supplied at three-phase low voltage with a load not exceeding 100 ampères to small-scale industries

Retail tariff unit charge	UShs189.80 per kWh
Fixed monthly fee per consumer	UShs 1000.00 per month

CODE 20: LOW-VOLTAGE SUPPLY FOR MEDIUM-SCALE INDUSTRIES
For electricity supply to medium-scale industries taking power at low voltage, with a maximum demand of up to 500 kVA

Retail tariff unit charge   UShs171.60 per kWh
Fixed monthly charge per consumer   UShs10,000.00 per month
Maximum demand charge   UShs 5000.00 per kVA

CODE 22: OFF-PEAK, LOW-VOLTAGE SUPPLY FOR MEDIUM-SCALE INDUSTRIES
For electricity supply to medium-scale industries taking power at low voltage during off-peak
hours (11 pm–6 am), with a maximum demand of up to 500 kVA
Retail tariff unit charge   UShs96.60 per kWh
Fixed monthly charge per consumer   UShs10,000.00 per month
Maximum demand charge   UShs5000.00 per kVA

CODE 30: HIGH-VOLTAGE SUPPLY TO LARGE INDUSTRIAL USERS
For electricity supply to large industrial users taking power at high voltage and with maximum
demand exceeding 500 kVA
Retail tariff unit charge   UShs104.40 per kWh
Fixed monthly charge per consumer   UShs15,000.00 per month
Maximum demand charge up to 2000 kVA   UShs3300.00 per kVA
Maximum demand charge above 2000 kVA   UShs3000.00 per kVA

CODE 32: OFF-PEAK, HIGH-VOLTAGE SUPPLY TO LARGE INDUSTRIAL USERS
For electricity supply to large industrial users taking power at high voltage during off-peak hours
(11 pm to 6 am) and with maximum demand exceeding 500 kVA.
Retail tariff unit charge   UShs68.30 per kWh
Fixed monthly charge per consumer   UShs15,000.00 per month
Maximum demand charge up to 2000 kVA   UShs3300.00 per kVA
Maximum demand charge above 2000 kVA   UShs3000.00 per kVA

CODE 50: STREET LIGHTS
For supplies of electricity for purpose of street lighting in cities, municipalities, towns, trading
centres and community centres
Retail tariff unit charge   UShs176.40 per kWh
Fixed monthly charge per consumer   UShs4000.00 per month

Appendix 8.14 New tariff rates for electricity consumed in Uganda with effect from 1 September 2002

The Uganda Electricity Distribution Company Limited (UEDCL) is pleased to inform its esteemed customers that the Electricity Regulatory Authority (ERA) has approved new tariff rates of charge for electricity consumed in Uganda with effect from 1 September 2002. The rates are as follows:

CODE 10.1: LOW-VOLTAGE SUPPLY FOR SMALL GENERAL SERVICE

For electricity supplies to residential houses, small shops, kiosks, etcetera, metered at low-voltage, single-phase retail tariff unit charge

The first 30 kWh	UShs50.00 per kWh
Above 30 kWh	UShs168.00 per kWh
Fixed monthly fee per customer	UShs1000.00 per month

CODE 10.2: LOW-VOLTAGE SUPPLY FOR SMALL GENERAL SERVICE

For electricity supplied at three-phase low voltage with a load not exceeding 100 ampères to small-scale industries

Retail tariff unit charge	UShs168.00 per kWh
Fixed monthly fee per consumer	UShs1,000.00 per month

CODE 20: LOW-VOLTAGE SUPPLY FOR MEDIUM-SCALE INDUSTRIES

For electricity supply to medium-scale industries taking power at low voltage, with a maximum demand of up to 500 kVA.

Retail tariff unit charge	UShs152.40 per kWh
Fixed monthly charge per consumer	UShs10,000.00 per month
Maximum demand charge	UShs5000.00 per kVA

CODE 22: OFF-PEAK, LOW-VOLTAGE SUPPLY FOR MEDIUM-SCALE INDUSTRIES

For electricity supply to medium-scale industries taking power at low voltage during off-peak hours (11 pm to 6 am), with a maximum demand of up to 500 kVA

Retail tariff unit charge	UShs80.60 per kWh
Fixed monthly charge per consumer	UShs10,000.00 per month
Maximum demand charge	UShs5000.00 per kVA

CODE 30: HIGH-VOLTAGE SUPPLY TO LARGE INDUSTRIAL USERS

For electricity supply to large industrial users taking power at high voltage and with maximum demand exceeding 500 kVA

Retail tariff unit charge	UShs93.50 per kWh
Fixed monthly charge per consumer	UShs15,000.00 per month
Maximum demand charge up to 2000 kVA	UShs3300.00 per kVA
Maximum demand charge above 2000 kVA	UShs3000.00 per kVA

CODE 32: OFF-PEAK, HIGH-VOLTAGE SUPPLY TO LARGE INDUSTRIAL USERS

For electricity supply to large industrial users taking power at high voltage during off-peak hours (11 pm to 6 am) and with maximum demand exceeding 500 kVA

Retail tariff unit charge	UShs57.40 per kWh
Fixed monthly charge per consumer	UShs15,000.00 per month
Maximum demand charge up to 2000 kVA	UShs3300.00 per kVA
Maximum demand charge above 2000 kVA	UShs3000.00 per kVA

CODE 50: STREET LIGHTS

For supplies of electricity for the purpose of street lighting in cities, municipalities, towns, trading centres and community centres

Retail tariff unit charge	UShs153.00 per kWh
Fixed monthly charge per consumer	UShs4000.00 per month

Appendix 8.15 Performance indicators for Uganda Electricity Board (UEB)

Year	Current assets	Current liabilities (000)	Stores (000)	Debt (000)	Monthly sales	Months of billing	Current ratio	Acid ratio	Debtor days	Equity + retained earnings(000)	Long-term debt (000)	Debt service coverage ratio
1991	15,606.9	20,997.0	5,170.8	3,797.1	746.8	5.1	0.7	0.5	153	224,675.4	62,914.2	0.28
1992	21,968.0	28,727.6	5,170.1	10,512.7	1,738.0	6.0	0.8	0.6	181	267,819.9	52,189.9	0.19
1993	37,382.9	26,388.2	9,656.4	15,877.2	2,420.3	6.6	1.4	1.1	197	513,584.5	76,423.8	0.15
1994	46,898.3	28,816.6	10,521.3	26,397.1	3,843.9	6.9	1.6	1.3	206	525,666.8	90,852.9	0.17
1995	56,588.9	32,752.8	9,950.9	47,470.7	4,002.5	11.9	1.7	1.4	356	537,502.4	138,148.2	0.26
1996	77,076.0	46,026.0	10,230.2	51,298.8	4,658.3	11.0	1.7	1.5	330	471,732.4	157,658.9	0.33
1997	81,769.4	63,193.0	14,411.8	44,528.8	5,154.6	8.6	1.3	1.1	259	357,832.0	189,034.9	0.53
1998	82,504.2	67,488.2	10,306.3	55,721.7	5,193.8	10.7	1.2	1.1	322	333,047.2	277,347.7	0.83
1999	96,667.0	80,268.1	9,928.9	66,092.8	5,458.5	12.1	1.2	1.1	363	324,162.1	512,758.1	1.58
2000	128,209.3	76,954.3	23,973.0	82,095.4	6,666.9	12.3	1.7	1.4	369	350,361.3	620,332.0	1.77

Source: UEB, 2000

Appendix 8.16 Selected time series data – Uganda

Year	1992	1993	1994	1995	1996	1997	1998	1999	2000	2001
National population (millions)	17.50	18.10	18.70	19.30	19.80	20.47	21.04	21.62	22.20	22.79
National population growth rate (%)	3.6	3.4	3.3	3.2	2.5	1.0	2.9	2.8	2.7	2.6
Urban population (millions)	2.13	2.27	2.41	2.58	2.76	2.95	3.14	3.35	3.57	3.79
GDP (US$ millions)	4,478	4,851	5,161	5,756	6,278	6,576	6,944	7,466	7,728	8,086
GNP per capita (US$)	200	190	190	250	290	320	310	320	310	260
Total modern energy consumption ('000 toe)	417	421	430	300	320	380	410	430	440	540
Modern energy consumption per capita (kgoe)	24	23	15	16	16	19	20	20	20	24
Modern energy production ('000 toe)			380	390	450	560	590	610	640	840
National debt (US$ millions)	2,928	3,029	3,372	3,573	3,674	3,913	4,016	3,494	3,602	3,733
Merchandise exports, f.o.b (US$ millions)	172	157	254	595	590	671	458	549	439	446
Installed capacity (MW)	166.0	171.1	174.0	180.0	183.3	183.3	183.3	183.3	263.0	263.0
Electricity generation (GWh)	994.0	978.4	1,017.4	1,057.8	1,130.1	1,218.5	1,233.6	1,341.7	1,539.2	1,577.0
Total electricity consumption (Gwh)	709	717	772	865	976	1,024	1,073	1,165	1,285	
Electricity consumption per capita (kWh)	40.50	39.60	41.30	44.80	49.30	51.20	51.00	53.90	57.90	
National electrification levels (%)	2.54	2.61	2.89	2.45	2.89	3.08	3.35	3.26	3.56	3.93
Urban electrification levels (%)	21.90	23.20	20.80	18.30	20.80	21.40	22.40	20.30	21.70	23.65
Rural electrification levels (%)	0.7	0.8	0.8	0.6	0.6	0.7	0.8	0.9	1.0	1.2
System losses (%)	31.7	33.2	36.2	39.5	30.8	33.1	34.2	39.7	34.4	36.0

Sources: AFREPREN/FWD, 2003; EIU, 1995; EIU, 1996; EIU, 1997; EIU, 1998; EIU, 1999; EIU, 2000; EIU, 2001; EIU, 2002, EIU, 2003; Engorait, 2001; IEA, 2003; Karekezi et al, 2002; Kyokutamba, 2002; Phelan, 2003; UNDP, 2003; World Bank, 2003a; World Bank, 2003b

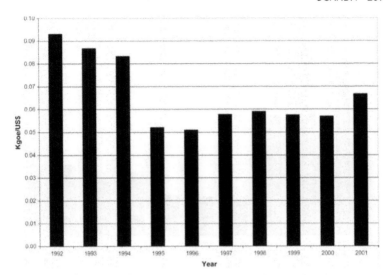

Figure A8.16.1 Uganda: Modern energy consumption (kgoe) per US$ of GDP, 1992–2001

Sources: AFREPREN/FWD, 2003; EIU, 1995; EIU, 1996; EIU, 1997; EIU, 1998; EIU, 1999; EIU, 2000; EIU, 2001; EIU, 2002, EIU, 2003; Engorait, 2001; IEA, 2003; Karekezi et al, 2002; Kyokutamba, 2002; Phelan, 2003; UNDP, 2003; World Bank, 2003a; World Bank 2003b

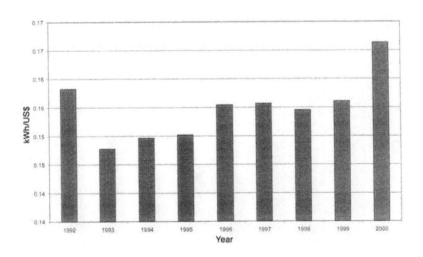

Figure A8.16.2 Uganda: Electricity consumption (kWh) per US$ of GDP, 1992–2000

Sources: AFREPREN/FWD, 2003; Engorait, 2001; Kyokutamba, 2002; World Bank, 2003a; World Bank, 2003b

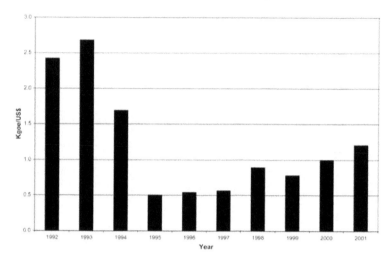

Figure A8.16.3 Uganda: Modern energy consumption (kgoe) per US$ of merchandise export, 1992–2001
Sources: AFREPREN/FWD, 2003; EIU, 1995; EIU, 1996; EIU, 1997; EIU, 1998; EIU, 1999; EIU, 2000; EIU, 2001; EIU, 2002, EIU, 2003; Engorait, 2001; Kyokutamba, 2002; World Bank, 2003a; World Bank, 2003b

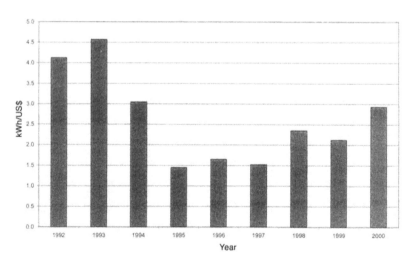

Figure A8.16.4 Uganda: Electricity consumption (kWh) per US$ of merchandise export, 1992–2000
Sources: AFREPREN/FWD, 2003; Engorait, 2001; Kyokutamba, 2002; World Bank, 2003a; World Bank, 2003b

Index

Addis Ababa 160-1, 166, 168, 177-80
Africa, East 20, 31; North 15, 18;
    Southern 20, 31, 33
African Energy Policy Research
    Network (AFREPREN) 3, 8, 33, 51,
    140
AGIP 57
agriculture 52-3, 97, 124, 133, 191,
    211, 225, 234
aid 19, 85, 159, 213
air conditioning 18
Angola 89, 128
animate power 30
Argentina 16
Asia 18; Central 15; East 15; South 15
Australia 242

backyard dwellers 8
Bahr Dar 160, 177-80
Banda 264
biomass 9, 18, 20-1, 23-4, 33, 96, 158,
    160-1, 163, 233, 265, 270-1, 284
Bolivia 16, 23
Botswana 17, 20, 26, 29, 34, 89, 105,
    128, 242; Labour Force Survey
    (LFS) 26
BP (Zambia) 57
Brazil 242, 272
Bulawayo 16-17
Bulawayo City Council 139
Bunda 216
Burkina Faso 17, 23
butane gas 160-1, 164-5

Cairo 15
Caltex 57
candles 25, 55, 61-5, 80, 96, 164, 264
Cape Verde 24
Care International 85

Central African Power Corporation
    (CAPCO) 57
charcoal 2, 9, 18, 20-1, 24-5, 28, 30, 33,
    44, 55, 60-7, 71, 73, 80-2, 84-5, 96-
    7, 160-5, 222, 236-9, 260-1, 264-6,
    270-1, 274, 278, 283-4
Chile 16
Chinhoyi 16
Chitipa 216
Chomachankola 216
Chunya 216
coal 20, 24, 55-6, 108
Colombia 16
compact ready boards 8, 10n, 22, 33,
    93, 113, 115, 140
cooking 24-5, 28-30, 55, 66-7, 81, 83,
    85, 94, 97, 106, 162, 167, 238-9,
    266, 268, 270-1, 274
cookstoves 4, 9-10, 27-8, 30, 66-7, 70,
    81-2, 84-5, 97, 164, 167, 169-71,
    266, 270-1, 274
Copperbelt Energy Company (CEC) 57
corruption 5, 193-4
Côte d'Ivoire 242, 272
credit 5-6, 9-10, 26, 81, 83, 85, 93-5,
    173-4, 193-4, 225, 243-4, 269-70

Dar-es-Salaam 15, 57, 221
data shortage 3
Debre Zeit 166, 177, 179-80
demand-side management (DSM) 117,
    138, 267-8, 274
Democratic Republic of Congo (DRC)
    52, 89
Dessie 177-80
development, economic liberalization
    and 52; energy issues at different
    levels of 3; and poverty 19
diesel generation 90

diesel oil 182, 264, 283-4
Dire Dawa 160-1, 171, 177, 179-80
drought 52-3
dry cells 164
dung cakes 2, 158, 160-2, 164-5
Durban Municipality 139

economic growth 3, 7, 51-3, 128-9, 163, 173, 195, 260
economic liberalization 52-3
education 26, 91, 108, 136, 256, 269
Elandskraal 31
Electricity Supply Commission (ESKOM, South Africa) 139-40
electricity, cheaper than traditional energy 70; exports 76; devices 116-17; distribution problems 261-2; grid 81, 90, 246, 254-7, 264; lighting 28, 55, 81, 94, 96-7, 124, 137, 162, 182, 184, 213, 224, 238, 242-3, 249-51, 268, 283-5; metered supplies 108; preference for 119-20; subsidies see theft of 261, 268, 273-4; see also fixed costs, diesel generation, hydropower, tariffs
employment/unemployment 2-3, 17, 21, 22, 26-7, 34, 107, 188, 225, 254, 259-60, 265
energy efficiency 6, 9, 82, 84-5, 117-18, 136-9, 144-5, 235, 243, 265-8, 274
energy ladder 161
energy service providers 2
Engen 57
Entebbe 264
entertainment 108
environment 51, 96-7, 128
Ethiopia 1; economic reform in 162; GDP 158, 206-7; Interconnected System (ICS) 182-7, 188-90, 194-6; National Bank 171-2; regional equity in 179; rural electrification in 158, 186, 195, 206; Self-contained System (SCS) 182-7, 188-90, 195-6; state role in 19; structural adjustment programme 182; subsidies in 6, 8-9; tariff structure in 6-7; urban electrification in 20, 158, 186, 195, 206; urban population growth in 16, 158, 206; urban poverty in 17-19; Zambia compared with 67-70, 161; Zimbabwe compared with 3, 105
Ethiopian Electric Power Corporation (EEPCO) 182, 193-4, 196
Europe 15

fixed costs, 2-3; amortization of 2, 5, 68-70, 81-3, 85, 93-5, 113-16, 136, 139-40, 144-5, 171-4, 193, 196, 225, 240, 243-5, 269-71, 280-2; connection fees 2, 4-5, 22, 33, 44, 68-70, 80-1, 83, 85, 91, 93-5, 113-14, 125-6, 128, 169, 193, 196, 225, 233, 240-4, 246, 255-6, 265, 269, 271, 280; and cookstove dissemination 9-10, 28, 81, 85; and credit 5-6, 9-10, 81, 85, 173-4, 244, 269; equipment costs 2, 4-6, 22, 33, 44, 64, 66-8, 70, 81, 83, 85, 94, 97, 113-15, 164, 167, 169, 171, 173, 193-4, 240-4, 265, 267-9, 280; internal wiring 4-5, 10n, 68-70, 80-1, 83, 85, 91, 113-14, 139-40, 169, 240-4, 269, 271-2, 279-80; of kerosene use 113-16, 119, 125-6; of LPG use 25-6, 113, 114-16; technological innovation and 136, 140-1, 145; woodfuel use 119
foreign exchange 52, 93, 107, 137, 139, 141-2
forests 55, 96-7, 128, 162, 191, 197n; deforestation 96-7, 128, 162, 197n
Francistown 17
Fuel oil 182
fuelwood 2

Gabon 242, 272
Gaborone 15, 17
Gairo 216
Gambia 17
Gasoline/petrol 8, 182, 264
Gatsby Trust (Uganda) 264, 268, 275n
Geita 216
Ghana 16
Gondar 160-1, 168, 177-80
gross domestic product (GDP) 3, 45, 50, 52-3, 76-9, 100-1, 104, 125, 127-9, 154-5, 158, 206-7, 211, 228-30,

253-4, 256-7, 288-9
gross national product (GNP) 34, 100, 50, 104, 154, 206
Gweru 16

Harar 160, 177, 179-80
Harare 15-17
health 51, 91, 108, 136, 256, 269
heating 96, 137, 243, 283
Household Energy Project Programme (HEPP) 270-1
hydropower 55-6, 90, 158

Igunga 216
Ileje 216
illegal connections 22, 33
imported power 137, 139, 158
INDENI Petroleum Refinery Co. Ltd 57
independent power distributors 82-3, 85
Indonesia 23
industrialization 18, 254
industry, 53, 75, 77, 92, 124, 131, 133-4, 184-7, 188-92, 195-6, 219-20, 224-5, 249-51, 254, 258, 260, 262, 285; chemicals and plastics 131; construction 53, 131, 190-1; food and beverages 131; manufacturing 53, 131, 190-2; metal fabrication 131; services 53, 77, 131, 191; textiles 131; wood and wood products 131; *see also* mining, transport
inflation 52-3, 93, 95, 107, 128-9, 173, 245
informal power distribution 8
informal sector 2-3, 7-8, 10, 20-1, 22, 26-32, 34, 45, 107, 124, 131-5, 144-5, 159-60, 188-92, 221-3, 225, 233, 259, 260-6; agricultural 29, 132, 134, 190-1, 283-4; bakeries 31-2, 261, 283-4; bars and restaurants 21, 30, 32, 131-3, 191, 261, 266, 283-4; beer brewing/selling 29-30, 32, 221-2, 261, 283-4; brickmaking 32; building services 29, 31-2, 131-3, 190-1; business services 131-3, 261, 263; butcheries 30, 32, 283-4; candlemaking 32; carpentry/furniture making 29, 31-2, 131,

133, 221-2, 261, 263, 283-4; catering 10, 21, 28, 30, 131-3, 221-2, 261, 266, 283-4; clothes making/tailoring 29-30, 32, 221-2, 261, 283-4; chemicals and plastics 131-3; communication/ entertainment 21, 30, 32, 221-2, 283-4; craftwork 29, 31, 263; electrical goods 32, 283-4; fabricating workshops 8, 21, 27, 31, 131-3, 190-1, 261, 263, 283-4; fishing 29, 191; grain milling 31, 221-2, 261, 263, 283-4; hairdressing/beauty salons 29, 32, 221-2, 261, 283-4; hawking/vending 29, 283-4; laundry 30, 261, 283; livestock/poultry selling 29; pottery 31; printing and publishing 132-3, 261; property rentals 29, 131-3; repair services 21, 29-30, 32, 131-3, 221-2, 261, 283-4; shoemaking 32; shops 29-30, 32, 131-3, 261, 283-4; smithing 29, 31, 221-2; taxi service 29-30; textiles 131-3; transport 21, 30, 191; upholstering 32
institutional/management capability 136
investment, 19, 27, 51-2, 82, 106, 127, 138-40, 212, 225, 242, 254, 256, 270; in energy 19, 27, 82, 106, 139, 212, 242, 256, 270; in energy efficiency 138; in human capital 51

Jimma 160, 177-80
Jovenna 57

Kabalagala 264
Kadoma 16
Kampala 15, 260, 264; Kampala Metro 264
Kanyigo 216
Kariba North Bank Company Ltd (KNBC) 57
Kariba North Bank Power Station 57
Kenya 8, 16-17, 20, 24-30, 34, 105
Kenya Ceramic Jiko (KCJ) 9, 27-8
kerosene 2, 4, 6, 8-9, 18, 20-1, 24-5, 27-8, 30, 33, 44, 55, 59, 61-7, 70, 71-3, 80, 91, 96, 106, 108-11, 113-16, 118-19, 121, 125-6, 128, 135-6, 141-

2, 144-5, 150-3, 160-9, 171, 174,
175-80, 193-4, 196, 199-200, 211,
222, 236-7, 262, 264, 278, 280,
283-4
Kibakwe 216
Kiira Power Station 273
Kilimanjaro district
Kiomboi 216
Kitintale 264
Kwekwe 16
Kyela 216

Lagos 15
Latin America 15-16, 18
Lesotho 20, 52, 89, 105
lighting 24-5, 28-30, 55, 80-1, 94, 96-7,
124, 137, 162, 167, 182, 184, 213,
219, 224-5, 236, 238, 242-3, 249-51,
268, 283, 285; street/public 182,
184, 213, 219, 224-5, 249-51, 285
liquefied petroleum gas (LPG) 4, 18,
20, 23-6, 30, 108, 113-16, 119, 136,
142, 144-5, 211, 280, 283-4
long-run marginal cost (LRMC) 4, 7-9,
46, 58, 61, 65, 69-71, 82, 84, 106,
109, 122-4, 131, 133-4, 182-7, 188-
9, 195-6, 212-13, 217, 219, 221-3,
246, 249-51, 254, 257, 262-3
Lugoba 216
Lupembe 216
Lusaka 15

Mafinga 216
maintenance 265
Mahenge 216
Makete 216
Malawi 16-17, 20, 89, 105, 128
Mali 16
Manyoni 216
Marondera 16
Masvingo 16
Matare 16
Mauritania 23, 33
Mauritius 20, 89, 105
Mbinga 216
Mbozi 216
Meatu 216
Mekele 160, 171, 177, 179-80
metering systems 272-3
methodology of the study 34, 43-6

Middle East 15
mining 52-3, 57, 124, 133-4, 190-1,
211, 225
Mobil 57
Morocco 242, 272
Mozambique 20, 89, 105, 128
Mpanda 216
Mpigi 264
Mufindi 216
Mwakaleli 216
Mwenge 221

Nairobi 8, 15, 24, 27-8
Najjanankumbi 264
Nakulabye 264
Nalubaale 265
Namibia 89, 105, 128
Nassa 216
Natete 264
National Oil Company of Zimbabwe
(NOCZIM) 125-8, 142
natural gas 158
Nazret 160, 177, 179-80
Ndola 25, 57, 94
new and renewable energy 55
Nigeria 1, 16-17
non-governmental organizations
(NGOs) 5, 84-5, 194
Nyasa, Lake 211

Ody's 57
Overseas Development Assistance
(ODA) see aid
Owen Falls Power Station 265, 273;
Extension Project 273

Pacific region 15
Pamodzi Low Cost Electrification
Project 81, 83, 93-8
Pamodzi Ndola 25, 94
petrol see gasoline
petroleum companies 142
petroleum fuels 22, 30, 56-7, 59, 76,
90, 125, 158, 164, 193, 233, 264;
gas oil 76; see also kerosene
Philippines 23-4
pipelines 57
population growth 1, 14, 15-20, 33, 50,
52, 55, 100, 104, 154, 158, 206, 211,
232, 288

poverty, and access to modern energy 1-6, 19, 21, 22, 26, 43-5, 51, 60-70, 71-5, 80-5, 106, 108-12, 113-24, 135-42; alleviation programmes 2, 51-2, 159, 180-1, 195, 265; and appropriate technology 93; and amortisation/credit schemes 2, 5-6, 9-10, 26, 68-70, 81-3, 85; and development 19, 51; energy policy and 51; energy poverty 51; and human capital investment 51; and informal sector 7-8, 21, 22, 26, 29-30, 33, 107, 225; measurement 53-4; and SMEs 3, 46, 107; state and 19; and subsidies 2-8, 19, 26, 43-5, 52, 57, 61-70, 71-5, 80-3, 106, 108-12, 113-24, 135-42

pricing 3

private sector 5, 52, 138-9, 141, 194

privatization 52, 136, 271

public utilities 2, 45, 57, 76-9, 81-5, 93-8, 107, 123, 125, 127-8, 131-4, 136-42, 182, 193, 212-18, 224, 233, 235, 240-1, 243-5, 246-7, 249-59, 262-3, 268-9, 271

radios 18, 97, 108, 117

refrigeration 18, 30, 117, 137

Ruangwa 216

sawdust 160, 164-5

Scientific and Industrial Research Development Corporation 140

Senegal 16

Sengerema 216

Seychelles 89

Shinyanga 216

Single Wire Earth Return (SWER) wiring system 11n, 242-3, 271-2

Sinza 221

small and micro- enterprises (SMEs), data on 3, 46, 124, 131-4, 144-5, 159-60, 188-92, 221-3, 234, 260-6, 267, 273-4, 283-4; *see also* informal sector

solar power 30, 56, 137, 284

South Africa, amortization schemes in 139; coal use in 20; compact ready boards in 93, 140; GDP growth 89; power utility 8; electrification in 20, 31-3, 105, 139-40, 242, 272; SWER in 242, 272; Zimbabwe compared with 105, 128

Southern African Development Community (SADC) 52, 89

structural adjustment 52, 94, 159, 182

subsidies, to agricultural sector 124, 191; captured by privileged groups 6, 23, 34, 45, 57, 71-5, 79, 83-4, 121-4; on charcoal 71, 73; to commercial sector 75, 92, 124, 184-7, 188-91, 195-6, 219-20, 224-5, 233, 249-51, 262, 264-5, 273; consumption/production bias in 7-8; cross-subsidization 2, 8-9, 107, 124, 134, 182, 187, 195, 212, 217, 224, 252; electricity 2, 4, 6-8, 24, 34, 45, 58, 61-70, 71-2, 74-5, 76-8, 80-3, 92, 108-12, 115-24, 125-8, 135-46, 159, 162, 164-6, 169-74, 175-80, 182-7, 188-91, 193-6, 197n, 201-5, 211, 212-18, 219-23, 224-5, 236-45, 246-8, 249-59, 260-6, 273; financial burden of 2, 5, 8, 45, 58, 76-9, 83-4, 125-30; for fixed (upfront) costs 4-7, 26, 81, 113-15, 125-6; to industrial sector 75, 92, 124, 184-7, 188-91, 195-6, 219-20, 224-5, 249-51, 254, 258, 262, 264-5, 273, 285; on kerosene 2, 4, 6, 8-9, 59, 71-3, 91, 108-13, 121, 125-8, 141, 159, 162, 164-9, 171, 174, 175-80, 182, 193-4, 196, 197n, 199-200, 211; lifeline 106; leakage of 2, 5-7, 23, 34, 45, 57-8, 71-5, 79, 83; and LPG 4, 211; and SMEs 3, 7-8, 46, 124, 131-4; redesign of 82-4, 136-9, 142, 144-5, 195, 220, 224-5; and rural electrification 84; social costs and benefits of 45, 92, 127-8, 136, 143, 159, 181, 193; on woodfuel 71; in Zambia 58-70, 71-5, 76-86, 92; in Zimbabwe 106, 108-12

supply companies (SUPCOs) 136

Sustainable Energy Use in Households and Industries (SEUHI) 270-1, 274

Swaziland 20, 89, 105

Swedish International Development Cooperation Agency (SIDA) 51, 93

Tandahimba 216

Tanganyika, Lake 211
Tanzania 1, 3, 16-17, 57, 69, 89, 105, 209-30; GDP 210, 228-30; Ministry of Energy and Minerals 213, 224; rural electrification 213, 216-18; urban electrification 210; urban population growth 210-11, 228;
Tanzania Electric Supply Company (TANESCO) 213-18, 224
tariff structures 2-3, 30, 44-5, 58-9, 61, 65-6, 69-70, 71, 82, 84, 106, 109, 121-4, 131, 133-4, 139, 144-5, 160, 162, 172, 182-6, 188-96, 197n, 211-13, 219-23, 224-5, 233, 236-9, 246-7, 249-59, 260-3, 268-9, 273-4, 284-6; average cost-based tariff (ACBT) 58, 61, 65-6, 69-70, 71, 82, 84; lifeline tariff 2, 4, 6-7, 24, 45, 82-4, 106, 109, 121-3, 136, 139, 142, 185-6, 188, 194-6, 197n, 211, 213, 219-20, 224-5, 233, 239, 246, 251, 253, 257, 268-9, 284; load-limited supplies 106, 108, 124, 133, 139
taxation 5, 10n, 26, 59, 71-3, 182, 193-4, 212, 225, 267
TAZAMA Pipelines Ltd 57
technology 27, 29-30, 117, 136, 140-1, 261, 268, 272-3, 283
television 18, 97, 108, 117
Thailand 16, 23-4
Total 57
Totalfinael 57
Tourism 211
training 26, 83-4, 93, 273
transport 73, 91, 108, 113
Tukuyu 216
Twapia Township 82, 95-8

Ubungo 221
Uganda 1, 3, 5, 10n, 16-17, 20, 23, 25, 69, 77-8, 105; Bank of Uganda 245, 248; Bureau of Standards 267-8, 272; Chamber of Commerce and Industry 268; Electricity Act 258, 268, 270, 273, 284; Electricity Regulatory Authority (ERA) 272-4, 284, 286; energy balance 233; GDP 232, 253-4, 256-7, 265, 288-9; Ministry of Energy and Minerals Development 267, 270-2, 274;

Ministry of Finance, Planning and Economic Development 268-9, 273; Ministry of Housing, Works and Communications 272; Ministry of Trade and Industry 267; Ministry of Works and Housing 242, 271-2; National Chamber of Commerce 268; population 232, 288; Revenue Authority 267; rural electrification 246, 256-7, 271-2, 288; urban electrification 232, 246, 256-7, 271-2, 288
Uganda Electricity Board (UEB) 5, 233, 235, 240, 243-5, 246-7, 249-59, 262-4, 269, 272-3, 287
Uganda Electricity Distribution Company Limited (UEDCL) 240, 243, 255, 268-9, 271-3, 284, 286
Uganda Bureau of Statistics (UBOS) 234
Uganda Institute of Professional Engineers (UIPE) 272
Uganda National Household Survey (UNHS) 234
Uganda Small Scale Industries Association (USSIA) 268
Urambo 216
urban electrification levels 1, 3, 20
urbanization 1-2, 15-16, 18-19, 21

Victoria, Lake 211

Wandegeya 264
water 76, 94, 256, 269
wind power 56
women/gender 97, 132
woodfuel 18, 20, 23-5, 28, 33, 44, 51, 55-6, 60-5, 71, 80-2, 96, 106, 108-9, 113, 118-19, 150-3, 160-5, 197n, 236-8, 260-1, 264, 278, 283
World Bank 159, 181, 271, 273

Zambezi River 57
Zambezi River Authority (ZRA) 57
Zambia 1, 3, 49-102; budget 77-9; Copperbelt 57; Department of Energy (DoE) 56; Electricity Act 57; Energy Regulation Act (No. 16 of 1995) 57; Energy Regulation Board (ERB) 57, 85; Ethiopia compared

with 67-70, 161; Forest Department 73; GDP 52-3, 76-9, 89, 100-1; Gini Coefficient in 17; income expenditure on energy in 23, 53-4, 59-70, 71-4; industries 53, 77; Ministry of Commerce and Industry 85; Ministry of Energy and Water Development (MEWD) 56, 85, 93; National Energy Policy (NEP) 56, 80; National Institute for Scientific and Industrial Research 85; organization of energy sector in 55-7; rural electrification 82, 84-5, 100; Rural Electrification Agency (REA) 82, 84-5; tariff structure in 7, 58-9, 61, 65-6, 69-70, 71, 82, 84; urban electrification in 20, 25, 33, 51-3, 55, 58, 80-5, 93-8, 100; urban poverty in 17, 51-3; wholesale and retail trade in 53; Zimbabwe compared with 69-70, 77-8, 105, 128

Zambia Consolidated Copper Mines (ZCCM) 52

Zambia Electricity Supply Corporation (ZESCO) Ltd 57, 76-9, 81-5, 93-8

Zambia National Oil Company Ltd (ZNOC) 56

Zanzibar 213, 219

Zimbabwe 1; access to energy 24; coal use in 20; compact ready boards in 22; Companies Act 139; Department of Energy (DoE) 125-6, 138-9; Electricity Act 137-9; Ethiopia compared with 3; Expanded Rural Electrification Programme 106; GDP 89, 104, 125, 127-9, 154-5; household fuels in 28; income expenditure on energy in 106-19; informal economy in

107; kerosene 8; Ministry of Defence 130; Ministry of Education, Sport and Culture 129-30; Ministry of Environment and Tourism 129; Ministry of Finance and Economic Development 129; Ministry of Health and Child Welfare 129; Ministry of Industry and International Trade 129; Ministry of Lands, Agriculture and Rural Resettlement 129-30; Ministry of Local Government, Public Works and National Housing 129; Ministry of Mines and Energy 129, 136; Ministry of Public Service, Labour and Social Welfare 129-30, 136-7; Ministry of Rural Resources and Water Development 129; Ministry of Transport and Communication 129; Ministry of Youth Development, Gender and Employment 129; Motor Trade Association of Zimbabwe (MTAZ) 141; Office of the Regulator 136-7; poverty in 38; power utility 8; rural electrification in 105-6, 109, 154; Rural Electrification Agency 106; rural electrification levy 109; SMEs in 28, 107; South Africa compared with 105, 128, 140; Standards Association 140; tariff structure in 7; urban electrification in 20, 33, 104, 105-6, 154; urban population growth in 16-17, 104, 154; Zambia compared with 69-70, 77-8, 105, 128

Zimbabwe Electricity Supply Authority (ZESA) 105-6, 113, 122-3, 125-8, 131-4, 136-43

www.ingramcontent.com/pod-product-compliance
Ingram Content Group UK Ltd.
Pitfield, Milton Keynes, MK11 3LW, UK
UKHW020731280225
455688UK00012B/604